DEFEAT
of
NA✦I
GERMANY

Flying with the 453rd Bomb Group in 1945

Chester Fong

LJ Strange
PO Box 2705
Olympic Valley, CA 96146

ISBN 979-8-9895392-0-8 (paperback), 979-8-9895392-1-5 (laminated hardcover), 979-8-9895392-3-9 (paperback), 979-8-9895392-2-2 (jacketed hardcover)

LCCN 2023922952

Publisher's Cataloging-in-Publication data

Names: Fong, Chester, author.
Title: Defeat of Nazi Germany: flying with the 453rd Bomb Group in 1945 / Chester Fong.
Description: Includes bibliographical references and index. | Olympic Valley, CA: LJ Strange, 2024.
Identifiers: LCCN: 2023922952 | ISBN: 979-8-9895392-0-8 (paperback) | 979-8-9895392-1-5 (hardcover) | 979-8-9895392-3-9 (paperback) | 979-8-9895392-2-2 (hardcover)
Subjects: LCSH Fong, Chester. | United States. Army Air Forces. Bombardment Group (Heavy), 453rd. | United States. Army Air Forces. Bombardment Group (H), 483rd--History. | World War, 1939-1945--Aerial operations, American. |BISAC BIOGRAPHY & AUTOBIOGRAPHY / Military | HISTORY / Wars & Conflicts / World War II / European Theater
Classification: LCC D790 .F66 2024 | DDC 940.54/4973/092--dc23

Book design by Kelly Carter

First edition 2024

ACKNOWLEDGEMENTS

Foremost, I would like to thank Hunter Chaney at collingsfoundation.org for granting me permission to use a series of photographs that were taken at the Wings of Freedom tour in 2015. They held the tour at the Moffett Federal Airfield in California. The Collings Foundation has been one of the leading historical institutions with the goal of establishing activities in remembrance of our combat veterans for their sacrifices in the service of our country. The air show was a splendid chance for all visitors to experience a part of our nation's aviation history. It was a fitting event to honor all of us who served in the armed forces.

Lyman Reid at the Textural Reference Archives II Branch, National Archives and Records Administration (NARA) in College Park, Maryland was very helpful in securing the Army Air Force material and photographs used in this book.

Much appreciation goes to Jack R. Lopez at Archival Research Service in Potomac, Maryland. His dogged determination to get every one of the mission reports written by our pilot, Lt. Raymond Swingle, was amazing. Mr. Lopez spent many hours seeking the needed information and diligently emailed the results of his efforts to us. There was a ton of material on the 453rd Bomb Group as well, but only a miniscule portion of their entirety made its way into the book.

A heartfelt thank you for all those involved in making this book's journey from manuscript to print such a success. Kristy Phillips provided excellent editorial help and constructive criticisms that were much appreciated. Louise Bouzari for her focused proofreading of the manuscript with eagle eyes, and her nice creation of the index for the book. Also, I would like to thank Kelly Carter for her expertise in graphic design, which created a delicate touch of beauty on each page.

Very special thanks to my nephew Dennis Wong for his tireless efforts and meticulous detail in creating all the exquisite maps and illustrations. They certainly gave the book that extra dimension of quality. With our common interests in military history, Dennis and I began our long trek from my first draft to the finished product. I certainly appreciated his efforts.

Much appreciation goes to my extended family, especially Diane Nakagawa, along with her cousin Wendy, my brother's daughter, for their interest in my wartime experiences and their help with providing Edmund's photo and heroic accomplishments during the war for my use in this book.

Finally, this endeavor would not have been possible without the love and support provided by my wife Jeannie, and my two wonderful and vivacious daughters Letty and Kathy.

CONTENTS

LIST OF PHOTOGRAPHS

LIST OF ILLUSTRATIONS

CHAPTER 1

OFF TO WAR

SITTING AT MY DESK AT Samuel Gompers High School on a warm and sunny day in the summer of 1942, I watched with building excitement as the clock's second hand steadily moved closer and closer to 3:00 p.m. I rushed out even before the school bell rang its familiar tune for the end of class. It was my final class before graduation, and I was looking forward to the start of a new adventure in my life.

But I couldn't imagine how it would entirely change the perception of the world as I knew it.

When war broke out in December 1941 between the United States and the Axis powers of Germany, Italy, and Japan, notices were put out for people to join and volunteer for the armed forces. Similar to other states, when a young man reached the age of eighteen in California, he was required to contact the local draft board to register for possible induction into the armed forces. Under wartime conditions, the Selective Service enlisted all qualified men into the army for active duty. However, since I'd just turned seventeen and hadn't yet been inducted into the army, I had the opportunity to look into other options, such as the merchant marine, which is separate from the army and navy. In fact, I'd strongly considered applying for the

1

US Maritime Academy but decided against it. Instead, my leaning was toward the US Army Air Force (AAF). I wanted to become a pilot.

I'd always been interested in airplanes and aviation. After spending three years at Galileo High School in San Francisco's Chinatown, I transferred to Samuel Gompers High School for my final year. Gompers at the time was located on Valencia Street between 22nd and 23rd Streets in the city's mission district. Gompers was a technical school, and I wanted to learn how to design airplanes. I took courses in the arts, such as drawing and painting. I'd intended to go to college after graduating to enhance my technical skills. But the Second World War changed all that. Or rather, it significantly delayed my future aspirations.

As soon as I was old enough to enlist, I met with two of my close friends, Howard Quan and Albert Fong, both of whom I'd known since our grammar school days together. I still remember that day when all three of us walked into the army recruitment office to join the AAF.

During World War II, the US Air Force was part of the army. It didn't become a separate arm of the services until after the war. It was an easy choice because Howard and Albert had always talked to me about joining up and going to China to become members of the Flying Tigers, a group of American pilots fighting the Japanese.

When Japan invaded China in 1931, China was totally unprepared for war against Japan's modern army, navy, and air force. By 1938, China was isolated from the rest of the world. The Japanese controlled the vital seaports on the east coast of China. Many of China's great cities—such as Peking, Nanking, and Shanghai—had fallen. Generalissimo Chiang Kai-shek, who was China's military leader, was desperate to establish a necessary supply pipeline to other countries in order to survive. So China built the Burma Road, winding more than 12,000 miles through the mountains and jungles of Burma. The supply route began at the port city of Rangoon, Burma's capital. There it penetrated central Burma through a network of rail lines. From there, the Burma Road finally snaked its way into southern China.

It was through this tortuous and tenuous link that China was able to receive military aid and supplies from the United States under the Lend-Lease Act.

Enter Col. Claire Lee Chennault and the beginnings of the Flying Tigers.

Chennault had been sort of a renegade fighter pilot in the AAF since 1917. When he arrived in China in 1937 to help them establish a more viable Chinese air force, he was actually retired from the AAF. However, Chennault became a prominent name in the annals of military history when he formed a very successful volunteer group of American fighter pilots called the Flying Tigers. They were given that name because of how the aircraft were painted.

There was a large and menacing image of a shark's mouth, including brilliantly painted sharp white teeth, on the nose of the fuselage of each of the group's Curtiss P-40 Warhawk fighter aircraft. The concept of an insignia in the form of a large shark's mouth had been borrowed from the British. They had a squadron of fighter planes in North Africa that were painted in such a manner. But the distinguishing feature of the P-40 Flying Tigers was an additional symbol of a Bengal tiger with wings jumping through a *V* (for *victory*). According to legendary sources, a Walt Disney studio artist conceived the symbol of the flying tiger.

Walt Disney himself was supposed to have been enamored with Chennault's Flying Tigers, who were proven to be ferocious fighters. Many Japanese fighter pilots who survived an encounter with the Tigers in the Burma-China zone of military operations were fully cognizant of their formidable reputation.

At that time, the Flying Tigers was an all-volunteer force because the United States hadn't yet entered the war in 1937. With the approval of President Franklin D. Roosevelt in 1942, Chennault was able to recruit as many as 112 pilots from all branches of the armed forces.[1] Each was asked to go to China to join the Tigers and defend the Burma Road against the Japanese invasion. All were excellent pilots and itching for a taste of adventure and combat experience. Some came from all walks of life, like navy pilot David "Tex" Hill, a proud son of a Texas Ranger, and some became famous, like Greg "Pappy" Boyington of the famed Black Sheep Squadron, who was the Marine Corps's top ace in World War II, with 24 kills, six as a Flying Tiger. Boyington's accomplishments ultimately earned him the Medal of Honor during his service in the war.[2]

Though outclassed by the Mitsubishi A6M2 Model 21 Type 0—the mainstay of the Japanese naval fighters, which the Americans called the Japanese Zero—the American P-40s became an equivalent adversary because of the outstanding flying skills demonstrated by the Tiger pilots. The Zero topped out at 332 mph with a 14,390-foot ceiling and carried heavy armaments, including two 20 mm cannons and two 7.7 mm machine guns. It could outclimb and outmaneuver the American P-40 with ease. The P-40 was no match for the Zero in the classic head-to-head confrontation regularly taught by our country's training schools back home.

Chennault was well aware of this disadvantage, so he changed the rules of engagement. He told his pilots to avoid a dogfight at any cost and to not turn with them, but to use hit-and-run tactics. The Tigers would attack from above in pairs, with the sun behind them, and then quickly dive away at speeds of up to 400 mph. Such tactical maneuvers proved so deadly that the Flying Tigers instilled terror in their adversaries in the skies over China and in time earned the respect of many Japanese pilots.

Stories of the exploits of the Flying Tigers in China were well known here in the States and especially in our Chinese community. In July 1943, at the age of eighteen, I enlisted with the US Army Air Force, together with Howard and Albert,

My older brother, Edmund

with the goal of becoming a pilot and going to China. Before leaving home to enter active duty, I said goodbye to my two older sisters, Lorraine and Elva, and my mother, Choy Ying Wah. My brother, Edmund, who was the eldest of the children in our family, was already in the US Army Air Force, training as a cadet pilot in Burma. He'd joined in early 1942, soon after our country declared war on the Axis powers.

They all understood why I wanted to go, but it was my mother who took it the hardest because I'd left the family once before. The last time I'd parted from my mother was during the Great Depression in 1933. I was nine years old at the time. Many people today don't realize how hard it was just to survive during this period in our history. Back then, my father, Lowe Tai On, and his brother, Hung On, owned a sewing factory at 678 Clay Street, right below Kearny Street in San Francisco's Chinatown. When the factory closed, we had a hard time making ends meet. I had to find odd jobs to help pay the bills. I had a shoeshine box, and I would go to Portsmouth Square to shine shoes for five cents a shine. Then I did all kinds of odd jobs, such as sweeping out apartment houses, washing windows at apartments and offices, and emptying out office wastebaskets.

I finally ended up with a real job at a photo engraving shop that was situated right next to my dad's sewing factory. It was called Chan Quong Photo Engraving, and I learned a lot about photography, the engraving process, and printing with a press. But my job wasn't enough to sustain the family. My father then decided that my sister Lorraine and I would need to live with our cousins in San Diego for a while. Uncle Hung had passed away during the Depression, but he had a son, Albert, who was a successful businessman in San Diego. He agreed to take us in. Leaving my mother at that time was especially difficult for me and for her. But in 1943 it was harder for me, going off to war, because I didn't know if I would come back.

When Howard, Albert, and I enlisted, there was an agreement between the army recruiter and us that we would be sent to Kentucky with a Chinese group and ultimately go to Kunming, China, where the Flying Tigers were stationed. However, as so often happens in the military, our orders got screwed up, and we all ended up with the infantry at Fort Ord in California for initial processing into the army. Eventually, Howard's and Albert's orders did come through, and they were sent for training elsewhere. But my revised orders never came. I was to remain in the infantry. I was so angry. This wasn't what I'd volunteered to do.

CAMP WOLTERS

I was sent for basic training to Camp Wolters, located near Mineral Wells in the northwestern region of Texas. Built in 1940 as a training center, it was a huge place, where over 200,000 trainees passed through on their way to the front lines. Officially, Wolters was called the Infantry Replacement Training Center, but to all of us it was simply known as basic training, or boot camp. It was here we learned the basic skills of becoming an essential cog in the vast machinery of army operations.

First piece of training was learning how to accept commands from superiors— or rather, just taking orders, period. If you've grown up taking orders from your parents without question, then you'd fit right in. If not, then there's a very real possibility that you can be discharged from the army in what's known as a Section 8. That is, you're mentally unfit for active duty.

My most memorable experience of West Texas on that first day, as I stepped out of the bus and walked to the barracks, was the oppressive July heat. It was 115 degrees Fahrenheit in the shade. I dropped my gear on the first bunk I came across, and that became my home at Camp Wolters.

Standing next to me was a towering Cherokee Native American. His bunk was next to mine. I remember him telling me his Native American name, but I'm pretty bad with names, so I just called him Lemon. You meet a lot of guys in boot camp. There were, I would guess, 10,000 or more fellows at Wolters back then. But some of them just click with you, and that's what happened between Lemon and me.

We became fast friends. He was a nice-looking guy, and he got along with everyone. Like many of the guys, Lemon just loved the taste of liquor, especially beer. He would invariably get very drunk while visiting a local hangout called the Beer Garden, and I would help him back to the barracks and look after him. Although boot camp lasted only eight weeks, we spent a lot of time together discussing this and that.

I never saw him again after I left Wolters, though I still remember him clearly to this day.

In boot camp, I was trained to become a scout in the field—basically army reconnaissance. I also had to learn everybody else's job, one of which was driving an army truck. Once I acquired the necessary skills involved in driving a truck, I could manage anything, from a jeep or wagon to a two-

Our gang at Camp Wolters

and-a-half-ton monster vehicle. I learned just about everything that comes with handling trucks, including simple engine repairs and how to pull things out of the mud with a winch. In terms of recon skills, I was taught to be a radioman, learning how to position myself to look for enemy troops and radio back information as well as how to quickly cut through barbed wire and other duties associated with field activity.

At the end of my training, I got a letter from my brother, Edmund. He'd joined the US Army Air Force in 1942 and was training to be a pilot in New Delhi, India. He was learning how to fly cubs, gliders, and other types of aircraft. He knew I'd wanted to become a pilot, but then he heard I was ordered into the infantry. He wrote, "You have got to get out of the infantry. Get yourself into the Army Air Force." He knew I wanted to be a pilot. I was convinced, and from that point on, I was determined to leave the infantry as soon as I could. My brother was right in saying that the infantry wasn't the right place for me.

There was also a bit of bad news from Edmund. He'd been removed from training in the AAF and immediately reassigned to Army Intelligence in Burma. He was really disappointed. Apparently, the army needed his skills with the Chinese language. Edmund was to spend the rest of his time in the service as one of the army's intelligence operatives in the jungles of Burma. This was a very difficult transition for him because he wanted to fly above the jungle rather than be stuck on the ground.

As for me, I found out that the Amarillo AAF air base was nearby, so I went and applied as an air cadet. Back at company headquarters, I informed the commanding officer, Lt. White, that I'd been accepted into the AAF and would be leaving Camp Wolters. I told him that if I had to give my life for my country, I'd rather die falling out of an airplane than as an infantryman. He wasn't too happy about the situation, but it was the top sergeant who was really mad at me for leaving. All that training wasted. He and I had never gotten along from the beginning because since I'd first arrived, I was always the last one out of the barracks for reverie. It was my way of letting out my anger and blaming the army for screwing up my orders. I felt I should have never ended up in the infantry in the first place. So the sergeant got his revenge by sending me to KP (kitchen patrol) until I was transferred out of Wolters.

Actually, we'd finished our eight weeks of basic training, and all of us were ready to leave camp anyway. We had all the required medical shots and received orders to be shipped overseas. I never saw any of the guys again. This was toward the end of 1943, so my guess is that a lot of them ended up on the beaches of Normandy during D-Day in June 1944.

At Amarillo, I was evaluated as an air cadet candidate to be assigned to a specific area of training. I took all kinds of tests. I wanted to become a pilot, but the flight surgeon told me that I would likely be unqualified for such a position because of my eyesight. There's a test involving depth perception where you look into a box and attempt to line up two blocks next to each other. Well, I failed that one by a wide margin. I was told I would never be able to land a plane successfully because of my unbalanced eyesight.

My dream of becoming a pilot just vaporized into thin air.

When you're disqualified as a pilot, you automatically become assigned to a crew position on a bomber. I was then told I would be assigned as a gunner, and I was promptly shipped out to Florida for training.

Processing individual orders in the army must be the most inefficient procedure in the armed forces, because it took months for me to get my orders to go to Florida. While waiting, I was sent to Pueblo, New Mexico, where they trained pilots and copilots. They needed some clerical help at the divisional office, so that duty came to me.

Needless to say, I did plenty of paperwork. One of my tasks was pinning up on the bulletin board the schedule for flight training sessions. As I was doing that one morning, a nice young fellow came up to me with a big smile and asked me if I could modify the schedule to suit his needs. His name was Collin Chong. He was training to be a navigator on a bomber. I told him I didn't have anything to do with scheduling. I only put up the schedule on the board. He then went on to tell me his regrets about applying to be an air cadet and said he wanted to be reassigned out of flight school. I gave him the only answer I knew, which was to have a talk with his commanding officer. Apparently, he failed to convince his commander, because shortly after training, Collin was shipped out as a navigator.

After a very long time in Pueblo, I was ordered back to Amarillo. I was next sent to Salt Lake City, Utah, in the middle of the winter, and it was freezing. The only experience I remember there was emptying frozen garbage cans.

After months of being sent to various places for an unending number of assignments, I was then abruptly ordered back to Amarillo. I'd finally received my orders to go to Florida for gunnery training. By this time, it was the summer of 1944, and the British and American invasion of Europe had already taken place in Normandy, France.

Gunnery school was located in Panama City, not far from Pensacola, in northwestern Florida. It was a hot, humid place, full of big bugs and flies that bit with a vengeance. We started out learning to shoot moving targets with a shotgun. It was a lot different from gunnery practice in the infantry, where we were on the ground shooting at stationary targets. Skillful practice with skeet shooting taught us how to lead a moving target, which is crucial in a dynamic combat situation. At first we were trained to shoot from a stationary position on the ground. Then we advanced to a moving position, where we shot moving targets from a moving vehicle, most often from the rear end of an open army truck.

Here is where the importance of leading the target before pulling the trigger comes into play. To successfully hit the moving target, you have to fire in front of the target so that it travels into your line of fire. Technically, this is termed a "deflection shot." Timing is of the essence in hitting your intended target. It isn't an easy task, but the more experience you gain, the luckier you become in accomplishing that goal.

This all appears to be low-tech training, but in those days, it proved its worth and was much better than on-the-job training. Ultimately, I learned how to use and shoot a heavy machine gun. The one used on four-engine bombers was the M2 Browning .50-caliber machine gun. It was a big gun, measuring 56 inches long and weighing 64 pounds. The rate of fire was between 750 and 850 rounds per minute, and it had a muzzle velocity of 2,650 feet per second. Its effective range was 3,500 feet, which meant anything within about a half a mile out could be hit, theoretically. In practice, it was another story. Much depended on various uncontrollable factors, a major one being the weather.

There were a variety of different rounds available for the gun. On the aircraft, the gun was mounted on a movable platform, and the ammo was automatically machine fed. You could tell what type of shell was loaded onto the ammo belt by a distinctive color painted on the tip of each round. If black, the round was armor piercing. Red meant tracer, blue was incendiary, and black with a light-blue tip designated an armor-piercing incendiary round. Each round was fairly large, with a length of 5.47 inches and a weight of 1.71 ounces. Because the ammunition belt was automatically fed into the gun in the turret, you couldn't tell what type of ammo was actually being loaded into the breech at any one time. The type of ammo that was belted mainly depended upon what was available to the ground crew when the aircraft was loaded with ordnance.

After each mission, all the guns were removed and stripped. They then had to be cleaned, reassembled, and oiled for the next mission. The ground crew normally performed these functions in the field, but in training school I learned how to break the gun down, clean it, and put it back together again, just like you do with your rifle in the infantry. So while we were out on a mission, I was able to handle any malfunction that might occur with the gun. Well, probably not any, but I had enough training to deal with simple common problems. Luckily, I didn't have any major problems with the guns on any of our missions. But other gunners have told me that such training did come in handy when their guns didn't function properly.

When my training ended, I was to report to Dover, Delaware, to wait for further orders. But before I had to go there, I was given two weeks leave so I could see my family. I made it home as fast as I could, and my mom was so happy to see me. But even happier was Betty Lee, my sexy girlfriend, whom I'd been thinking about all the time I was gone. We'd been the best of friends since childhood. When I joined the army, she promised to write me every day, and she pretty much kept her word. She was my constant contact to the events happening back home. I found out that most of my friends had joined up. Ted Tang and Frank Yip ended up in the merchant marine, while Howard and Albert were somewhere in China.

To get to Dover, I hopped on a Northern Pacific railroad car and headed east. Since my future was so uncertain, I wanted to see as much of the country as I could before I reached Dover. So I jumped off the train to explore at every stop. I found Chicago the most interesting. It was a great sightseeing experience.

My next stop was New York City, and I couldn't wait to see the Big Apple. But when I got to Grand Central Station, I was stopped by two burly MPs (military police). One of them asked for my papers. This was a routine procedure, but there appeared to be some issues. So they took me to headquarters and contacted Dover.

As it turned out, I was five days late. Technically I was AWOL, or absent without leave, which during wartime conditions could result in severe repercussions. Then one of them handed me back my papers and said, "You'd better get there soon, or we're going to come after you." That was my cue to head for Dover with no more delays.

I was put on the next train to Dover, arrived there in a short time, and waited for my departure date to Charleston, South Carolina. I had orders to go there to meet the crew I would be serving with, and all of us would then begin training as a unit. While I was in Dover, the city experienced the worst hurricane ever to hit Delaware. It was a terrible storm. I watched with awe as small single-engine airplanes were blown off the tarmac. Debris was flying all over the place. I couldn't wait to leave, and before I knew it, I was on my way to South Carolina.

FLIGHT TRAINING WITH THE FLIGHT CREW

Charleston is a nice place with a lot of history. In the fall of 1944, the countryside was very pretty as the leaves started to turn color. There I met the members of our crew: 1st Lt. Raymond R. Swingle, pilot; 2nd Lt. Theodore Clark, copilot; 2nd Lt. F. Campbell, bombardier; 2nd Lt. John T. Harrington, navigator; S.Sgt. Ralph S. Gordy, aerial engineer/left waist gunner; S.Sgt. John M. McCarl, radioman; S.Sgt. Melvin Weaver, assistant radioman/right waist gunner; S.Sgt. William F. Hicks, aerial engineer/nose gunner; and S.Sgt. Arthur W. Simpson, armorer/top turret gunner.

Being the smallest guy in the group, I was assigned as a tail gunner, which usually goes to the smallest guy in the crew. There wasn't much space on the bomber, and the tail gunner needed to be small enough to easily climb onto the seat of the tail gun turret. The pilot, copilot, bombardier, and navigator were officers, while the rest of us automatically got promoted to the rank of staff sergeant when we were assigned as members of the flight crew.

Normally, a full crew consisted of nine people, including the pilot, copilot, nav-

MEMBERS OF OUR CREW
Top row, left to right: 1st Lt. Raymond R. Swingle (pilot), 2nd Lt. Theodore W. Clark (copilot), 2nd Lt. John T. Harrington (navigator), 2nd Lt. F. Campbell, (bombardier), T.Sgt. Ralph S. Gordy (aerial engineer/gunner)

Bottom row, left to right: T.Sgt. John M. McCarl (radio operator/gunner), S.Sgt. Arthur W. Simpson (armorer/gunner), S.Sgt. Melvin Weaver (armorer/gunner), S.Sgt. William F. Hicks (aerial engineer/gunner), and S.Sgt. Chester Fong (armorer/gunner).

igator, engineer, and five gunners. Sometimes there might be fewer, depending on circumstances, but there were usually no fewer than nine. On other occasions, there would be two or three other observers who flew with us on our missions. These additional personnel could be communications officers, target assessment operators, intelligence officers, or a number of other functionaries. Since each flight could last more than seven or eight hours, there had to be a good reason why they were on board because it started to be really cramped inside the craft!

We trained on a Consolidated B-24 Liberator, which was one of the two four-engine bombers used in the European Theater of Operations (ETO). The other heavy bomber was the Boeing B-17 Flying Fortress. The B-24 Liberator had the distinction of being the most mass-produced heavy bomber used during the Second World War. It was first produced in late 1941 as the B-24D Liberator, and of this series, a total of 2,728 were built. Production increased during the war, and a whole series of B-24s with different configurations were generated, including the B-24E, G, H, J, L, and M. Of the series, the B-24J was the most numerous, with 6,678 aircraft constructed at various production and assembly plants throughout the United States. A total of 19,256 Liberators were built from 1941 to 1945.[3]

A unique and defining attribute of the B-24 Liberator was the incorporation of the Davis wing, designed by aeronautical engineer David R. Davis. Unlike most other aircraft of its time, the Liberator's wing was attached to the top of the fuselage with an airfoil design that gave the aircraft substantially more lift than other bombers of a similar weight class. In addition, the increased space available in the wing itself allowed the plane to carry more fuel on missions, resulting in a longer target range. The wings carried a total of eighteen fuel cells, while an additional two fuel cells could be placed in the forward bomb bay of the twinned-bay aircraft. Consequently, the maximum fuel load was 3,576 gallons, with a maximum range of 3,300 miles, less with a full bomb load.

A fully restored flying B-24J Liberator heavy bomber by the Collings Foundation, exhibited at the Wings of Freedom Air Show in the San Francisco Bay Area in 2016. After restoration in 1989, it was repainted as All-American to honor the 461st Bomb Group of the US 15th Air Force, which flew in Italy. She was finally repainted as Witchcraft in 2005 to honor the veterans of the US 8th Air Force who flew in the ETO in World War II.

A view of the twin .50-caliber guns at the rear of the aircraft. The person inside is where the tail gunner sat. There's about six inches of clearance from the top of his cap to the top of the turret.

Left: Inside view of the aircraft looking aft into the tail gun turret. The .50-caliber ammunition rounds were fed into the turret by moving along the stainless steel track situated just left of the 18-inch-wide center catwalk. The belted rounds were then fed into the guns from underneath by flexible chutes. (Collings Foundation)

Right: The tail gunner is seated facing out, looking for enemy aircraft. The left and right .50-caliber guns can be seen pointing down in front of the armor-plated panels. The movement and firing controls for the guns sit in front of the gunner, and as you can see, there's not much leg room underneath the controls. (Collings Foundation)

Finally, the day came when I flew for the first time. On the first three flights, I got airsick because of all the exhaust and gasoline fumes. Unlike modern-day aircraft flying at high altitudes, the B-24 wasn't pressurized, and there were two large openings on each side of the fuselage, where the waist gun turrets were located. These openings were cut into the aircraft frame and exposed to the elements, although there was a loose cover that could be opened and hinged above on the outside of the craft during long flights. But anything outside the plane literally blew right inside, such as fumes, smoke, rain, ice, and debris.

Our normal cruising altitude was around 25,000 feet, and the temperature outside and inside the aircraft often dropped to -30 degrees Fahrenheit or more. To keep warm, we usually wore a heated nylon suit and as many clothes as we could put on. Heavy gloves, a hat, thick jacket, and a tight-fitting oxygen mask rounded out our flying outfit.

My flight position as the tail gunner was in the rear gun turret, which was located at the very end of the plane. It was extremely cramped inside the turret itself, which was absolutely not built for comfort. In fact, the comfort level inside the entire plane wasn't suited for anything other than combat—specifically, for carrying a maximum bomb load.

After several months of training on the essentials of our duties aboard a B-24 and working coherently as a team, we were finally ready to ship out to our assigned destination.

We traveled from South Carolina to New York City by train. Then most of our crew went aboard the *Queen Mary* bound for England. In early 1945, there were two large troop ships, HMS *Queen Mary* and HMS *Queen Elizabeth*, both of which ferried troops and supplies to and from the United States to England or France. Transit across the North Atlantic involved two hazards. First was the unpredictable weather—especially in the winter. The greater hazard was avoiding detection by and attack from German U-boats (submarines). To minimize detection, these large ships traveled a route that crossed the Atlantic in a zigzag pattern.

Our destination was Liverpool, England, and when we got on board, there were thousands of troops, almost all of them from the army. The *Queen Mary* could carry more than 15,000 troops, so there were a lot of people on the ship. As AAF personnel, we were bunked on the top deck, A Deck. This was the best part of the ship, and I felt sorry for all the army guys squeezed together below decks. They were from all branches, including the infantry, artillery, tank, and many others. We were the only US Army Air Force flight crew members on the whole ship. I wasn't so surprised about this after experiencing, with some regret, how efficient, or more likely inefficient, the army is with processing orders.

DECEMBER 16, 1944:
THE GERMAN COUNTEROFFENSIVE IN THE ARDENNES

As we boarded the ship in mid-December 1944, events on the ground in Western Europe were about to heat up significantly. Allied forces had made considerable gains throughout the Western Front and were now on the offensive in Belgium. The capture of Belgium, which bordered Germany, was being bitterly fought by both sides—especially by the Germans, who wanted at all costs to prevent the Allies from entering the Rhineland. The *Wehrmacht* (German armed forces) was in a weakened state from years of fighting and attrition. Facing the Allies in the west and the Russians in the east, it was only a matter of time before Germany was defeated. In fact, Hitler was about to order his last major offensive in the West.

Ever since the Allied invasion of Normandy on June 6, 1944, the Germans had been relentlessly pushed back on all fronts. By late 1944, the US 9th Army in northern Belgium was on the winter offensive at the Roer River, which was about 30 miles west of the Rhine River. The Rhine was the last natural defense preventing the Allies from gaining easy access into the heart of Germany. Farther south, the US 3rd Army was on the advance in the Saar region in Luxembourg.

On the Eastern Front, the Russians were within reach of the Oder River, the last natural obstacle into Germany from the east. With the Russians only about 35 miles from Berlin, Adolf Hitler was facing determined enemies on two fronts, and his armies were caught in a vise that was slowly squeezing the life out of the Werhmacht. In desperation, he conceived of plan known as *Operation Wacht on dem Rhine* (Watch on the Rhine), a counteroffensive that he believed would change the tenor of the war.

In a bold move to break through the Allied front line, the goal was to drive his attacking forces all the way to Antwerp, Belgium, and split the Allied forces in two. Antwerp was a vital port city for the Allies, where they received supplies and munitions for the entire Western Front. It was one of many cities that stretched over 350 miles from Normandy to Belgium. Because the Allied drive toward Germany had been so swift and successful, American units on the front lines were short of everything, from fuel, food, and ammunition to even clothing. Many soldiers were still wearing the outfits that had been issued during the summer Normandy invasion. They were totally unprepared for the harsh winter weather conditions prevailing

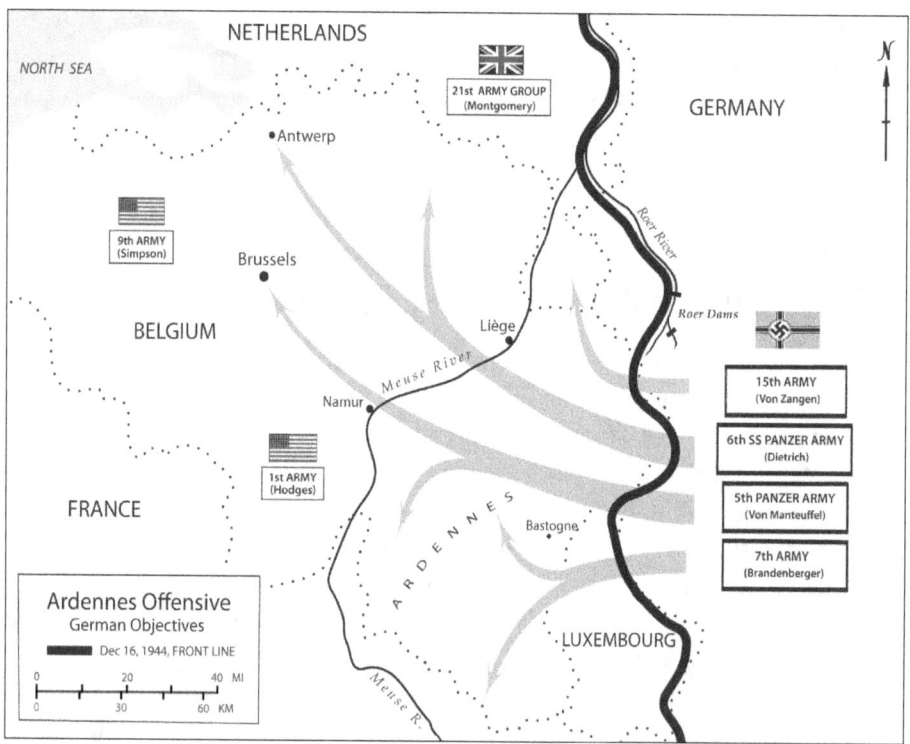

DEFEAT OF NAZI GERMANY

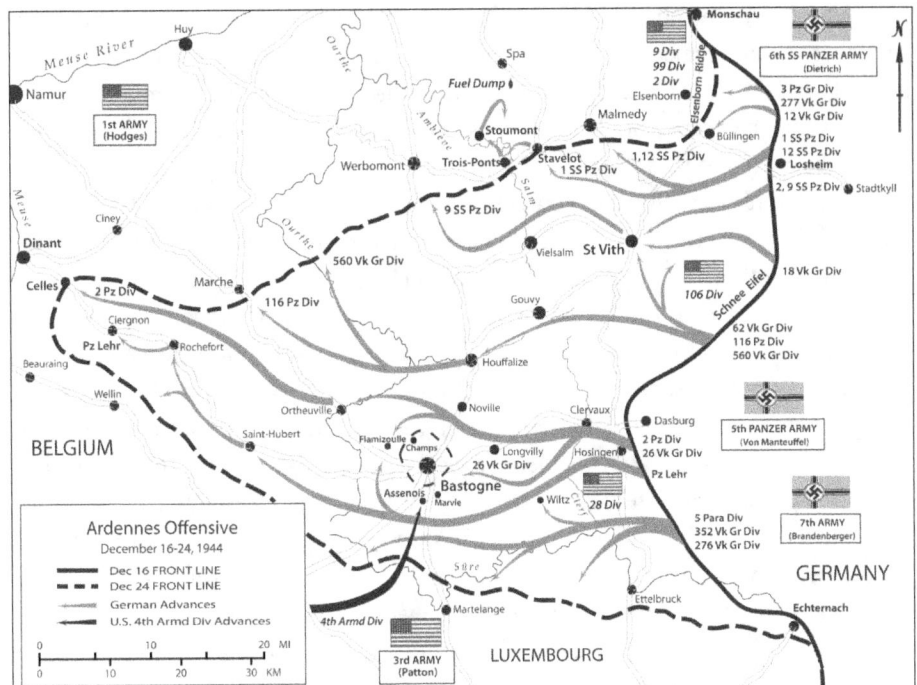

Ardennes Offensive
December 16-24, 1944

———	Dec 16 FRONT LINE
– – –	Dec 24 FRONT LINE
	German Advances
	U.S. 4th Armd Div Advances

throughout northern Belgium.

Hitler announced his plan on September 16, 1944, and Field Marshal Gerd von Rundstedt was ordered to head the offensive. To provide the necessary manpower, Hitler ordered all men between the ages of sixteen and sixty to serve in newly formed divisions, which he called *Volksgranadiers* (the people's army). Unlike regular German Army divisions, these were composed of fewer men, 10,000 instead of the usual 17,000, who were less trained, if at all, and less well-equipped for frontline duty. The plan listed a total of 13 infantry divisions, two parachute divisions, and six panzer divisions. As time drew nearer to the counteroffensive, the name of the operation was changed from *Wacht am Rhein* to *Herbstnebel* (Autumn Mist).

Hitler chose to attack the most vulnerable sector of the entire Allied Western Front, a heavily forested sector known as the Ardennes, which was lightly defended by the VIII Corps of the US 1st Army. The commander was Maj. Gen. Troy H. Middleton. Located in the northern sector of the front line were the 2nd and 99th Infantry Divisions. The 2nd Infantry Division had made a major thrust into Germany in an attempt to reach the Roer River, while the 99th Infantry Division was there for training and had been there for only about a month.

The 106th Infantry Division held the central sector of the front. They'd arrived just five days earlier to gain some combat experience. Probably the most experienced divisions were in the southern sector, which included the 28th and 4th Infantries. These two divisions had been sent there primarily for rest and recreation after suffering extremely heavy losses in November during the Hürtgen Forest campaign in northern Belgium. General Courtney H. Hodges, who was the commander of the US 1st Army, had sent Middleton's corps to the Ardennes, where the German forces weren't expected to be active.

Middleton's five divisions represented one-third of the 1st Army. The remaining 10 divisions were situated farther north, attacking the Roer River dams with the intention of linking up with Lt. Gen. William H. Simpson's 9th Army on the banks of the Roer. Securing the dams was of vital importance to prevent the Germans from opening the floodgates and inundating the region south of the Roer River. Just south of the Ardennes, Gen. George S. Patton's 3rd Army, with 10 divisions, had recently pierced the German defensive barrier known as the Siegfried Line on the east side of the Saar River. Patton's objective was to advance east to the Rhine River.

Hitler's plan was simple and straightforward: smash through the front lines with massive infantry and armor, cross the Meuse River, and wrestle Antwerp from the Allies. However, it depended on two critical factors. First was shock and surprise, and second was speed. For the plan to work at all, it was necessary to cross the Meuse in the shortest possible amount of time before the American forces could regroup and counterattack with overwhelming force. This task was assigned to German Army Group B, commanded by Field Marshal Walter Model.

Model was in charge of operations, but it was Hitler who actually assigned the attacking armies and controlled the events in the field. The main strike force was delegated to the 6th SS Panzer Army, commanded by Oberstgruppenführer der Waffen SS Josef Dietrich, more commonly known as Sepp Dietrich.

He'd started his military career as a tank soldier and served with distinction in World War I. His relationship with Hitler went back as far as 1928, when he was one of the Führer's most ardent followers. Dietrich had previously served as Hitler's bodyguard and commanded his personal protective force, the SS Leibstandarte Adolf Hitler Regiment. This force eventually evolved into a Waffen SS Panzer Division. Hitler rewarded Dietrich's loyalty by making the 6th SS Panzer one of the best equipped in Model's Army Group B.[4]

Dietrich had little formal military training. He wasn't regarded very highly by other generals of the German Army, but both Von Rundstedt and Model provided the 6th SS Panzer Army with competent staff officers, one of whom was the brilliant tactician Fritz Kraemer, who was the chief of staff. What Dietrich lacked in traits common to the aristocratic commanders dominating the German Army, he made up for as a natural fighter and leader of men on the front line. Provided with 120,000 men, 500 tanks, and assault guns, in addition to 1,000 artillery pieces, the 6th SS Panzer Army was expected to easily break through the front lines, cross the Meuse, and reach Antwerp in a matter of days.

Supporting Dietrich on the left flank was the 5th Panzer Army, commanded by General der Panzertruppen Hasso von Manteuffel, a competent and capable officer. Coming from a military family with generations of generals, Von Manteuffel graduated from the Cadet Academy in Berlin-Lichterfelde. A cavalryman who excelled as an equestrian, Von Manteuffel served in World War I as a second lieutenant in the 3rd Brandenburg Hussar Regiment von Zieten. He served with distinction in Russia and North Africa in the 7th Panzer Division under Field Marshal Erwin Rommel. When Hitler told him on September 1, 1944, that he was to be promoted to command the 5th Panzer Army, Von Manteuffel became one of Germany's youngest panzer generals. It was the 5th Panzer Army's task to break through the front lines in the southern sector of the Ardennes, race across the Meuse River, and take Brussels.

The attack came in the early-morning hours of December 16, 1944, when at 5:20 a.m., the 6th SS Panzer Army began its heavy artillery bombardment. The Germans threw everything they had against the thinly stretched Ardennes Front. This was immediately followed by the first wave of tanks smashing through Middleton's shocked and unprepared divisions. Von Rundstedt counted on speed and surprise to punch a hole through the line, and it was a resounding success. Many of Middleton's troops were overrun and had to fall back to defensive positions. The weather was terrible, with sleeting rain turning into thick snow on the ground. The weather had grounded all Allied planes, and there was absolutely no air support. Hitler had been waiting exactly for this scenario. The first phase of the German counteroffensive was complete.

The success or failure of the entire counteroffensive was to depend on crucial battles for two key cities in the Ardennes. The first was St. Vith, located in the northern sector, while the second was Bastogne, situated in the southern sector. Both were at critical road junctions with many roads leading in and out of them. Two main roads from St. Vith led directly through Malmedy and Werbomont to Huy on the Meuse River. Bastogne had a direct link to St. Vith and no fewer than seven main roads coming in from Germany and northern Luxembourg, then straight to Dinant on the Meuse River.

The fight at both St. Vith and Bastogne would determine the outcome of the battle for the Ardennes.

THE BATTLE FOR ST. VITH

The spearhead of Dietrich's army was the 1st SS Panzer Division. It was formed around the 1st SS Panzer Regiment, which was commanded by a young fanatical Nazi, Lt. Col. Joachim Peiper. At twenty-nine, Peiper was one of the youngest regimental commanders in the German Army. He came from a military family and was schooled as the supreme SS officer. His brutal reputation for conquests during the Russian invasion in 1941 and 1942 included burning villages and their inhabitants alive, without mercy.

On the morning of the attack, 1st Lt. Lyle J. Bouck Jr. was in command of a reconnaissance platoon in the 14th Cavalry Group attached to the US 99th Division manning the front line. Bouck's unit was located on a main road leading out of Losheim Gap, a key strategic location from which Peiper's infantry was to break through the front line. As the forward column of enemy infantry approached Bouck's position, his unit opened fire and stopped the Germans dead in their tracks. Despite heavy frontal attacks and repeated waves of enemy infantry attempting to overrun his position, Bouck and his men stood their ground. Finally, out of ammunition and with most of his men wounded, Bouck surrendered.

The fierce resistance demonstrated by Bouck's unit and many such acts of heroism along the entire American front line against overwhelming German attacks eventually determined the outcome of the battle for the Ardennes. The efforts of just that single platoon to stop an entire German column for almost an entire day put such a crimp in the German offensive timetable that it had vital repercussions in the coming weeks.

No one was more upset than Peiper, who had further troubles moving his columns through the Losheim Gap. His schedule was to break through the front lines by the end of the morning. However, his tanks were now just sitting there, caught in a massive traffic jam of vehicles and men, all barely moving along the narrow bridges and roadways. It wasn't until midnight that Peiper even reached the main road through the Losheim Gap.

Just north of Peiper's attack in the area around the town of Elsenborn, a bigger battle was brewing. Both the 1st and 12th SS Panzer Divisions had an easy time breaking through the front lines of the inexperienced troops of the US 99th Division. But they ran into fierce resistance when forward elements of the 99th and 2nd Divisions regrouped at Elsenborn Ridge. The long, steep ridgeline provided a natural defense structure, preventing the German advance from continuing its quick run toward Malmedy, a key road junction leading to the Meuse River. A fierce fight ensued and lasted well into the night.

The next day, December 17, Peiper decided to make a detour to Büllingen because of fuel concerns. Before the offensive began, two trainloads of fuel had failed to arrive on time, and the attacking divisions were told they would need to replenish their supplies by capturing enemy fuel depots. German intelligence had provided maps of fuel dumps at Büllingen and Stavelot. On the way to Büllingen, small groups of American troops were overrun, and they surrendered. Peiper's SS troops immediately executed them. The worst scene occurred in Baugnez, where 120 men of Battery B of the 285th Field Artillery Observation Battalion surrendered with their hands up. They were subsequently shot by SS troopers with machine guns and machine pistols. Then, SS officers walked among the wounded and shot each of them in the head. This was to be called the Malmedy Massacre.

The news of this terrible incident spread quickly through all the American units. As a result, revenge and retribution were on the mind of every American trooper in the Ardennes. Not only did this stiffen their resolve to fight back the German advance with renewed vigor, but many American troops exacted revenge on German soldiers belonging to SS units. As Peiper's column advanced from one town to another, SS troops murdered American prisoners and many innocent civilians. These atrocities were repeated over and over again.

While Dietrich's 2nd and 9th SS Panzer Divisions were heading toward St. Vith from the north, Von Manteuffel's 5th Panzer Army Division was approaching from the south. Two regiments of the US 106th Infantry Division, the 422nd and 423rd, were trapped at the Schnee Eifel. They were inexperienced but fought back with vigor and determination.

Similar to Peiper's situation in the north, Von Manteuffel's advancing columns were bogged down by roads clogged with vehicles, horses, troops, and fleeing civilian refugees. To make matters worse, the horrendous road conditions caused by heavy mud, sleet, and snow, with drifts accumulating up to three feet, made progress extremely slow. Hitler had waited until the exact moment when the weather conditions in the Ardennes would be at their worst to prevent the Allies from using lethal air strikes. But such a tactic came to be a double-edged sword. Von Manteuffel's tanks and vehicles began to suffer fuel shortages. His schedule was to capture St. Vith on the first day. He now realized this wouldn't happen.

By December 18, Peiper's forces had taken Stavelot and headed west to Trios Points, where it would be a straight shot to Werbomont and the Meuse River. Both the Amblève and Salm Rivers met at Trios Points, and a series of bridges crossed the main roads. As the German approach appeared imminent, the 51st Engineer Battalion was ordered to go to Trios Points and blow up the bridges on the roads leading to Werbomont. At 11:15 a.m., the first of Peiper's tanks came rolling into Trio Points, and the engineers blew up the bridges over the Amblève and Salm Rivers. At the same time, reinforcements from the US 7th Armored Division arrived from the north to augment the defense of Trios Points. The 7th Division had been rushed south from Aachen on the first day of the attack. Peiper's way to Werbomont was now blocked, so he decided to go back to Stavelot and find an alternative route.

As the main forces of the US 7th Armored Division raced toward St. Vith, so too did divisions from Dietrich's 6th SS Panzer and Manteuffel's 5th Panzer Armies. The Germans made probing attacks against the defenders of St. Vith, but the main force of both armies was yet to reach the city. They were having some serious traffic problems on the roads leading west to St. Vith. The jammed roads were the result of the fierce resistance of the American troops on top of Elsenborn Ridge, which forced Dietrich's divisions to turn south instead of pushing through to Malmedy and securing a northern route to the Meuse River. As a result, Dietrich's divisions ran headlong into Von Manteuffel's northern forces heading for St. Vith.

Calling it chaos on the roads is an understatement.

General Dwight D. Eisenhower, the Supreme Commander of Allied forces in Europe, met with some of his top staff officers at Verdun, France, on December 19 to discuss the situation in the Ardennes. The meeting took place at the rear headquarters of the US 12th Army Group, commanded by Gen. Omar N. Bradley. The 12th Army Group consisted of the 1st Army (Gen. Courtney H. Hodges), the 3rd Army (Gen. George S. Patton), and the 9th Army (Lt. Gen. William H. Simpson).

When Hitler's counteroffensive began on December 16, both Bradley and Patton thought the attacks were just spoilers—that is, the main goal being to blunt the US winter offensive in the north and south of the Ardennes. Bradley himself couldn't believe the Germans even had enough manpower and material to launch an effective counteroffensive. His intelligence command had told him that the Wehrmacht was on the verge of collapse from fighting and attrition.

However, Eisenhower thought otherwise. One of the reasons President Franklin D. Roosevelt chose Eisenhower to become the supreme commander was the general's brilliance as a strategist. He was always thinking of the big picture. Eisenhower had a gut feeling about the German attack. He felt it might be something big. He was also aware that if this was a determined counterattack, it would come at the weakest point along the entire Western Front. True, the German armies were in a weakened state, but such an attack meant Hitler was using his final reserves for a last-ditch effort to stave off the Allied forces. Eisenhower was correct on all counts.

On the first day of the attack, December 16, Eisenhower had the foresight to order Simpson to send the 7th Armored Division of the US 9th Army south to Maj. Gen. Troy H. Middleton's VIII Corps sector, where the focus of the German attack was occurring. Eisenhower also sent two mobile divisions, the US 82nd and 101st Airborne Divisions, to the Ardennes. The 82nd was sent to St. Vith, and the 101st was sent to Bastogne. At the same time, Eisenhower asked Bradley to come to Middleton's aid. Bradley then telephoned Patton from Eisenhower's office and asked Patton to send the US 3rd Army's 10th Armored Division north to the Ardennes to attack the enemy's southern flank if they broke through Middleton's line.

Patton's insistence that the situation was nothing more than a spoiling attack was duly noted, but Bradley assured him it would be prudent if Eisenhower was correct. Patton finally relented, and, within a few minutes of talking to Bradley, he ordered the 10th Division to help Middleton.[5] The 7th and 19th Armored Divisions, along with the 82nd and 101st, were the only four divisions left as reserves on the Western Front.

The supreme commander's quick reaction had a tremendous impact on the outcome of the battle.

By December 19, at the time of Eisenhower's meeting, the situation in the Ardennes was getting worse by the minute. German divisions with infantry and tanks were pouring through large gaps on the front lines stretching from Monschau in the north to Echternach in the south, a span of over 85 miles. But Eisenhower calmly told his commanders that this attack wasn't a disaster for the Allies, but an opportunity. Patton, aggressive as ever, wanted to attack the Germans immediately.

Eisenhower agreed and told him it would come in due time. But he stated in no uncertain terms to his staff that the Germans must never be allowed to cross the Meuse River. He then turned to Patton and asked him when he would be able to start his attack. Patton, without hesitation, replied that it would occur in three days, on December 21, with three divisions—the 4th, 26th, and 80th Armored Divisions.[6]

To think that the bulk of the 3rd Army could make such a quick turn north to the Ardennes, a distance of over 60 miles, in three days seemed an impossible task. Even Bradley was skeptical that it could be accomplished. However, Eisenhower knew if anyone could do it, it would be Patton, who had a reputation for doing the impossible. Many campaigns throughout Italy and North Africa were a testimony to Patton's skills. Of all the commanders Eisenhower had in the field, Patton was the one the Germans feared the most. Eisenhower then decided to give Patton an extra day, so he told Patton that December 22 would be a reasonable date of attack.[7]

Eisenhower and Patton were longtime friends, and both had always been interested in mechanized warfare. Eisenhower commanded a tank battalion in the First World War but never had the chance to go overseas. At Camp Meade, Maryland, in 1919, Eisenhower and a young colonel by the name of George Patton belonged to a closely knit group of soldiers intensely involved in developing the use of tanks in combat field operations. To create the ideal tank, Patton and Eisenhower completely disassembled an entire tank, right down to individual engine parts, and put it back together again. Their redesigned visions influenced the father of the modern tank, J. Walter Christie, to develop an efficient and fast-moving prototype that exceeded the known capabilities of tanks being used in the army at the time. Christie sold his plans to the Russians, who in turn produced one of the best tanks in World War II, the T-34.[8]

The night before Eisenhower discussed strategy at his meeting, the 7th Armored Division arrived in St. Vith and began advancing eastward in an attempt to save the 422nd and 423rd Regiments of the US 106th Division. Both regiments and other elements from retreating American forces were encircled and trapped at the Schnee Eifel in Germany. However, the 7th Division couldn't get through the main roads. They were jammed with troops and vehicles going in the opposite direction during the wholesale retreat from the front lines. The 422nd and 423rd, having run out of ammunition, had no choice but to surrender. Over 8,000 men were taken prisoner in one of the largest Allied defeats on the Western Front.

Farther north, Peiper's tanks and armored vehicles were quickly running out of fuel. A large Allied fuel dump containing over 400,000 gallons of gasoline was located several miles southeast of Spa. Peiper's access to the fuel supply was thwarted when American troops created an impossible roadblock by setting 124,000 gallons of fuel on fire. Knowing that the Germans desperately needed fuel, the American quartermaster corps was hard at work removing all available supplies. Between December 17 and December 19, over 1.5 million gallons of fuel had been removed from all the depots located in the Stavelot and Spa vicinity. But this was to be the least of Peiper's problems.

A break in the cloud cover enabled a US Army Air Force observation plane to locate Peiper's tank and infantry columns. This meant that the US 1st Army's headquarters at Spa knew exactly where his forces were located. A trap was set to encircle Peiper's forces. The US 30th Division had retaken Stavelot, and with the US 82nd Airborne Division closing in, Peiper was trapped at Stoumont. The spearhead of the 6th SS Panzer Army was now fighting for its life, and Stoumont would be Peiper's farthest western intrusion into the Ardennes. Peiper's forces were now cut off from Dietrich's main force.

At Elsenborn Ridge, more and more units retreating from the front lines were coming to the aid of its defenders. Reinforcements also began to trickle in, including units from the US 1st, 2nd, and 9th Divisions. The mass of artillery on the top of the ridge included the 155 mm Long Toms, which could reach any village now occupied by the Germans below. Repeated attacks by enemy forces were repulsed with heavy casualties. Taking Elsenborn Ridge seemed impossible. In fact it was, and time wasn't on the Germans' side. As more and more American reinforcements were streaming in from the north, the bulk of Dietrich's 6th SS Panzer Division was being diverted south, clashing into Von Manteuffel's 5th Panzer Army and impeding both armies on their way to the Meuse River.

By December 20, the Germans were still having no luck trying to capture St. Vith. The German High Command, frustrated with the constant delays, ordered an all-out attack the next day. The defenders of St. Vith included units of the US 7th and 9th Armored Divisions. Remnants of the US 106th Division (St. Vith was the divisional headquarters of the 106th) had implemented a 15-mile horseshoe-shaped defense perimeter around the city. So far, repeated attacks by the German divisions had been successively repulsed. But on December 21 at 11:00 a.m., the Germans began their determined assault on St. Vith. A total of 21 attacks came in from the north, south, and east, preceded by a massive bombardment using Nebelwerfer rocket launchers and artillery. The barrage was followed by multiple attacks by infantry and tanks. The defenders were overwhelmed.

The fierce battle lasted well into late evening, when the German tanks broke through and entered St. Vith. The next day, December 22, Maj. Gen. Matthew B. Ridgeway, commander of the US XVIII Airborne Corps, sent a message to Brig. Gen. Robert W. Hasbrouck, commander of the US 7th Armored Division, which stated that a new defense line was being formed west of St. Vith. Hasbrouck's forces joined the US 82nd Airborne Division to form a defensive ring called the fortified goose egg. It had a diameter of about 10 miles and was located between St. Vith and Vielsalm, just east of the Salm River. Hasbrouck's artillery was down to its last rounds when reinforcements and 90 truckloads of artillery shells with 5,000 rounds for the 105 mm howitzers arrived just in the nick of time. St. Vith had fallen, but its defenders had delayed the German advance for six crucial days. It proved to be enough time for reinforcements from the north to hold the German advance along the newly established front line.

Farther north, Peiper was in a desperate situation. His forces remained cut off at Stoumont and were quickly running out of fuel and ammunition. Then, on December 23, Peiper received orders to break out and try to make his way back to the main German force. Under the cover of night, Peiper and his troops silently slipped into the forests surrounding Stoumont and made their way heading southeast toward Trios Points. They were forced to leave all their heavy equipment and vehicles behind, along with their wounded and their American prisoners. In the early-morning hours of December 24, Peiper and his men swam across the icy and dangerous Salm River to reach the German lines, several miles east of Trios Points. Of the original 5,000 men under Peiper's command, only 800 made it back alive.[9]

With Dietrich's 6th SS Panzer Army blocked from securing a northern route to the Meuse, all eyes then turned south, about 30 miles southwest of St. Vith, to Bastogne, the other key city in the battle for the Ardennes. It was now up to Von Manteuffel's 5th Panzer Army to forge ahead and continue efforts to reach the Meuse River. Hitler realized early on the vital importance of Bastogne, with seven main roads leading out of Germany and toward the Meuse. Eisenhower also knew the importance of this city, and on December 17, he'd ordered the US 10th Armored, 82nd Airborne, and 101st Airborne Divisions into the Ardennes.

THE SIEGE OF BASTOGNE

Hitler's original plan was to have Von Manteuffel's 5th Panzer Army break through the Allied front lines in the southern sector of the Ardennes, then quickly capture Bastogne and race to the Meuse River. Once reaching the Meuse, the German 5th Army would head northwest to support the left flank of Dietrich's 6th SS Panzer Army's drive to Antwerp. Von Manteuffel's attack on the first day was a complete success, routing the forward units of the US 106th and 28th Divisions on the front line, but then the Germans began to run into stiff resistance. The first impasse occurred in a small resort town called Clervaux. There, at the headquarters of the 110th Regiment of the US 28th Division, their regimental commander, Col. Hurley E. Fuller, was ordered by Maj. Gen. Norman D. "Dutch" Cota, the commander of the 28th Division at Wiltz, to hold Clervaux at all costs. Fuller, a tough veteran of World War I, assured Cota that there would be no retreat.

Von Manteuffel's 5th Panzer Army was spearheaded by two of his best divisions—the 2nd Panzer Division and the formidable Panzer Lehr Division. They made short work of the brave and fierce soldiers of the US 110th Regiment. Surrounded on all sides and with most of his men dead or wounded, Fuller was forced to surrender on December 17. Cota's forces at the US 28th divisional headquarters at Wiltz were also heavily outnumbered and quickly being decimated by German forces. They held out until the evening of December 19, when Middleton, the corps commander, ordered the remaining survivors to abandon Wiltz. Retreating units of the US 28th Division at Clervaux and Hosingen fought so fiercely that even Mantueuffel himself was surprised at the ferocity and tenacity with which American troops were so determined to stand their ground against overwhelming odds. The Germans had to fight for every inch of ground. By delaying Manteuffel's divisions for two entire days, the result was a severe crimp in the Germans' timetable of attack. Von Manteuffel had expected to capture Bastogne by the second day, but he wasn't even within reach of the city by December 19.

Those precious days gave Brig. Gen. Anthony C. McAuliffe, the acting commander of the US 101st Airborne Division, sufficient time to bolster the defenses around Bastogne. When Eisenhower sent the 82nd and 101st Airborne Divisions to the Ardennes, the 82nd headed for St. Vith and the 101st to Werbomont. On his way to his assigned destination, McAuliffe happened to drop by Middleton's VIII Corps headquarters in Bastogne. Middleton told McAuliffe that the corps's headquarters would be moved to Neufchâteau, located southwest of Bastogne. McAuliffe's new orders were to defend Bastogne with the 101st. He was told to hold the city at all costs.

Forward units of another division, the US 10th Armored Division, sent by Patton's 3rd Army had arrived. McAuliffe decided to split the units to defend three key road junctions leading into Bastogne from the east. The first was at Noville, the second at Longueville, and the third, which was coming in from Wiltz, was located at Wardin, just southwest of Bastogne. When the Germans arrived, the fiercest fighting occurred at Noville, which was directly in the path of Von Manteuffel's 2nd

Panzer Division. On December 20, German tanks broke through the city's defenses and into Noville. Major William R. Desobry, who was commanding the unit at Noville, was then ordered to fall back to Foy, a small town just south of Noville.

When the main force of the 2nd Panzer Division entered Noville, the entire division was ordered to bypass Bastogne and head straight for the Meuse River. The Panzer Lehr Division was told to do the same. It was to be a fatal mistake. Hitler and the German High Command still insisted on crossing the Meuse, but now it was already too late. With the 2nd Panzer Division in the north and Panzer Lehr in the south, Bastogne would have been completely surrounded. This key city could have easily been taken. Now Von Manteuffel was left with the 26th Volksgranedier Division, just one full infantry division, and a unit of tanks from Panzer Lehr to capture Bastogne while his main forces moved on.

However, by this time, the main forces of the US 101st Airborne and 10th Armored Division were defending Bastogne. In addition, the 705th Tank Destroyer Battalion from the north had arrived with more than seven battalions of artillery. Von Manteuffel had a difficult task ahead of him. McAuliffe's only concern was the dwindling supplies of munitions. Fortunately, there was a lull in the next two and a half days as the Germans repositioned their troops and planned their attack. During that time, on December 22, an ultimatum was sent to McAuliffe asking him to surrender. His reply—"Nuts"—to the German commander was the cry of every American soldier's voice in the Ardennes, and his answer was recorded in the annals of military history.[10]

On that same day, Patton's 3rd Army was on the attack, fighting its way toward Bastogne as he'd promised Eisenhower at the meeting in Verdun. This astounding feat surprised everyone. Patton was able to move the bulk of his 3rd Army, including 133,000 tanks and trucks, through 60 miles of rough terrain to attack the German 7th Army's southern flank. McAuliffe received word that Patton's 4th Armored Division was battering its way to the besieged city. It wouldn't be an easy task because the southern approaches were defended by the German 5th Parachute Division, one of the Wehrmacht's most battle-tested divisions.

As the sun came up on December 23, everyone looked up to see clear blue skies. The weather finally broke, and the sound of airplane propellers soon filled the air. Shortly before noon, the sky above Bastogne was filled with hundreds of parachutes drifting slowly down, dropped from 241 huge C-47 cargo carriers. With hundreds of tons of supplies in over 1,000 packages, this was the most beautiful sight for every beleaguered soldier in Bastogne. Those silk parachutes also made excellent sleeping bags!

Perhaps the happiest sight for McAuliffe was the eighty-two P-47 Thunderbolts that came as escorts for the C-47s. As soon as the carriers dropped their loads and flew off, the P-47 fighter-bombers went to work. Their enthusiasm for bombing and strafing any German positions in the open even went so far as attacking friendly artillery positions. American troops had to fend them off by waving identification panels. Allied air support was now in full operation, as over 1,200 sorties were flown against enemy positions. For the Germans, havoc and chaos reigned the day. Major General Heinz Kokott, commanding officer of the 26th Volksgrenadier Division, first saw the planes at 9:00 a.m. and instantly knew the consequences. He bitterly complained that he didn't see one Luftwaffe fighter in the sky. In fact, there were a few, but they were vastly outnumbered and ineffective.[11]

Kokott had to wait until dusk—for an absence of planes in the air—before launching an attack on Marvie, just outside the defensive perimeter southwest of Bastogne. A fierce battle ensued, and the defending troops were on the verge of being overrun by the waves of charging German infantry. Then huge fires erupted, caused by burning armored vehicles and other targets hit by German artillery. The landscape was lit up. Kokott's troops were illuminated and silhouetted against the burning background of fires. They were cut down by machine-gun fire from American troops. The attack was repulsed with heavy losses.

The next day, on Christmas Eve, massive waves of 2,000 American bombers with 800 escort fighters dropped tons of bombs on 31 enemy targets, in which columns of tanks on the road were exposed in the open like sitting ducks. Lead columns of the 2nd Panzer Division stretched for over 12 miles along snow-covered roads. Without their own air support, the Germans would now suffer the consequences. Operations during the day became more hazardous, and air attacks by Allied fighter-bombers became a constant and dangerous menace.

Von Manteuffel and Kokott agreed that with Patton's 4th Armored Division within 20 miles of Bastogne, it was necessary to take Bastogne as quickly as possible. An all-out attack was to be made on Christmas Day. In the early-morning hours of December 25, Kokott's plan was to attack on the western side of Bastogne at Champs and Flamizoulle. The goal was to penetrate the outer defense perimeter and fight their way into the center of Bastogne. The first wave of German infantry and tanks overwhelmed the defenders at Flamizoulle. Cries of help flooded the incoming communication lines of the headquarters of Lt. Col. Steve Chappuis, commander of a parachute regiment. But Chappuis waited for his moment of attack. As Kokott's forces turned north to Champs in an attempt to attack the suburban district from behind, Chappuis sent his forces to lay a trap alongside a wooded forest. The result was a turkey shoot, destroying Kokott's infantry and tanks in a short amount of time. A total of 18 Panzer Lehr tanks were sent on the attack, and well-placed bazookas, high-velocity 76 mm anti-tank guns, and American Sherman tanks destroyed all of them. The Germans tanks were within a mile from the city limits of Bastogne before they were blown to pieces.

In the late afternoon of December 26, the 37th Tank Battalion of Combat

Command R of the US 4th Armored Division, commanded by Lt. Col. Creighton Abrams, was in sight of Assenois, a small village just a few miles south of Bastogne. Patton was informed that despite the danger of the 4th Armored being out-flanked by German forces, Abrams wanted to immediately smash his way through to Bastogne. Of course, Patton responded with an exuberant affirmative.[12] So, as the sun was setting on the horizon, Abrams and his lead tanks went roaring through Assenois with guns blazing, supported by corps artillery and American fighters bombing enemy forces with napalm. Patton called Bradley at 4:00 p.m. to inform his commander that the US 4th Armored Division breakthrough had ended the seven-day siege of Bastogne.[13]

When Kokott heard the news that Abrams's advanced unit of the 4th Armored had entered Bastogne, he knew it was all over. Indeed, the height of the German advance had already peaked on December 23, when the 2nd Panzer Army reached Celles. That morning, as they rolled into town, the troops were exhausted and the tanks suddenly stopped, having run out of gas. A desperate cry for more fuel went out. It would never arrive. Celles was only four miles from Dinant, easily within walking distance to the Meuse River. However, by now the US 2nd Armored Division had arrived from the north and would eventually counterattack and surround the 2nd Panzer Army at Celles. Neither Dietrich's 6th SS Panzer Army nor Von Manteuffel's 5th Panzer Army would ever reach the Meuse. The new front line created on December 24 by the German counteroffensive formed a distinct "bulge" from the previous front. It was due to this configuration of the battlefield that military historians would forever call the Ardennes campaign the Battle of the Bulge.

Hitler had gambled on a quick victory to regain the initiative from the Allies on the Western Front, and he'd lost. Realizing that the war would last only a few months more, his plan was to fragment the Allied forces and then initiate a separate peace treaty with the Western Allies. In this way, his armies would be better able to contend with the Russians on the Eastern Front. Of course, Hitler was the only one who thought the counteroffensive would succeed. His staff all knew the plan was doomed to fail. The German armies were just not strong enough, either in men or material, to accomplish such lofty goals. Von Rundstedt knew that if his armies didn't reach and cross the Meuse River as fast as possible, they would never get to Antwerp. It took four days for Von Manteuffel's 5th Panzer Army to reach just Bastogne. By December 19, Von Rundstedt realized it was too late. After the war, Dietrich also admitted that by December 19, his 6th SS Panzer Army had lost the forward momentum needed to reach the Meuse. Their advance was fatally stalled in the vicious fighting around Malmedy and St. Vith. In the end, the German Army suffered over 100,000 casualties, with the loss of 600 tanks and assault guns, and 1,600 combat aircraft. It would be the last major German offensive on the Western Front.[14]

The failure of the Ardennes counteroffensive would have great repercussions in the defense of Germany in the coming months. It would also have two major impacts on our future missions. First, the Germans would have no more reserves or material to stem the tide of the Allied advance into the Rhineland. All remaining manpower and resources would be transferred to the Eastern Front against the Russians when they began their winter offensive in January. Consequently, as Eisenhower and Bradley had both predicted, the war in Europe would be shortened considerably because of the German defeat in the Ardennes. Second, the near total dominance of Allied air power against the German Luftwaffe was vividly evident over the skies of Belgium. Like the German Army, the Luftwaffe was in rapid deterioration during the final months of 1944. And it would never recover. The skies over Germany would be ruled by the Allied air forces, and the Luftwaffe would no longer be a significant threat. For us, this would be a godsend.

As our troops fought for their lives on Christmas Eve in the inhospitable and frigid winter conditions of the Ardennes, my fellow servicemen and I had the good fortune of being on the *Queen Mary*. It was crowded but comfortable. We arrived in Liverpool, England, on January 1, and I was glad to be on land again. Sailing across the North Atlantic in the winter isn't like ocean cruising in the summertime. There were times when the sea got a little rough. We soon arrived at our final destination—Old Buckenham Airfield, just a few miles southwest of Norwich in the south of England.

CHAPTER 2

OUR FIRST MISSION

OUR JOURNEY ACROSS THE ATLANTIC ended on January 1, 1945, as we docked at Liverpool, England. We then celebrated New Year's Day as soon as we got off the Queen Mary. After that it was a cross-country trip by rail to our final destination, Royal Air Force (RAF) Station Old Buckenham, also known as United States Army Air Force Station 144. Affectionately called "Old Buck," the large air-field is located a couple of miles just southeast of a small town called Attleborough in Norfolk County on the southeastern tip of England. Constructed in 1943 by the AAF 8th Air Force, Old Buckenham was one of many airfields for launching strategic bombing missions against Germany.

Our crew was assigned to the 735th Bombardment Squadron of the 453rd Bombardment Group (Heavy). The 453rd Bomb Group was formed from a starting group of 50 officers and 23 enlisted men from the 29th Bombardment Group (Heavy) on June 29, 1943, at Gowen Field in Boise, Idaho.[1] The 453rd became operational in the ETO in England at Old Buckenham in December 1943. It then commenced combat operations in February 1944, and the bombing missions of the 453rd Bomb Group continued throughout the war until April 1945. Its first operational mission began on February 5, 1944, and the 453rd successfully completed a total of 259 combat missions.

The US 8th Air Force consisted of three air divisions: the 1st Air Division,

2nd Air Division, and 3rd Air Division. All three were stationed in southeastern England. Our 453rd Bomb Group was one of three, along with the 389th and 445th Bomb Groups, within the 2nd Combat Bomb Wing of the 2nd Air Division. While our group was based at Old Buckenham, the 389th Bomb Group had its home base at Hethel and the 445th at Tibenham.

Lieutenant General James Doolittle was the commander of the 8th Air Force when we joined the 453rd Bomb Group. General Doolittle was well-respected and had received the Medal of Honor for leading the B-25 Mitchell bombing raid on Tokyo in 1942. He was responsible for the day-to-day operations of the 8th at the headquarters (Pinetree) of our air command located at High Wycombe, just west of London. Prior to the appointment of Doolittle as head of the 8th Air Force on January 1, 1944,[2] it was Brig. Gen. Ira C. Eaker who contributed much of the planning and formulation of the strategic bombing campaign of the 8th Air Force from 1942 to 1944.

THE CASABLANCA DIRECTIVE

Origins of a cohesive Allied strategic bombing plan took form at the Casablanca Conference in Morocco on January 14, 1943. A summit meeting was scheduled at that time for the Big Three Allied commanders, who were Prime Minister Winston Churchill of England, President Franklin D. Roosevelt of the United States, and Marshal Joseph V. Stalin of Russia. Their military chiefs of staff would also be present at the meeting. Unfortunately, Stalin was unable to attend because he needed to resolve the dilemma of the siege of Stalingrad in Russia, which involved the Red Army and the German 6th Army. However, Stalin was able to send his deputy chief of the Russian general staff, Col. Gen. Alexey I. Antonov, in his place.

Discussions by the Allied leaders at the meeting focused on the military goals and objectives for the coming year. At the top of the agenda was the anticipated cross-Channel invasion of France from England, code-named Operation Overlord. The invasion was originally scheduled to take place in the spring of 1943. However, the operation needed to be rescheduled because there weren't enough American troops or materials for a successful invasion to occur. The new date was to be set in the spring or summer of 1944.

The primary reason for the lack of American resources was the well-entrenched and extremely effective German submarine forces. Enemy U-boats were destroying large numbers of US transport ships traversing the Atlantic Ocean. Before any invasion could be launched, this threat had to be eliminated. Although the Allied bombing raids during 1942 were successful in destroying numerous targets, including enemy submarine bases in Axis-occupied Europe and Germany itself, there was no unified policy among the Allied air forces on what a successful anti-submarine bombing campaign would entail. Worse yet, there was no type of official military liaison to coordinate efforts between the RAF and the AAF in targeting objectives or determining what type of bombing operations would be more effective in defeating the Axis powers. A direct establishment of informational exchange between the two air forces was sorely needed.

Another important topic at the meeting was what type of Allied bombing strategy was required to defeat Germany. It was here in the discussions between the Allied air commanders that serious disagreements arose on the basic concepts of a successful strategic bombing campaign. The commander of the RAF bomber command, Air Chief Marshal Sir Arthur Harris, was at odds with Lt. Gen. Ira Eaker, who was the commander of the US 8th Air Force at the time. Harris believed that indiscriminate bombing, known also as area bombing, of cities and industrial sites would eventually force the Germans to surrender. The ongoing RAF bombing campaign was relegated to daily night bombing raids because of the unacceptable loss of bombers to the Luftwaffe during the day. On the other hand, Eaker and Gen. Henry "Hap" Arnold, the AAF chief of staff, put forward the American policy of strategic bombing. They believed strongly that a strategy of daylight precision bombing of specific industrial targets would destroy Germany's ability to wage war. Both Eaker and Arnold believed that the massed formations of heavy bombers, with their multiple high-caliber machine guns, would be sufficient to ward off attacks by Luftwaffe fighter planes. Thus, the American air commanders were convinced of the effectiveness of precision bombing as opposed to Harris's doctrine of area bombing.

This difference in the concept of strategic bombing held by the American and the British bomber forces brought about a clash between the two Allied air force commanders. An impasse was reached at the conference when Harris attempted to convince Eaker of the merits of area bombing as the most promising method of strategic bombing warfare. The British chiefs of staff, in particular, were skeptical of the American doctrine of daylight bombing. The Luftwaffe was so strong in the early years of the war that bombing raids by the RAF during the day had resulted in unacceptable losses. They had little choice but to switch to night raids. Churchill sided with Harris and was aware that there was little data to suggest precision bombing would be any more effective than area bombing under the combat situations in the ETO. Eaker's concept was new and untested.

In the attempt to convince Churchill of the merits of precision daylight bombing raids, Arnold asked Eaker to draft a document noting the major advantages of this type of strategy. Eaker was then flown to Morocco to meet with the prime minister. At the conference, Churchill read Eaker's notes carefully and listened intently to what the general had to say. What impressed him most was Eaker's suggestion of a round-the-clock bombing campaign with the RAF continuing its nightly raids and the AAF its daylight raids. It would put tremendous pressure on the Luftwaffe fighter force. Both Churchill and Eaker agreed that the resulting attrition rate of German air forces couldn't be sustained over the long term.

Churchill and his air staff intended to convince the Americans to join them in an overall campaign of nightly bombing raids. But the prime minister finally conceded to Eaker's plan of a continuous day-and-night bombing strategy because this was the compromise that could break the impasse confronting the two Allied air commanders. Churchill decided to give the American doctrine of precision daylight bombing strategy a trial run to prove its merits. Out of this meeting were sown the seeds of a strategic bombing plan, one of which was to lead to a truly combined bomber offensive involving both British and American air forces.

Although this was the first time Churchill had ever heard of Eaker's plan, the concept of an effective bombing strategy against Germany had been in the works long before it was formally discussed at the Casablanca Conference. In September 1942, President Roosevelt received a document, known as AWPD-42, from the AAF outlining a strategic bombing plan in preparation for the coming Casablanca Conference. The plan stipulated that the American air forces were to concentrate all their efforts on a systematic destruction of specific and vital elements of the German military and industrial complexes, both in occupied Europe and Germany. Precision daylight bombing raids on selected targets critical to the German war effort would be central to the air campaign. An initial list of 177 targets was included in the operational plan. The focus was on factories and facilities necessary in the production of German aircraft, oil, transportation, armament, and munitions, as well as vital communication networks.

The plan included the expected inclusion of a cooperative effort by the RAF, which was to assist the American efforts by continuing its ongoing night raids. As Eaker detailed his talking points around AWPD-42, he was thus able to convince Churchill of the necessity for a specific policy of an Allied combined bomber offensive that would continue around the clock. At the end of the meeting, the two men came to an agreement on what was required to move the plan forward. The next day, January 21, 1943, Air Vice Marshal John Slessor, the RAF assistant chief of staff, drafted an official directive employing a combined bomber offensive by British and American air forces in a day-and-night bombing campaign.

Slessor's document was then presented to the Combined Chiefs of Staff, composed of both the British and American Chiefs of Staff. The Casablanca Directive was approved on January 23, 1943, and released as the policy document CCS 166. (See Appendix 2.) In the end, both the aspirations of the British and American air force commanders for a joint Anglo-American bomber offensive finally came to fruition. However, CCS 166 was more of a policy statement than a directive with explicit instructions on how a combined offensive would be carried out by each of the Allied air forces.

The first paragraph of CCS 166 stated the primary purpose of the Combined Bomber Offensive with two important considerations. The first was essentially to achieve the total destruction of the German military and industrial complex, and the second was to undermine the morale of the German people to the extent that they would be unable or unwilling to continue to fight. Slessor had intentionally drafted a loosely worded document as a compromise to appease the contentious air war strategy between the American and British air forces. Each of the commanders—Harris for the RAF and Eaker for the AAF—was left to interpret and implement how the stated objectives would be accomplished.

When the Casablanca Directive was issued to the air force commanders, Harris interpreted the directive as a vindication of his doctrine of area bombing. He therefore continued to bomb targets on the long list of large German cities to accomplish his objective to destroy the will of the German people by inflicting mass casualties. Eaker, along with his superiors, Gen. Arnold and Gen. Carl Spaatz (commanding general of the US Strategic Air Forces), held the belief that the British doctrine of area bombing was no more than terror bombing with no visible evidence of success. The American commanders were sure that precision bombing against legitimate military targets would eventually lead to the defeat of the German armed forces.

The major weakness of the Casablanca Directive was that it was just a statement of policy on what was necessary in identifying strategic bombing objectives, but it wasn't a concrete operational plan on how to accomplish these goals. As an agent of the Combined Chiefs of Staff, which dictated policy issues to commanders of the RAF and AAF, Air Chief Marshal Charles Portal was responsible for their bombing operations. However, Portal left the interpretation of the directive to the discretion of commanders Harris and Eaker. They were to implement the stated objectives in whatever manner they saw fit.

Although each of the air forces, the RAF and AAF, had a liaison staff at their respective headquarters, there was never a command structure to integrate the two air forces in operational terms. Each continued to conduct independent bombing campaigns. The American air staff wanted a single commander to oversee and direct air operations for the entire European Theater. The British thought otherwise and insisted upon separate commands for operational independence. This was primarily due to the dogged determination of Harris, who vehemently opposed any interference with his area-bombing campaign. As a result, in the months following the establishment of CCS 166, both Anglo-American allied air forces resumed their own separate bombing operations. It was a combined bombing offensive in name only.

THE POINTBLANK DIRECTIVE

General Arnold was well aware of the deficiencies present in the Casablanca Directive. For him, it represented a good step forward in establishing an Allied strategic bombing strategy that he'd envisioned for a long time. To Arnold, CCS 166 was just the beginning of a lengthy process of formulating a concrete plan. It was going in the right direction. The basic structure was intact; the plan just needed to be fleshed out. To do this, Arnold instructed Eaker to draft a plan to make CCS 166 work. It turned out that CCS 166 was only part of the puzzle to accomplish the final Combined Bomber Offensive that would satisfy all the parties involved. The first part was the previous document, AWPD-42, which Eaker had used to help convince Churchill of the feasibility of a combined offensive. Of course, the second part was CCS 166 itself, in which some of the ideas presented in AWPD-42 were incorporated into the Casablanca Directive. The final and last piece of the puzzle began when AWPD-42 was completed back in September 1942.

At that time, in their analysis of target selections, the US Joint Intelligence Committee found AWPD-42 too limited. The document represented a major step in providing a working framework for initiating a plan for the systematic bombardment of Germany. However, it fell short of providing enough details to satisfy the Joint Intelligence Committee. So, on December 9, 1942, Gen. Arnold sent Col. Byron E. Gates, of the AC/AS Management Control, a directive. Gates was to assemble a group of operational analysts to begin a study on what would be required for a bombing campaign that would deteriorate the German war effort to the point where a successful invasion of Western Europe could take place. This would be the birth of what would be known as the Committee of Operations Analysts (COA).[3]

COA members included military personnel as well as civilian experts from both academia and the wartime industrial sector. Notable members included Edward M. Earle, of the Institute for Advanced Study at Princeton, and Thomas W. Lamont, of J.P. Morgan and Company. The British Ministry of Economic Warfare and the Air Ministry were also incorporated into the study program to provide valuable data for the committee. A large number of subcommittees were formed to study which German industries would be the most critical in sustaining the war effort. The results of this effort eventually provided the basis for an analytical determination of target selection that led to a successful bombing campaign.

The COA study was completed in the spring of 1943, and the results of its findings were sent to Gen. Arnold on March 8, 1943. With regard to the degree of deterioration of the German war effort needed for a successful invasion of Europe, the committee failed to deliver a firm answer. It couldn't be determined what available air forces would be on hand for a sustained bombing campaign, and the operational experience of the US 8th Air Force was found to be lacking for such an effort. Since the 8th had been in operation for less than a year, the committee found it difficult to assess its operational efficiency moving forward. However, in terms of target selection, the study provided compelling evidence to identify and destroy key German industrial systems in a worthwhile effort to eliminate the enemy's ability to continue the war.

The COA concluded that it was better to concentrate on a high degree of destruction in the critical industries needed to sustain the war effort than effect a small degree of destruction on a wide variety of unrelated industrial targets. In the end, members decided that a persistent and unrelenting effort to completely destroy these essential industries would be cumulative, which would ultimately lead to a severe, if not complete, impairment of Germany's military strength. With respect to target selection, the committee, after an intensive study of 19 German industrial systems, identified 60 targets. The committee believed that the destruction of these specific targets would be enough to cause the collapse of Germany's economic base—and with it, the Wehrmacht's ability to continue its military operations.

The committee provided a list of target systems, with each system listed in preferential order. Strictly speaking, it wasn't a priority list as such but one the committee deemed to be of importance in the target selection process. First on the list was the German aircraft industry. Before a bombing campaign could be successful, this vital industry had to first be eliminated or neutralized. From 1942 to 1943, Luftwaffe fighters had been very effective in causing unsustainable losses in the US 8th Air Force's personnel and aircraft. There was some debate over which would be more effective—focused attacks on final-assembly plants or engine-assembly plants. The committee decided that final-assembly plants and component-producing plants took precedence over engine-assembly plants. It was estimated that the destruction of 20 targets within these two types of industrial base would have a profound effect on the production of single-engine aircraft.

The next system considered was the manufacture of ball bearings. The widespread use of this material was essential not only to the aircraft industry but also in the production of many types of war material, spanning specialized test equipment to high-speed machinery. The committee believed only a few large plants were capable of producing ball bearings. The Schweinfurt plants, in particular, were reputed to produce one-half of the total production of this critical war material.

The third system in the order of preferential target selections was the oil and petroleum industry. Importation of crude oil was essential for Germany's energy requirements, almost two-thirds of which came from the rich oil fields of Ploesti in Rumania. Without access to external sources of crude oil, Germany would need to generate its own within its borders. Synthetic oil production was localized in thirteen Bergius hydrogenation plants and fewer than a dozen major synthetic oil plants.

Destruction of these plants, along with 26 petroleum refinery facilities, would almost totally eliminate Germany's ability to meet its essential energy requirements.

Based on army intelligence information at that time, the COA came up with a list of 76 specific targets within six critical military systems that were listed in terms of their importance in the ability of the Western Axis to continue the war effort:

PRIMARY OBJECTIVES:

1. Submarine construction yards and bases
2. German aircraft industry
3. Ball bearings
4. Oil

SECONDARY OBJECTIVES:

1. Synthetic rubber and tires
2. Military transport vehicles

Both British and American air staffs agreed that the elimination of the submarine threat posed by the German navy was the most important military target system to be addressed before there was any chance of success with Operation Overlord. The COA studies were completed and reported to Gen. Arnold in March 1943. At last, a thoroughly detailed analytical evaluation of target selection for an effective combined bomber offensive had been accomplished. This list of industrial target systems was the last piece of the puzzle necessary for completing a comprehensive operational plan for the Casablanca Directive, CCS 166. In April 1943, per Gen. Arnold's request, Eaker incorporated the results of the COA studies to formulate the final plan. Eaker's final work came to be known as the Plan for the Combined Bomber Offensive for the United Kingdom, or simply the CBO plan.

The CBO plan had many elements in common with CCS 166 and didn't replace the Casablanca Directive. Instead, it added to its policy objectives. It provided a concrete operational plan for a truly combined bomber offensive with an organized list of targets for each of the critical German military industrial systems. In addition, the plan consisted of a timetable operating in four successive phases from June 1943 to June 1944, which was the anticipated date of the invasion of Western Europe, known as Operation Overlord. Each operational phase would build upon the other as the numbers of flight personnel and bombers of the American air forces increased with time.

In early May 1943, Eaker's CBO plan was submitted to the American Joint Chiefs of Staff, who approved it, as did the Allied Combined Chiefs of Staff. Churchill endorsed the CBO plan on May 18, 1943. On June 10, 1943, the new directive, termed the Pointblank Directive and code-named Operation Pointblank, was officially issued to the commanding officers of the RAF Bomber Command: Air Marshal Harris and Gen. Eaker of the US 8th Air Force.[4]

General Arnold and the American air staff had finally accomplished their goal of achieving a long-term strategic bombing program that integrated the efforts of both the RAF Bomber Command and AAF in the ETO. The Pointblank Directive was really an extension of the Casablanca Directive because Pointblank incorporated much of the policy and objectives initiated by the previous directive. However, the important addition of a cohesive and well-developed CBO operational plan was what was needed for the Casablanca Directive to achieve meaningful results. The target priorities listed in the Pointblank Directive were assigned primarily to the US 8th Air Force, but Operation Pointblank was established to actually integrate the air operations of both Allied air forces in a combined bombing program. This was accomplished by issuing clear-cut assignments to each of the participants. The American air forces would bomb targets established in Operation Pointblank in daylight raids using precision-bombing techniques, while the RAF complemented and completed the 8th's missions by continued bombing attacks against the same target area at night. Such an effort would ensure a near-total destruction of the target. In this manner, Harris would be able to achieve a place for his area-bombing campaign within the framework of Operation Pointblank.

As with the Casablanca Directive, the RAF chief of staff oversaw the direction and progress of Operation Pointblank. The Combined Chiefs of Staff requested regular reports of ongoing operations to determine the correct time frame for proceeding with Operation Overlord in the following year. Elimination of the two top-priority enemy systems listed in the Casablanca Directive—the submarine fleet and German Luftwaffe—was deemed critical for the success of a cross-Channel invasion into France. By June 1943, when Operation Pointblank became operational, the submarine menace had been neutralized. It wasn't through bombing raids but due to rapid technological advances in anti-submarine warfare by the Allied naval forces. Improved sonar detection of enemy U-boats and an ever-increasing deployment of naval submarine destroyers provided much better protection of trans-Atlantic military convoys.

With the diminished threat of enemy submarines, defeat of the German Luftwaffe took precedence as a top-priority target in the Operation Pointblank bombing campaign. Not only was Allied air supremacy critical for the success of Operation Overlord, but Eaker knew that effective precision bombing of industrial targets by the 8th Air Force couldn't be accomplished without destroying the German Air Force. The COA had compiled a list of 22 targets for attacking the German aircraft industry, which the 8th air staff now incorporated for its Operation Pointblank bombing operations. These included aircraft final-assembly plants; critical component production facilities, such as ball-bearing factories; and other types of manufacturing plants necessary for the generation of enemy fighter aircraft. This was to continue nonstop from June 1943 to June 1944 in preparation for Operation Overlord.

THE OIL CAMPAIGN

A high-priority industrial system targeted by Operation Pointblank was the oil industry. General Arnold and his staff realized early on that this system was the enemy's Achilles' heel. Eliminating the access to and production of oil would be the key in destroying Germany's ability to sustain the war effort. General Eaker was eager to initiate a concentrated effort to bomb oil targets as soon as Operation Pointblank went into effect in June 1943. His efforts were thwarted, however, by the urgent need to eliminate the threat of the German fighter forces prior to Operation Overlord. It wasn't until June 1944, a full year later, when Allied air supremacy had been achieved, that the oil industry became the primary target system in Operation Pointblank.

On June 8, 1944, two days after the Normandy landings in France, Gen. Carl Spaatz, the commanding general of US Strategic Air Forces in Europe, officially ordered the American air forces to bomb targets of the oil industry as their prime objective going forward. The US 8th Air Force was to focus on oil targets in eastern and central Germany, while the 15th Air Force was to bomb the oil fields of Ploesti in Rumania as well as in Vienna, Austria and Budapest, Hungary. The oil campaign advanced with renewed energy and ferocity. It was to be known as the Fall Oil Offensive of 1944.

Germany had very scarce natural oil resources within its borders. Almost all of its crude oil supply came from the vast oil fields located in the Nazi-occupied countries of Rumania and Hungary. Because of the lack of this precious resource, the Germans began to develop and produce synthetic oil from coal in the 1940s using two methods. Friedrich Bergius developed the first method in 1913. Called the Bergius process, the coal was directly converted into hydrocarbon liquids by a technique known as hydrogenation, where the coal is heated and liquefied in the presence of hydrogen gas. In 1925, Franz Fischer and Hans Tropsch developed a second method that indirectly converts coal to synthetic oils. It's a two-step process in which carbon monoxide and hydrogen are generated from liquefaction of coal through gasification. This second step involves a series of chemical reactions that convert these gases into synthetic oils and fuels.

Of the two methods, the Bergius process—a direct conversion of coal to synthetic oil—was more advanced and found to be the most efficient. Furthermore, brown coal called lignite was the only coal available in many parts of Germany, and hydrogenation was easily accomplished by the Bergius method. Consequently, a series of Bergius hydrogenation plants was built in Germany before the war started. As the demand for oil increased, numerous Fischer-Tropsch plants were also built throughout Germany to augment the supply of crude oil being imported from Axis-occupied countries. The huge deposits of coal in the Ruhr Valley allowed the Germans to produce more than three times the amount of petroleum products than they could get by importing crude oil.

General Spaatz was well aware that synthetic oil production was highly concentrated in certain locations, especially in the Ruhr. It was discovered that more than 90 percent of the output of oil was represented by 54 crude-oil refineries and synthetic petroleum plants, of which 27 were deemed the most important. These 27 were found to be located in Ploesti, Rumania, and Silesia, and in the Ruhr Valley.[5] The numerous crude oil refineries surrounding the massive oil fields located in Ploesti became the focus of the summer and autumn oil campaigns. It would become an all-out effort to destroy these critical facilities, but it wouldn't be easy. Ploesti was one of the most heavily defended areas of German-occupied Europe.

When the US 15th Air Force, commanded by Maj. Gen. Nathan Twining, began its heavy bombing raids on Ploesti, the Germans quickly increased their defensive posture. Heavy antiaircraft artillery was brought into the fight. The hills overlooking Ploesti were peppered with multiple batteries of heavy 88 mm, 105 mm, and 128 mm artillery, supported by more emplacements of light antiaircraft weapons. Over 500 guns pointed upward toward the skies above. In addition, at least four Gruppen[6] of Luftwaffe interceptor fighters, represented by over 200 aircraft, were stationed around the oil fields. However, the Germans didn't expect such a determined air attack on Ploesti and were unprepared for the onslaught to come.

All through the summer, Ploesti was pounded again and again by massive bombing raids, often numbering well over 1,000 bombers per raid by the US 15th Air Force. The oil fields around Ploesti became fiery cauldrons of smoke and fire that continued to burn for weeks. By the middle of August 1944, Ploesti had received 24 Allied bombing raids. The last of them came on August 17, 18, and 19. Soon afterward, the Russians occupied Rumania. All they found at Ploesti were smoldering ruins. The Russians invited Gen. Eaker himself to survey the site at the end of August. Taken aback by what he saw, he couldn't have imagined the devastation that had been wrought by the Allied air forces. Destruction was complete.

Bombing raids were also carried out against oil refineries and synthetic petroleum plants throughout other Nazi-occupied territories, such as Hungary, Poland, Czechoslovakia, and elsewhere. But Ploesti was the biggest prize and represented as much as one-fourth of Germany's total crude oil imports. Nor was Germany itself immune from the destruction. From September to November 1944, multiple Allied bombing raids were concentrated in cities with large oil industrial facilities, such as crude oil refineries, synthetic petroleum production factories, benzol chemical plants, and oil storage depot sites. No part of Germany was spared. Bremen, Hanover, Hamburg, and Politz were targeted in the north, while Böhlen, Ludwigshafen, Lützkendorf, Merseburg, Leuna, Ruhland, and Zeitz were bombed in the south. Magdeburg in central Germany was especially hard hit, as were Düsseldorf and many other cities in the Ruhr Valley, such as Dortmund and Gelsenkirchen.[7]

By the end of November 1944, all of the synthetic oil plants in western Germany were put out of commission, and only one crude oil refinery remained operational in the entire country. The German war machine was starving for oil and petroleum products, especially fuel oil and gasoline. This was made most evident when the mechanized advance units of the German armies came to a complete standstill during the Ardennes Offensive in December 1944. They literally ran out of gas. The offensive's failure was due to many factors, some of which were related to poor planning, but the most critical component was the lack of fuel.

The oil campaign was a complete success. From January to December 1944, importation of crude oil and refined petroleum products fell dramatically from 179,000 tons to 22,000 tons, a drop of 91 percent. During the same time period, both synthetic oil production and refined oil products within Germany decreased by 98 percent.[8] The Germans were now forced to acquire all their needed energy through an ever-decreasing production of synthetic oil. This would have serious repercussions on the Wehrmacht's ability to continue the war. But also more profoundly, the marginal availability of aviation fuel would completely compromise the Luftwaffe's capability to sustain airborne operations to adequately defend its homeland.

MISSION #1: JANUARY 16, 1945
TARGET: MAGDEBURG

When we entered combat operations, the oil campaign was coming to an end. "Mopping up" is what they termed the elimination of the remaining oil production facilities. Although complete destruction was evident in all the major oil production sites, the resourceful Germans were able to repair, rebuild, and sustain the production of a limited amount of synthetic oil in the largest facilities. One of these was in Magdeburg. It would be our target on our first mission. We were all eager to get started as soon as we got situated at Old Buckenham, but we had to wait two weeks because of constant delays due to the uncontrollable forces of Mother Nature.

As soon as we arrived at Liverpool and disembarked from the troop ship on New Year's Day, the first thing we noticed was the atrocious weather. It was cold, foggy, and raining. Then it started to snow. For an entire week, our base was del-

Our first day at Old Buckenham was cold and dreary, but all of us were in high spirits!

uged with intermittent bouts of heavy sleet and turbulent snowstorms. The winter of 1944–1945 was one of the worst ever recorded in the British Isles. It had a severe detrimental effect on the training routines given to new crew arrivals at Old Buck. Probably the most challenging sessions were for our pilot, Lt. Swingle, who was learning the flight routines of taking off and getting into combat formation with other units of our squadron. Adverse weather conditions, like fog, rain, and sleet, made these procedures extremely hazardous. There were many instances of midair collisions between aircraft that uncontrollably flew too close to one another under these stressful conditions.

The day we arrived on base, there was a fatal crash of an aircraft from the 735th Squadron as it attempted takeoff under freezing conditions. There were only three survivors.

Operations continued, but the weather conditions remained hazardous and unaccommodating. There were many accidents and mission cancellations, including ours, during the first two weeks. However, the weather began to let up a bit during the second week, and we were scheduled for takeoff on January 16. The 8th's primary targets were oil and industrial facilities.

Our division, the 2nd Air Division, was assigned two primary and two secondary targets. Primary targets were the main focus of a raid. But due to certain circumstances, such as inclement weather conditions, that prevented the bomb group from reaching its designated target, the group was normally diverted to its secondary targets. For the 2nd Division, the synthetic oil production industrial complex in Rothensee, Magdeburg and the oil plants in Ruhland were the primary targets. The secondary targets included munitions factories in Magdeburg and railway stations in Dresden.

During the war, Magdeburg was a fairly large city with well over 300,000 inhabitants. It was an important industrial center in east-central Germany. Ideally situated on the Elbe River, just 80 miles from Berlin in the east and highly accessible to the Ruhr industrial center in the west, Magdeburg was a prime target for

Allied bombing raids. It had been bombed many times during the war. Despite the constant air raids, industrial activity within the city remained productive up until the end of the war even though most of the city was in total ruins.

One of the primary targets for the 8th in Magdeburg on this mission was Braun-kohle-Benzin-A.G. (BRABAG), a large and highly productive Bergius hydrogenation plant processing lignite into synthetic petroleum. BRABAG was situated in the Rothensee industrial zone of the Magdeburg Port Basin I alongside the Elbe River. BRABAG was one of the first Bergius plants built in 1936, specializing in the production of synthetic fuels. The company built and operated two more Bergius plants, as well as one Fischer-Tropsch plant, before the war started. During the war, at least twelve Bergius plants and nine Fischer-Tropsch plants operated within Germany. The other primary target was a large Fischer-Tropsch plant located in Ruhland. That plant, known as BRABAG II, was constructed in 1937. It began producing gasoline and diesel oil in modest quantities when it first became operational, but its amounts grew substantially during the war to become Germany's largest Fischer-Tropsch plant.

The attack on these two industrial targets consisted of 627 heavy bombers that were dispatched from the 2nd and 3rd Air Divisions. This number of bombers was about the average for January. The total number ranged from 117 to 1,158 bombers per mission. This wide range represented the cumulative effects of the awful weather conditions during this time. Of the total on this mission, three hundred sixty-four B-24s from the 2nd Air Division were directed to their primary targets. Our squadron and two other squadrons of the 453rd Bomb Group, with a combined total of 33 aircraft, were directed to attack the Krupp Tank Manufacturing plant located in Magdeburg. The company Krupp AG was probably a giant armaments industry within itself. Its factories produced a wide variety of weapons and munitions, from battleships and submarines to howitzers and artillery shells. This particular Krupp factory in Magdeburg specialized in building panzer tanks for the German Army.

When our crew received news that our first mission would be on January 16, we were all inundated with a shower of mixed emotions. I felt both extreme elation and apprehension at the same time. The crew would be able to put to good use the many months of training that led up to this day. In the early-morning hours of the 16th, we quickly went to the mess hall to have breakfast before going to the operations briefing. On every mission, before we went to our aircraft, we had an extensive presentation and discussion of the assigned targets and mission details.

Each bombing mission was determined the previous day by Gen. Doolittle and his operational staff at 8th Air Force headquarters in a secured underground war room at High Wycombe (code-named Pinetree), which was located just 30 miles northwest of London. There, the specific targets were assigned to the bomb crews, and the intelligence staff assessed the potential success of the mission and determined if the weather conditions were good enough for a go-ahead the next day. If all the conditions were positive, the details of the bombing mission were then transmitted from Doolittle's headquarters to the air divisional headquarters at each of the air bases that were to participate in the bombing raids.

At the operations briefing, our group commander usually began by informing us of the nature of the target's location and strategic importance, along with other facts necessary for a successful mission. Next up, the operations officer described the flight formations, who would fly lead in the formation, the attack routes, communication requirements, and other pertinent information. The intelligence officer then informed us of the critical components of the target area, such as the presence of anti-artillery defense installations, details of aerial reconnaissance photographs, and the probability of attack by Luftwaffe fighters. Finally, the meteorological officer assessed the prevailing weather conditions—not only that of the prescribed target area but also, more importantly, the local environment on base. Conditions of the latter determined whether or not we would even be able to take off and assemble properly in the formation before we began flying toward our destination.

After the operations briefing, our crew then put on our flight clothing and equipment. Flying at a cruising altitude of 25,000 feet in an unheated aircraft required us to dress for extreme cold, with temperatures falling as low as -25 degrees Fahrenheit in most cases. Underneath our regular flight uniform we wore an electronically heated undergarment complete with a wire and electrical input plug. Then, finally, we put on the familiar fleece-lined leather flight jacket. Along with a pair of silk gloves underneath a pair of leather ones, there was also a tight-fitting skullcap to keep the head warm and a towel or heavy scarf around the neck to keep out the cold. On top of all these items was the essential oxygen mask to enable us to survive the high-altitude environment in an unpressurized aircraft. Packed like well-dressed polar bears, we then entered our aircraft in preparation for takeoff.

Depending on the current weather conditions, a decision was made at 8:00 a.m. to either begin or abort the mission. If the decision was an affirmative, then the bomber crews received permission to take off and proceeded to their assigned group formation assembly coordinates. Once in the air, each bomb group, with their squadrons, assembled into combat formations within a designated area in the sky above the airfield. The assembly point for the 453rd Bomb Group in good weather was usually a few miles from our airfield. But in less-than-ideal weather conditions, our group assembled much farther out, as far as 25 to 30 miles north of Old Buck, by the edge of the North Sea.

Assembly was the most hazardous part of getting into formation because bad weather conditions could result in disastrous midair collisions between close-flying aircraft. Rendezvous coordinates for each bomb group in a combat wing were assisted by the use of radio beacons sending out specific radio frequencies that were monitored by the group formation leaders. The different bomb groups then orbited the beacon signal for assembly.

For new pilots, such a procedure was a challenging and potentially danger-ous learning experience. To visually distinguish the different circling formations of various aircraft, a special assembly plane was often used. Its exterior surface was painted in all types of colorful designs. The entire plane was decorated with bright-green, yellow, or orange splashes of polka dots, stripes (zebra stripes were a favorite), or other types of wild and distinctive patterns.

Squadrons within each bomb group assembled at different altitudes, as did dif-ferent bomb groups, to position themselves within the combat formation. If you looked up from the ground, a bomber formation flying overhead might just look like a massive traffic jam of flying aircraft. However, each bomber had a specific position in the bomb group formation. Likewise, each bomb group had a similar po-sition in the combat wing formation. A single combat wing was usually composed of three or four bomb groups.

A specific pattern of bomber positions was formed within each combat forma-tion, which came to be known as a combat box. This pattern was originally devel-oped for two important purposes. The first was to design the proper configuration of bombers for maximizing the massed firepower of the entire bomb group for defense against German fighters. Since each bomber carried at least ten .50-caliber machine guns, the combined firepower of a single bomb group within the formation repre-sented a formidable defense structure against enemy attack. The second advantage of a closely knit configuration of bombers was to concentrate and tighten the release perimeter of the massive unloading of bombs onto the target.

The evolution of heavy bomber formations began in 1942 when the US 8th Air Force initiated its bombing raids. An effective defensive formation of bombers with-in the combat box was modified through costly battles against attacking Luftwaffe fighters. As a result, the configuration of bombers within the formation, with re-spect to the number of aircraft and the pattern or position of each aircraft, gradually changed from 1942 to 1945. The term *box* was used in a figurative sense to represent an area of airspace occupied by bombers flying in combat formation in a squadron or bomb group. It was coined as a tool for operational planning purposes, which proved to be very useful for developing different patterns of aircraft in the formation.

For example, a squadron of nine aircraft consisted of three groups of aircraft in *V* formation, with each group occupying a specific area of airspace. The three groups were arranged in a specific pattern to form a squadron box. A bomb group normally consisted of three squadrons of bombers. Each squadron occupied a des-ignated area of airspace within the bomb group box. The first squadron might be flying in a lead squadron position ahead of the two other squadrons. The second squadron, flying to the right and above the first squadron, would be in the high-right squadron position. Finally, the remaining squadron might be flying to the left, below the lead squadron, and thus was called the low-left squadron. To visualize objects in 3D space in one's mind can be mind-boggling, so in this case a picture is really worth a thousand words.

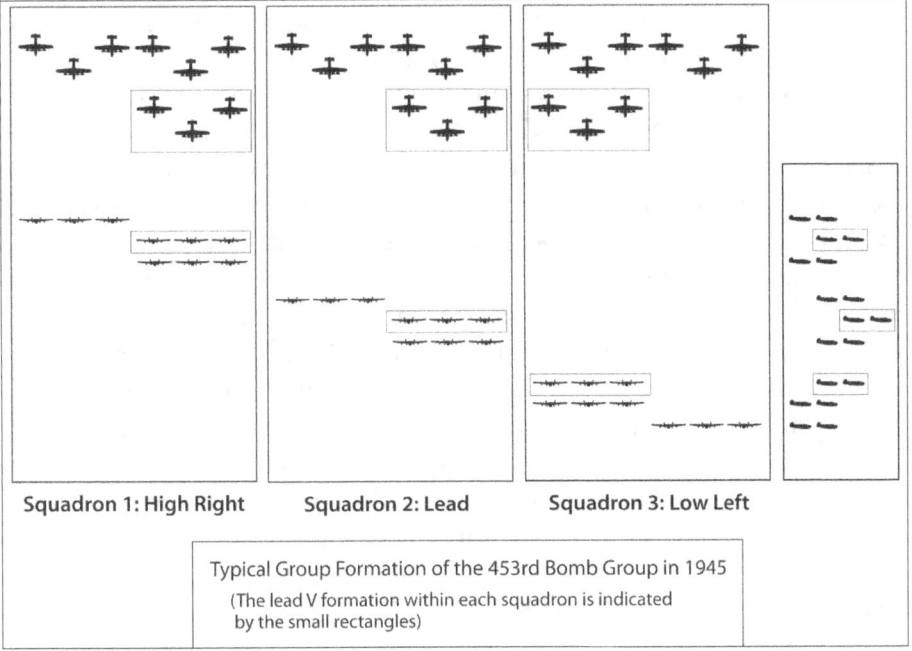

Squadron 1: High Right   Squadron 2: Lead   Squadron 3: Low Left

Typical Group Formation of the 453rd Bomb Group in 1945
(The lead V formation within each squadron is indicated by the small rectangles)

If we extend and expand this concept to a combat wing consisting of three or more bomb groups, we begin to realize how large an area an entire wing formation encompassed. Because each aircraft was 50 to 75 feet from its closest companion, a single bomb group formation most often spanned a horizontal distance of half a mile and a vertical displacement of roughly a quarter mile. The airspace occupied by a single combat wing could extend for many miles. Furthermore, in a big raid, each air division might dispatch three or more combat wings. The 2nd Air Division usually sent four: the 2nd, 14th, 20th, and 96th combat wings. It's no wonder the enemy on the ground looking up was amazed to see our attacking bombers covering the entire sky.

As the number of heavy bombers increased dramatically in 1944, very large bombing raids were composed of multiple attacking combat wings. To allow for proper maneuvering of the bomb groups within the wing, especially during a bombing run, the distance separating the combat wings was increased from three to six miles. The number of aircraft in the bomb group also increased, from 27 to a high of 36 aircraft or more on each mission. Varying types of bomber formations changed depending on the tactics German fighters employed in their attacks. Throughout 1944, it was found that the most effective defense against German fighters was the configuration of a lead, high-right, and low-left squadron within the bomb group. Additional squadrons could be added to the bomb group in high high-right and low low-left positions to accommodate more bombers. This pattern of the group bomber formation continued to the end of the war.

During the winter of 1944–1945, conditions in the field once again changed. Coinciding with the defeat of the Luftwaffe in the spring of 1944, the increase in bomber losses was now due to the Germans' renewed effort to use heavy concentrations of antiaircraft batteries as their main defense against bombers. A change in the positioning of aircraft within the squadron box was initiated. The distance between individual bombers was increased to minimize the threat of closely spaced artillery shell bursts, while the three squadrons came closer together so the entire bomb group became more compact to present a smaller target to antiaircraft fire. In most bombing raids during the final months of the war, the 2nd Air Division regularly employed a bomb group formation composed of 27 aircraft within each bomb group.

In terms of ordnance, our bomb bays were loaded with nine 500-pound general purpose bombs on this mission. The 8th used four main types of bombs, depending upon the requirements for maximizing the destruction of the target. The general purpose, or GP, bombs carried a high-explosive charge intended to provide the most damage through blast and concussive effects. We carried GPs as our main bomb load on almost all our missions, and they came in a wide variety of sizes, from 100 pounds to 2,000 pounds. Although the B-24 Liberator could carry a maximum bomb load of 12,800 pounds, our average bomb load per mission was about 6,000 pounds. There was always a compromise between the bomb load and the amount of fuel required on each mission. On some missions we carried incendiary bombs in addition to GPs. Two other types, the armor-piercing and fragmentation bombs, were employed for special targets and used less often on our massed heavy bomber raids. The US 9th Air Force made good use of frags on its tactical raids against armor and infantry.

Before we took off, the ground crew loaded the bombs on board, and an armorer inserted the bomb fuses into the bombs. Attached to each fuse was a cotter pin with an attached label, commonly called the bomb tag. The cotter pin prevented premature detonation on board, especially while taking off. Once we were in the air and on our way to our designated target, it was necessary to manually remove the attached cotter pin to arm the bomb. This was done when we were well on our way toward our target, usually as we were crossing the English Channel into France before reaching Germany.

Being the smallest member of the crew, I was most often assigned to remove the bomb tags. This was because the bomb bays were very cramped spaces. I had to walk on a narrow (less than a foot in width) catwalk extending through the lower center divide of each of the two tandem bomb bay compartments. I wouldn't say it

The narrow catwalk through the bomb bays looking forward toward the cockpit. The bombs were stacked vertically on each side of the bay. They could be released automatically or manually only when the bomb bay doors were fully opened. Occasionally the doors became jammed, and one of the crew had to go into the bay and manually open them. This could be most dangerous, and regulations required the crew member to be fully suited with a parachute. However, that rarely happened because the space was so cramped that there was no room to put on a parachute. (Collings Foundation)

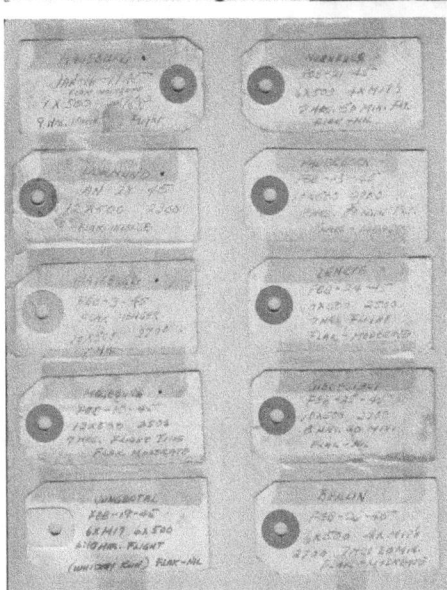

I wrote down quick notes on a bomb tag for each of our missions. Missions No. 1–10.

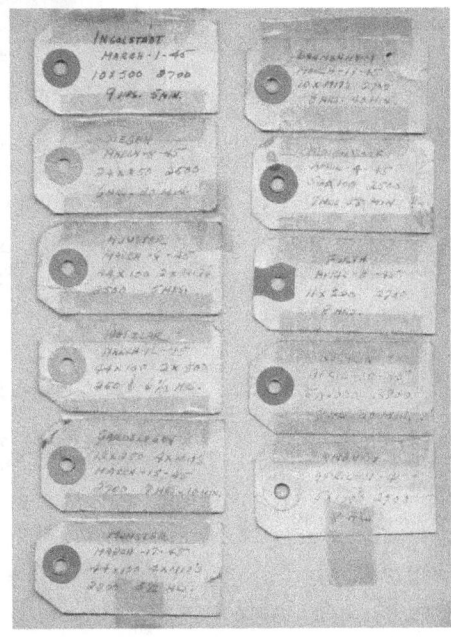

Missions No. 11–22. (No bomb tag for No. 18, which was an airdrop supply mission.)

was like walking a tightrope, but at times it did take some maneuvering—especially when we ran into air turbulence. Since I did this pretty often, I kept a bunch of bomb tags and wrote some mission details on them during each of our missions, such as the name of our target and the load of bombs we carried. Many of the guys on base kept a diary of all their missions, and this was perhaps the only personal record I kept during my tour of duty. The average time to our target and back was around eight hours, so I had plenty of spare time.

As soon as we crossed into Germany, we started to receive enemy anti-artillery fire, what we called flak. The Germans had a sophisticated network of radar systems to detect any enemy aircraft entering their airspace. They knew our exact location and intended target area. Heavy antiaircraft artillery guns mounted on specially built railway cars made the guns mobile, which meant they could intercept the bomber streams on their way to their target. I remember the first time my plane was hit by flak. I thought we were passing through some kind of airborne debris. I could hear the exploding shells around us. As we approached Magdeburg, the amount of flak increased exponentially. The sky soon filled with large black puffs of smoke from numerous exploding artillery shells. There was some armor plating around the cockpit and turret guns for protection against explosive shrapnel, but otherwise the skin of a B-24 was basically just a thin layer of aluminum. It was like flying around in a big Coke can. Along with a direct hit, any exploding shell within about 200 yards of an aircraft could be lethal, especially if large fragments struck an engine or one of the fuel tanks.

Any breach by shrapnel was immediately evident, but most often you could just hear the bits of shrapnel hitting the sides of the aircraft. It sounded very much like someone throwing a bunch of pebbles or rocks against the riveted panels covering the outside of the plane. The other dramatic effect was the turbulence caused by the concussion of exploding shells. A shell exploding very close to the aircraft could cause the plane to be buffeted around quite a bit, like a canoe on a stormy lake. Because we were always flying in tight formation, midair collisions were a constant danger. But perhaps the most dangerous time was when we were on our bombing run over the target.

As we approached the target, it was critical for the aircraft to fly at a constant altitude and airspeed without the slightest deviation, while the bombardier was synchronizing the bombsight onto the target. Our bombers carried the Norden bombsight, which calculated the most important parameters required for a successful hit during the bombing run. The unit was really an analog computer. It received inputs from the bombardier, such as wind force and direction, air and ground speed, drift, and the type of bombs being dropped. Then the Norden automatically calculated what speed and altitude were necessary to release the bombs while flying directly over the target.

Because the plane was moving at a cruising speed of about 250 to 300 mph, the load of bombs released followed a forward trajectory path that curved downward onto the target. Hence, the bombs were dropped ahead of the target, and the aircraft actually passed over the target before the bombs hit and detonated on the ground. The Norden bombsight made all the necessary calculations to put the bombs on the correct path during the bombing run. John Harrington, who was our navigator and resident math wizard, explained all the gory details to me. But it was, in a nutshell, pretty complicated.

As soon as the target was visible, the bombardier looked through the optical part of the Norden bombsight, which was basically a telescope with vertical and horizontal crosshairs, and manually made the fine adjustments necessary to keep the flight path on course. He was actually affecting the flight controls, either through the PDI (pilot's directional indicator, located on the cockpit instrument panel) for the pilot to follow or through the Norden's AFCE (automatic flight control equipment), which controlled the aircraft in autopilot mode. As the bombardier aimed the sight at the target, the Norden automatically computed the time for the release of the bombs. When all the necessary conditions were met, the bombs were automatically released. However, there was a manual override in which the bombardier could bypass and control the bombsight's automatic release system. He could then use a toggle switch to release the bombs.

When the Norden was first introduced in 1942, it was hailed as the most perfect bombsight ever invented, at least up to that time. It was touted as able "to drop a bomb into a pickle barrel from an altitude of 30,000 ft."[9] This might have been true under ideal testing conditions in the clear blue skies of the American Midwest, but in the cloudy skies over Europe under battle conditions, we were no longer in Kansas. It was quickly discovered that the Norden couldn't live up to such glowing expectations. Probably the greatest impediment to its use was the requirement that the bombardier have a clear, visible view of the target. In the winter months, the skies over the European continent were almost always cloudy or overcast with patchy clouds.

The second problem with the Norden bombsight was its automatic pilot controls. To keep each aircraft on the true flight path over the target, small adjustments had to be made in the flight controls. These small adjustments quickly added up in large bomber formations composed of many aircraft. As a result, individual bombers veered around in the tight formation and thus increased the likelihood of midair collisions. To circumvent this problem, Col. Curtis LeMay, who was the commander of the 305th Bomb Group, came up with a possible solution. He introduced the togglelier system, in which the bomb group's bombardier who was best at using the Norden flew in the lead aircraft of the lead squadron of the formation. When he released his bombs, then all the bombardiers in the formation did likewise and toggled their load. The system worked very well under combat conditions. As a result, the 8th Air Force adopted the togglelier bomb release method, which vastly improved the results obtained by precision bombing.

Of course, there was a backup targeting method to the Norden that we used when bad weather conditions obscured the target area with heavy cloud cover. It was called the H2X target system, and it used radar to locate and pinpoint the target. Perhaps *pinpoint* is an exaggeration, because the accuracy of the aerial radar systems used during that time was often less than ideal. The H2X was developed by the Massachusetts Institute of Technology in Boston and was based on the H2S radar system the British used during their nightly bombing raids. Images from H2S could clearly discern land and water but fell short of identifying structural objects, like buildings and industrial centers, on the ground.

Improvements to the H2S model led to the development of the H2X, which had a higher image resolution, resulting in a much greater definition of structures on the ground. Images from H2X, popularly called the Mickey scope, gave a clear indication of landmarks associated with surface areas, such as seas, coastlines, and rivers. This gave trained radar operators the ability to distinguish industrial targets just outside cities or alongside river junctions. During the final months of the war, it was a useful added component to the Norden bombsight. This gave bombardiers the advantage of using either a visual targeting bombsight with the Norden or blind bombing with H2X. During those cloudy and stormy weather conditions over Germany in January and February, we used H2X on quite a few missions.

Photo of clear skies at 25,000 feet with optimal conditions for visual targeting by the Norden bombsight.

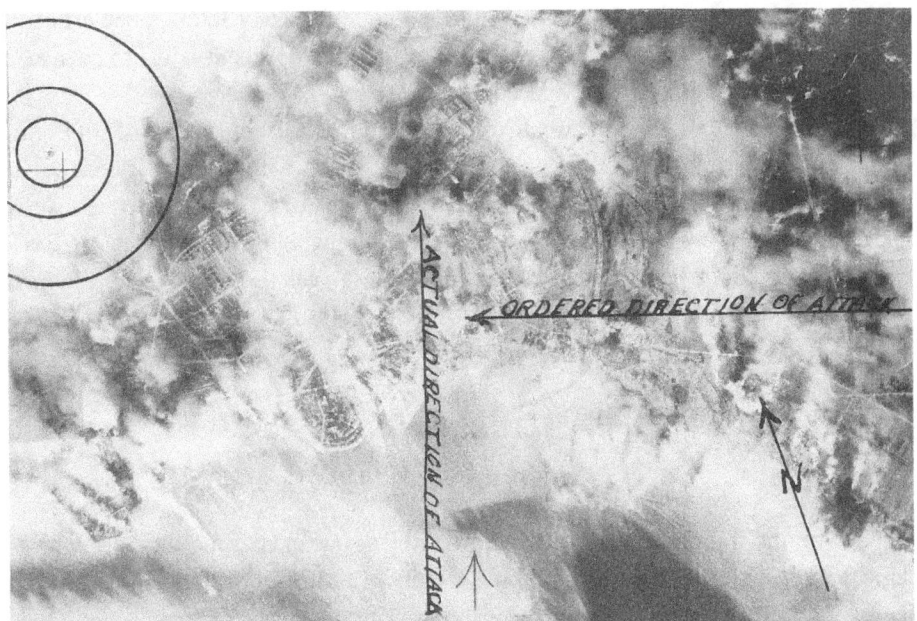

Low-altitude scattered clouds over the target area, requiring the acquisition of the target by H2X radar.

Even though weather conditions over Germany were very bad, our division was able to obtain some good bombing results on primary targets. The Bergius hydrogenation plant in Rothensee was especially hard hit, exhibiting extensive damage. During the oil campaign, these types of synthetic oil plants were priority targets because of their ability to produce large volumes of high-grade aviation fuel supplying the Luftwaffe. The good results obtained at Rothensee were somewhat tarnished, however, by our bombing efforts on the Krupp tank manufacturing plant in Magdeburg. Because of extensive cloud cover over the target area, we had intended to bomb by H2X, but at the last minute the weather suddenly cleared up, so we were able to hit our target. We did have a minor problem with the rear bomb bay door being jammed for a while, but we soon fixed that. Overall, our first mission was a success, and it was a telling experience for what we could expect on future missions.

As soon as we landed, I was glad to be back on base. After every combat mission, all members of the flight crew were given their allotment of "medicinal alcohol," as dictated by the flight surgeon. It was usually bourbon, scotch, or gin. Since I wasn't a drinker, I saved mine for our crew, and they gladly accepted my gift. After the celebratory event, operations officers or intelligence officers debriefed us. They wanted to know how the mission went and if there were any significant observations or incidents that were out of the ordinary. Frequently, the debriefing session was mostly short and sweet—more or less just another routine mission. Once in a while, in addition to our regular crew on board, our mission was accompanied by a number of people, such as guest visitors, photographers, or intelligence officers, who would fly with us. We weren't told much about any of them—just to be aware that we had other personnel on board.

After our first mission, the weather took a turn for the worse, so the 453rd Bomb Group was told to stand down for a week. Air operations with other divisional bomb groups continued, but their missions were few and far between. For the next week and a half, there were only three missions by the 8th involving all air divisions. Reliable flying conditions didn't materialize until the last week of January. We were then told that our next assignment would be a synthetic oil refinery plant in Dortmund.

MISSION #2: JANUARY 28, 1945
TARGET: DORTMUND

Dortmund was one of the largest cities as well as one of 8th's most important strategic targets in the Ruhr Valley. This bustling city is located in western Germany near its border with Belgium. The Ruhr was the industrial heart of Germany, and it was sprinkled with a number of large cities that supplied critical military material to the German war machine. Dortmund, especially, was a major transportation hub, with a network of rail and road junctions connecting all the other cities in the area. A large German force was reported to be making its way through the Ruhr to Berlin, and then to the Eastern Front. The 1st, 2nd, and 3rd Air Divisions dispatched over 1,000 bombers to attack railways, bridges, and benzol petroleum plants in the eastern Ruhr. The 2nd Air Division's specific targets were the synthetic fuel plants in Dortmund.

Our primary target was the Hoesch Benzin GmbH plant, located approximately two and a half miles northeast of Dortmund. It was one of the very few plants remaining in operation producing benzol from coke in the Ruhr. Because of the abundance of oil refineries and petroleum plants located near and around Dortmund, RAF Bomber Command attacked the city many times in 1944. They routinely dropped not only bomb loads in the 1,000-pound-class range but also the huge 4,000-pound cookie bombs, which were devastating in their blast effects. By the time we got our chance to hit Dortmund, there wasn't much left.

However, the entire Ruhr Valley was still heavily defended. It was called the Happy Valley, and for many bomber crews in the earlier years, it felt more like the Valley of Death. On the hills surrounding the valley were placed more than 200 heavy 88 mm flak batteries, each containing six to eight big guns. The Luftwaffe employed sophisticated radar equipment that could hit a target as high as 25,000 feet. This didn't even include the hundreds of smaller-caliber antiaircraft guns placed around the large industrial centers within the valley. Before the demise of the Luftwaffe, scores of German fighter groups also defended the valley.

As we approached our target, the sky began filling up with dark black puffs of bursting shells. The flak was pretty intense. Our ship shuddered from the shock waves of nearby explosions. We managed to overcome the clouds of flak and unload our full load of twelve 500-pound GP bombs over the target. The weather wasn't perfect, with patchy clouds hanging over the city. We were one of nineteen B-24 Liberators from the 453rd Bomb Group to hit Dortmund. We were hopeful that the synthetic oil refinery was put out of business. Visual confirmation of the degree of destruction applied to our target couldn't be determined that day. Our second mission was over, and we were finally getting into the routine of how things worked on base. This would be our last mission during the first month of 1945, and we looked forward to what might come next in February.

JANUARY 12, 1945: THE RUSSIAN WINTER OFFENSIVE

As January came to a close, the ground war was again heating up on a grand scale. On January 12, the long-awaited Russian attack, with the goal of reaching the Oder River, finally materialized with an unbelievably massive force, the size of which hadn't been seen at any time in military history. Stalin had assembled four huge army groups forming an attacking front that extended more than 450 miles along the Vistula River in central Poland. In the center was the 1st Belorussian Front commanded by Marshal Georgy K. Zhukov. South of the 1st Belorussian Front was Marshal Ivan S. Konev's 1st Ukrainian Front. Together they had 2.25 million troops, 6,500 tanks, 32,000 assault guns, and 4,500 aircraft.[10] Zhukov's armies were to smash their way through Poland, take Warsaw, and push ahead west to the Oder River. Konev, coming up from the south, was to advance toward Breslau and take control of Silesia in the southwest of Poland. Upper and Lower Silesia was one of the most important industrial centers of the Third Reich.

Marshal Konstantin K. Rokossovsky's 2nd Belorussian Front and the 3rd Belorussian Front, commanded by Col. Gen. Ivan D. Chernyakhovsky, were the two attacking groups in the north. Their combined forces were composed of 1.7 million troops, 3,300 tanks, 28,000 guns, and 3,000 aircraft. Chernyakhovsky's objective was to drive westward through East Prussia to Königsberg. Rokossovsky was to advance in a northwesterly direction from the Narev River in Poland and through Danzig on his way to the East Prussian coast.

Plans for the Russian offensive were developed months ahead of time, beginning in November 1944. The upcoming battle was so important that Stalin himself personally took command of the 1st and 2nd Belorussian Fronts and the 1st Ukrainian Front from the *Stavka*, the Russian High Command. Commanders of these three army groups were to report directly to him. Zhukov's 1st Belorussian Front was ordered to attack along the Warsaw-Berlin axis, which was the most direct route into the heart of Germany. Therefore, it would be the most heavily defended by German forces. Facing Zhukov's armies was German Army Group Center, commanded by Col. Gen. Georg-Hans Reinhardt and consisting of the German 3rd Panzer Army, 2nd Army, and 4th Army. Reinhardt's order was to hold East Prussia and the northern sector of Poland. South of Army Group Center stood Army Group A, commanded by Gen. Josef Harpe, with the German 4th Panzer, 9th, and 17th Armies situated just north of Warsaw.

Altogether, the German defense consisted of approximately 1 million troops, with fewer than 2,000 tanks and 800 aircraft. Reinhardt's Army Group Center, with 41 divisions and just under 600,000 men, would bear the brunt of the attacking Russian armies. With such an overwhelming force against them, the Germans knew they couldn't stop the Russian advances to the Oder River. They could only slow them down. Outgunned and outmanned, the outcome was inevitable. Hitler, with his usual insensitivity to the pleas of his own field commanders, resisted any signs of retreat. The Führer expected his armies to stand and hold their positions. They were ordered to never yield any ground to the Russians. This would cost the German armies dearly in the weeks to come.

Konev's 1st Ukrainian Front, from bridgeheads at Sandomierz and Baranów on the Vistula River in southern Poland, began its offensive in the early-morning hours of January 12 with an unrelenting artillery barrage. The bombardment by heavy artillery lasted almost two hours. This was followed by a devastating attack by Russian T-34 heavy tanks smashing their way through the front lines and crushing the resistance of the German 4th Panzer Army. The breakthrough was overwhelming, and nothing could stop the rapidly advancing Russian armies. All German resistance was swept aside. The defending German forces were in chaos, and by evening, spearheads of Konev's tank armies had penetrated the front lines 12 miles deep. Within thirty-six hours, three of Konev's armies closed in and captured Kielce on the 1st Ukrainian Front's right flank, while more armies were advancing on the left flank toward Kraców. In the north, advance units had already reached the Pilica River.[11]

The next day, on January 13, Chernyakhovsky's 3rd Belorussian Front began its attack at 6:00 a.m. After a massive artillery barrage between Pillkallen and the Goldapa River, Chernyakhovsky's armies immediately advanced westward toward Königsberg, the capital of East Prussia, which was their final objective. Their immediate aim was to eliminate the Tilsit-Insterburg group of German armies facing their advance. All the Germans' defensive measures were swept aside as the attacking Red Army's armored divisions raced through the Insterburg Gap toward Königsberg.

Now it was Zhukov's turn to begin his attack. On the morning of January 14, he ordered his armies to advance from two bridgeheads on the Vistula. The first assault came from the Magnusze bridgehead south of Warsaw along the Pilica and Radomka Rivers. Another assault sprung from the Pulawy bridgehead farther south. The ferocious artillery barrage preceding the attacks lasted less than thirty minutes, but its effect was so crushing that the German forces on the front line fell back in confusion and disarray. The breakout was so complete that by evening, Zhukov's tank armies had quickly advanced westward as far as 10 miles beyond the front line.

Zhukov's armies managed to punch two huge holes through the German front lines, and his rapidly advancing armored units were quickly clearing the German forces between the Vistula and Bug Rivers. By the next day, the Russian armies' envelopment of Warsaw began. German resistance fell apart, and on the night of January 16, their garrison withdrew from the city. Russian troops entered the city at noon the next day, January 17. The fall of Warsaw got Hitler's attention in Berlin.

The Führer was furious that his explicit orders to hold the city weren't carried out to the fullest. General Harpe was immediately removed from his command of Army Group A and replaced with Col. Gen. Ferdinand Schörner, one of Hitler's favorite Nazis. Schörner's unwavering loyalty and reputation of being a ruthless commander even to his own troops made Hitler's decision an easy one. Hitler was now personally engaged in every aspect of military operations. Every field commander, from the top down to the divisional level, was required to report his progress directly to the Führer.

On January 19, only a week after the offensive began, the German armies on the front lines were on the verge of total collapse. A coherent German Front was no longer viable as its armies were swept aside, fractured, or splintered into smaller units as they fell back toward the Oder River. In the north, the German 3rd Panzer Army and 4th Army had been either overrun or bypassed as armies from the Russian 2nd and 3rd Belorussian Fronts raced northward toward Königsberg and the Baltic Sea. It was no better in the south as Konev's armies decimated the German 4th Panzer Army. The German 17th Army had been bypassed and was on the verge of being encircled. Konev's armies had taken Kracòw. Zhukov's 8th Guards Army captured the industrial city of Lodz and was well on its way to Poznan.

As armies from the 1st Ukrainian Front advanced toward Breslau, Konev had received strict orders from Stalin to leave the Silesian industrial area intact. In order to flush the German forces out of the cities, Konev decided to encircle the region with Col. Gen. P.S. Rybalko's 3rd Guards Tank Army and move around the cities instead of moving through them to prevent the potential destruction of the vital factories within. Konev's 21st Army proceeded to engage in a heavy frontal attack from the northwest, while Rybalko's army moved up south along the Oder River. As the German troops retreated in a southwesterly direction, they met the tanks and infantry of Rybalko's 3rd Guards Tank Army. Of the 100,000 German soldiers caught in the Silesian trap, only about 30,000 made it to the Oder River. By the end of January, Silesia had been cleared of all German forces. The loss of Silesia was a big blow to Germany's war effort because almost two-thirds of its coal production came from Upper Silesia.

Konev's 4th Tank Army was the first to reach the Oder River at Goben, north of Steinau, on January 22. Soon, two bridgeheads were secured—one in the north, near Steinau, between Breslau and Glogau, while the other was located farther south, between Breslau and Oppeln. After securing the Neisse River, which was the main tributary of the Oder, the Red Army had eliminated the last major obstacle on its path to Berlin. Much like a giant moat, the Vistula and Oder Rivers have provided a natural defensive barrier against invading armies from the east throughout Germany's turbulent history with Poland and Russia. North of Konev's 1st Ukrainian Front, advance units of Zhukov's 5th Shock Army made their first assault crossing of the Oder on the morning of January 31, capturing a vital bridgehead at Gross Neuendorf, near Kienitz, a small village less than 10 miles northwest of Küstrin. Within days, the 1st Guards Tank Army from Zhukov's 1st Belorussian Front entered the southern suburbs of Küstrin.

With Konev's and Zhukov's forces occupying the Oder, the next important objective in the Stavka's winter offensive plan was the capture of East Prussia. While Chernyakhovsky's 3rd Belorussian Front was rapidly advancing toward Königsberg, the capital of East Prussia, Rokossovsky received an order from the Stavka. The 2nd Belorussian Front, under his command, was to isolate East Prussia from Germany. Rokossovsky then advanced his armies in a north-to-northwesterly direction through East Prussia in a drive toward Elbing and Marienburg to the Baltic Sea. Tannenberg fell on January 21, and then the Allenstein fortified zone fell on January 23. This opened up a path to the Baltic. At that point, Rokossovsky ordered his 5th Guards Tank Army to advance forward with all haste. Captain Dyachenko's 3rd Tank Brigade, in the lead of the 5th Guards Tank Army, moved so quickly that he merely drove as fast as his tanks would permit through downtown Elbing, amid evening shoppers unaware that the speeding tanks were even Russian. Dyachenko reached the Frische Haff, a huge lagoon along the shores of the Baltic Sea stretching from Elbing to Königsberg, at midnight on January 23. Other units of the 5th Guards Tank Army linked up with Dyachenko's brigade soon after.[12]

Coming in from the north, Chernyakhovsky's 3rd Belorussian Front reached Königsberg on January 29. Just outside the city, the Russian troops were shocked when they heard that Gen. Chernyakhovsky had been struck and killed by a stray artillery shell. Stalin then immediately ordered Marshal Aleksandr Vasilevsky, the former chief of the general staff, to take command of the 3rd Belorussian Front. Soon after Vasilevsky's arrival, Königsberg was surrounded and under siege. Less than seventy-two hours after Rokossovsky received his orders from the Stavka on January 21, his armies were able to cut off all German forces in East Prussia.

When Russian troops were advancing to the Baltic coast, the German armies were forced to retreat and found themselves with their backs against the sea. The German 4th Army was encircled along the Frische Haff, the 2nd Army pushed back into the Vistula estuary, and the 3rd Panzer Army was trapped on the Samland Peninsula. In total, close to half a million troops of Reinhardt's Army Group Center were now trapped by the Red Army.

General Friedrich Hossbach, commander of the German 4th Army, received permission from Reinhardt for an attempted breakout east of Elbing. Reinhardt agreed it would be the only choice possible. The attempt was made on January 30, but Hossbach's forces were cut to pieces by tanks and artillery from Rokossovsky's 5th Guards Tank Army. Hitler, fed up with Reinhardt's failures, replaced him with Gen. Lothar Rendulic. He ordered Rendulic to hold Königsberg at all costs, which Rendulic did for another two months until the capital of East Prussia fell to the Russians on April 9.

With the demise of Army Group Center, Hitler decided to raise a new army group designated as Army Group Vistula. Since there were no reserves remaining after the failed Ardennes Offensive, Vistula was composed of the surviving remnants of the German 2nd and 9th Armies. For the commander of the newly formed Army Group Vistula, Hitler named his longtime Nazi associate Heinrich Himmler, Reichsführer-SS and chief of police. Colonel General Heinz Guderian was shocked that a person with absolutely no military field experience would be commanding such an important army group. A bitter argument arose between Guderian and Hitler, but the field marshal failed to persuade the Führer to appoint a more competent commander. Differences of opinion between the two men had become more robust since the Ardennes Offensive, but it would only increase in severity during the final months of the war, to the point where Hitler finally dismissed Guderian as his army commander of the west. Yet later, Guderian was able to replace Himmler as commander of Army Group Vistula when the fanatical Nazi failed miserably in his role as a competent military commander.

As Rokossovsky's forces smashed their way through northern Poland and East Prussia, they left a wake of death and destruction not seen since the German invasions of Russia in 1941 and 1942. The murders and atrocities German SS troops committed as they plowed through Russian territory toward Moscow during those years still lingered in the minds of Russian soldiers. Now the roles were reversed as the Russian armies fought their way to the Oder River. The vengeance Stalin's troops inflicted on the helpless and unarmed German citizens was acutely evident wherever the Russian armies advanced. Whole villages and small towns were put to the torch. Persons with any evidence of ties with the Nazi Party were mercilessly shot, and entire families paid the price. Many women were tortured, raped, and murdered.

Rumors of the disintegration of the Eastern Front sent hundreds of thousands of refugees fleeing westward from East Prussia and Silesia. The largest German population living east of the Oder River was in Silesia, a place where more than 4.5 million people lived. At least 3 million were able to reach German-held territory in Czechoslovakia or other parts of the Reich. The flood of refugees was so great that upward of 40,000 to 50,000 people were arriving in Berlin each day, mostly by train. Those were the lucky ones.

In Breslau, the capital and largest city in Silesia, orders were issued for its citizens to leave the city as the Red Army approached. Many of the refugees fled from their homes by any means available—some on horses, carts, or whatever they could scavenge. Most had to travel laboriously on foot, with the majority being women, children, and old men. In the harsh and severe winter months of January and February, many thousands of these refugees died along the roads leading to the west. Temperatures dropped to well below freezing, and there was no shelter. It was a ghastly trek, with women delivering babies on the sides of roads and nearby ditches filled with dead children. Thousands of bodies littered the snow-filled roads throughout Poland.

By January 31, Konev's 1st Ukrainian Front was firmly established on the Oder and Neisse Rivers, while Zhukov's 1st Belorussian Front was well on its way to building strong bridgeheads on the Oder. Across the river was Germany. All of Silesia was now in Russian control. Chernyakhovsky's 3rd Belorussian Front and Rokossovsky's 2nd Belorussian Front had cut off East Prussia from the rest of the Reich. In less than three weeks, the Red Army had pushed so fast and so far beyond the Vistula River that even Stalin himself was surprised. The Stavka's plan was for an anticipated advance rate of less than 10 miles a day. But the Russian forces' massive attacks were so great that advances of up to 10 to 20 miles a day were common, and in many cases it was much greater. Immediately after the start of the offensive, Col. Gen. Vasily I. Chuikov, the commander of Zhukov's 8th Guards Army, was to advance at a rate of almost 20 miles a day, and at their peak on January 17, this rate exceeded 25 miles per day.

When Chuikov's forces reached the heavily fortified city of Poznan, he stayed behind to capture the city while the bulk of his army quickly moved forward toward the Oder River. He discovered that his main problem wasn't the resistance of the German forces, but the Red Army's long and tenuous supply lines that stretched across Poland. Shortages began to occur more frequently, to the extent that fuel was being siphoned off some vehicles to supply others. Tanks were being abandoned along the roads from the lack of fuel. Then the ammunition supply began to run low, and Chuikov's troops had to scavenge around for abandoned German guns and shells.

On January 25, Stalin called Zhukov and told him to slow down because his forces were now too far from the left flank of Rokossovsky's 2nd Belorussian Front and were becoming highly susceptible to German counterattacks. Despite Stalin's concerns, the natural high of victories coursing through Zhukov's veins prompted him to decide to continue his advance straight through to Berlin. Zhukov reported that his armies were facing little resistance from the Germans. Konev was equally euphoric over his quick advance to the Oder River, and he'd already made plans to attack Berlin from the south. In a surprising move, Stalin gave Zhukov the approval to advance on January 27, and Konev on January 29.

However, the Stavka intervened. All the Russian armies were running short of fuel and supplies, so the Russian High Command told Stalin and his generals to temper their exuberance with prudence. Three arduous weeks of sustained fighting had taken a toll on manpower, and many of the Russian divisions were substantially below normal strength, in some cases down below 50 percent. Russian intelligence indicated that German reinforcements were being transferred from the Western Front, and an increasing number of German troops were observed in Pomerania and Silesia. It was decided that the Russian forces should resupply, regroup, and consolidate their positions on the Oder River as their first priority.

The risk of German counterattacks was very real. In fact, as soon as Zhukov's advanced forces had reached the Oder River on January 31 and began to secure the bridgehead at Gross Neuendorf, just north of Kienitz, the Germans quickly counterattacked. Because of the frigid and dangerous weather conditions, the Russians weren't able to send their armor across the river. As a result, the German attack successfully drove the attackers back to the other side. When Hitler heard that Zhukov's forces had reached the Oder River at Küstrin, he ordered that the city be fortified and held at all costs. Reinforcements were quickly sent to Küstrin. The city was only 48 miles from Berlin, and the closest and most direct route to the capital was through the Küstrin bridgeheads. Hitler was well aware of this strategic locale, as was Zhukov. The siege of Küstrin was to last for another two months before the city was captured and the bridgeheads secured enough for Zhukov's forces to resume their advance into Germany.

On the Western Front, US forces soon took back all the territory lost to the Germans during the Ardennes Offensive. The British and American allies pondered their next move as they advanced toward the Rhine River. Eisenhower's assessment of the German opposition going forward determined his next plan of operations. The German Army had 80 divisions, many of which were decimated during and following the Ardennes Offensive. This was all they had to defend against 85 Allied divisions. The numerical superiority thus gave the Allies a distinct advantage.[13]

The Allied strategy for the defeat of Germany first entailed a series of attacks along the entire front with the goal of destroying all German forces west of the

Rhine River. Although Hitler didn't succeed in securing his ultimate objective of splitting the Allied forces during the Ardennes Offensive, his plans definitely upset their schedule and delayed their advance to the Rhine. At the time, Eisenhower suspected but didn't actually know that the Germans had no more reserves remaining to launch another major offensive. So he decided to move forward at a more cautious pace. Upon crossing the Rhine River, Allied forces were to establish major bridgeheads before advancing eastward into the Rhineland to link up with the Red Army coming from the Eastern Front.

The Germans were soon fighting on two fronts simultaneously within Germany itself, and they knew the end result could only be total defeat. It was the beginning of the end for the Third Reich. In mid-January, shortly after the start of the Russian offensive, Hitler returned to Berlin for the last time and prepared for the final battle to come. He was determined to fight to the very end and cared little about what would eventually become the ashes of the city of Berlin. The Führer wanted to see Berlin engulfed in flames, an apocalyptic event representing a gigantic funeral pyre to honor the death of a great leader. The end was near. The Red Army was on the Oder River and within reach of Berlin. As January came to a close, the three Allied leaders—Premier Joseph Stalin, President Franklin Roosevelt, and Prime Minister Winston Churchill—were preparing to meet at Yalta to coordinate Germany's final defeat.

CHAPTER 3

MAXIMUM EFFORT

THE YALTA CONFERENCE 1945

With the imminent defeat of Germany in sight, the Big Three Allied leaders—Roosevelt, Churchill, and Stalin—along with their chiefs of staff, met at Yalta to discuss the Allied strategy for the final phase of operations in the defeat of German forces and postwar occupation of Germany. The conference took place on February 4–11, 1945, at the resort city of Yalta, located in the Crimea Peninsula along the coast of the Black Sea. Plenary sessions were held in the fabulous white granite Summer Palace built by Tsar Nicolas II. One of the first sessions dealt with a report of the Russian winter offensive and a discussion concerning the Allied forces' invasion of Germany.

Colonel General Alexey I. Antonov summarized the accomplishments the Russian forces had made in their drive to the Oder River. His main concern was the strengthening and increased resistance of the expected German forces in the defense of Berlin—the city that was the Red Army's next objective. Antonov indicated that they'd already detected movements of a number of German armored and infantry divisions being transferred to the Eastern Front. The Russians estimated that up to 35 to 40 divisions could potentially be moved from Italy, Norway, and the Western Front to fortify defenses within Germany against the anticipated advance of Russian forces from the east.

In order to hinder the movement of German forces, Antonov formally asked the Allied command for assistance in the form of bombing raids in eastern Germany, particularly on Berlin and Leipzig. An immense number of refugees fleeing from Poland and East Prussia were flowing into these cities. Heavy bombing raids on the German transportation network would cause plenty of disruption and chaos, perhaps enough to affect the movements of German reinforcements to the Eastern Front.

The Allied air commanders had expected this request before the Yalta Conference. The British and US Chiefs of Staff met in Malta on January 30 and 31, 1945, in anticipation of the forthcoming Yalta Conference to discuss this very matter. A British colony located in the Mediterranean just 58 miles from the coast of Sicily, Malta was originally the proposed site of the Yalta Conference. However, Stalin insisted that the conference be held in the Crimea, primarily due to his aversion to air travel.

Churchill and his chief of the air staff, Air Chief Marshal Charles Portal, also attended the Malta meeting to talk to the American military officials. At the Malta Conference, a plan was proposed to incorporate both the US 8th Air Force and RAF Bomber Command in a series of attacks on cities in eastern Germany. Their primary targets would consist of major communications centers and transportation networks within Berlin, Leipzig, Dresden, Chemnitz, Cottbus, and others. Thus, the Combined Chiefs of Staff decided to support the Russian advance from the Eastern Front. These discussions were eventually formalized as the Allied transportation campaign against Germany. The Allied leaders at the Yalta Conference endorsed the Malta plan for the Allied air forces to attack Germany's transportation system a few days later.

The Russian delegation at Yalta made one clarification regarding the widespread bombing raids proposed. They asked that the Allies agree to implement a formal bomb line to prevent American or British bombers from crossing over and possibly bombing Russian forces advancing from the east. The proposed bomb line would run through Berlin and Leipzig in the north to Vienna in the south. This discussion also led to the question of direct contact between Anglo-American ground forces advancing from the Western Front and Red Army forces from the east. Roosevelt approached Stalin and expressed his concerns in this regard. The president wanted to avoid any conflicts that might arise between the two Allied forces, whether they were accidental or otherwise. He proposed to Stalin that General Eisenhower directly communicate with the Russian Army staff related to military operations on the ground instead of going through the Combined Chiefs of Staff in London. Stalin agreed and told the president that his staff would work out the details. This procedure was a deviation from normal protocol, since major changes in military operations initiated by the supreme commander were usually addressed to the Combined Chiefs of Staff through Gen. George Marshall, the chief of staff of the US Joint Chiefs of Staff, for discussion and approval. This meeting and agreement between Roosevelt and Stalin later had broad implications during the final months of the war.[1]

THE TRANSPORTATION PLAN

Timing means everything, and it just so happened that the Russians' request for a bombing campaign targeting German communication networks was uniquely favorable in February 1945. As proscribed in the Casablanca Directive and later in the Combined Bomber Offensive directive of Operation Pointblank, transportation targets came immediately after the German aircraft industry and oil production had been eliminated. With the oil campaign coming to its end, February was to be a transition period, from intensive attacks on the oil industry to attacks on communication and transportation centers within Germany.

Bombing raids continued on both aircraft industry and oil industrial targets to maintain constant pressure and prevent resurgence, but the main focus in the strategic objective to end Germany's capacity to wage war was now the transportation networks. This important target had actually been under investigation long before the Casablanca Conference in 1943. Early in 1939, the Research and Experiments Department of the Ministry of Home Security in England was formed to study the bombing effects on certain target systems, such as oil storage, power stations, aircraft, motorized vehicle factories, and transportation facilities. The goal was to estimate the maximum damage that various types of ordnance—including high-explosive, fragmentation, and incendiary bombs—could inflict on German industrial structures.

Dr. Reginald Stradling, the director of the Research and Experiments Department, recruited a colorful assortment of scientists and statisticians to staff the department. Included were Professors Solly Zuckerman, a noted zoologist, and physicist J. D. Bernal. A report from the department came out in September 1940 to indicate that the extensive use of certain types of bombs could inflict considerable damage to and even total destruction of different types of heavily constructed buildings and factories. The report's impact had the far-reaching consequences of developing a coherent and useful bombing strategy for the RAF Bomber Command. Professor Zuckerman was particularly interested in how bomb damage to transportation networks affected the viability of enemy personnel and military equipment movement. For example, in comparing the extensive German railway system to an animal's nervous system, the professor concluded that destroying this vital nexus could completely paralyze enemy transportation activities.

Zuckerman had his chance to prove his theory in July 1943 during the invasion of Sicily, Italy, while he was a member on the planning committee as a scientific adviser. His recommendation was to bomb the critical Sicilian and southern Italian transportation centers, especially railway repair shops, depots, and marshalling yards. Marshalling yards in particular were vitally important in the transportation of war material and movement of enemy troops. Bombing surveys after the invasion proved that the plan had been an outstanding success. Zuckerman had made his reputation as the expert on targeting transportation systems.

Zuckerman's expertise once again came to the fore when Air Marshal Arthur Tedder, Eisenhower's Deputy Supreme Commander of the Supreme Headquarters Allied Expeditionary Force (SHAEF), and his staff met in January 1944 to discuss the bombing campaign in support of the upcoming invasion, Operation Overlord. Zuckerman, now a scientific adviser to SHAEF, no doubt came up with a plan for attacking vital transportation and communication systems in France and Belgium. The goal was to disrupt and impede the German force's ability to organize counterattacks on the invading Allied troops. The professor produced a paper titled "Delay and Disorganization of Enemy Movement by Rail," outlining his plan's critical features. Tedder, who was duly impressed with Zuckerman's achievements during the invasion of Italy, was also an ardent supporter of the value of attacking enemy transportation systems. Tedder happily contributed his own ideas. Together, Tedder and Zuckerman formulated what would be known as the Transportation Plan. It eventually formed the basis of the pre-invasion bombing campaign for Operation Overlord.

The plan to bomb rail targets raised immediate objections from Maj. Gen. Carl Spaatz, Commander of US Strategic Air Forces (USSTAF) in Europe. Spaatz was just initiating an increased effort to target the oil industry, as proscribed in Operation Pointblank. Spaatz had always felt that targeting the oil and petroleum industries was the key in defeating the German military machine, even before it was one of the top priorities in the Casablanca Directive. In his view, the spring of 1944 was the right time to begin the oil campaign with maximum effort. The resistance by Spaatz and his air staff to the reassignment of targets in favor of Tedder's Transportation Plan for Operation Overlord was so great that the supreme commander had to intervene.

On March 25, 1944, Eisenhower held a meeting with his Allied air staff. Operation Overlord was so important and demanded so many resources to succeed that Eisenhower totally agreed with Tedder's plan. The Transportation Plan for disrupting rail traffic in northwestern Europe took precedence over the oil campaign as a top priority for the Allied air forces. Spaatz's oil campaign would have to be delayed until after the invasion.

The plan's basic premise was to attack and destroy rail centers in France and Belgium. Transportation targets thus included rail yards, train stations, rail sheds, repair shops, signal systems, switching stations, and other necessary rail facilities that kept the railway networks operational. It was determined that the most important components of a rail network system were the marshalling yards, a more specific term for railway yards, where large numbers of locomotives and rolling stock are concentrated. Marshalling yards in large industrial centers can be highly complex, with a number of roundhouses, turntables, and switch systems necessary for organizing, loading, and distributing freight or troops and sending them efficiently on their way to their final destinations. These marshalling yards can contain hundreds of tracks to accommodate and control every train coming into or going out from these huge rail centers.

It was estimated that just over 100 railway centers needed to be destroyed in order to cripple the Germans' ability to move troops and material to reinforce the Normandy invasion area. Zuckerman's associate, E. D. Grant, a British rail expert, also indicated the importance of other railroad communication facilities, such as bridges and tunnels that required the attention of any bombing plan. However, these structures were difficult to destroy, and large amounts of ordnance were required. Thus it was necessary to consider all possible transportation targets, but to first concentrate directly on the railway systems whenever possible.

In early April 1944, the pre-invasion transportation campaign was initiated with the US 9th Air Force assigned to attack 30 targets in Belgium and north central France. The US 8th Air Force was given 23 targets in Belgium, northeastern France, and western Germany. Large bombing raids continued throughout April and into May 1944, when the attacks on rail centers intensified. As a result, many hundreds of locomotives and moving stock were destroyed, and more than 150 rail lines and rail centers were extensively damaged. American B-26 Marauder medium bombers and fighter-bombers dropping 2,000-pound bombs and air-to-ground rockets completely destroyed all railway and highway bridges over the Seine River.

The bombing campaign was a resounding success. Disruption of enemy traffic and troop movements was enormous. Railway traffic in France fell dramatically, and by July it was at a standstill. The Allied attacks opened up the way for a successful invasion. Field Marshals Gerd von Rundstedt and Erwin Rommel were effectively unable to move the necessary reinforcements into the Normandy area to initiate any significant counterattacks. The destruction of railroad crossings on key bridges across the Seine proved decisive in preventing the movement of both troops and supplies to the German front lines in Normandy. The Allied invasion force had achieved its primary objective: to build up their forces streaming from England across the Channel into Normandy more quickly than the Germans were able to reinforce their positions on the front lines. Consequently, American and British forces were able to secure the invasion beachheads and move into France much faster than it would have been possible without the attritional bombing and interdiction of enemy railway systems.

The Transportation Plan was deemed so successful that discussions began in the late summer of 1944 about the possibility of extending the campaign. Eisenhower anticipated moving his forces across the Rhine River and advancing deep into the heart of Germany. The question arose as to how the strategic air forces could be best employed to help accomplish this goal. A debate then began over whether or not attacks on the German transportation system would have any real effects on the movement of German forces on a wide scale. The British Air Ministry believed it would be an important supportive factor and was inclined to sustain a transportation bombing campaign in Germany. Air Marshal Tedder, who was the most vocal in support of continuing the attacks, was also in favor of the idea. The oil campaign had just begun in earnest, and Gen. Spaatz predictably voiced his reservations, insisting that the oil campaign should remain as a top priority.

Although no clear-cut plan was adopted, everyone agreed that attacks on the German transportation system should be continued, but at a lower priority than the oil industry. Throughout the autumn of 1944, bombing raids were carried out, specifically targeting marshalling yards in Stuttgart, Karlsruhe, Mainz, Frankfurt, and many other cities in the Ruhr industrial area. However, by November, these air attacks didn't seem to improve the progress of Allied forces in their advance to the Rhine River. Tedder then pushed for a more concrete plan for the transportation campaign against Germany. So the Combined Strategic Targets Committee met in early November to establish a group of experts to come up with a more comprehensive transportation plan.

The result was the decision to divide Germany and other Axis-occupied territories into nine designated zones in their order of importance:

1. Northwestern approaches to the Ruhr Valley
2. Frankfurt-Mannheim
3. Cologne-Koblenz
4. Kassel
5. Karlsruhe-Stuttgart
6. Magdeburg-Leipzig
7. Upper Silesia
8. Vienna
9. Bavaria

Strategic bombing raids would be carried out by heavy bombardment groups of the US 8th and 15th Air Forces in the defined areas, which would repeatedly target railway centers to deny the enemy a chance to repair damaged facilities and restore their use. Tactical roles employed by medium bombers and fighter-bombers of the

9th Air Force would then attack the rail centers to destroy objectives that the heavy bombers might have missed. These could include train depots, repair installations, electric power stations, and other ancillary targets. Also, fighter-bomber attacks on railway lines and moving rail traffic, as the opportunity arose, would augment the bombing campaign.[2]

By the end of 1944, the transportation campaign was well underway and actually intensified as Allied ground forces pushed the Germans from Belgium back toward Germany after the failed Ardennes Offensive. Eisenhower, in particular, pressed for more attacks as he prepared his forces to advance to the Rhine River. Although the oil campaign had accomplished its major task of significantly reducing oil and petroleum production to drastically affect the German war machine, oil industrial targets remained on the bombing list as long as the Germans continued to repair and replace damaged factories and facilities in their desperate attempt to produce more fuel.

MISSION #3: FEBRUARY 3, 1945
TARGET: MAGDEBURG

One aspect of the Transportation Plan discussed at the Yalta Conference was the psychological effect a heavy bombing raid would have on the population in general. Panic had already gripped the residents of Berlin as tens of thousands of refugees streamed into the city with their horror stories of death and destruction inflicted by the rapidly advancing Russian armies invading East Prussia and Silesia. It was thought that massive bombing raids on the city would cause an increase in the chaos and perhaps speed up the demise of Hitler's Nazi regime, or at least decrease its hold on the civilian population. Those raids were to begin on February 3.

The 8th Air Force bombers had two primary target objectives, one in Berlin and the other in Magdeburg. The biggest raid would be on the marshalling yards in Berlin, specifically those in the Tempelhof area located in the western sector of the city. The 1st and 3rd Air Divisions dispatched just over 1,000 heavy bombers to bomb Berlin. Attacks would also be made on Tempelhof Airfield and in the central district of the capital, where the government buildings were located. Berlin had always been a prime target for the Allied air forces due to its large industrial complexes and it being the heart of the Nazi regime, but it was now even more so because it was a major transportation hub to all parts of Germany.

The second primary target in Magdeburg was given to the 2nd Air Division. It was the Rothensee synthetic oil plant, which was just one of four remaining oil plants in active production. Ancillary targets were the many storage depots located near the industrial site. It seemed our first bombing mission against Rothensee had not been quite enough to completely destroy the plant. So now, the 2nd Division was back to make sure it never again resumed production, or at least to put it out of action for the duration of the war.

Over four hundred B-24 Liberators were dispatched to Magdeburg. Most of the bomb groups were directed to attack Rothensee, while some groups hit marshalling yards in the city. Our squadron, along with a couple of others, was assigned to attack Brunswick, where seven tank manufacturing plants were rolling out new shipments of tanks that were being sent to the front lines.

At the operations briefing, we were given instructions regarding the possibility of a forced landing. At the Yalta Conference, Allied and Russian officials had agreed to honor a designated bomb line, where Allied air forces wouldn't cross over into the Red Army front lines. However, there was no discussion about the possibility of our bombers encountering Red Army aircraft. The Eastern Front was now less than 50 miles from Berlin, and they were ramping up their air attacks along the entire front. We were told that if our aircraft was damaged, we were to implement the following options:

1. Proceed to home base if possible.
2. Land at friendly bases west of the Western Front line if necessary.
3. Land in Sweden if friendly bases cannot be reached.

We were also told: "If it can be avoided do not attempt to land behind Russian front lines as aircraft approaching those lines may be regarded as hostile and may be attacked by either German or Russian ground and fighter forces. In the event one cannot land on those bases mentioned and in order to avoid landing in Germany, the Russian line should be crossed at as high an altitude as possible and landing should be made as far east of the Russian lines as possible. If the safety of the crew is in jeopardy by Russian aircraft, crews may abandon their aircraft in flight. The friendly signal to approaching Russian fighter aircraft would be for our pilot to dip the right wing of our aircraft two or three times, and when their aircraft did likewise, then rock our wings three to five times."

Hopefully, we would never need to use any of these options. Luckily, we didn't encounter any problems, and our bomb group was able to completely destroy the tank manufacturing plant in Brunswick. Our second mission to Magdeburg was a complete success. All the bomb groups from the 2nd Division inflicted severe damage to the targets they were able to reach. We didn't experience any enemy air opposition and received very little flak. The other bomb groups in our division sent to attack Rothensee were a total bust, as the target area was completely covered with clouds. As a result, they went on to bomb marshalling yards in Magdeburg. Rothensee was to be dealt with at a later date.

As expected, the Germans concentrated most of their opposition on the bomber streams over Berlin. The 1st and 3rd Air Divisions took a lot of the damage. Together they lost 21 heavy bombers. However, the mission to Berlin was extremely successful, with many targets hit in strength. Their bombers inflicted some severe damage to many of the marshalling yards and railway stations all around the Berlin area. Perhaps the most successful hits occurred in the government district. The Reich Chancellery, Air Ministry, Foreign Office, Ministry of Propaganda, and Gestapo headquarters sustained major damage to their buildings.[3] It was one of the biggest raids the 8th had ever made on Berlin, and it was just a taste of what was to come.

MISSION #4: FEBRUARY 15, 1945
TARGET: MAGDEBURG

After our last mission, the weather became very unaccommodating, and a couple of our missions were scrubbed, that is, aborted. But on February 15, another big raid was on the board. This time, the 2nd Air Division was again going back to Magdeburg to attack oil refining and processing plants at Rothensee that had been repaired and were trying to resume partial production. The Germans had made the mistake of building and concentrating many of their synthetic oil plants together in large cities. This made them easy to locate. Also, because of the delicate and complicated machinery necessary to produce synthetic oil, these plants were highly susceptible to bomb damage. With most, if not all, of these plants damaged or destroyed during the oil campaign in the summer and fall of 1944, Hitler became furious when Albert Speer, the minister of armaments and war production, told him there were no more oil reserves and that the war effort couldn't continue much longer. Speer then came up with an accelerated rebuilding plan for the synthetic oil industry by constructing factories in smaller units and in different locations, making them more difficult to find.

In this effort, Speer was able to recruit hundreds of thousands of workers—mostly foreign slaves, refugees, and prisoners of war from Nazi-occupied territories—to reconstruct and repair those factories that had been damaged or destroyed by Allied bombings. These workers were all transported to many of the large industrial cities in Germany for the express purpose of rebuilding and repairing damaged plants and factories. Such efforts were so efficient and intense, with work shifts continuing day and night, that bombed-out plants became operational in a matter of days or weeks.

Consequently, as soon as our air intelligence units discovered functioning oil facilities, wherever they might be, they were put on the target list. These included Essen and Dortmund in the Ruhr, along with Rothensee, Gelsenkirchen, Böhlen,

Ruhland, and Zeitz. Although the oil industry was deemed to be of a lower priority than transportation, it continued to receive bombing raids throughout the final months of the war.

Only the day before our mission, the 2nd Air Division was sent to bomb an oil refinery at Magdeburg, but the raid had to be diverted to secondary targets because of bad weather conditions. Now we were going back to finally finish the job. Oil targets in Böhlen and Ruhland were assigned to the 1st and 3rd Air Divisions, but again the bad weather conditions prevailed, and attacks were made against secondary targets, including marshalling yards in Cottbus, Münster, and Dresden. The 2nd Air Division dispatched 372 heavy bombers to hit the Rothensee synthetic oil plant in Magdeburg. The 2nd Combat Wing in this raid included squadrons from the 389th and 445th Bomb Groups as well as ours, the 453rd. Altogether, the 8th Air Force sent over 1,000 heavy bombers to their designated targets.

As we approached our target, the flak was moderate, but the area was covered with low clouds and ground fog. However, the target area was just visible enough, and we were able to make a very successful bomb run. The 389th Bomb Group, being the high group in the wing formation, had to bomb from 27,000 feet because they ran into more cloud cover than our group. As a result, it was difficult to determine the degree of the division's success on the primary target. It took some time for air reconnaissance to discover that the Rothensee oil plant had finally been put out of commission, at least for the time being. So we were happy the mission was a success.

This was the last of our three missions to Magdeburg, which had been a prime target for bombing raids throughout the war. Ideally situated on the Elbe River near Berlin, this large industrial city and its surrounding suburbs contained large complexes of oil plants, munitions, and aircraft-component manufacturing factories as well as a vast array of rail centers. It was a vital transportation hub linking the Ruhr and Berlin to other parts of Germany.

I've heard that Magdeburg claimed the honor of being the most bombed city by the 8th Air Force, and I believe it. Even as our aerial photo reconnaissance team showed that most of the city itself was destroyed, forced labor crews desperately tried to keep the few plants and rail lines running in some state of usage. To discourage them even more, RAF Bomber Command bombed the city again the next day.

MISSION #5: FEBRUARY 19, 1945
TARGET: JUNGENTHAL

Another large raid was initiated with a wide range of targets spanning oil and vehicle manufacturing plants, along with marshalling yards, which were the main focus of attacks. Over 1,000 heavy bombers participated in these raids. The bulk of the heavies were sent to hit transportation targets in the Ruhr area. The 1st Air Division attacked oil targets in Dortmund, Bochum, and Gelsenkirchen. A group was also sent to bomb marshalling yards in Münster. The 3rd Air Division concentrated on marshalling yards in Osnabrück, Münster, and Rheine. Groups were also sent to attack a rail bridge at Wesel.

For our division, the primary targets were manufacturing plants and marshalling yards. Ten squadrons from the 20th and 14th Combat Wings were sent to attack rail yards in Siegen, while the same number from the 96th Combat Wing bombed the Meschede-Henschel aircraft manufacturing plant. Our wing, the 2nd Combat Wing, with nine squadrons from the 389th, 445th, and 453rd Bomb Groups, was sent to bomb the Jung tank assembly plant and repair depot at Jungenthal.

All of Germany's large industrial cities had been bombed repeatedly at this stage of the war. In a desperate attempt to keep war material flowing to the armed forces, Albert Speer had decentralized factories critical to maintaining the war effort in remote areas throughout Germany. Wooded hills and thick forests were especially chosen to prevent detection by enemy reconnaissance aircraft. Included in Speer's dispersal program was Jungenthal. Tucked away in the secluded wooded hills east of Cologne and just seven miles southwest of Siegen were several small factories, which were busy building and assembling the Wehrmacht's Tiger tanks. These were the Germans' most formidable tanks, and they were being produced and repaired at this location on their way to the Western Front.

Our bomb load on this mission consisted of two types—the usual 500-pound GP high-explosive bomb and a load of incendiary bombs. This was our first mission carrying an incendiary bomb load. The Allied air forces' development and use of incendiary devices have a varied and interesting history. Although GP bombs have been used since the First World War, widespread use of incendiary bombs didn't occur until the Second World War. During the Blitz in 1940, when the Germans attempted to bomb England into submission, the British Air Ministry was well aware of the death and destruction caused by fires resulting from bombing raids. This led to the idea that, by studying the effects of enemy raids on their own cities, the Air Ministry could incorporate the knowledge gained and use incendiary devices on bombing raids against German cities. These studies were done very scientifically.

It all began in November 1941, when the Research and Experiments (R&E) Department of the Ministry of Home Security asked J. D. Bernal, a key member of the research team, to set up a special studies division known as RE8 within the R&E Department to study the damage German bombs inflicted upon British cities. Bernal then enlisted the Road Research Laboratory and the Building Research Laboratory to assist him in these studies. He also employed a fellow physicist, Frederick Lindemann, to form a statistical section to analyze the effect of German bombs on various parameters, such as population density and the destruction of houses, buildings, and other standing structures within different city zones.[4]

The results of a number of RE8 studies indicated that the most destructive agent against houses, buildings, and factories was fire. The uncontrollable spread of fire from the concentrated use of incendiary devices was found to be the key to complete destruction of large industrial sites, and possibly even the cities themselves. Firefighters and fire engineers were consulted to determine how fires spread from room to room, house to house, and block to block in large fires. Domestic architecture in Germany was studied in detail, including roof construction, material used for stairwells and staircases, and interior furnishings. It was found that German houses were highly vulnerable to aerial bombardment by incendiary weapons.

This was music to the ears of Air Marshal Arthur Harris, who wanted his bombing raids to exert maximum destruction on every town and city that would be attacked in force. In his doctrine of area bombing, the use of incendiaries as the prime weapon in the destruction of German cities would evolve into a high degree of sophistication. Many different types of incendiary devices were developed and employed in enormous quantities throughout the war. However, the standard weapon of choice was to become the MK-I, better known as the stick-type incendiary device.

The MK-I was small and simply constructed, but it proved to be extremely destructive when used in massive quantities. Its main component consisted of thin, hexagonally shaped rods, approximately 21 inches in length, composed of a magnesium-zinc alloy casing. The shape was designed to make it easy to pack them into small bomb containers. The sticks separated when dropped. Upon impact, percussion caps triggered them, igniting 17 thermite pellets. The magnesium alloy shell then melted into a flaming mass of material capable of reaching very high temperatures. The flames extinguished in eight minutes, but they burned anything flammable that they came into contact with.

Intensive research on the use of MK-I incendiary bombs revealed that when they were used in quantity, these weapons were four to five times more destructive than high-explosive bombs. While seven tons of high-explosive GP bombs could cause significant damage to approximately 20 square miles, an equal amount of incendiary bombs increased the destruction to more than 90 miles.[5] Moreover, the use of both types of bombs in combination resulted in even greater destruction.

The British had a 4,000-pound high-explosive bomb they called the blockbuster, which was capable of destroying several blocks of buildings. Its blast effects caused considerable damage and created such an intense shock wave that any standing structure within its range was blown to pieces. However, the big bomb's main use was blowing out all the roofs and windows of buildings miles beyond the blast zone. This ventilated the structures to create enough flammable debris so that when the next wave of bombers attacked with incendiaries, there was total destruction by fire.

The critical test of what the judicious use of fire as a weapon could accomplish came on the night of July 27, 1943. The target was the city of Hamburg, in northern Germany. It just happened to be on top of Harris's list for his bombing raids. Like many large cities in Germany, Hamburg's center had an area commonly termed Old Town, with buildings and dwellings that stretched in age as far back as the eighteenth and nineteenth centuries, some with structures dating back to medieval times. Houses had wooden roofs and were primarily constructed both inside and outside using old timber. Rows upon rows of tightly packed housing units without firewalls lined the winding narrow streets. Such areas of densely populated sectors were what the British incendiary experts called Zone 1—an area ripe for an incendiary bombing attack.

The weather was also ideal for an attack, with one of the hottest and driest summers in decades. With high temperatures and low humidity, the city was primed to burn. It was late in the evening when over 700 British bombers dropped 2,326 tons of GP and MK-I incendiary bombs with a concentration of 1,200 tons of incendiaries within an area of two square miles. It had been calculated that between 100,000 and 200,000 incendiaries dropped in large salvos would curtail firefighters' ability to control the resulting fires. On this attack, there were more than enough bombs to start a major conflagration—an uncontrollable fire.

The entire raid lasted a little over an hour, and the fire spread rapidly. As predicted, the thousands of small fires grew larger and coalesced into an inferno. The blockbusters had done their job, and now the roofless houses and blown-out windows acted like an open chimney that fed the flames. Soon entire blocks were on fire, and as the inferno grew in size and intensity, a firestorm erupted.

More than just a raging inferno, a firestorm actually exponentially increases in ferocity and takes on a life of its own. Hot, flaming debris and thick smoke can rise as high as two or three miles above a city. The tremendous updraft draws the cooler air on the ground into its flames. This updraft can cause winds of up to a 100 mph or greater. This swallows up more and more combustible material into the flaming body.

Trees are uprooted, damaged structures disintegrate, and people are all sucked into the flames. The most destructive component of a firestorm is not the actual fire itself but the available oxygen being depleted to feed the fire. People fleeing the flames found their shoes melting on the superheated asphalt, lost consciousness from the lack of oxygen, and became incinerated. Those unlucky victims sheltering in their cellars or underground fire bunkers died from asphyxiation and carbon monoxide poisoning. The vast majority of deaths, over 70 percent, were due to suffocation. The heat was so intense—up to thousands of degrees Fahrenheit—that metal became molten and anything flammable was quickly turned into ash. Shelters packed with many people, when opened, revealed nothing left but ash. Because of this, it was never determined how many people died from this one bombing raid in Hamburg. Estimates exceeded 40,000.

This was, however, only one bombing raid of many on Hamburg during the British Operation Gomorrah in 1943. Harris was very pleased to hear the results of the raid on Hamburg. He believed that this kind of devastating attack, at such a ghastly cost to human lives, on all the cities on his bombing list would finally be the panacea needed to defeat Germany. But that was not to be. Most cities escaped the firestorm phenomenon. But the cities that did succumb to such horrendous destruction included Essen, Kassel, Pforzheim, Dresden, and Magdeburg.

On January 16, 1945—the day our group bombed the Krupp tank factory in Magdeburg—fifteen-year-old Dieter Becker was on the ground watching our bombs fall. Becker was likely a member of the Hitler Youth, an organization of young recruits dedicated to helping the war effort. Along with other members of the Ottersleben fire brigade, he was at his post looking out toward the Krupp-Gruson plant as the explosions rocked the area. He could see women running from the Krupp Aschenberg air raid bunker near the factory. Only German citizens were allowed into the air raid shelters. Young French women who were slave laborers at the plant were refused entry, and they were running into the open fields to escape the falling bombs. Some escaped to safety. But most did not. It was Becker's first experience with corpses, and he helped collect them from the fields nearby. But for the city of Magdeburg, the worst was yet to come.[6]

That evening, as Becker was on his way home, the air raid sirens began wailing once again. Then all around him it became as bright as day. It was the RAF Bomber Command's turn to bomb Magdeburg.

Like Hamburg, Magdeburg housed many old structures and was highly susceptible to fire. Of all the major cities in Germany, Magdeburg had the unenviable distinction of being the one to suffer the most destruction by aerial bombardment. It wasn't a big raid, but enough blockbusters and incendiaries—over 1,000 tons—were dropped in an area of less than one square mile. As wave after wave of bombers released their deadly payloads, an enormous firestorm erupted. In less than half an hour, the city center was totally destroyed. Only the rubble of brick and stone remained. It was estimated that 4,000 lives were lost that night.

Upon hearing the results of the July 1943, firebombing of Hamburg, Churchill himself was appalled at the death and destruction inflicted by Bomber Command. However, there was little he could do to ameliorate the situation because it was Harris who commanded the RAF bombing campaign against Germany. It had always been American policy, ordered by Gen. Arnold and the American Joint Chiefs of Staff, that bombing raids by American air forces would restrict attacks to military and industrial targets in an attempt to reduce civilian casualties as much as possible. Like the British, our air forces developed and used a wide variety of incendiary devices. However, in most instances, incendiaries weren't massively employed in the hundreds of thousands. Instead, they were used in lesser quantities in specific situations against certain types of targets.

On all our missions that required the use of incendiary bombs, we carried the M-17A1 cluster bomb. It was essentially a hollow 500-pound bomb container packed with one hundred and ten M50A1 bomblets inside. The M50A1 is actually the same stick-type incendiary as the MK I British device, composed of a four-pound hexagonal magnesium alloy body with steel fins containing an explosive thermite charge and a fuse. Between five and ninety seconds after the M-17A1 was dropped from the aircraft, a timed fuse burst the bomb container and released the clustered M50A1 bomblets. When ignited upon impact, each M50A1 incendiary device burned from six to eight minutes at extremely high temperatures, up to 2,500 degrees Fahrenheit. A single M50A1 exploding upon inflammable material burned so fiercely that water couldn't extinguish it. It merely evaporated upon contact with the burning material.[7]

The maximum number of M-17A1 incendiary bombs we carried on board was usually six or fewer, in addition to our GP load. A load of medium-size GP bombs, along with M-17s, was found to exert maximum destruction on structures built from concrete and steel, such as railroad marshalling yards, bridges, canals, viaducts, surface bunkers, and other highly vulnerable targets. On the mission to Jungenthal, our bomb load consisted of six M-17 and six 500-pound GP bombs, an ideal load for a munitions target hidden in the forest. Located in such a remote area, the target was lightly defended by antiaircraft batteries, and we received very little flak during our bomb run. However, the area was covered with clouds, so we had to bomb by instruments. Therefore, damage to the factory complex couldn't be immediately assessed. We figured it would likely be repeatedly targeted in the future until there was clear evidence of its destruction.

FEBRUARY 20, 1944: BIG WEEK

The day after our mission to Jungenthal, we were reminded of what had happened exactly one year before, on February 20, 1944, when the American air forces defeated the Luftwaffe and took command of the skies above Germany. Eliminating the threat of the German Air Force had been a top priority in Operation Pointblank when operations began in June 1943. At that time, the Luftwaffe was at the top of the list of systems targeted for two reasons: first as a prerequisite for Operation Overlord, and second as a requirement for a successful daylight bombing campaign in Germany. In 1943, the Luftwaffe had a massive interceptor force, and it was able to send hundreds of fighters to intercept American bomber forces. Losses were overwhelming, and the bombing raids couldn't be sustained for long. Therefore, the German Air Force and the aircraft industry had to be destroyed.

General Ira Eaker, who was the commander of the US 8th Air Force at the time, always believed that bombers heavily armed with .50-caliber machine guns and flying in tight combat formations would be an adequate defense against any enemy interceptor attack. This was Eaker's doctrine of "defense by force." The British air commanders repeatedly told Eaker, based on their own experiences, that such a policy was doomed to failure. The RAF had tried such a method and suffered severe losses as a consequence. That was why the RAF Bomber Command had to resort to night bombing raids. The Luftwaffe was just too powerful for daylight raids to be successful.

Eaker thought otherwise, and throughout the summer and fall of 1943, the 8th Air Force suffered horrific losses. He was adamant that his policy of a self-defending well-armed bomber force would rule the day. Brigadier General Frank Hunter, commander of the 8th Air Force's Fighter Command, supported Eaker's concept.

However, Lt. Gen. Henry Arnold didn't share Eaker's views. Arnold realized that for daylight raids to succeed, the bomber force would need fighter escorts. There was no alternative. The existing American fighter forces in 1943, consisting of the P-47 Thunderbolt and P-38 Lightning, had a limited range of operations. They were constrained by the size of their fuel tanks. Each fighter had a maximum range of 500 miles, which meant it could get only as far as the Rhine River and not very far into Germany. Consequently, this meant the bombers were on their own in reaching their targets and returning to base. The Germans knew this, and they were able to develop tactics that decimated the American bomber forces. This was clearly evident during the first raid against the Schweinfurt ball-bearing factories in August 1943, when the loss rate of bombers exceeded 10 percent. Such severe losses totally jeopardized the bombing operations of the 8th Air Force. It wasn't able to effectively sustain its bombing campaign. The end result: no more daylight raids.

Clearly, Eaker's self-defending policy needed to be reassessed. Arnold then had Eaker replace Gen. Hunter with Maj. Gen. William Kepner, an experienced fighter pilot who was a staunch advocate of actively pursuing and destroying the German Luftwaffe. Arnold had issued an order in early 1942 to equip all new fighters with auxiliary tanks to extend their range as bomber escorts. Kepner wanted to accelerate the program, but Eaker was reluctant to do so. Tensions began to escalate among the top commanders in the 8th, and Arnold finally decided that an organizational change was needed for the US Army Air Force to establish a more unified command structure for strategic air operations in Europe.

In December 1943, the Combined Chiefs of Staff granted Arnold's request to reorganize the American air forces in the ETO. Arnold created a new air force command called the United States Strategic Air Force (USSTAF), consisting of the US 8th and 15th Air Forces. Arnold brought in Maj. Gen. Carl Spaatz, who took command of USSTAF on January 1, 1944. Spaatz also had some authority over the US 9th Air Force. He brought with him Maj. Gen. Jimmy Doolittle, who replaced Gen. Eaker as commander of the US 8th Air Force. Doolittle, who earned fame in the famous raid against Japan from the aircraft carrier USS *Hornet* on April 18, 1942, was an aggressive advocate of bomber escorts and exactly the type of commander Arnold was seeking for the 8th.[8]

As early as June 1943, Arnold had pushed for the development of the next generation of American fighter aircraft known as the North American P-51 Mustang. The new aircraft became operational in December 1943, and by January, they were readily available to USSTAF. The timing couldn't have been more perfect. Spaatz, Doolittle, and Kepner were all aligned with the importance of fighter escorts to accompany and protect the bombers all the way to their targets and back.

If there was ever such a thing as a silver bullet in the American air campaign against the Luftwaffe, the P-51 Mustang was it.

The Mustang was the most advanced Allied fighter aircraft at the time of its deployment in the beginning of 1944. It was developed in the United States and designed by the British. Powered by an advanced Merlin engine—the same type used by the British Mark IX Spitfire—the P-51 was the fastest and finest piston-engine fighter of the war. Its performance, rate of climb, and maneuverability outclassed the Luftwaffe's Messerschmitt 109 and Focke-Wulf 190 fighter class interceptors. Fitted with external fuel tanks, the P-51 had an operating range of over 900 miles, making it easily capable of escorting the bomber forces all the way to Berlin and back.

America's newest fighter aircraft totally transformed the air war over Germany.

After establishing the first P-51 Mustang fighter groups Arnold then sent messages to the commanders of the US 8th and 15th Air Forces—Gen. Doolittle and Lt.

The P-51 Mustang was the mainstay of the heavy bomber escort aircraft. Its introduction to the US Strategic Air Forces in the ETO in 1944 changed the dynamics of aerial warfare against the German Air Force. The P-51 played a key role in the AAF's ability to achieve absolute air superiority in the skies over Germany. (Collings Foundation)

Gen. Nathan Twining, respectively—to destroy the German Air Force wherever it existed, whether in the air, on the ground, or in the factories.[9]

Doolittle, in turn, wrote to his commanders and stated as commander of the 8th Air Force that their prime objective was to neutralize the enemy fighter opposition as soon as it presented itself. Even before Doolittle had assumed command, Kepner was in the process of transforming fighter support tactics. Their foremost purpose was to protect the bomber force, but they were encouraged to actively engage and eliminate any enemy forces they encountered. As a consequence, Doolittle and Kepner adopted a new tactic known as Freelance, in which groups of escort fighters were allowed to leave the bomber stream and aggressively seek out and destroy enemy aircraft wherever they might be found. A major component of Freelance operations was having American fighters fly to known German airfields to strafe enemy aircraft on the ground or while they were taking off or landing. Attrition of enemy forces from Freelance operations was key in defeating the Luftwaffe.

By early 1944, the US 8th Air Force had over 2,000 heavy bombers and more than half that number of fighter escorts in operation. The Republic P-47 Thunderbolt was the mainstay of the fighter force and remained so during the spring of 1944, until the numbers of P-51 Mustang could be ramped up. Eventually, the escort fighter force was composed almost entirely of P-51s. With such a large force, Doolittle wanted to initiate an aggressive air offensive as soon as he arrived at 8th Air Force headquarters, but the weather didn't permit serious air activity until mid-February 1944. On February 20, 1944, the weather cleared, and Operation Argument was immediately launched.

Operation Argument was a sustained bombing campaign against German aircraft factories. Precision attacks were directed against all known aircraft-component manufacturing factories and final-assembly plants of single- and twin-engine enemy aircraft. These included the Fw 190, Me 109, Me 110, Ju 88, and Ju 188 aircraft. A series of concentrated attacks on 12 specific targets in central and southern Germany began on February 20 and continued daily until February 26. This was known as the Big Week Bombing Campaign of 1944. During that span of time, the German aircraft industry suffered some very heavy damage. However, it wasn't only the damage from the bombing raids that was so destructive, but also the aggressive attacks by American escort fighters on German interceptors. Selected targets were specifically chosen for the express purpose of luring enemy fighters into the sky. As soon as they were in the air, the P-51 fighter escorts decimated them. The German fighters were being shot out of the sky. By the end of February, the Luftwaffe had lost more than 1,000 fighter aircraft.

The Luftwaffe High Command was so concerned about such severe losses that they abruptly changed their attack strategy. They knew they were losing control of the skies over Germany. Instead of massed interceptor attacks on every

American bombing raid, the Germans sent up fighters to intercept the bomber force only on particular targets. On other occasions, there was no enemy air resistance to bombers at all. The American air commanders knew that the Germans' active conservation of strength was a clear indication of trouble for the Third Reich's war effort. So the American air offensive was increased to an even higher level in March 1944.

General Spaatz had always believed that if vital targets were attacked, such as the refineries and petroleum factories, the Germans would send up a large attacking force in their defense. All through the spring of 1944, oil targets were bombed again and again. The Bergius hydrogenation plants were especially targeted. Much of the Luftwaffe's high-octane aviation fuel was being generated through the synthetic fuel processes. As predicted, the Germans sent interceptor forces against the bombers, and their fighters were shot down. To further increase the pressure on the Luftwaffe, American escort fighters expanded their efforts in Freelance operations. Small groups of four or more fighters would leave the bomber stream and scour the area nearby to seek out and destroy any enemy aircraft in the air or on the ground at German airfields. Freelance was becoming extremely successful, and on March 4, 1944, the 8th Air Force began for the first time a series of large bombing raids against the most heavily defended city in Germany: Berlin.

There were many Luftwaffe airfields surrounding the capital, and sure enough, the enemy sent up interceptors in force to defend the city. Targets within the city, such as the ball-bearing factories at Erkner and aircraft component plants, were especially targeted. All through March and April 1944, bombing raids against Berlin and other high-value targets destroyed an increasing number of German fighters. In March, German losses amounted to a total of 1,591 aircraft, even more than in February.[10]

In practically every case of air-to-air combat with American fighters, the Germans were outnumbered and outclassed. It was in March 1944 that a significant deterioration in the quality of German pilots first became evident. As envisioned by the American air commanders, the constant and rising attrition rate of German fighter aircraft was bad enough, but it was the loss of its best pilots that eventually doomed the Luftwaffe.

The 8th Air Force's intensified attacks on oil targets had depleted the aviation fuel reserves to such a level that German fuel conservation was paramount in sustaining ongoing Luftwaffe operations. As Germany attempted to replace the large number of pilots being killed in combat, a bottleneck appeared in their air force academies. Young pilot cadets in flight school were receiving a quality of training that was far below the norm. The German high command had two choices to make with regard to the shortage of fuel being allocated to their air academies: either decrease the number of pilots being trained or decrease the amount of flight training per student. They chose the latter. As a result, the required hours of flight training were drastically reduced. These new Luftwaffe recruits never had a chance against the experienced American fighter pilots. The German Air Force was now caught in a vicious cycle of an increasing shortage of aviation fuel, an inadequate level of training for new pilots, and an ever-increasing loss of fighter pilots who couldn't be replaced.

The attrition rate of aircraft and pilots only accelerated in April. The Luftwaffe lost almost half its fighter force in that month alone. It was no better for them in May. On May 12, 1944, the US 8th Air Force attacked synthetic oil plants in the Ruhr. The Germans sent wave after wave of interceptors against the bombers, but the P-47 and P-51 fighter escorts virtually eliminated them. As many as 150 enemy aircraft were lost in a single American bombing raid. The German interceptors had become increasingly reluctant to tangle with the bomber fighter escorts.

It was evident that March was the turning point in the air war against the Germans. Luftwaffe resistance decreased dramatically from a peak in April, which was reflected in a steep decline of American bomber losses due to enemy fighters. By June 1944, the attrition cycle in the destruction of the German fighter force was complete.

The Luftwaffe had been defeated.

On D-Day, June 6, 1944, Gen. Eisenhower told his commanders, "If you see fighter aircraft over you, they will be ours."[11] On the first day of Operation Overlord, the Allied air forces had absolute air supremacy over the skies of France. More than 16,000 Allied aircraft sorties supported the invasion forces landing on the beaches of Normandy. Fewer than 100 Luftwaffe aircraft were even observed on that day. Lieutenant General Werner Junck, who was the commander of the German fighter forces in the Normandy area, had 160 aircraft available, but only 80 were operational.[12]

The top priority in the Casablanca Directive and Operation Pointblank had been achieved: The threat of the German Air Force had been eliminated, ensuring the success of Operation Overlord.

MISSION #6: FEBRUARY 21, 1945
TARGET: NUREMBERG

While the 8th Air Force had been targeting the German transportation system since the beginning of February, this mission would be our first crack of many to hit enemy rail targets. Similar to the massive effort to defeat the Luftwaffe in February 1944, the push to accelerate the current transportation campaign would be our Big Week of 1945. Allied bomber forces were instructed to exert maximum effort to destroy the German transportation systems. Daily bombing raids by Allied air forces continued in full effect through the month and well into March. The goal of these raids was to simply crush the German armed forces' ability to effectively sustain military operations.

Germany has three natural transportation areas of importance. The first is the North and Baltic Sea coastlines. Next come the west-east geographical route along the foothills of a low mountain range called the Mittelgebirge, and then the Rhine

German Rail Centers Targeted by Allied Air Forces

River. Of course, the most important network of transportation and railroad network centers is located in the Rhine-Ruhr Valley region, where trains travel north toward Osnabrück to the Baltic Sea, eastward through Hanover to Berlin, and to central and southern Germany by way of Paderborn and Kassel. Vital railway centers span the east-west axis connecting the three major industrial regions of the Ruhr, Upper Silesia, and Saxony.

Located in southern Germany, Nuremberg held importance in the bombing campaign as a major nexus of rail centers leading to all the large cities of the country's eastern and southern provinces. Nuremberg was a large industrial city with an abundance of manufacturing centers specializing in munitions, electrical works, ordnance, diesel engines, and aircraft components. Factories producing tanks, trucks, and armored vehicles were also located in the metro area. The US 8th Air Force hadn't bombed the city for some time. Its rail marshalling yards were now crammed full of locomotives and freight trains supplying the Eastern Front.

Bomb groups from all air divisions were to attack rail centers throughout the entire metropolitan area. This was a large raid totaling over 1,200 heavy bombers. Over 800 heavy bombers from the 1st and 3rd Air Divisions and approximately 400 from our division were dispatched to hit targets in Nuremberg. Every bomb group in the 2nd Air Division, except the 491st Bomb Group, participated in the attack. German resistance was very light over our target, and the weather conditions were perfect for visual bombing. Practically every bomb group scored direct hits. The city suffered severe damage from the raid. Photographic results from air reconnaissance showed major destruction not only in the critical rail centers permeating the city but in many of the industrial sites as well. It was an excellent start to an intensive bombing campaign that was to last for months.

OPERATION CLARION

Operation Clarion was launched the next day, February 22, 1945. It was a combined British and American daylight air offensive including both tactical and strategic air forces. Originally proposed in July 1944, Clarion was to be a single-day bombing raid by all Anglo-American air forces against communications and transportation targets throughout Germany. But it took until February 1945 before the air forces actually commenced operations. No surprise there. The types of targets chosen included marshalling yards, railroad grade crossings, railway stations, railroad tracks, bridges, canals, barges, docks, and wherever there was movement of military traffic. Clarion's goal was to stymie the activities of German forces, with the purpose of helping Eisenhower's armies advance to the Rhine River.

The Allied air forces sent thousands of heavy bombers to target areas all over Germany. The US 8th Air Force dispatched more than 1,400 heavies to targets in central and northern Germany, while the 15th Air Force concentrated its efforts over a wide area in the south. RAF Bomber Command attacked targets in the Ruhr. American tactical air forces were assigned targets in western and northwestern Germany. This mighty effort was a resounding success, with the vast majority of the targets totally destroyed or put out of commission.

MISSION #7: FEBRUARY 23, 1945
TARGET: PADERBORN

The results of Operation Clarion were so good that another very similar operation was scheduled for the next day.

Now it was our turn.

Again, all Allied air forces were involved. RAF Bomber Command went after rail targets in Gelsenkirchen and Essen in the Ruhr with daylight raids, while at night their target was Berlin. In the south, the US 15th Air Force attacked eight transportation targets. Tactical air forces were assigned targets similar to the ones they'd attacked the previous day.

It was another big raid for the 8th, as more than 1,200 heavy bombers were dispatched. All three divisions of the 8th Air Force were to attack marshalling yards, rail facilities, and other transportation targets in a wide sweep across western and central Germany. The 1st and 3rd Air Divisions together dispatched almost 1,000 heavy bombers to attack six major rail targets. More than 300 bombers in our division were sent to Weimar, Fulda, and Gera. The 453rd and other bomb groups of the 2nd Combat Wing were directed to bomb marshalling yards in Fulda.

In contrast to the previous day, the weather turned really bad, and we were almost unable to take off. The cloud cover extended up to 12,000 feet, and visibility was so limited that we had to take off by instruments. High-altitude bombing runs were precluded. Instead, for increased accuracy of target location and bombing, we had to bomb at a lower altitude—less than 10,000 feet—instead of a normal run of 20,000 to 25,000 feet. However, layers of thick clouds and bad weather extended way beyond the higher altitudes, so our wing was directed to a secondary target—a rail bridge in Paderborn.

Probably on the list of the most destroyed cities in Germany from scores of bombing raids, Paderborn is centrally located just east of the Ruhr Valley and has an extensive array of railroad lines spreading eastward to Magdeburg and Berlin. Because of the weather conditions, German resistance was nil. Thick clouds covered the entire target area. Without the ability to see the target, H2X radar was the only option. When we returned to base, the weather was no better. The area was covered with fog and rain. It was a tense and tricky landing by instruments, but Lt. Swingle, our pilot, did a fantastic job. We all treated him to drinks that evening.

I can't say enough about our pilot. To me he was one of the best pilots in the wing because there were many times when we didn't think we would make it, but his skill as a pilot and determination to look out for our crew saved the day. Our closest brush with disaster occurred on one of our earlier missions, when we had to abort because one of the engines caught fire while we were crossing the Channel into France. Some of our fighters escorted us back to base, and Swingle had to make a hard landing. We all prayed on that day. Despite the many mechanical problems our Libs had, which was a common occurrence in combat, bad weather took down the greater number of our aircraft.

Despite the most atrocious weather we'd ever experienced, the second day of Clarion was deemed a success. The 8th was able to strike 26 of its assigned targets, and the Germans suffered some heavy damage to their railway systems, again. Damage inflicted by the Allied air forces included at least 150 marshalling yards, hundreds of railway lines, and 300 locomotives. In many parts of Germany, rail traffic was at a complete standstill. But even with such devastation, Speer's army of hundreds of thousands of laborers began work on the damage wreaked during Clarion. Ongoing repairs were observed by aerial reconnaissance the very next day. Thus, constant pressure by repeated bombing raids was necessary in the coming months, a familiar theme heard in the oil campaign. Germany's transportation system soon experienced what the Luftwaffe had in the spring of 1944.

After Clarion, the transportation campaign entered a new phase. While the operation encompassed a variety of targets over a wide expanse, the Allied air forces now concentrated their bombing efforts on specific areas of concern. One was the Ruhr region. After reaching the Rhine River, Eisenhower's next strategic objective was the Ruhr Valley. The Russian occupation of Upper Silesia had drastically affected the German war machine's industrial capability. The Ruhr Valley then became the largest and most vital coal and steel industrial area remaining in Germany.

Allied and American ground forces were advancing quickly to the Rhine River, reaching it within a month at the most. In preparation for assisting Eisenhower's forces in their anticipated advance to the Ruhr, the American air forces were to isolate the Ruhr from the rest of Germany. The first objective was to cut every line of communication to the Ruhr region, which included railway trestles, bridges, canals, and viaducts in a wide arc beginning in the north, at Bremen on the Wesel River, to Koblenz, south of the Ruhr. With this first phase of operations accomplished, all vital marshalling yards in the Ruhr and rail lines running through bridges on the Wesel and Rhine Rivers were then repeatedly attacked to prevent them from being repaired, reconstructed, and used. Tactical air forces concentrated on railroad crossings and rolling stock. This was a very ambitious campaign, although there was a strong precedent for success in northern France prior to the launch of Operation Overlord in 1944.

MISSION #8: FEBRUARY 24, 1945
TARGET: LEHRTE

This was another day of miserable weather, which is very typical of northern Germany this time of the year. Nonetheless, another big raid was launched against oil and transportation targets. More than 300 heavy bombers from the 1st Air Division were launched against oil targets in northern Germany, specifically in Hamburg and Albrecht. Four hundred heavies from the 3rd Air Division were sent to the Bremen area to bomb a submarine pen and rail bridge in that area as well as a bridge across the Wesel River. For our division, close to 200 Liberators were sent to attack an oil plant in Misburg and marshalling yards in Bielefeld and Lehrte.

At the beginning of the oil campaign in the spring of 1944, 81 oil targets were on the target list. Fifty-eight were oil refineries, and 23 were synthetic oil plants. By February 1945, no refineries were known to be in operation. Only four synthetic oil plants were known to be still functioning. One of these was in Misburg, in the Hanover region of northwestern Germany. All three of our division's targets were in the vicinity of Hanover, which was the third-largest city in Germany after Hamburg and Bremen. Hanover was an important industrial center and a key transportation hub bridging the Ruhr in western Germany and Berlin in the east. Its extensive rail systems ran to Hamburg in the north and as far south as Munich.

Bielefeld is just southwest of Hanover, while Lehrte is just 10 miles east of the Hanover metropolitan area. The heavily traveled passenger and freight Lehrte-Berlin railway line began in Hanover and ended in central Berlin. Severing that link would greatly disrupt traffic and impede movement through the entire region between these two major cities.

As our combat wing of 85 Liberators approached Lehrte, the target area was immersed in cloud cover. There was a moderate amount of flak, and we had to bomb by H2X. Though not as accurate as the Norden bombsight, improvements in the H2X terrain-scanning radar technique allowed a clear distinction of rivers and waterways from land formations.

Hanover is located next to the Leine River, an offshoot of the Wesel River. The large city was clearly visible on the Mickey scope. Because of the cloud cover, bombing results from our attacks remained unobserved. Bombers from the other air divisions also encountered bad weather, and it wasn't a great day for the 8th. Tactical operations by the 9th Air Force, with nearly 500 fighter-bombers, had better luck. Their attacks resulted in accurate hits of five communication centers, two marshalling yards, and three rail bridges in northern Germany.

MISSION #9: FEBRUARY 25, 1945
TARGET: GIEBELSTADT

The weather in northern Germany remained bad, but in southern Germany, the weather was exceptionally good—perfect, in fact—for the Norden bombsight. It was an opportunity not to be missed. So the 8th sent more than 1,100 heavy bombers to attack oil and transportation targets in the southern regions of the country. The 1st and 3rd Air Divisions attacked a train station, marshalling yards, and oil storage depots in Munich. Also on their target list were marshalling yards in Ulm, Neuburg, and the Maybach tank factory in Friedrichshafen. The 2nd Air Division, with 368 Liberators, concentrated on destroying a marshalling yard and tank factory at Aschaffenburg and airfield installations at Giebelstadt. Our combat wing, consisting of 96 Libs, went after the Giebelstadt Army Airfield located in Bavaria, just southeast of Frankfurt and approximately 250 miles south of Berlin.

Giebelstadt was one of the very first Luftwaffe airfields built in 1935. It had training facilities for pilots and ground crew. More importantly, it became a vital testing and staging ground for all of the Luftwaffe's newest aircraft, including the Me 262 jet fighter and Me 163A Komet rocket fighter. The airfield was expanded in 1944 to accommodate longer runways and was used for servicing, maintaining, and repairing the newer types of interceptor jet aircraft. It was so important that the Germans tried their utmost to completely camouflage the entire airfield from Allied aerial surveillance. Only the highest officials in the German Air Ministry knew about its location. It caught the attention of the 8th's commanders because they hadn't seen much air activity from the Luftwaffe all during February, and it was reported that they were regrouping and preparing for a heavy assault on our bombers. Giebelstadt was one place where there was a beehive of activity.

As we approached the airfield, we encountered only light flak. Tactical fighter-bomber units from the US 9th Air Force had already begun their attacks on the field with 500-pound GPs, unguided rockets, and .50-caliber machine guns to keep the interceptors grounded so they wouldn't be able to take off to attack our bomber force. Apparently, our fighters were also doing a good job destroying their heavy artillery.

We were running into some light cloud cover, so we descended to 17,000 feet to release our bomb load of ten 500-pound GPs. The entire airfield was plastered with ordnance, and nearly all the hangars and barracks were completely demolished. There was also considerable damage to the runways and adjoining ground support facilities. At least three of Luftwaffe's newest Me 262 jet fighters were observed vigorously burning on the runway.

Our mission was a complete success. In fact, the 2nd Air Division's destruction of all the targets was so impressive that our divisional commander, Maj. Gen. William E. Kepner, posted a message on our bulletin board congratulating the division: "Evaluation of today's results on important communications and A/C centers conclusively shows that each of 2nd Division's targets was superlatively hit. I consider this to be one of the outstanding performances in the history of precision bombing."[13]

MISSION #10: FEBRUARY 26, 1945
TARGET: BERLIN

On February 26, the 8th sent another massive bomber force to hit the Third Reich where it hurt: Berlin. It might have been just another target on the 8th's list, but we were all eager and excited to have a chance to attack the very heart of the Nazi regime. It was Lt. Swingle's dream to have a chance to bomb Berlin, so his enthusiasm for this mission just permeated throughout our crew. We were psyched, but we knew it would probably be our most dangerous mission so far.

In the earlier years of the war, Berlin was a target all airmen from the 8th dreaded. The city was one of the most heavily fortified cities in Germany, ringed with more than 100 antiaircraft artillery batteries composed of heavy 88 mm, 105 mm, and 128 mm flak guns. A single battery unit contained 16 to 24 guns, with each gun manned by a crew of 11 specialized artillery Luftwaffe personnel.

The 88 mm cannon was a fearsome weapon capable of throwing a 20-pound fragmentation shell up to five miles into the sky. Because of a highly sophisticated radar-controlled aiming mechanism, its accuracy and precision in hitting an attacking bomber stream was quite accurate. Under ideal conditions, these heavy flak guns used a system called "predicted flak," which enabled the guns to hit a single bomber flying at a high altitude.[14]

Berlin was included on the roster as being a Flak City, like other important cities in the Ruhr Valley, more notably Hamm and Essen. These cities were surrounded by a ring of flak batteries. Berlin was probably even more formidable in terms of air defense because of the addition of three huge flak towers placed in the city center. Each tower stood more than 30 feet above ground and was constructed of thick concrete and steel, enabling it to withstand a direct hit by a high-explosive bomb. On top of the flak tower were three to four gun batteries, with each battery composed of six to eight cannons ranging in size from the usual 88 mm to mega cannons of 105 mm and 128 mm. (See Appendix 4.)

The purpose of all this antiaircraft firepower was to knock heavy bombers out of the sky and, more importantly, cause extensive damage to the aircraft. Bombers hit by shrapnel from the multitude of exploding shells had to fly behind or out of formation. Virtually defenseless, these stragglers were the ones German interceptors sought out and easily destroyed. During the bomber raids of 1942 and 1943, before the advent of fighter escorts that protected the bombers against marauding German fighters, Allied aircraft and crews suffered extensive losses.

We were very fortunate during the final months of the war that the German fighter forces had been rendered ineffective and no longer posed a significant threat to our bomber forces. Of course, German fighters were still a real danger, and on every mission, we received intelligence reports on the possibility of enemy interception. But we were accompanied by large numbers of fighter escorts on all our raids. Ideally, Doolittle wanted a one-to-one ratio of fighter escorts to bombers. However, this often wasn't the case in practice, and probably was overkill.

For example, the 8th dispatched 1,207 heavy bombers, accompanied by 726 escort fighters, on this mission. The lack of fuel meant that the Luftwaffe could muster only a small number of interceptors to attack the bomber streams at any one time. Besides being outclassed by the P-51s, enemy interceptors were woefully outnumbered. It was difficult enough for them to attack bombers, but with such massive numbers of fighter escorts, it was almost impossible to be successful. In fact, the majority of bomber losses were now due to flak rather than attack by enemy fighters.

Two to three hundred escort fighter aircraft accompanied each of the 8th's air divisions, with the majority being P-51 Mustangs. The rest were P-47 Thunderbolts. The escorts flew high above the bomber streams, keeping a vigilant eye out for enemy interceptors. Our escorts then swooped down to attack as enemy fighters aimed for our bombers. On occasion, our escorts flew alongside our aircraft, so close that we would easily see them waving to us. We referred to them as "Little Friends," while they called us "Big Friends." The P-51s that flew with us to Berlin most likely carried 108-gallon drop tanks under each wing, which enabled them to make a round trip of 1,700 miles. They easily got to our target and back. With so many escort fighters flying over us, we seldom saw any German interceptors on most of our missions.

The primary targets on February 26 were three rail stations in Berlin. The 1st Air Division, with 377 bombers, was sent to hit the Schlesischer rail station in the Friedrichshain district, while the 3rd Air Division, with 466 bombers, went after the Alexanderplatz station in the Mitte district. Our division had 361 Libs dispatched to attack a railway network center just northwest of the downtown district of Berlin, the largest of which was the Berlin-Lehrte train station. Of the 726 fighter escorts sent with the three divisions, the 2nd Air Division was accompanied by one hundred ninety P-51s and twenty P-47s.[15]

As previously mentioned, the Berlin-Lehrte rail line coming from Hanover enters directly into Berlin's central district, known as the Mitte. There the rail line branches out into various directions. The Alexanderplatz and Schlesischer stations were situated in the eastern sector of the city. The terminus for the Berlin-Lehrte line was at the large Anhalter Bahnhof station in the southern sector, where it became the Berlin-Halle line, which continued on to Halle, 93 miles south of Berlin, and other southern cities, such as Leipzig. The main surface rail lines going through the city ran alongside a dense patchwork of Berlin's S-Bahn and U-Bahn, the surface and subterranean rapid transit rail systems. These transit lines were connected to a vast number of large rail stations situated throughout the capital. The larger stations included Lehrter Bahnhof, Leipziger Platz, Alexanderplatz, Anhalter Bahnhof, and Schlesischer stations.

The 8th's heaviest bombing raid on Berlin took place just a couple of weeks earlier, on February 3. Nearly 1,500 heavy bombers and 1,000 fighter escorts attacked communications targets around the capital as well as the government sector in the city's central district. The massive destruction that ensued would now be repeated. As our combat wing entered the target area, the flak increased dramatically. On our approach, the sky became immersed in flak, and we were flying through a thick cloud of bursting shells. The concentration of exploding artillery shells increased proportionately as we came to the IP, or initial point—the point at which our bombing run began over the target. The entire group formation needed to fly straight and true right over the target. The Germans knew this, so they concentrated all their antiaircraft fire into tight rectangular patterns termed "box barrages." In effect, it's like carpet-bombing in reverse, in the sky, as opposed to ground targets. We were hit by many large shrapnel fragments from nearby exploding shells, but luckily we didn't sustain any major damage.

The target area was partially covered with low, patchy clouds, precluding visual targeting, so we had to bomb by H2X. Once we dropped our bomb load of six 500-pound GPs and four M-17 incendiaries, our ship banked left in a wide arc to return to base. From the rear of the aircraft, I had a perfect view of the city, with hundreds of bombs bursting on the ground amidst thick plumes of rising smoke. There were a few scattered clouds over the target area, but I could clearly see the secondary explosions and the beginnings of a number of violent conflagrations. It was an amazing sight that I would never forget. Hit by tons of high-explosive and incendiary bombs, Berlin was being engulfed in huge roaring fires. That evening, when it was RAF Bomber Command's turn to attack the city and drop more incendiaries, they had an optimal view of their targets because the raging fires were still burning bright and the extreme heat had cleared away the cloud cover.

After the unbelievable destruction incendiary raids caused in Hamburg, it was

Harris's dream that a huge firestorm would cause the same devastation in Berlin. But it never happened. Berlin just didn't burn like other cities. Being one of the most modern cities in Europe at the time, Berlin's huge and sprawling metropolis encompassed nearly 25 square miles. Hitler had ordered a vast number of buildings in the city to be solidly constructed of steel and concrete. Unlike the older and more densely populated cities, like Hamburg, Magdeburg, and Dresden, the population and housing structures in the capital were dispersed over a wide area. The city itself was honeycombed with parapeted firewalls that restricted the spread of fire. A well-designed civil defense system, with hundreds of elaborate underground bomb shelters throughout the city, was another factor that spared the city from destruction by a firestorm. Plus, the capital's firefighting resources were considered the most modern and sophisticated of any city in Germany.

The 8th dropped nearly 3,000 tons of bombs on Berlin, and our post-mission assessment indicated it had been another successful raid. The most severe damage occurred at the Schlesischer station, with moderate effects on the other railway targets, power stations, and buildings in the government sector. The Reichstag building sustained major damage; there was complete destruction of a wing of the Ministry of Propaganda. Some industrial centers surrounding the city center were put out of commission. Surprisingly, despite the use of H2X radar to locate the targets, the accuracy of bombing was very good, especially in our division's attacks on primary targets.

Being our last mission in February, the crew was in good spirits upon hearing about the excellent job the 8th had accomplished at the very end of the Big Week of February 1945, exactly one year after the Big Week of 1944. We were totally exhausted after eight straight days of combat, but all of us were still eager to continue, with high hopes that our efforts would lead to the defeat of Hitler's Third Reich. None of us knew at the time of our attack on Berlin that Hitler and his close associates were sheltered more than 60 feet below the street's surface in the Führerbunker deep underneath the Reich Chancellery. But I'm sure he undoubtedly felt our presence.

As February came to a close, the transportation campaign was still going strong and would continue throughout the next month. The goals remained the same: to completely paralyze Germany's industrial economic structure and severely restrict the movements of military troops and material to the Ruhr region.

On the Western Front, the big Allied push to the Rhine River came on February 8, 1945, when the British 21st Army Group, commanded by Field Marshal Bernard Montgomery, began its assault on the Rhine from the Nijmegen region in the north. After a month of overcoming fierce enemy resistance and destroying 19 German divisions, Montgomery's Army Group was able to secure the west bank of the Rhine, extending from Nijmegen to Düsseldorf. At the same time, Gen. Omar

Official Army Air Force photo of our crew. These photos were usually taken after completing seven successful bombing missions.

Bradley's 12th Army Group, farther south, secured 80 miles of the west bank from Düsseldorf to Koblenz.

Eisenhower was thus able to accomplish his first phase of operations by eliminating the German forces west of the Rhine River and securing the bridgeheads along the river. The next phase entailed crossing the river in force and advancing into the Rhineland. Foremost on the supreme commander's mind was whether or not he had enough Allied forces to defeat the Germans and end the war in the west. He knew the Allies had at least 85 divisions, with another eight new French divisions being equipped to full combat strength. The Germans had only 80 divisions, most of which were vastly below normal strength.

Since their defeat at the Ardennes Offensive, the German armies on the Western Front had deteriorated to such a level that they could never stop the Allied advance. Many of their divisions had only about 8,000 men, scarcely half the strength of a full division. Many men and much material had been lost during the offensive in Belgium just two months earlier. Worse yet, large numbers of tanks, artillery, and aircraft had been rushed to the Eastern Front, where the Red Army was overrunning the German defenses in its advance to the Oder River. The majority of German Army units had no more fuel reserves; ammunition stockpiles were at very low levels, and the army had no available troop reinforcements except for very young and untrained recruits. Expecting little or no significant change in the Wehrmacht forces facing him, Eisenhower was confident that the Allied campaign against Germany would be a success.[16]

After its rapid advance to the Oder River at the end of January, the Red Army had been busy consolidating and regrouping its forces. The right flank of Zhukov's 1st Belorussian Front was more than 100 miles from Rokossovsky's 2nd Belorussian Front. Fearing German counterattacks, Stalin ordered Zhukov to link up with Rokossovsky's armies before advancing any farther from the Oder River. The threat of enemy counterattacks was very real and became increasingly so. On February 19, units of the German 4th Army trapped at the Frische Haff, a large water lagoon on the Baltic Sea in northern Poland 38 miles southwest of Konigsberg, launched an attack to link up with remnants of the 3rd Panzer Army in Königsberg, which had been cut off from the Samland Peninsula in East Prussia. But attacks from both sides were successful, and the Germans were able to secure a land bridge between the two armies.

It was evident that the German forces in East Prussia had been either surrounded or heavily decimated, but not defeated. Consequently, Stalin ordered Rokossovsky to launch an offensive to destroy the German forces in East Pomerania. The attack began on February 10, but because of the worsening weather conditions of rain, sleet, and snow, the offensive bogged down. It took more than five days for Rokossovsky's forces to advance more than 10 miles. Farther south, at the bridgeheads on the Oder River around Küstrin, Zhukov's forces faced the same conditions as they attempted to move forward to secure the area. As soon as Hitler heard that Zhukov's armies had reached the Oder, he ordered Küstrin to become a fortified city. German reinforcements were immediately sent to Küstrin while local German forces kept the Russians at bay. This eventually led to the siege of Küstrin and prevented Zhukov's forces from crossing the Oder River into Germany until the end of March.

With the Red Army so close to Berlin, an atmosphere of panic began to seep into the minds of the German people. Everyone had heard the horror stories of atrocities the Red Army had committed as they pillaged and raped their way across Poland and East Prussia. The Russians' attacks were so overwhelming that the German armies were unable to set up a defensive line to stem their advance. Consequently, many units were annihilated or simply disintegrated as soldiers, officers, and men from the *Volkssturm*[17] just melted into the woods and joined the ranks of the vast horde of refugees fleeing westward from East Prussia, Silesia, and Pomerania. Deserters were hunted down by the German military police, which were empowered with summary court-martial authority. Tens of thousands of deserters were sent back to the front lines and many hundreds executed without trial.

To suppress the coming crisis of faith in the Nazi regime, many towns throughout the Reich were subjected to their own form of horror. The increasingly rampant spread of defeatism forced Nazi officials to employ Waffen SS troops and the secret police to exact justice from people who were charged with undermining the war effort. Summary court-martials outside the legal system were established with the power to apply death sentences to public officials or anyone who dared question the authority of Nazi officials or in any way act against the Party. In the final months of the war, many German citizens were incarcerated or executed by the Nazis.[18]

In Germany, everyone except Hitler knew the war was lost and accepted that reality. Even high-ranking Nazi Party officials were busy planning their future lives with the coming of a defeated Germany.

They wouldn't have to wait long. Albert Speer, the armaments minister, sent Hitler a memorandum stating that, with the industrial region of Upper Silesia taken by the Russians, Germany's economy would soon become unsustainable. If the last remaining coal-producing area in the Ruhr was lost, then the armaments industry would no longer be able to adequately compensate for the loss of weaponry and material occurring on the front lines. The German industrial capacity to wage war would then collapse in a matter of months.

CHAPTER 4

THIRD REICH CRUMBLES

ON PRACTICALLY EVERY MISSION WE flew in February, there were few reports of massed attacks by Luftwaffe interceptors on our bombers. However, the Germans had plenty of fighter aircraft. Despite the horrendous German losses during the air war of 1944, Albert Speer's dispersal of hidden aircraft factories throughout Germany actually resulted in an increase in fighter production. In September 1944 alone, more than 3,000 single-engine fighters were generated, the majority being the Messerschmitt Me 109 and Focke-Wulf Fw 190 aircraft. The problem was that there weren't enough experienced pilots to fly them. The tremendous loss of personnel each month in 1944 amounted to more than 1,400 flight officers and men.[1]

Although it was possible to replace aircraft, the pilots could never be replaced during the final months of the war. The drastic decrease of military manpower at the beginning of 1945 meant that younger and younger recruits were being trained as fighter pilots, many of them only sixteen or seventeen years of age. The acute shortage of aviation fuel merely exacerbated this problem. Flight training hours were cut from 150 hours to a mere 40 hours, which was only about 30 percent of the time American pilots were trained. There was practically no training in aerial combat techniques. As a result, these young German pilots became no more than just cannon fodder for the experienced Allied pilots.

By March 1945, the skies over Germany were crowded with hundreds of Allied fighter aircraft. The 8th's Freelance operations enabled large groups of P-51s and P-47s to roam freely, seeking enemy aircraft in the air or on the ground. It was a hunter's paradise. A scouting American pilot who spotted an enemy aircraft in the air wouldn't report the sighting unless he knew he could get to it first. Doing otherwise would mean hordes of his fellow fighters rushing in for an easy kill. Because of the lack of fuel, most enemy aircraft were grounded anyway. The few groups of German fighters that took to the air to intercept bombers had to confront the hundreds of fighter escorts accompanying the bombers on every raid. Every German pilot, even the most seasoned, knew that each sortie was becoming more and more like a suicide mission.

However, this didn't mean that there were no more casualties from enemy fighters in early 1945. In fact, it was far from it. The Germans had launched a new interceptor called the Messerschmitt Me 262, which represented the next generation of fighter aircraft. The Me 262 was the first jet aircraft ever deployed for air combat. With a Junkers Jumo 004B turbojet engine under each wing, the new jet fighter was a quantum leap in design, structure, and combat effectiveness. No other piston-driven fighter aircraft could match the Me 262—not even the American P-51 Mustang. With a top speed of 540 mph at 19,685 feet and armed with four 30 mm MK 108 cannons, the Me 262 could fly faster and outgun any Allied aircraft flying over Germany. Upon takeoff, the jet could climb at a rate of 3,700 feet per minute to a maximum altitude of 37,565 feet.

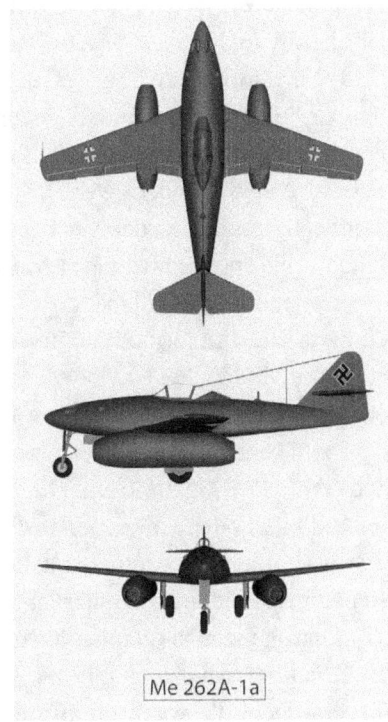

Me 262A-1a

The Me 262 came in different versions, of which the Me 262A-1a was used primarily as a fighter interceptor. The Me 262A-1a, though limited in numbers, became operational in late 1944. The development of jet aircraft had started as early as 1942. However, because of Hitler's obsession with using jets as an offensive fighter-bomber instead of a world-class fighter interceptor, a variation of the A-1a was developed. It was designated as the Me 262A-2a fighter-bomber. This version of the jet could carry a single 1,102-pound bomb or two 551-pound bombs under each wing. However, the Me 262A-2a was poorly adapted as a fighter-bomber. Its low attack speed nullified its speed potential, and the aircraft's limited aerial maneuverability made it very difficult for it to destroy its targets with much precision. This was made worse by the fact that many of the Me 262 jets, when modified as fighter-bombers, were rushed to the front and didn't even include bombsights!

Standing at a height of 12 feet, 7 inches and a length of 34 feet, 9.5 inches, the Me 262A-1a had a wingspan of 40 feet, 11.5 inches. Its empty weight was 8,378 pounds, with a maximum takeoff weight of 24,110 pounds. Unlike conventional piston-engine fighters, the Me 262 jet had a tricycle landing gear, which enabled the pilot to have a full view of the runway in front of him during takeoffs and landings. The weight of the four 30 mm MK 108 cannons in the nose section of the aircraft enabled a stable weight configuration for this type of landing gear. A unique feature of the Me 262 among its peers of conventional fighter aircraft was its modified wing structure, which was swept back at an angle of about 18 degrees to improve the jet's aerodynamic speed performance.

MISSION #11: MARCH 1, 1945
TARGET: INGOLSTADT

US Air Force Intelligence had known about the Me 262 jet fighter since 1944, when the first experimental jet unit, Erprobungskommando 262, known more commonly as Ekdo 262, was established to test the new aircraft's combat effectiveness. Hauptman Werner Thierfelder, who commanded Ekdo 262, received the unit's first jet aircraft in June 1944. After several months of getting the pilots and aircraft ready for combat-active sorties, the first encounter between German jets and the US 8th Air Force heavy bombers occurred on September 11, 1944. Shortly after, RAF bombers, particularly Mosquitos, were also attacked by small numbers of Me 262s. Several Allied bombers were lost, and Ekdo 262 proved its effectiveness against bombers. Tragedy struck on September 18, when Thierfelder was attacked and killed while engaged with P-51 Mustangs from the US 15th Air Force over Bavaria.[2]

General Adolf Galland, commander of the German fighter force, then disbanded Ekdo 262 and formed the first combat-operational Me 262A-1a jet fighter unit. He chose Maj. Walter Nowotny as commander. As the fifth-ranking German fighter ace in the Luftwaffe, Nowotny was only twenty-three years old when he achieved his 255th confirmed aerial victory on the Eastern Front. Galland chose him to lead and train pilots, many from Thierfelder's Ekdo 262 unit, in order to establish his unit into immediate operational status. On September 26, 1944, Nowotny's fighter unit was officially designated as Kommando Nowotny. One jet unit was based at Achmer Airfield, near Osnabrück, and the other at Hesepe.[3]

During the next month, Nowotny's jet-fighter force became a growing menace to Allied bombers. It caught the attention of the US 8th Air Force commanders. General Doolittle was well aware of the threat imposed by the German jets. He issued an order to form an Allied aerial photoreconnaissance unit to track which airfields the jet units were using as their home bases. These air bases were easy to locate because the Me 262's turbojet engines had an exhaust blast that left distinctive scorch marks on the surface of runways as they took off. Doolittle also wanted to know where the jets were built and how they were being transported to the air bases. His plan was to destroy the enemy jets by attrition. The German jets were to be targeted wherever they were found, in the sky or on the ground. It was then that groups of American fighter escorts routinely flew ahead of the attacking bomber streams to search the airfields, bombing and strafing any jets before they could take off to intercept the bombers.

Despite these efforts to dampen the frequency of Kommando Nowotny's jet attacks, Allied heavy bombers continued to be engaged and shot down by experienced pilots who were becoming more and more skilled at flying the Me 262.

Then disaster struck once again. On November 8, 1944, Maj. Nowotny, who'd led a group of jet fighters on a successful attack against an 8th Air Force bombing raid, was heading back to his home base when he was jumped by a group of P-51 Mustangs. General Galland was at Nowotny's headquarters for an inspection tour of the air base when Nowotny was heard over the radio stating that American fighters were attacking him and his aircraft was on fire. Galland and several of the group's officers ran out and saw Nowotny's aircraft fall from the sky, hitting the ground. Then they heard the sound of an explosion behind some trees. They raced to the crash scene, where a thick column of smoke rose, but found little left of the aircraft and Nowotny. Only his left hand and pieces of his air medals were recovered. The commander of Kommando Nowotny died after claiming his 258th victory.[4]

In early December 1944, Nowotny's unit was disbanded, and its pilots formed the nucleus of a new jet fighter group designated as Jagdgeschwader 7, known as JG 7. During its brief existence, Kommando Nowotny was extremely successful in demonstrating the effectiveness of Me 262 jet fighters against Allied bombers and their fighter escorts. Altogether, Nowotny's experienced group of pilots destroyed 22 Allied aircraft, the majority of them heavy bombers. As more and more Me 262A-1a aircraft were received and the unit grew in size, the JG 7 group of fighter interceptors became one of the most formidable jet units in the Luftwaffe against the Allied air forces.

The American and British efforts to develop a jet fighter were years behind the Germans. As soon as the Me 262 became operational in the latter part of 1944, Allied air force commanders realized the superiority of the German jet as the future development of combat aircraft. Fearing that the new threat would severely compromise American bombing raids, Gen. Spaatz pushed for the speedy development of the American jet fighter known as the Lockheed P-80. However, although a few of the new P-80 jets did become operational at the end of 1944, it was too late to have much of an impact in the ETO.

The British saw their jet fighter, the Gloster Meteor, operational at about the same time as the German Me 262 in late 1944. The British RAF had ordered 120 of the jets, but only limited numbers made it to operational status.[5] The Gloster Meteor was used mainly against the German V-1 rocket bombs and ground targets in Holland and northern Germany. Lacking the speed of the Me 262, the Meteor would have likely proved less effective in aerial combat against the German jet. However, this was a moot point since no British jet fighter had any encounters with the Me 262.[6]

However, there was one instance on record of a German Me 262 fighter attacking an American jet aircraft. Oberst Hermann Buchner, who was one of Germany's top Luftwaffe aces, managed to shoot down an US Army Air Force reconnaissance jet aircraft, an F-5E Lightning, which had just finished taking photographs of bomb damage by an Allied bombing raid near Munich on November 26, 1944. It was Buchner's first combat victory in the Me 262. He was to become a very successful jet pilot, first with Kommando Nowotny's Me 262 jet unit and then later with JG 7. Buchner flew more than 300 missions in Russia and finished his amazing wartime career as a fighter pilot with more than 600 Luftwaffe missions.[7]

At the operations briefing, we were told that the frequency of attacks by the German Me 262A-1a jet fighters had begun to increase in late February. Our air force commanders were getting uneasy about their presence. The suspicion that the Germans were planning something big was one reason Giebelstadt Army Airfield was bombed on February 25. These jets were being assembled and grouped there for missions against Allied bombers. We were warned on several missions during February to be on the alert for possible Me 262 attacks. We were warned again on this mission of an increased likelihood of interception by enemy jets.

Ingolstadt is an important industrial city deep in the south of Germany. It's located just 30 miles north of the Munich metropolitan area, and Ingolstadt's most important railway networks are situated on the banks of the river Danube in the center of Bavaria. The main rail center contained a number of rail repair shops and rail sidings actively engaged in repairing and rebuilding damaged steam locomotives. At least 50 locomotives had been sighted at the location.

With the Swiss border less than 100 miles south of Munich, we were also briefed on the possibility of encounters with Swiss fighter aircraft. Although a neutral country, Switzerland had been accidentally bombed by both Allied and Axis bombers. There were a number of Swiss airfields close to German airfields near the border. As a result, Swiss fighters had attacked, without warning, two or more foreign aircraft flying in formation. If our bomber was in trouble and approached by Swiss fighters, we were told to lower our landing gear and we would be escorted to an airfield. An order to land would be signaled by the fighter firing green flares and lowering its landing gear. We were also reminded that Swiss aircraft insignia had a white cross on a red field. Some of our crews had been directed to German airfields because the Germans had painted a similar insignia of a red cross on a white field, thus misleading our pilots to follow them. Swiss fighters looked very much like German Fw 190s, so this was an easy mistake to make.

This was another massive mission, with more than 1,200 heavy bombers from all three divisions of the 8th dispatched to transportation targets in central and southern Germany. The 1st Air Division, with 452 bombers, was to attack marshalling yards in Heilbronn, Bruchsal, Göttingen, Reutlingen, and Neckarsulm. The 3rd Division, with 449 bombers, was to hit the marshalling yards at Ulm. Our division's primary targets were marshalling yards at Ingolstadt, with a secondary target of a jet airfield at Neuburg. Sixty-two Liberators were sent to the airfield located approximately 2.5 miles southeast of Neuburg on the southern bank of the Danube River. Results obtained from aerial photoreconnaissance indicated the airfield was loaded with jets.

The remaining 253 bombers in our division, including our wing, were sent to attack Ingolstadt. We carried a full load of ten 500-pound GP bombs and, because of the distance, this was one of our longest missions—over nine hours of flight time. With wing formations so large at this point in operations, each wing was flown a certain distance away from the others. Our wing was scheduled to be three minutes behind the 2nd Air Division's 96th Combat Wing, and three minutes ahead of the 14th Combat Wing. At an average cruising speed of 200 mph, a distance of approximately three miles separated the wing formations from each other in the bomber stream. Our pilot, Lt. Raymond Swingle, was assigned position #8 in the lead squadron of our group, the 453rd Bomb Group.

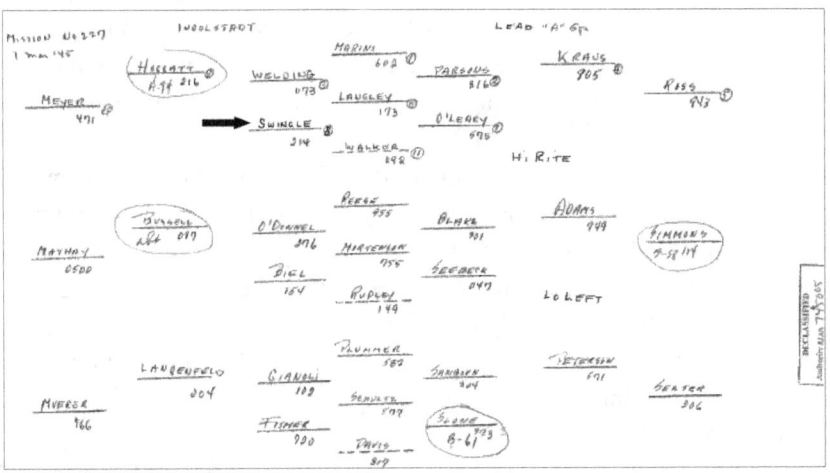

A copy of the dispatch that's posted before each mission to indicate the position of each aircraft in each of the three squadrons of the bomb group. On our mission to Ingolstadt, our pilot (Swingle) is #8 in the lead squadron (top group). (NARA)

As we approached the target, there was almost no flak. German efforts to transport much of their 88 mm antiaircraft artillery to the Eastern Front resulted in much less protection around their major cities against bombing raids. The 88 mm guns were one of the most versatile pieces of German armory. They were incorporated into their formidable Tiger tanks and proved to be an excellent anti-tank destroyer when using armor-piercing shells. However, not only were the Germans short of 88s, but they were also severely undermanned in terms of military personnel. Most, if not all, of the existing antiaircraft batteries on the Western Front were now being operated with the help of young volunteers known as *Flakhelfers* and *Flakhelfer-innen* (flak helpers), male and female Hitler Youth recruits in their teens. Consequently, the shortage of specialized technicians in the gun batteries contributed to the increasing reports of the inaccurate targeting these flak batteries were having on the bomber streams. This was good news for us. During the final months of the war, bomber losses attributed to flak decreased dramatically.

Just before initiating our bomb run, three Me 262 jet fighters were seen coming into our group, one of which came in at four o'clock high, just within 1,000 yards of our group's high-right squadron formation, but it didn't attack. The enemy jets took only a few seconds to make their pass before our escort fighters quickly chased them away. These Me 262s probably came from the jet airfield in Neuberg, which was near our target area. The German jet unit I./KG (J) 54[8] was stationed at the airfield. JG 54 was originally a bomber unit, but some of its bomber pilots were trained to fly the Me 262A-1a jet against attacking Allied bombers.

On this mission, our division had two hundred fifty-three P-51 escorts, more than enough to handle any enemy attacks. Perhaps we were just lucky. But recent reports had indicated that encounters with the jets didn't result in many attacks. It seemed as if their pilots were developing different attack formations and tactics against heavy bombers. Because the Me 262s flew and attacked at such a high rate of speed, their pilots had to adjust their tactics, which were very different from conventional piston-driven fighter aircraft.

Enemy jet attacks could come from any direction. Most of their pilots preferred to attack from a twelve o'clock high position (front of our aircraft), coming in from the sun so they'd be difficult to spot. Another choice direction was a fast attack at six o'clock low, toward the rear of the bomber, where they'd be out of sight of the top turret and waist gunners. Only the tail and belly gunners had a shot, but both turrets were situated in such a cramped space with limited maneuverability that accurate enemy target acquisition was nearly impossible against an attack from such a fast-moving Me 262 jet.

Ingolstadt was completely covered by clouds, so we had to bomb by H2X. It appeared that bad weather conditions extended throughout southern Germany that day. As a result, the other air divisions had similar problems with the weather.

Many of the bomb groups resorted to attacking secondary targets. Despite the lousy weather, massive bombing raids by the 8th Air Force again targeted marshalling yards and rail centers over the next two days. In addition, synthetic oil plants in Dresden, Ruhland, and, of course, Magdeburg were bombed again. The raid on Magdeburg was so destructive that there was little chance the 8th would return in the future.

On March 3, two days after our mission to Ingolstadt, the Germans sent up more than fifty Me 262 jet fighters to intercept a large bombing raid by the 8th Air Force. Yet there were only a handful of attacks by the German jets, which downed six bombers before being chased away by P-51 escort fighters. Air Force Intelligence was befuddled as to why there were so few attacks by such a large enemy interceptor force. Perhaps they were experimenting with methods of attack, or maybe they couldn't get through the defense shield of our escort fighters. We'll never know. Whatever it was, it sure kept our air commanders on edge.

THE LAST BRIDGE AT REMAGEN

After the failed German Ardennes Offensive in late December 1944, the Allied forces resumed their advance to the Rhine River. By early March 1945, the German forces west of the Rhine had been defeated. To prevent Eisenhower's armies from easily crossing the Rhine River into Germany, Hitler had ordered all bridges across the Rhine to be demolished by any means necessary. On March 6, German troops retreating from the Allied advance had blown up the Hohenzollern Bridge, one of the last intact bridges across the Rhine.

Only a single bridge remained standing. It was located in the small town of Remagen, adjacent to the Rhine. The large railway trestle bridge was called the Ludendorff Bridge. The entire structure was mined with high-explosives ready to be detonated. As one of the last vital links to Germany across the river, it was being heavily used by troops from the retreating German 15th Army. The US 1st Army wasn't expected to reach this sector of the Rhine for at least another day or two, when suddenly, shortly after noon on March 7, 1945, advance units from the US 9th Armored Division appeared on a hill overlooking the city of Remagen.

Second Lieutenant Emmet J. Burrows, leading an infantry platoon, was surprised at the sight of the rushed movement of German troops and vehicles across the bridge, which was situated on the southern edge of the town. Burrows contacted his company commander, Lt. Karl H. Timmermann, who immediately understood the implications of an intact bridge over the Rhine River. Timmermann was commanding Company A, one of three with the 14th Tank Battalion, which was part of a larger tank task force of the US 1st Army's 9th Armored Division, heading toward Remagen. Timmerman in turn contacted his superiors, and when the commander of the tank task force, Lt. Col. Leonard Engemann, was apprised of the information, he issued an order to capture the bridge as soon as possible.

Timmermann was told to descend the hill and follow the tank force as it attacked the city. By 2:00 p.m., the tanks had cleared the lightly defended town and were moving toward the western approach to the bridge. Timmermann's three platoons found the center of town virtually deserted. They could see American tanks moving toward the bridge. On each end of the bridge stood twin towers armed with German machine gun emplacements. The tanks began firing at the western bridge towers. They were also aiming toward the other side of the bridge, where a locomotive, which was just pulling out from a train station, was struck. Suddenly there was a loud explosion, and Timmermann's men hit the ground.

Heinz Schwartz, who was sixteen years old at the time, clearly remembered what happened that day. He was assigned as a member of the auxiliary flak battery unit atop one of the two bridge towers on the eastern side of the bridge. He was one of the many Hitler Youth recruits manning the antiaircraft flak unit. His job was to work the telephones connecting the communication links among the commanding officers. Earlier that morning, he'd heard the conversation between Capt. Willi Bratge, the German commander in Remagen, and the bridge commander, Capt. Karl Friesenhahn. Bratge had informed Friesenhahn that the American forces had taken Rheinbach, which was only 15 miles away. Bratge then told Friesenhahn to be prepared to blow up the bridge.[9]

Friesenhahn was in charge of the demolition explosives set to detonate, and he was assigned to bring down the bridge when it became necessary to do so. Between Bratge's and Friesenhahn's commands, there were approximately 1,000 German defenders at Remagen. The defensive force consisted of a motley contingent of men from Luftwaffe antiaircraft units, convalescing soldiers, ill-equipped and poorly trained non-German conscripts, and several hundred civilian Volkssturm soldiers. Also included were 180 Hitler Youth recruits.

Both commanders were surprised when Maj. Hans Scheller arrived to relieve Bratge of his command and assumed full control of the German forces in Remagen. Scheller was anticipated to arrive with a full battalion of reinforcements but came with much less. He'd been ordered to allow as many German retreating troops to cross the Rhine as possible and prevent the American forces from capturing the bridge. If this couldn't be avoided, Scheller was instructed to destroy the bridge.

Bratge and Friesenhahn were at the western end of the bridge, directing traffic, when they heard the American tanks coming from the center of town. Then everyone started to run across the bridge, and Friesenhahn immediately ordered the explosive charges at the western approach to be detonated. A large explosion erupted, which left a gaping 30-foot crater in the road, a defensive measure intended to prevent enemy tanks from accessing the bridge. Schwarz was with his friend at the eastern end of the bridge, working to prepare explosives. Like any curious kid, he told his companion that he wanted a better look at what was happening. So he ran up one of the eastern flak towers to get a better view of the action coming from the other side of the bridge.

As the smoke and dust from the explosion dissipated, Timmermann could clearly see American tanks supplying cover fire onto the bridge. Now was the moment for action. Timmermann ordered his men to fix bayonets, and they began their charge across the bridge. On the eastern side of the bridge, confusion and chaos reigned among the German defenders as a hail of gunfire from the American Pershing and Sherman tanks descended upon them. Friesenhahn was knocked unconscious by an exploding shell. When he regained his senses fifteen minutes later, he heard Scheller screaming at him to detonate the charges. Friesenhahn then ran into the railroad tunnel behind the eastern twin towers, where the main detonation switches were located.

Meanwhile, Schwarz, realizing that the American forces would soon arrive, immediately cut the telephone wires with an axe so they couldn't be used again. Quickly scurrying down the circular stairway and out the tower entrance onto the bridge, Schwarz came under heavy fire from the other side of the bridge. Trying his best to avoid the exploding shells, he ran as fast as he could into the tunnel where Friesenhahn had just completed the final connections to the explosives.

Everyone was told to brace for the explosion. When Friesenhahn turned the key to ignite the explosives, nothing happened. Friesenhahn did it again, and again there was silence. After the third failed attempt, the captain asked for a volunteer to ignite the secondary charges by hand at the eastern end of the bridge. A trooper came forward, ran close to 100 yards across the bridge to light the primer fuse, and ran back into the safety of the tunnel.

As Timmermann and his men rushed across the western section of the bridge, a tremendous explosion erupted in front of them, about two-thirds of the way across to the east bank. Debris and large pieces of the bridge flew high into the air. The bridge churned and trembled as if it were about to collapse. But when the smoke cleared, the bridge remained standing! The wooden planks over the rail tracks were blown to pieces, and parts of the tracks remained as twisted pieces of iron, but the main steel structure of the bridge was still intact.

The footpaths across the bridge were still passable. Timmermann prodded his men to continue forward, but fearing another explosion, they hesitated. With little cover, they were taking heavy fire from enemy machine-gun emplacements located on the eastern towers. Timmermann knew that if they stayed where they were, they would be cut to pieces. He yelled at Sgt. Joseph DeLisio of the First Platoon to get his men moving, immediately. Without hesitation, DeLisio sprinted forward, dodging the intense fire directed at him. His men followed, then the Second Platoon lurched forward. Running at full speed, Timmermann and his men reached the other side of the bridge, where an intense firefight ensued. Hand-to-hand combat with pistols, bayonets, and knives finally defeated the bridge defenders. Several of DeLisio's men headed for one of the eastern towers while he fought his way up the stairwell of the second tower and took out the machine-gun emplacement.

With an imminent attack coming to the tunnel, Schwartz and his young companions were told to run home as fast as they could. The tunnel was now packed with retreating German soldiers and civilians taking shelter from the barrage of enemy fire. Attacking American troops were throwing grenades into the tunnel, so Bratge and Friesenhahn were forced to surrender. An improvised white flag was used to stop the attack. Scheller was nowhere to be found; he'd long escaped through the tunnel. Heinz Schwartz was also able to avoid being captured. He practically ran the entire five miles from the bridge to his house, where he remained with his parents until the end of the war. Fifteen years later, he met an American soldier who was also on the bridge that day. That soldier was Joe DeLisio.

MISSION #12: MARCH 8, 1945
TARGET: SIEGEN

The capture of the Ludendorff Bridge by the American forces was an unexpected breakthrough for the Allies. When Hitler heard the news, he became uncontrollably furious, so much so that he ordered the officers responsible for failing to blow up the bridge to be court-martialed without delay. Major Hans Scheller and four other officers were executed by a firing squad. Both Capt. Karl Friesenhahn and Capt. Bratge escaped execution because they became prisoners of war when they surrendered during the battle for the bridge.

In contrast to Hitler's reaction, Eisenhower was elated when Gen. Omar Bradley, commander of the US 12th Army Group, told him they'd captured the bridge intact. Bradley was immediately ordered to get as many divisions across the Rhine as possible. Although the events at Remagen didn't fit into Eisenhower's plan for his forces in the north, he wouldn't miss this opportunity to establish a foothold on the Rhine. He thus ordered Bradley to secure the bridge area and wait until Patton's 3rd Army reached the Rhine farther south. Not only was the first phase of Eisenhower's plan for defeating the German forces west of the Rhine complete, but his forces had broken through the last remaining defensive barrier leading into the heart of Germany. The supreme commander wrote that it was one of his "happy moments of the war."[10]

While an unending stream of American soldiers was crossing the Ludendorff Bridge into Germany, the US 8th Air Force was sending another large force to bomb oil and transportation targets in the Ruhr area. Over 1,300 heavy bombers and more than 300 fighter escorts were dispatched, which was now commonplace during the closing months of the war. So many bombers and crew were arriving each day from the States that all the bomb groups were more than fully staffed. March would be our final push to destroy the major communications and transportation centers in western and central Germany.

The 1st and 3rd Air Divisions were targeting a slew of benzol plants, which included the Robert Muser and Bruchstrasse plants in Langendreer, the Gneisenau plant in Dortmund, the Emil plant in Essen, the Stinnes plant in Bottrop, and the Viktoria plant in Hüls. Also on the primary target list was the synthetic oil plant at Buer-Scholren and the Heddernheim chemical factory located in Frankfurt. Secondary targets included marshalling yards in Essen, Giessen, Frankfurt, and Wetzlar. Our division dispatched 360 heavies to attack vital rail targets east of the Rhine River area, which included Siegen, Betzdorf, and Dillenburg. Our wing, with three squadrons from each of the 389th, 445th, and 453rd Bomb Groups, with a total of 97 aircraft, was assigned to hit the rail marshalling yards in Siegen. Escorting our division were one hundred and two P-51 Mustangs.

The large rail centers in Siegen were located in a heavily forested area just southeast of Cologne. They represented the base of a major railway network with multiple rail lines running to the south of the Ruhr and through Cologne, connecting this large city with other cities in eastern Germany. Destruction of these targets would not only cause main-line traffic to be rerouted to the east or south but also greatly strain facilities needed to repair and rebuild the damaged or destroyed rail centers.

On this particular mission, we were issued extra supplies, such as food and other survival materials, in the event that we were downed in enemy territory. We were told that if we came down more than 20 miles from our front lines, we were to avoid capture until we could locate and surrender to either soldiers from the German Army or Luftwaffe personnel. If at all possible, we were to avoid all civilians, Hitler Youth, Nazi SS troopers, and the Gestapo.[11] If within 20 miles of the front lines, we were to make an attempt to pass through the front lines to friendly territory. There had been reports of downed Allied pilots or crew being confronted by extremely angry civilians who had lost so much in the intense bombing raids. Often, these people decided to take matters into their own hands. Bomber personnel captured by such vengeful German citizens didn't fare very well.

We were also warned that small forces of Me 262s might be seen along our route, but no large forces of enemy fighters were to be expected. Luckily, our Little Friends kept a vigilant eye above us, and we experienced no encounters with enemy fighters. There was also no flak when we entered the target area. Visual acquisition of the rail center was perfect, and we dropped our load of twenty-four 250-pound GPs right on target. Our mission was a success, and all aircraft from our division returned without incident.

MISSION #13: MARCH 9, 1945
TARGET: MÜNSTER

This day's targets focused on important marshalling yards north and south of the Ruhr area. The 1st and 3rd Air Divisions, with a total of 759 heavy bombers, were sent to hit rail and industrial targets in the Kassel-Frankfurt area, approximately 100 miles southeast of the Ruhr. Kassel was home to one of the largest complex of tank factories in western Germany. Our division sent three bomb groups—the 389th, 445th, and 453rd—to three key cities on the transportation target list: Münster, Rheine, and Osnabrück, just north of the Ruhr. Our target was a large rail center in Münster, which was one of the most important of all rail junctions north of the Ruhr. Direct rail lines from this city connected to Rheine, going to northern Germany and running through Osnabrück eastward to Hanover and Berlin.

Rail facilities in Münster became even more important when freight in that area had to be rerouted by train due to the destruction of sections of the Dortmund-Ems Canal. The Ems Canal ran from Emden, a port on the Baltic Coast in the north, through Rheine and Münster, to Dortmund in the Ruhr. It had been a very important transportation route for the Germans.

Now, much of the traffic from the northern Ruhr was being moved by rail through Münster, Osnabrück, and Rheine. Marshalling yards in these cities became critical elements on the target list in the transportation campaign to isolate the Ruhr from northern and eastern Germany.

Our wing of the 2nd Air Division, with nine squadrons, was to attack Münster, while the 96th Combat Wing, with 10 squadrons, was directed to Osnabrück, and the 20th Combat Wing, with nine squadrons, to Rheine. The weather was predicted to be much better than what had transpired earlier that month, so hopes were up that these targets would feel the impact of the 2nd Division raids. Our bomb group was assigned to special operations, and on this mission, S.Sgt. R. H. Infield accompanied us as an observer. Aside from Lt. Swingle, who was certainly briefed before the mission, none of us ever found out the purpose of our guest.

We were fully loaded with forty-four 100-pound GP and two 500-pound M-17 incendiary cluster bombs. We were put on alert for possible harassing attacks from small groups of Me 262s, although there were no encounters with enemy aircraft on this mission. We were again given survival material and warned to avoid capture by civilians, the Gestapo, or SS troops. If captured, our orders were to demand placement at the nearest prison camp. There were large numbers of POW camps in the Ruhr area for the use of prison labor to repair damaged factories and rail networks.

Although Münster isn't within the Ruhr Valley, this particular region was noted for its high concentration of antiaircraft batteries. As we approached our target, the intensity of flak increased. Flying through the intense fire of an enemy artillery box barrage is unnerving, and we took some hits but suffered no appreciable damage. Unfortunately, a heavy from the 389th Bomb Group in our wing took a direct hit and went down in flames with no chutes seen coming from the aircraft.

The mission was a success, with many of the targets severely hit by the three air divisions, which caused extensive damage to marshalling yards throughout northwestern Germany. The large tank factory at Kassel was completely demolished and remained unusable for the remainder of the war. It was now close to mid-March, and the Germans were beginning to dramatically feel the effects of the transportation bombing campaign. Ruhr rail traffic, along with shipping by barges and other vessels on the Rhine River and adjacent canal systems to other parts of Germany, was becoming more and more restricted. Essential coal and steel products from the Ruhr were being stopped in their tracks. The movements of critical war material, troops, and equipment were drastically affected. The attacks on the enemy's communications and transportation networks only increased in the following weeks to completely strangle the German war effort.

MISSION #14: MARCH 12, 1945
TARGET: WETZLAR

On March 12, the 8th Air Force received a last-minute request from the Russians to attack Swinemünde, a major port on the Baltic coast just north of Stettin, close to positions of the advancing Red Army. Apparently, the Germans were sending seaborne troop reinforcements that were being ferried through the port on their way to the Eastern Front. There were also large oil depots at the port, and the harbor was crowded with German naval and merchant vessels. As a result, half of the forces of each of the 1st, 2nd, and 3rd Air Divisions, consisting of 677 heavy bombers, were being diverted from the 8th's planned operations to bomb Swinemünde. The remaining half from each division, totaling 678 heavies, was to attack rail targets in Wetzlar, Siegen, Frankfurt, Betzdorf, and Dillenburg.

The 2nd Air Division dispatched 154 heavies to marshalling yards in Wetzlar and Friedberg. Our wing of 97 Liberators in three squadrons was sent to attack a major rail center in Wetzlar, a town approximately 30 miles north of Frankfurt on the Rhine. The center was both a tactical and strategic key point in the German defense of the lower Rhine, and while our troops hadn't yet reached the city, they were getting closer by the day. We carried a full bomb load of forty-four 100 GP and two M-17 incendiaries. There was no enemy air resistance and meager flak at the target area.

There was extensive cloud cover over the target, and we had to attack by H2X. But post-mission aerial photoreconnaissance indicated that our mission was a success, with our target completely destroyed. The results of the 8th's divisional forces sent to Swinemünde were even better. Bombing by H2X radar resulted in substantial damage to vessels in the harbor, quays, and slipways, as well as destruction of adjacent industrial areas. Oil depots were reported to be burning fiercely. Large columns of smoke were observed billowing up through the dense cloud layer. It was believed that the use of H2X had clearly identified the targets on the Mickey scope with considerable precision and thereby increased the accuracy of bombing. A focused attack was necessary because the port city of Swinemünde was only about 15 to 20 miles from the front lines of the Russian armies.

MISSION #15: MARCH 15, 1945
TARGET: GARDELEGEN

This mission was a big one, with the focus of attacks on Zossen, the military headquarters of the German armed forces, as well as multiple marshalling yards in the Berlin area. These targets were also at the request of our Russian allies.

Red Army intelligence had discovered the hidden location of the main operations base of the OKW (Oberkommando der Wehrmacht), which was the German High Command of the Armed Forces.[12] The base was situated approximately two miles southeast of Zossen. This target had long been on the 8th's strategic target list as one of the most vital communications networks in all of Germany. It was said to be invulnerable to the heaviest explosives because of its extensive fortifications and deep underground bunkers. But now, at the request of the Russians, our air commanders thought it would be worth accommodating their needs with a systematical attack on the OKW base's above-ground facilities. It was reported that the German High Command was in the process of feverishly preparing for an evacuation from Zossen, as the Russians were closing in on the base from the east. This was our chance to put a crimp in their plans.

The second primary target was an important rail center in Oranienburg, located about 25 miles northwest of Berlin. Its main rail lines branched out to crisscross the entire Berlin area, and these railways were vital links leading to the Eastern Front. The Germans had been actively moving troops and equipment to the front lines in eastern Germany for the past two months, and these railway lines had been extremely busy. In fact, any major marshalling yard in our assigned target area was game for an attack as secondary, or rather opportunity, targets. On every heavy bomber mission, the US 9th Air Force had its own tactical operations to attack moving trains and rolling stock at every chance encounter. So the Germans were now reeling from the intense pressure on their transportation systems.

This was perhaps our biggest raid yet, with 1,353 heavy bombers dispatched from all air divisions. The 1st Air Division sent 300 heavies to Zossen and 149 to Oranienburg, while the 3rd Air Division targeted marshalling yards in Oranienburg, Wittenberg, Havelberg, Duderstadt, Mellendorf, and Schmarsau, as well as an airfield in Dedelstorf, with a total of 526 heavy bombers. Our division dispatched 372 Liberators to Zossen, consisting of a full nine squadrons in each of the division's four combat wings. The 453rd Bomb Group had the distinction of leading the 2nd Combat Wing in front of the entire force of the 2nd Air Division to Zossen, and we were happy to be in the lead squadron of our wing.

During the extended briefing we had before we took off from Old Buck, we were told to be on the lookout for Red Army aircraft in the vicinity of Berlin. The Russians were now bombing Berlin almost constantly, and their fighter aircraft were actively pursuing any German aircraft in the area. Zossen was just 28 miles southwest of central Berlin, and the skies overhead were beginning to get a bit crowded.

In the event of an encounter with Red Army fighter aircraft, our friendly signal was to dip the right wing three to five times, then the same with the left wing. Although adverse incidents of friendly contacts between Allied bombers and Russian fighters hadn't been reported, some tragic friendly fire contacts between their fighters and American fighter aircraft had occurred recently.

Contact with Russian soldiers on the ground was a little more of a problem. We carried Russian identification cards in our left breast pockets, since many Russian troops didn't readily recognize American uniforms. More likely than not, they tended to shoot anyone in a uniform that wasn't their own, and we were told that our uniforms closely resembled those of the German Army. Many Russian soldiers were untrained conscripts from the gulags in Russia or prisoner of war camps in occupied Nazi territories, so their first tendency was to shoot on sight any enemy coming their way. If approached by Russians, we were given explicit instructions to raise our hands and halt when we heard the word *stol*, which in Russian means "stop," and to not make any suspicious or quick movements, such as reaching into our pockets.

As for German interception, intelligence reports indicated scores of enemy fighters in the air, but most of them were supporting their ground operations against the Russians. Small groups of Me 262 jet fighters were sighted over northwest Germany, and the largest group of 30 jets was observed. However, many made no attempt to attack. And when they did, the P-51s were on their tails. P-51s engaged two Me 163 rocket jets over the Wittenberg area, and one of the jets was shot down. Although a number of widely scattered Me 262s and Me 163s jet fighters were observed along our entire route to our targets, they weren't aggressive and offered no organized opposition to our wing. Most were engaged in tactical ground or reconnaissance activity. In fact, the Me 262 jet was found to be the perfect recon aircraft, with its tremendous speed and high-altitude capabilities, as nothing in the sky at the time could catch them.

On this mission, we were carrying a full bomb load of twelve 250-pound GPs and four M17 incendiary bombs for maximum destructive effect on surface building structures. The German base in Zossen had originally been built to house all the staff officers in large underground bunkers. However, because of the increase in military personnel through the years, many of the offices, messes, and barracks were housed above ground. It was a large military installation containing many troop units and vehicles. A large German communications network infrastructure was built at the center of the base, which was the most modern of its time. Since they were in the process of evacuating the base, our goal was to disrupt and disorganize the administrative processes of the German general staff as much as possible.

The weather over Zossen was forecast to be clear and optimum for visual bombing, but as we approached the city, the ground was covered with a very thick haze of fog or low clouds, with visibility limited to only two or three miles. As a result, we couldn't visually identify our target soon enough for an attack. Instead, upon withdrawal from our assigned target, we were able to accurately bomb a rail center in Gardelegen, which was on the mission list as a target of opportunity. The town was located in the district of Saxony-Anhalt, 20 miles west of Stendal, and situated on the right bank of the Milde River. The Stendal and Gardelegen rail networks were the most important rail hub of the Berlin-Lehrte railway, which ran from Hanover in the west to Berlin in the east. Stendal was also on the list of targets of opportunity for the 1st Air Division, and a group of bombers from their division was able to destroy its marshalling yards. We did the same in Gardelegen. We encountered little flak, and our bomb group demolished the city's rail center with 71 tons of bombs.

While the 453rd Bomb Group was unable to succeed in the attack against Zossen, the remaining two bomb groups of our wing, the 339th and 445th, were able to identify their targets and make a successful attack, as did the other three combat wings of the 2nd Air Division. Together with the 1st Air Division's bombers, they dropped more than 1,300 tons of high-explosive and incendiary bombs onto the headquarters of the German OKW base in Zossen. All attacking bomb groups were able to successfully zero in on their targets, and the results of their efforts were excellent. Buildings above ground were either totally destroyed or severely damaged. The raid by the 8th had caused a massive disruption of activity on one of the most important military communication centers in the Reich.

On the ground that day was Maj. Bernd Freytag von Loringhoven, who was ADC (aide-de-camp) to the chief of the general staff, Col. Gen. Heinz Guderian. The young major was having lunch with his ADC, Capt. Gerhard Boldt, when they heard the air raid sirens. As they bolted out of the mess hall, bombs were already exploding. Running full speed toward the air raid bunkers, both men made it to the shelter as buildings exploded all around them. One of those was a large concrete building housing the operations department. With the ground violently trembling from the rain of bombs, the shelter's steel door slammed shut just in the nick of time. Several senior officers were injured in the raid, including Gen. Hans Krebs, who was Guderian's deputy chief of staff. Maj. Von Loringhoven was to play an important role during the final weeks of the war in the Führerbunker as the military liaison between the OKW and Hitler.[13]

MISSION #16: MARCH 17, 1945
TARGET: MÜNSTER

The order of the day for all bomb groups of the 8th Air Force was to once again hit oil, industrial, and rail targets in northwestern Germany. Continuing with unrelenting pressure on the oil industry, the 1st Air Division dispatched 449 heavy bombers to attack targets in Mölbis. Especially targeted was one synthetic plant in Böhlen that had been reported to be active and operational again. The 3rd Air Division sent 527 heavies to bomb oil plants in Ruhland and Bitterfeld. Our division dispatched 346 bombers to hit marshalling yards at Münster and the Hanomag tank factory at Hanover. Of the 170 Liberators sent to attack Münster, our wing consisted of a total of 88 aircraft.

This was our second strike on Münster, the first happening about a week earlier. Apparently, it hadn't been enough to completely put the rail centers out of action. This time, twice the number of bombers was sent because the Münster rail networks had suddenly become one of the last remaining rail links from the Ruhr to northern and eastern Germany.

The two most important railway lines leading out of the Ruhr area were on the Schildesche viaduct in Bielefeld and the large viaduct in Altenbeken. Each of these huge viaducts was over 1,000 feet in length and contained twin railway lines. Both were just east of Münster and had been prime targets in the transportation campaign. Thousands of tons of conventional high-explosive bombs had been used in an attempt to destroy them since February, but the only damaging effects appeared to be some bent rails that could easily be replaced. The Altenbeken viaduct was destroyed during Operation Clarion in late February, but the one in Bielefeld remained standing.

A Consolidated B-24 Liberator from the 458th Bomb Group releasing its load of heavy bombs over Bielefeld, Germany, on February 24, 1945, during Operation Clarion. Despite the repeated efforts of Allied bombing raids to destroy the Schildesche viaduct, it remained operational well into March. (NARA)

The Schildesche viaduct was finally rendered unusable just three days before our second mission to Münster, on March 14, when a squadron of heavy bombers from the RAF Bomber Command dropped their loads of the new 22,000-pound Grand Slam and 12,000-pound Tallboy deep-penetration bombs. These bombs were designed to slam through the stone and concrete structures and explode deep within the ground to cause extremely destructive seismic effects. Known affectionately by the British as "earthquake bombs," a Grand Slam explosion created a wide 100-foot crater at the base of the Schildesche viaduct, causing a large section of it to collapse into a pile of rubble.

Therefore, the Münster rail networks became our most important target of the day. As we approached the rail yards in the city, there was no enemy interception, and the flak was minimal and ineffective. However, a thick cloud cover extended from about 15,000 feet all the way down to 1,000 feet. Visual acquisition of the target was therefore impossible, and we had to resort to H2X. In good weather, with clear skies, our bombardiers, using the Norden bombsight, could drop a full load of bombs within 1,000 feet of the aiming point. But with less accommodating weather conditions, the results could range from less than optimal to dismal, depending upon the terrain.

Although we couldn't immediately determine the results of our raid, post-mission reconnaissance indicated that our target had received considerable damage. We figured it probably wasn't enough to put rail traffic completely out of commission, but we were sure other raids would follow ours. Other units of our division sent to bomb targets farther east in Hanover encountered the same miserable weather that plagued us. However, results of their bombing raids were considered good, with severe damage to all targets. The 2nd Air Division's missions were thus deemed a success.

Such an important transportation center had to be neutralized. Münster had always been a key target in the Allied bombing raids. The first attack on this ancient city was against its industrial factories in 1940, and they continued throughout the war. It received more than 100 air raids. Like other German cities with structures dating back to the fourteenth century, the city center was almost totally destroyed, with very few structures left standing. Our second attack was a significant contribution to its destruction, and when Allied forces captured the town in early April, it was evident that it had little left to contribute to the German war effort.

ME 262 JET ATTACK WITH R4M ROCKETS

The next day, March 18, we were down between missions, but other crews from our squadron were sent on the biggest daylight-bombing raid on Berlin of the war. All three divisions participated, with 1,329 bombers and seven hundred thirty-three P-51 Mustang escort fighters dispatched to hit transportation and industrial targets in the German capital. The target was the northwestern portion of Berlin, known as the Tegel District, where railway stations and tank-producing factories were located. Also in this industrial area were multiple armaments factories, producing all types of weaponry, ammunition, and armored vehicles. This section of the city hadn't been bombed since the early part of 1944, and a steady flow of military material was being supplied to the front lines. One major objective of the raid was to aid the Russians by negatively affecting the German forces' ability to resist the advancing Red Army. Very heavy ordnance was used on this raid, including 1,000-pound GP bombs and a massive amount of incendiary bombs.

All through the early half of March, the 8th Air Force had encountered very little or no interception from Me 262 jet fighters. But this was about to change, dramatically.

The Germans appeared to be waiting for a big raid on Berlin, like the one on March 18, before sending up a large force of Me 262 jets to attack our bombers. Air Force Intelligence had warned group commanders at almost every operational briefing since early March to be aware of possible interception by enemy jets. Now, that threat materialized with full effect. Chance appeared to favor the Germans on that day because of bad weather and poor visibility, which enabled the Me 262 attack forces to easily evade the fighter escorts. Many of the enemy jet fighters broke through the escort's defensive shield to attack the bomber streams. Once that happened, all hell broke loose.

As many as thirty-six Me 262 jets from JG 7 units located at the Oranienburg and Parchim Airfields were scrambled to intercept the American bomber forces. The Luftwaffe attacking force was composed of two main groups, with the first consisting of 10 to 15 jet fighters zeroing in on the 8th Air Force's 1st Air Division bombers while they were on their way to attack the Schlesischer railway station in Berlin. Under intense 30 mm cannon fire, five heavy bombers went down on the first attack. Then a P-51 Mustang was hit.

With four nose-mounted cannons, the Me 262 jets were capable of inflicting enormous damage. Known as the "pneumatic hammer," the cannon's eleven-ounce explosive shell had a blast radius of almost two feet. Three direct hits on a heavy bomber were enough to bring it down. A single hit was capable of slicing a P-51 in half. Bombers of the 1st Air Division had suffered some heavy damage. But the worst was yet to come.

It was the heavies from the 3rd Air Division that would bear the brunt of the day's attack by enemy aircraft. The second group of German interceptors began their attack on the bombers from this division. Six Me 262 jets, led by Oberleutnant Günther Wegmann of JG 7's nine staffel, took flight from Parchim Airfield to intercept the 3rd Division's bomber streams. All the jets were carrying a new type of weapon system, the R4M air-to-air rocket.

Luftwaffe fighters had used primitive antiaircraft explosive projectiles in the past, the most notable being the Werfer-Grenate 21 rocket, which had been used as early as 1943. It was composed of a rocket-mortar type system that was fired from a distance. The Werfer-Grenate 21 was step in the right direction, but it proved to be highly unreliable, inaccurate, and not very effective in hitting its intended target. Its limited use made little impact on the destruction of Allied heavy bombers.

However, the R4M rocket was a totally different beast. The weapon system was developed by Dr. Kurt Heber at the Deutsche Waffen und Munitions Fabrik, and then implemented for combat use by Professor Willy Messerschmitt's research team. The simple design and structure of the R4M belied its truly devastating effect on enemy aircraft. A tubular steel casing approximately three feet in length housed a solid-fueled rocket engine, which carried a 55 mm warhead containing high-explosive hexogen. Weighing a mere seven pounds, the R4M's tail end was fitted with eight slender fins to impart directional control of the rocket during its flight to the target.

As the new and improved version of past air-to-air rockets, the R4Ms were much more sophisticated, with a timed proximity fuse and aerodynamic guidance system. The great advantage of these new rockets was the extreme range of their effectiveness. The attacking German fighters could launch them as far as 1,000 feet from their target, well beyond the most accurate range of the bomber's .50-caliber gun turrets. It was the perfect weapon system for high-speed jet attacks. Approaching from any direction, the pilot could fire the rockets and break away before they could even be detected. A single rocket exploding less than 50 feet away could bring down a bomber. A direct hit was fatal.

In the haste to make the rocket system operational, Messerschmitt himself designed and implemented the formation of wooden racks that were fitted under each wing of the Me 262 to hold the R4Ms. Each of the two wing racks housed 12 rockets that the pilot could manually fire through electronic controls connected to the rocket's release system. The rockets could be fired in salvos of six or twelve at a time. Like the jet aircraft itself, the R4M system didn't have time to go through all the normal developmental cycles required to ensure its operational effectiveness in the field. Thus, many problems resulted in its use in combat situations. However, when it worked as planned, the R4M rocket worked extremely well. (See Appendix 5.)

Oberleutnant Wegman, in the lead, was the first to approach the formation of bombers from the rear, at six o'clock. When he was within range, he fired all twenty-four R4Ms in two salvos directly into the bomber formation. As the rockets streaked toward the bombers at over 1,700 feet per second, it took only moments before one of the bombers took a direct hit. A blinding light flashed through the formation as the tremendous explosion of the R4M and the plane's bomb load sent concussive blast waves, striking other aircraft nearby.

Wegman wasn't finished, as he fired his cannons at another bomber, where he could see several hits on the aircraft's starboard engine. Suddenly, a volley of machine-gun fire from the defending bombers hit Wegman's jet with a vengeance. Smashing through the canopy and destroying the front instrument panel, a shell pierced Wegman's leg. Now with a number of P-51 fighters chasing him through the formation, Wegman pushed his jet to maximum velocity to quickly escape their range of fire. Bleeding badly and with his jet on fire, he was still able to bail out. He landed safely, but when taken to the hospital, the doctors couldn't save his leg. Never to fly again, Wegman was lucky to be alive.[14]

The 8th lost 24 bombers and 10 fighters in the air battles over Berlin that day. Fifteen bombers were so badly damaged that they were written off after returning to base. Ten heavies never made it back to base but crash-landed in Russian-held territory. Another 21 escort fighters also never made it back to base. Flak over Berlin was extremely heavy and accounted for some damage and losses. In fact, more than 700 bombers suffered heavy damage through enemy air attacks and flak. It was one of the highest numbers of casualties of any mission.

MISSION #17: MARCH 19, 1945
TARGET: BÄUMENHEIM

We had heard that a big attack against 8th Air Force bombers occurred the day before, and there were heavy losses. Although the 2nd Air Division's bomb groups came out relatively unscathed, the 1st and 3rd Air Divisions weren't so fortunate. It was at the operations briefing that the full extent of the German attack hit home. It really riled up our commanders. Not only were the enemy Me 262 jets more vicious in their attacks, but they were also using the new R4M rocket system with full effect. This gave them a tremendous offensive capability that they didn't have before. The tactics they employed were also improving to a point where a real threat to our bombing raids was becoming a reality.

With the great speed advantage and improved firepower, the Me 262 pilots developed a new tactic termed the "roller-coaster attack." The attacking fighter would approach the bomber stream from astern at about 6,000 to 8,000 feet above the formation, and at a distance of three or four miles behind the formation. It would then begin its attack run. The jet would dive down through the bomber formation to increase its speed and come up to level out behind a selected bomber at a distance of 3,000 feet, where the pilot could attack with extreme speed and fire his cannons.

Because of the closing speed of attack, the jet pilot had time for only about a three-second burst of cannon fire before he had to break away from the attack. This had to be at no less than 600 feet from his target to avoid a collision. Such a short burst of cannon fire might not seem like much, but it proved to be exceptionally deadly if the pilot scored a direct hit. This tactic required a high degree of timing and flying skill, which the experienced enemy pilots readily picked up. They also learned that the best position for a successful attack was to come in fast at the rear of the bomber, slightly below six o'clock, where there would be the least chance of defensive fire by the tail and belly gunners.

Only the Me 262 jets could accomplish a successful roller-coaster attack, since

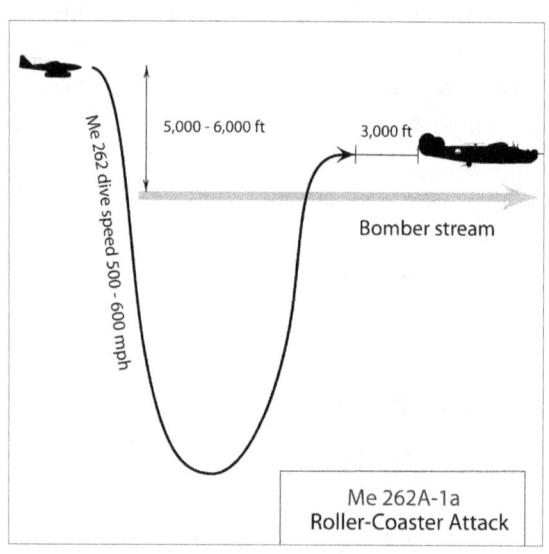

Me 262 dive speed 500 - 600 mph

5,000 - 6,000 ft   3,000 ft

Bomber stream

Me 262A-1a
Roller-Coaster Attack

conventional piston-engine fighter aircraft couldn't gain sufficient recovery speed after the steep dive to come up from below and initiate the attack. Time and time again, enemy jets could be observed diving through the formation at a scorching rate of speed, with bomber crews only catching a glimpse of the attacker. The jet would then come up rapidly from below to initiate its attack on the bomber. In this way, a skilled pilot was almost assured of a kill before our fighter escorts had a chance to come to the rescue of their Big Friends.

Armed with R4M rockets, this tactic proved exceptionally lethal. It gave the jet interceptors an advantage that no other Luftwaffe fighter aircraft could match. Oberst Johannes Steinhoff, the commander of JG 7, was just as amazed as the other pilots when he used the rockets for the first time. Steinhoff favored the hit-and-run ambush technique. Coming in fast, he would release the full payload of all twenty-four R4Ms on the first pass, and then speed away before being jumped by enemy fighter escorts. Being loaded down with two wing racks of rockets impeded the Me 262's speed and maneuverability, so most pilots chose to release all of them as quickly as possible. Steinhoff also liked to use a flanking approach, speeding in at the five or seven o'clock position, where the enemy bomber's silhouette would be at its widest, then releasing the R4Ms well beyond the maximum range of the bomber's .50-caliber machine guns.

The manner in which each salvo of rockets was released from under the wings of the jet was designed to converge at a distance of about 2,000 feet. At the convergence point, the field of fire encompassed a kill area of 100 feet by 50 feet. With this shotgun pattern, it was hard to miss. When two or more jets released their rockets into the tight bomber formation, chaos often ensued. One or two bombers would be hit, lose control, and in some cases collide with other bombers. Then the jets would come back and finish off the stragglers or the ones that had been severely damaged. The R4M appeared to be the ideal weapon for causing enough confusion to weaken the integrity of the bomber formations and make them critically susceptible to further attacks by other raiding jets.

The success of these attacks by JG 7's jet fighters shocked our air commanders. A real threat to our bombers, with a potential for disaster, was in the works. Something had to be done, with haste.

General Doolittle spoke to the survivors of rocket attacks by enemy jets. He could see the panic and strained expression of anxiety in their faces as they retold their experiences. Consistent with the many reports was the speed of the attacks. It all happened within seconds, and many bomber crews never knew what hit them. Some thought it was a direct hit from flak. Others knew better from the massive destruction that followed. Loaded with bombs and fuel, the bomber almost always violently exploded when struck by the R4M.

A crew member described how a rocket exploded under his ship and the force of the blast lifted the aircraft 200 feet above the formation. One pilot observed a direct hit on the wing of a nearby aircraft. With propellers moving in slow motion, the entire right wing was ripped off the fuselage, from front to rear, while the entire aircraft was engulfed in flames. He could clearly see the crew in the cockpit, immobilized as if in shock or from the concussion of the blast, the stricken pilot still gripping the controls as pieces of the twisted aircraft slowly spun downward into its death spiral.

Bombers that were hit by rockets exploded and collided with others in the tight formation. When one was struck, the blast effects caused massive damage with an almost immediate loss of flight controls, and fire quickly spread throughout the aircraft. There was little time to escape, and consequently few survivors. With the entire formation in disarray, individual bombers became easy prey for the attacking jets. Aircraft damaged during the first pass were annihilated when the jets came around for a second.

This was also when most enemy jets met their fate. A swarm of bomber fighter escorts would come diving down on them from above. As formidable as the Me 262 fighter was against heavy bombers, it was no match in a dogfight against either the P-51 Mustang or P-47 Thunderbolt. Most often, there were so many pursuing American fighters that the attacking jet would be hit by gunfire multiple times. If the jet couldn't escape with speed, it was doomed to be shot down. Many of them were, and the loss of jet aircraft and their pilots would soon take its toll.

Although the Me 262 now posed a very significant threat, Gen. Doolittle knew there were too few of them to change the outcome of the war at this late date. His major concern was the devastating psychological effect that these types of crushing attacks had on the bomber crews. They felt that the fighter escorts could no longer protect them from enemy interceptors. Morale was starting to take a dive. So Doolittle immediately issued orders for an all-out assault on the jet fighters. He was determined to wipe them out, wherever they might be.

The aircraft industry had been extensively bombed since November 1944, when the threat of Me 262 jets was evident. By March 1945, practically all known factories and assembly plants had been bombed to rubble. The Luftwaffe was able to receive newly built Me 262s only through hidden factory sites under Albert Speer's decentralization efforts. These locations included underground facilities, caves, and heavily wooded forest environments. So a new bombing campaign began to root out these covert locations.

One area where the jets were especially vulnerable was their air bases. Our air force intelligence team knew exactly where the major operational jet airfields were located. When the Me 262 fighters took off, they left distinctive scorch marks on the runways from the exhaust of their turbine engines, which was clearly evident from reconnaissance photos. Such runways were also longer than normal because it took time for the jet to gain sufficient speed to take off and to accomplish a safe high-speed landing. This would prove to be their most vulnerable weakness. The jets were attacked in the air and on the ground. Major operational Me 262 airfields—such as Parchim, Brandenburg-Briest, Neuberg, Munich-Riem, and Bäumenheim—were bombed again and again until they were virtually useless.

This airfield bombing campaign was accelerated on March 19, with our air division attacking airfields at Neuberg, Leipheim, and Bäumenheim. While a large force of 932 heavy bombers from the 1st and 3rd Air Divisions were assigned to attack industrial targets in Jena, Plauen, Zwickau, and marshalling yards in Fulda and Saalfeld, the entire force of 341 heavies from the 2nd Air Division went after the jet airfields in Neuberg and Leipheim. A jet aircraft factory in Bäumenheim was also on the target list.

Neuburg had large jet aircraft installations and an airfield. The large industrial city was located less than 10 miles southwest of Ingolstadt, near the Danube River, in southern Germany. The largest Me 262 assembly plant and production factory making aircraft components was in Neuburg. Nearby was a large airfield, where the jets were operational. The aircraft factories at Bäumenheim were on the top of the list of industrial targets producing the necessary components for the jet aircraft, supposedly one the few factories still functioning. Bäumenheim also had an active airfield nearby. The aircraft factories in both Neuberg and Bäumenheim were above ground, which made them ideal targets.

TARGETS FOR THE 2ND AIR DIVISION		
COMBAT WING	SQUADRONS	TARGET
14th CW	8	Neuberg Airfield
2nd CW (Group A)	4	Neuberg Airfield
2nd CW (Group B)	4	Bäumenheim Jet Factory
20th CW	8	Bäumenheim Airfield
96th CW	9	Leipheim Airfield

Our wing had two attacking forces sent to two different targets. Group A consisted of two squadrons from the 453rd Bomb Group (Old Buck) and two squadrons from the 445th Bomb Group (Tibenham), all of which were sent to bomb Neuberg Airfield. Eight squadrons from the 14th Combat Wing joined Group A in the attack against Neuberg for a total force of 125 Liberators. Group B, with four squadrons—three from the 389th Bomb Group (Hethel) and our squadron, the 735th Bombardment Squadron from the 453rd Bomb Group—was sent to bomb the Bäumenheim jet factory. Group B had a force of 43 Liberators.

As we approached the city, we encountered very little flak. The weather was perfect for visual bombing, and 32 Libs from the 389th Bomb Group were the first to attack. They dropped their loads of 100- and 500-pound GP bombs right on target. Our squadron, with 11 Libs, followed their attack to finish the job by plastering the entire target area with full loads of ten M17 incendiary bombs. When we left, nothing was left of the jet factory except fire and smoke.

We were warned that groups of Me 262s would be operational along routes to the target areas of the three air divisions, and an attack by them might be expected. Although many of these enemy jets had been observed supporting operations against the Russians on the ground, we were nevertheless told to stay alert. Our fighter escorts must have done a good job of keeping these interceptors away from our wing, because we didn't run into any Luftwaffe interceptors.

After the successful coordinated attack by enemy jet fighters on heavy bombers the day before, Doolittle wanted an escort-to-bomber ratio of two to one, but this wasn't practical with such large numbers of bombers. He had to settle for a less-than-ideal one to one ratio. It proved to be enough to keep the threat of jet fighters manageable. For the bomber force of 1,273 dispatched on the day's mission, the majority of 675 fighter escorts from 14 fighter groups accompanied the divisional bomber streams. Of the 341 heavies dispatched in our division, we had one hundred ninety-four P-51 Mustangs as our fighter escorts. The remaining groups of fighters not assigned to bomber protection were involved in Freelance operations. Our Little Friends did their job in keeping the jets at bay. The other air divisions weren't as lucky.

Like the previous day, a large group of twenty-eight Me 262s from JG 7 and EFG2 jet units attacked bombers from the 1st and 3rd Air Divisions. Ten heavy bombers were lost in the first wave of attacks by the German jets, which were using cannon fire and R4M rockets. But the P-51 Mustangs were ready this time, and the tables were turned when the fighter escorts dived down on them with guns blazing. A number of enemy jets were shot down, and the remaining ones never got a chance for a second attack. Outnumbered by more than ten to one, the jets were chased away before more damage could be done. Increasing the number of escort fighters appeared to be a big factor in stemming the threat by enemy jets. Each attack resulted in more jets being shot down as our fighter pilots gained more experience with more aggressive tactics. The Me 262 jets were built for offense with a focus on speed at the expense of maneuverability. The P-51s could easily turn in on them in a dogfight, so their only option was to hit and run.

Jet aircraft were also being decimated on the ground as bomb groups of our wing attacked Neuberg Airfield with a vengeance. Eighty enemy aircraft could be seen parked neatly in rows on the tarmac. All but 10 of them were Me 262 jets. After tons of GP and fragmentation bombs were dropped in a low-level attack, the wreckage of what was left of at least 16 jets was observed by air photoreconnaissance the next day. Along with the aircraft, all the hangars and surrounding buildings in the airfield were severely damaged. The runways were all pitted with deep bomb craters. Not only Neuberg but also other jet airfields were bombed. These included Parchim, Brandenburg-Briest, and Munich-Riem, all of which suffered heavy destruction.

In the next several days, the American air forces undertook an all-out effort to demolish jet airfields. On March 21, the 8th sent massive bombing raids to 10 airfields, in which the 453rd Bomb Group bombed airfields in Achmer and Essen. The following day, on the 22nd, five more airfields were bombed, including Giebelstadt, which was on the assigned target list for the 453rd Bomb Group. The spring weather had arrived, and the skies were beginning to clear up in northern Germany, so bombing results were excellent.

Many of the airfields were put out of commission. Luftwaffe problems were exacerbated because most of its jet fighters were grounded anyway due to the lack of fuel. There was only enough fuel to send up small groups of Me 262 jets to attack the bombers. Wholesale destruction of the jets was also occurring on the ground as more and more American fighters strafed and bombed them in Freelance operations. The grinding loss of men and material on what remained of the Luftwaffe was once more beginning to take its toll.

MISSION #18: MARCH 24, 1945
TARGET: DZ-WESEL

Our last mission in March was a special one. The US 8th, 9th, and 15th Air Forces were to assist the Allied ground troops in the crossing of the Rhine River. We were to support their advance into Germany. After Gen. Hodges's First Army reached Remagen and captured the Ludendorff Bridge on March 7, his forces immediately began to secure a bridgehead on the Rhine. By March 12, as Hodges awaited Patton's 3rd Army in the south to reach the Rhine, the US 1st Army had secured a 14-mile front on the east bank.

Advance units from Patton's 3rd Corps of the 3rd Army reached the Rhine on March 22. They arrived at two small towns, Nierstein and Oppenheim, about 20 miles southwest of Frankfurt-on-the-Rhine. His army engineers built two pontoon bridges, and shortly before midnight, six battalions made a quiet assault across the river with very few casualties. The small numbers of German defenders immediately surrendered. Patton's troopers were totally unexpected.

When the main forces of the German armies retreated across the Rhine, they left few defenders to face the advancing Allied armies. The majority were aged Volkssturm recruits and young boys. By the evening of March 23, the entire 5th Division of the US 3rd Army was across the river. Patton called Bradley and gleefully told him that he'd crossed the Rhine ahead of Field Marshal Sir Bernard Montgomery's 21st Army Group farther north.

Montgomery had amassed a huge army group with well over 1 million men. After an initial furious artillery barrage, the 2nd British Army began its Rhine assault on the evening of March 23 and crossed the river in short order. Units from

Montgomery's two army corps attacked Rees and Wesel. Just south of Wesel, elements of the US 9th Army, which had been attached to the British army group for this attack, crossed the Rhine in the early morning of March 24 with little resistance. Unlike the Americans, the advance of the British forces was met by a much more determined defense by the German 1st Parachute Army. It took a full day before Montgomery's forces resumed their advance into Germany.

At 10:00 a.m. on March 24, the massive airborne assault, Operation Varsity, began. It was the biggest Allied airborne operation of the war. More than 20,000 British and American troops either were flown by gliders or parachuted behind enemy lines to support Montgomery's main forces as they crossed the river in their attack against the German defenders. As the airborne infantry captured the city of Wesel and cleared the surrounding area, the main Allied force was busy ferrying troops and equipment across temporary bridges over the Rhine. It was the job of the US 8th Air Force's 2nd Air Division to drop much-needed supplies to the troops on the ground.

This was also the biggest operation for the 8th, in which 1,749 heavy bombers were dispatched to support the Allied advance across the Rhine. An escort fighter force of more than one thousand three hundred P-47s and P-51s accompanied the bombers. To keep the Luftwaffe at bay, heavy bombers from the 1st and 3rd Air Divisions attacked more than 17 enemy airfields in western and northwestern

March 24, 1945, B-24 Liberator from the US 8th Air Force 2nd Air Division dropping supplies by parachute to airborne troops who had landed east of the Rhine River. (NARA)

Germany. For the 2nd Air Division, 182 heavy bombers were sent to attack airfields at Störmede, Kirtorf, and Ziegenhain east of the Ruhr. Another group of 240 Liberators was assigned to drop supplies for the Allied airborne forces on the ground. Our wing—with the 389th, 445th, and 453rd Bomb Groups, composed of a total of 80 Liberators—was included in the airdrop of supplies to the airborne troops on the ground.

All of the heavy equipment, such as artillery and armored vehicles, was dropped with the Allied troops on the morning of March 24. It was our job to supply them with small arms ammunition, grenades, rations, medical supplies, and whatever else they needed. Large bundles of supplies were packed into our bomb bays and pushed out when we reached our designated drop zone. In order to release the bundles accurately and gently by parachute, each aircraft had to fly very low, almost at treetop level. We were told that an altitude of 300 to 400 feet was optimal. However, this exposed us to dangerous antiaircraft fire. After the drop, it was necessary to make a tight turn, which brought us over enemy territory for approximately fifteen minutes. During that time, our aircraft was vulnerable to antiaircraft and small arms fire.

Consequently many of our aircraft sustained some heavy damage passing through this dangerous zone of enemy fire. There were reports that up to 20 bombers were lost. In our wing, the 453rd Bomb Group was fortunate to have all of her aircrew return safely. But the 389th Bomb Group lost two aircraft, and the 445th Bomb Group also lost two. Colonel Carl Fleming, who was the deputy division air commander of the 445th Bomb Group, was in one of the bombers that were hit. It burst into flames and crashed. There were no survivors. Despite this tragic loss, the 8th's 2nd Air Division was able to drop 600 tons of supplies to the troops of the American 17th and British 6th Airborne Divisions, which had parachuted behind the lines earlier in the morning. The mission was a complete success.

As our last mission in March came to an end, the Germans were facing overwhelming Allied forces on the Western Front that would be impossible to stop. In the defense of the Rhine River, the Germans had suffered appalling losses. Colonel General Paul Hausser's Army Group G had retreated across the river with more than 350,000 men killed, wounded, missing in action, or taken prisoner. Their divisional strength was reduced to almost half, and the tremendous loss of tanks, artillery, and other heavy weaponry could never be replaced. The Wehrmacht's capability to resist the advancing Allied forces was now drastically diminished and severely compromised. The lack of reserves meant that the army ranks were now being filled with raw recruits who had little training and were composed of ill-equipped Volkssturm volunteers, along with other units from the navy or Luftwaffe. Morale among the troops was collapsing, and stringent measures were taken to keep them in line.

On March 25, 1945, Himmler, as commander of Army Group Vistula, ordered that any straggler would be summarily court-martialed, sentenced, and shot on the spot. Such action was in effect throughout all the army groups. Hausser went so far as to recommend imprisonment of the family members of any soldier who deserted or was unwilling to fight. Furthermore, any German soldier seen crossing the front lines would be shot. Collapse seemed imminent on the Western Front as scores of soldiers began to desert despite such severe consequences. In fact, desertion was becoming more and more evident within the ranks. It finally spiraled out of control in the final month of the war when entire German Army units surrendered to the

Western Allies. This loss of faith in the Nazi regime's ability to maintain the war effort and sustain the will of the German people to carry on the fight also extended into the civilian population.[15]

After years of constant bombing raids on all of Germany's major cities, the economic and military infrastructure was breaking down. This was most evident in cities, where shortages of food and other essentials for life began to deteriorate to catastrophic levels. Because the transportation system was either beyond repair or confiscated for military use only, the civilian food distribution networks had collapsed. Hoarding and looting of food were beginning to become commonplace. People no longer believed the propaganda that Joseph Goebbels, the Reichsminister for Propaganda and Enlightenment, was spewing at them. In the most severely bombed cities, and in Berlin itself, the necessities of day-to-day living, such as food, water, gas, and electricity, were either being severely rationed or quickly running out.

Everyone knew Germany was going to lose the war, and they just wanted it to end. Severe repression was the only option left to the Nazi regime for controlling civil unrest. People who spoke against the regime or spread the notion of defeatism were arrested by the Gestapo and executed. Hitler ordered summary court-martials throughout Germany. Known as the People's Court, exactors of justice traveled around the country acting as judge, jury, and executioner for anyone accused of undermining Nazi rule and refusing to continue to support the war effort. In the vast majority of cases, the verdict was a death sentence. There was no appeal process. The disintegration of the rule of law clearly indicated that the Nazi Party was progressively losing control of the German population.

Hitler could see the Third Reich disintegrating before his eyes. He realized the end was inevitable when Armaments Minister Albert Speer sent him a memorandum on March 18, 1945. It informed Hitler of the imminent collapse of the German economy. Speer wrote that it would happen "with certainty" within four to eight weeks. Germany wouldn't be able to continue the war effort. Speer wasn't as concerned about the end of the Wehrmacht as he was about the future of the German people. The postwar survival of the German people was at stake, and Speer emphasized the need to protect the country's vital infrastructures, such as the transportation and communication networks, from total destruction in the final weeks of the war. But on the very next day, March 19, in complete repudiation of Speer's concerns, Hitler issued his scorched earth policy known as the Nero Order.[16]

The order called for the destruction of any installation—such as military transports, communication lines, and supply depots—within the Reich territory that the enemy could use at any time, including the future. Explosives were to be employed to essentially eliminate all means of transportation. The extensive list of facilities included all forms of railway components, such as tracks, roundhouses, freight depots, rail work and repair stations, locomotives, freight trains, passenger trains, and roadway interchanges. Waterways were also on the list: canal sluices and locks, barges, cargo vessels, bridges, canals, and any form of transport within.

Speer was horrified. The wholesale destruction of such vital structures within Germany would undoubtedly guarantee undue suffering among the German people for many years to come. Hitler told Speer that if the war was lost, then so were the people. They wouldn't need to be concerned about any future existence. It wasn't for him to worry about their survival. If the Führer was to go down in flames, so would the German people. However, because of Speer's amicable relationship with Hitler, he was fortunate enough to be able to convince Hitler to allow him to oversee the implementation of the Nero Order through the Armaments Ministry. Speer then went on a personal crusade throughout Germany to stop, prevent, or ameliorate the destruction of Germany. Because of his efforts, Speer saved the German people from a horrific future.[17]

Speer was also proven correct about the collapse of the Third Reich, as the Russians were now preparing to launch their final offensive against Berlin. When Zhukov established bridgeheads on the Oder River at Küstrin on January 31, 1945, his armies met vicious counterattacks by German forces in the region. Upon Hitler's orders, Küstrin was reinforced and fortified.

The siege of Küstrin had begun.

As more and more German troops arrived to aid the city, a protracted struggle ensued along the eastern bank of the Oder River as the Russian armies attempted to take the city.

All through February, bad weather conditions prevented the Russians from capturing Küstrin. It wasn't until the beginning of March that weather conditions improved enough for the Russian forces to break through the German defenses and enter the city. After an intensely brutal bout of street-to-street fighting by Red Army troops within the city, the situation became hopeless, and the German garrison broke through the Russian lines on the night of March 29 to escape the city. Küstrin was now in Russian hands, and Zhukov's armies were soon able to cross the Oder River to begin their advance into Germany.

While the Russians prepared their advance on the Eastern Front, the Allied strategic air forces continued to eliminate major communications and transportation targets within Germany. The transportation interdiction operations of the 9th Air Force were occurring on almost a daily basis throughout February and March 1945. Through attacks by light and medium bombers—such as the Douglas A-20 Havoc, Douglas A-26 Invader, and Martin B-26 Marauder—a multitude of targets were destroyed or damaged beyond repair. These included road and rail overpasses and bridges, railroad junctions and marshalling yards, rail repair stations, communication centers, motor vehicle transport repair and storage depots, ammunition and munitions-filling plants and storage facilities, and light and heavy flak positions around important cities and industrial areas. Many of these raids occurred on the heels of heavy bomber raids. However, the majority of attacks were separate operations to hit targets of opportunity as they occurred. The number of locomotives and rolling stock destroyed was immense, running into the thousands. The ability of the German transportation system to operate effectively was now on the verge of collapse.

Such tactical operations by the US 9th Air Force also included providing close air support for the advancing American troops fighting their way to the Rhine River. The effect of such attacks in impeding the movement of enemy troops, vehicles, equipment, and supplies can't be underestimated. Meanwhile, the transportation bombing campaign against the Ruhr Valley was coming to a close. It was a total success. By the end of March, there was little or no movement of rail, road, or waterborne traffic in or out of the Ruhr. The strategic bombing raids had completely isolated the Ruhr from the rest of Germany.

Eisenhower's initial phase of operations to defeat Germany was now complete. All German forces west of the Rhine had been eliminated, and bridgeheads all along the Rhine River had been successfully established. The final phase of his plan was the destruction of the remaining German forces on the Western Front. The next step to achieve this goal was the encirclement of the Ruhr Valley. Eisenhower knew that the largest concentration of enemy forces would be there to defend the most vital industrial region in Germany: the Ruhr.

As the Allied forces advanced into Germany from the Rhine River, Gen. Simpson's US 9th Army was to advance along the northern border of the Ruhr to Paderborn. General Hodges's 1st Army was to drive from the Remagen bridgehead eastward toward Marburg and Kassel, and then swing toward the southeast to link up with Gen. Patton's 3rd Army coming up from the south. Patton's army was to cover Hodges's right flank as the 1st Army advanced to Paderborn and link up with Simpson's 9th Army. Hodges's mechanized advance with tanks, armored vehicles, and trucks was unexpectedly swift, meeting little resistance. The 1st Army moved forward at a rapid pace, up to 40 miles a day. Its 3rd Armored Division met the 9th Army's 2nd Armored Division at Lippstadt, approximately 12 miles southwest of Paderborn, on April 1, 1945. Encirclement of the entire Ruhr industrial region was complete.

Trapped within the Ruhr Valley was Field Marshal Walter Model's entire German Army Group B. It included the German 5th Panzer Army, the 15th Army, and elements of the 1st Parachute Army from Col. Gen. Johannes Blaskowitz's Army Group H. With seven corps and 19 divisions, nearly 300,000 German troops and 10 million civilians were trapped in the Ruhr Pocket. According to Eisenhower, the Ruhr campaign was the largest double envelopment of enemy forces in military

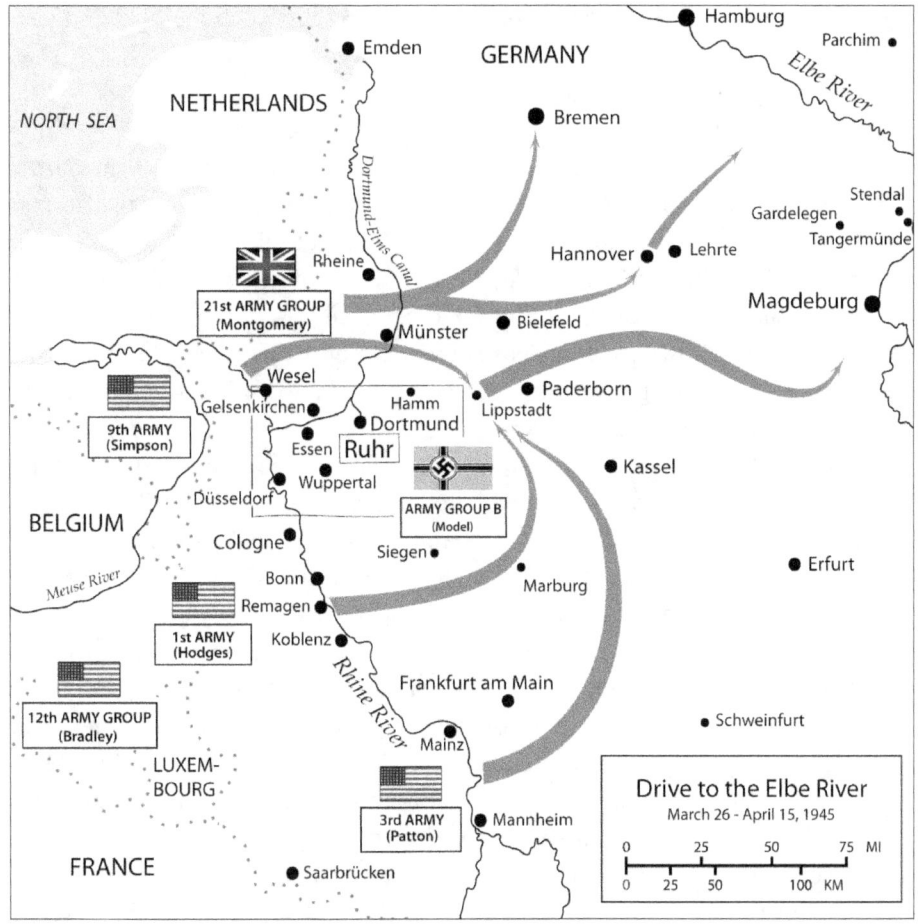

Drive to the Elbe River
March 26 - April 15, 1945

history. He also knew that the strength and fighting spirit of the Wehrmacht was in a state of collapse.[18]

It was a hopeless situation, but Model refused to surrender. Hitler had made it very clear that any of his trapped armies had to fight to the very last man. But the regular army troops were worn out, with no more fight left in them. They all knew the war was lost, and they continued to fight only for their own survival. Instead of being killed or captured as prisoners of war and sent to slave labor camps in Russia, the best way to accomplish this was to surrender to the Western Allies.

Within two weeks, Model's Army Group B surrendered. There was no other choice. Model couldn't contemplate a formal surrender, so he simply ordered his troops to go home when their ammunition and supplies ran out. Many did, some melting into the civilian population when given a chance, and entire units gave up their arms and refused to fight. American divisional commanders were shocked at the number of enemy soldiers putting up minimal resistance and surrendering in droves. Up to 50,000 German soldiers in one case gave up the fight and were taken prisoner.

One of Model's commanders, however, was fortunate enough to escape the Ruhr Pocket. It was Gen. Hasso von Manteuffel of the German 5th Panzer Army, whom Hitler had ordered to make his way to the Netherlands before Army Group B was completely encircled. Von Manteuffel was to take command of the German 3rd Panzer Army of Himmler's Army Group Vistula to face Rokossovsky's 2nd Belorussian Front in East Prussia. Von Manteuffel was one of the lucky ones. Model, on the other hand, adamantly refused to be taken prisoner. In a wooded forest outside Düsseldorf, the commander of Army Group B put a bullet into his own head. The Ruhr campaign was the last major battle between the Allied forces and German armies on the Western Front.

On March 28, 1945, Eisenhower made a fateful decision that changed the course of the war. It also infuriated Churchill and the British staff. The supreme commander sent a message directly to Stalin, informing the Russian leader of the Allied plans to invade Germany. The major focus of the Allied attack was to advance from the Rhine River to the Erfurt-Leipzig-Dresden region and meet the Red Army on the Elbe River. The British force under Montgomery then struck for the Baltic Sea. It was a clear message to Stalin that the Western Allies wouldn't advance to Berlin. Stalin then sent Eisenhower a reply on April 1, approving of the Allied plan and telling him that Berlin was no longer a strategic objective. Berlin was to be of secondary significance to the Russian forces, and his forces would advance in the direction Eisenhower so indicated.

When Churchill was informed of this conversation, he was furious. The prime minister had always seen Berlin as the ultimate prize in the fight against Germany. The Western Allies' capture of the capital would be paramount to the defeat of the German people, and thus add prestige to the British people. Churchill even encouraged Montgomery to advance to Berlin as soon as the British armies reached the Elbe River.

But that would never happen. In a flurry of messages between Churchill, Roosevelt, and Eisenhower, the prime minister pleaded with the Americans to secure Berlin before the Russians did. However, Roosevelt turned a deaf ear. The president was never really concerned with what would happen to the European countries after the war ended. Foremost in his mind was the goal to end the war as quickly as possible and bring American troops home.

The issue of capturing Berlin had already been decided at the Yalta Conference in February 1945. In a secret meeting with Stalin, without Churchill's knowledge, Roosevelt had agreed to Stalin's demand that the USSR take Berlin and much of East Germany. Roosevelt always thought he could handle Stalin's territorial aspirations with friendly persuasion. Instead, the Russian leader skillfully outplayed Roosevelt. Stalin received from the Western Allies everything he wanted. When the Big Three signed the Declaration on Liberated Europe, stating that any country liberated from Nazi rule would be allowed to determine the form of government under which its people would live, Stalin promised to allow free, democratic elections.[19]

Roosevelt believed him, but when Churchill heard about their private conversation, he was shocked and very upset. The prime minister knew well the Russian premier's insatiable territorial aspirations and tried to convince Roosevelt that it was the Russians who posed the most pernicious threat to a free and liberated Europe. It wasn't until later, when Stalin had crushed any attempt to establish a democratic form of government and forcibly instilled communist rule in the liberated countries, that Roosevelt finally realized the mistake of allowing Stalin to do what he'd always intended to do—build a totalitarian empire. Churchill's worst fears were to come true; the tyranny of Hitler's Third Reich would just be replaced by the tyranny of a communist dictator.

Eisenhower alleviated Churchill's objections by diplomatically persuading the prime minister of the futility of trying to reach Berlin before the Russians. The Red Armies were already less than 40 miles from Berlin. By the time Allied forces reached the Elbe River, they would still be almost twice the distance to Berlin. Even if Montgomery's forces could reach Berlin before the Red Army, which was unlikely, there was a possibility of a conflict with Russian forces, since Stalin was so determined to capture Berlin. Roosevelt told Eisenhower to avoid such a situation at all costs.[20]

Because Eisenhower had communicated directly with Stalin, which breached the normal established protocols of first informing the Combined Chiefs of Staff, Churchill believed the general had exceeded his authority. However, during the Yalta Conference, the British had already accepted the issue of a direct communication between the supreme commander and the Russian staff. Nonetheless, Eisenhower told Churchill that if the Combined Chiefs of Staff deemed it necessary to take Berlin based on military considerations, he would do so and comply with their decision.[21]

The Combined Chiefs of Staff decided to defer to the US Joint Chiefs of Staff on the final settlement of Eisenhower's decision. Eisenhower sent a message to his commander, Gen. George Marshall, on March 30, outlining his plan and stating that Berlin was no longer a strategic military objective. The capture of Berlin would be better accomplished by a quick and decisive elimination of the opposing German forces on the Western Front.

The next day, Marshall replied to the supreme commander, saying it was up to him as the field commander in the ETO to make any military decisions he saw fit. In addition, the US Joint Chiefs of Staff found Eisenhower's strategic concept sound and would support his decision. Lastly, Eisenhower would be allowed to continue to communicate freely with the commander-in-chief of the Russian Army. The issue of an Allied advance to Berlin was finally put to rest.[22]

Eisenhower had thought long and hard concerning the final defeat of Germany. On the Berlin issue, he sought the advice of his friend Gen. Omar Bradley, with whom he'd had a close relationship through the years. They'd met in 1911 at Jackson Barracks near St. Louis, Missouri, while taking the entrance examinations for the West Point Class of 1915. Eisenhower, who was twenty years old at the time, was a senatorial appointee from Abilene, Kansas. Omar Bradley, just eighteen, was a selected congressional alternate from the 2nd Congressional District of Missouri. It wasn't a formal meeting, but they might have noticed one another in the examination room. Who could have predicted that they would rise through the ranks to become two of the US Army's top generals, each playing a vital role in the Second World War?[23]

When Eisenhower and Bradley discussed the fate of Berlin, they agreed that destruction of the German forces was the prime military objective. Without the Wehrmacht, Germany's only option would be to surrender. They also knew how much the British wanted to capture Berlin as a symbolic victory for the Western Allies. If it was necessary to take Berlin, then Eisenhower would have chosen Bradley over Montgomery for the task. Bradley had a superior command of his armies and was more than capable to achieve the best results.

The supreme commander asked Bradley how many troop casualties it might take to capture Berlin. Bradley estimated the number to be about 100,000. However, both were also aware that the high casualty rates of street-to-street fighting to defeat Berlin's defenders would result in a much greater number of deaths and injuries. As the Russians would soon discover, both generals were absolutely correct in their assessment. Bradley then asked Eisenhower if such a cost in American lives merely for prestige purposes would be worth it. Eisenhower thought not.[24]

In the closing weeks of the transportation campaign, the main goal of destroying Germany's transportation systems was a resounding success. The Allied air commanders' theory that this final bombing campaign would cause the eventual collapse of Germany's economic and military might had been proven correct. Railway and other forms of transportation were at a virtual standstill.

The remaining German forces on the Western Front were now facing disorganization and lacked the necessary resources to sustain an effective resistance to the advancing American and British forces. Mobility of enemy troops was either crippled or, in some cases, in total paralysis. Acute shortages of fuel, along with the constant attacks by Allied fighters on all road traffic, prevented the much needed supplies and equipment from reaching the front lines. Although German resistance continued, and at times rose with determined intensity, it could no longer be considered a viable threat. The Allied advance to the Elbe River was rapid and inevitable.

On the Eastern Front, the massive Russian armies were poised to begin their final offensive against Berlin. The stage was now set for the complete destruction of Hitler's Third Reich.

CHAPTER 5

THE FINAL CURTAIN

AS THE WAR DREW CLOSER to its conclusion, the Luftwaffe was in a desperate state of combat fitness. At the beginning of April 1945, thousands of fighter aircraft, which included the Me 262 jet fighter, were still being manufactured and assembled in hidden enclaves all over Germany, following Speer's plan of decentralization. Yet these newly built aircraft weren't able to reach the airfields because of a severely damaged transportation system. The limited success of the few jet fighters that actually made it to their final destination was being relentlessly destroyed by American fighter aircraft. Along with the lack of fuel, which in itself was a critical factor, the major problem was the availability of experienced pilots.

General Doolittle's air warfare campaign in 1944 not only decimated the large numbers of aircraft needed to sustain a functioning air force, but more importantly, the vast majority of experienced fighter pilots. Oberst Johannes Steinhoff, one of Germany's leading air aces in the war, recounted the dismal state of the Luftwaffe during those final months. In early 1945, Steinhoff left as commander of JG 7 to join Gen. Adolf Galland's legendary JV 44 jet squadron. Steinhoff was the chief flight instructor for the unending stream of young replacements coming into the unit to fly Me 262 jets. Most were barely out of their teens. These new pilots received virtually no combat training in flight school. Their operational training time was less than 50 hours, in some cases only 20. With barely enough hands-on experience to just fly a fighter aircraft, these young recruits were sent directly into frontline combat. Steinhoff knew they didn't have a chance.

Attacking massive heavy bomber formations was suicidal at best, even for the most experienced fighter pilot. With up to sixty or more .50-caliber machine guns able to fire against an attacking aircraft, it was like flying through a blizzard of deadly projectiles. Even if one survived that ordeal and was able to complete a successful attack, the pilot would then need to fend off the hundreds of P-51 or P-47 fighter escorts, all looking to score an easy kill. The young, inexperienced pilots could survive, at most, only two missions before they were dead. The majority of them actually met their fate not due to the lethal attacks of American pilots but more often the ever-present hazards of just being a combat pilot, such as bad weather conditions, loss of aircraft control, or simply pilot error. Yet, Steinhoff did his best to train and teach them how to survive in combat. It was such a travesty and a waste of young lives. He blamed the Luftwaffe high command for this intolerable situation and their use of these young innocents as cannon fodder, which he viewed simply as a form of murder.

MISSION #19: APRIL 4, 1945
TARGET: WESENDORF

In spite of the weaknesses of the Luftwaffe, the few remaining experienced fighter pilots were extremely successful in attacking heavy bombers with Me 262 jets armed with cannons and rockets. They were still a formidable menace to our bomber forces, and they were to be severely dealt with by all means necessary. A concerted effort by the Allied air forces in April focused on eliminating this threat wherever it existed. For the US 8th Air Force, massive bombing raids were directed at jet airfields throughout northern and central Germany. On April 4, all air divisions targeted seven enemy airfields. It was one of the biggest bombing raids to date, with 1,431 heavy bombers dispatched, along with 866 escort fighters.

The 1st Air Division, with 443 heavy bombers, was assigned to attack airfields in Fassberg, Dedelstorf, and Hoya. Another 24 heavies targeted the U-boat facilities at Hamburg. The 3rd Air Division sent 526 heavy bombers to attack the airfield at Eggebek and the Deutsche U-boat shipyard at Kiel. Our division, with 438 heavies, was to bomb airfields at Parchim, Perleberg, and Wesendorf.

In our wing, there were three bomb groups—the 453rd, 389th, and 445th. Our bomb group was sent to bomb the Wesendorf Airfield, which was located approximately 20 miles north of Brunswick, an industrial city just over 100 miles west of Berlin. Elements of the 389th Bomb Group were also assigned to bomb the Wesendorf Airfield as well as the airfield at Parchim. JG 7, one of the largest and most aggressive operational jet units in the Luftwaffe, had multiple Gruppe units in Parchim, Brandenburg-Briest, and Oranienburg. These enemy air bases were relentlessly bombed by the 8th's heavies and strafed by American fighters on a weekly basis in April. Parchim Airfield, only 90 miles northwest of Berlin, was reported to have over 100 aircraft on the ground. It was primed for a heavy attack. The third bomb group in our wing, the 445th, went on to bomb the airfield at Perleberg.

The number of fighter escorts flying with the 2nd Air Division included two hundred ninety-three P-51 and fifty-eight P-47 escort fighters, so we were well protected. Being so near JG 7's air bases, we were warned of possible attacks by Me 262 jets. The threat was realized when 47 jets were scrambled to intercept our bomber divisions. A group of enemy fighters attacked the 1st and 3rd Air Divisions with cannon and rockets, destroying or doing irreparable damage to 10 heavy bombers. Our division was attacked by a group of about 20 enemy jets, some of which briefly pierced our fighter escort shield of protection.

Two of the jets came into our group formation for an attack. It was the first time in almost a year that enemy interceptors had an opportunity to fight their way through our fighter escorts to attack the 453rd Bomb Group. We were in the low-left squadron of our group, and one of the Me 262s came in fast at nine o'clock high and passed through the formation without firing. The second Me 262 started to make its attack run at eight o'clock level, straight to our position. Just before it got close enough to fire, it was jumped by a swarm of P-51 escorts and chased away. We were lucky. The two other bomb groups in our wing weren't as fortunate.

As the leading bomb groups in the formation ahead of us, the 445th and 389th received the brunt of the jet attacks. Three Me 262s made a successful attacking run with cannon and rockets. The 389th Bomb Group (Hethel) lost one aircraft and received major damage to a number of others. The 445th Bomb Group (Tibenham) was also attacked and lost two Liberators. Our pilot, Lt. Swingle, observed the attack on the Libs in the formation ahead of us. One bomber was hit and seen going down in flames. It was most likely the one from the 389th Bomb Group. Only three parachutes were observed. One of the German jets was hit by bomber defensive fire and observed to be on fire while it spiraled downward into the clouds. P-51 fighters chased away the other enemy jets before they could make a second run. Many of the attacking jets were followed all the way to their home base by our escort fighters and destroyed while trying to land. This was now standard procedure for any attacks by Me 262s.

Our division lost six Libs that day. Some of those were by flak. Wesendorf, like many of the Luftwaffe's jet airfields, was ringed by a number of antiaircraft artillery batteries, and we received an unexpected heavy volume of flak. The flak intensity increased quite a bit on our bomb run over the target area. We did sustain some heavy damage, mainly in the forward section of the aircraft, especially the nose gun turret. However, none of our crew was seriously injured. Our maximum load of fifty-two 100-pound GP fragmentation bombs hit right on target. The frags were deadly on any aircraft sitting on the tarmac. The explosions just tore them to shreds. On this raid, Wesendorf was bombed by almost 100 heavy bombers, receiving over 200 tons of bombs. The Germans were using the Wesendorf Airfield to train new pilots, and it was a known operational center for jet interceptor attacks. The airfield sustained heavy damage and lost much of its aircraft on the ground. Our mission was a complete success.

To make sure these jet air bases were put out of commission for good, both the Parchim and Wesendorf Airfields were again attacked on April 7, 1945. On that raid, Parchim received almost 400 tons of bombs. A number of other airfields were also on the bomb list, including Kaltenkirchen, Salzwedel, and Kohlenbissen, along with another visit to Fassberg. On that day, the Luftwaffe exerted a truly desperate attempt to intercept our bombing raids by sending up its dwindling number of operational fighter aircraft. It was a massive attack involving one hundred thirty Me 109 and Fw 190 conventional fighter aircraft, and fifty Me 262 jets.

Included in this force of enemy fighters was the Sonderkommando Elbe, a unit of German pilots assigned with specific orders to ram their target if they were unable to bring it down with cannon fire. The advised method was to strike the enemy bomber's aft section, just before the tail of the fuselage, in the hope of slicing the tail apart with the attacking aircraft's wing. This would, theoretically, enable the enemy pilot to bail out if he was lucky enough to survive the impact. In practice this seldom worked as planned, and both aircraft usually exploded into flames. At least eight heavy bombers succumbed to this type of suicidal attack. Altogether, the 8th lost a total of 17 heavy bombers. But the Germans came out far worse, with at least 100 aircraft lost, some of which were flown by the German Air Force's most experienced pilots.

MISSION #20: APRIL 8, 1945
TARGET: FÜRTH

The next day, the 1st and 3rd Air Divisions of the 8th Air Force continued to pound airfields and target marshalling yards. The 1st Air Division struck the Derben oil depot and an airfield at Schafstädt. Marshalling yards at Stendal and Halberstadt were also hit by large formations of heavy bombers. The 3rd Air Division targeted a slew of marshalling yards in Plauen, Hof, and Eger. The ordnance depot at Grafenwöhr also sustained an attack with a heavy tonnage of bombs. Our division concentrated on a munitions depot at Bayreuth and airfields at Unterschlauersbach, Roth, and Fürth. The 453rd Bomb Group's target was the Blumenthal jet aircraft factory in the city of Fürth, located five miles west of Nuremberg in southern Germany. Blumenthal was turning out aircraft components and the assembly of parts for jet aircraft. An airfield nearby was still providing one of the few remaining safe havens for the jets to take off and land.

On the way to Fürth, the weather was pretty brutal, and it took a long time to reach our target. Our total flight time on this mission exceeded eight hours. By the time we reached the target area, the weather had cleared up somewhat, and we were able to bomb by visual means. The flak was intense over the target. It seemed as if the Germans were finally increasing their efforts to protect their airfields—probably a little too late at this stage of the war. Of course, this would be at the expense of their cities, which by this time had fewer and fewer heavy antiaircraft batteries. A massive effort had been in place since February to send many of these heavy guns to the Eastern Front to counter the thousands of Russian tanks that had been employed during the winter offensive in January.

Despite encountering an unusually heavy barrage of flak, we were able to inflict a great deal of damage to the plant and destroyed a sufficient number of finished aircraft, making this mission a complete success. More enemy aircraft were now being destroyed on the ground than in the air. Our commanders were hoping this would keep the Luftwaffe at bay. To increase the pressure, the 8th sent more bombing raids on jet airfields throughout Germany the very next day, April 9. The three air divisions dropped more than 3,000 tons of bombs on the jet airfields at Oberpfaffenhofen, Fürstenfeldbruck, Schleissheim, Neuburg, Munich/Riem, Lechfeld, Memmingen, Leipheim, and Landsberg. As fast as the Germans were trying to repair damaged airfields, we were destroying them on a daily basis. On April 10, it was our turn again, and the raids were even more massive than the day before. General Doolittle wanted no airfields left for the jets to take off or land for the duration of the war. Although there were more than 300 airfields in Germany, Air Force Intelligence knew exactly where the jet airfields were located. Leaving nothing to chance, airfields even suspected of being available for the Me 262 jets were to be completely destroyed.

MISSION #21: APRIL 10, 1945
TARGET: RECHLIN

With so many major airfields under constant attack by heavy bombers and free-lancing P-51 Mustangs, we believed it was virtually impossible for the Luftwaffe to send up more jets for a massed attack. Yet they did it again on April 10. More than fifty-five Me 262 jets, along with 115 conventional Me 109 and Fw 190 fighters, were scrambled to intercept another massive bombing raid by the American air forces. The US 8th Air Force alone dispatched over 1,300 heavy bombers and more than 900 escort fighters to participate in one of the most destructive bombing raids of the war. Along with the 8th, both the 9th and 15th Air Forces attacked various targets throughout Germany. The focus was on enemy airfields, especially those bases supporting jet aircraft. This day turned out to be one of the most contested air battles in the skies over Germany in 1945.

The 3rd Division had the most targeted airfields, including Neuruppin, Brandenburg/Briest, Zerbst, and Burg bei Magdeburg. A small force was also sent to attack the marshalling yards in Stendal. The 1st Air Division struck an airfield in Oranienburg and a munitions depot in the city. Of the many airfields in the vicinity of Berlin, the one at Oranienburg housed one of the largest concentrations of jet aircraft in northern Germany. Despite numerous raids, the airfield was still operational, indicating its importance to the Luftwaffe. Being so close to Berlin, our bombers from the 1st Air Division were to take the brunt of jet attacks.

Our division's targets included a marshalling yard at Wittenberge and jet airfields at Rechlin, Rechlin/Lärz, and Parchim. The airfield at Parchim had been bombed so heavily in April that we wondered if there was really anything left standing there to destroy. But the Germans had built underground bunkers everywhere, and the main reason for this bombing raid was to apply sufficient pressure to keep the runways from functioning at all. The 453rd Bomb Group's main target was Rechlin/Lärz, where three of our squadrons were assigned to bomb the airfield complex, while another squadron was sent to attack the marshalling yards at Wittenberge.

The Rechlin/Lärz experimental aircraft facility was a huge complex encompassing two separate airfields in close proximity to each other—the larger one at Rechlin and a smaller one at Lärz, just south of the main airfield. The Rechlin Airfield was located approximately 65 miles northwest of Berlin, and it was made the official Luftwaffe testing ground for highly experimental aircraft in 1936. Throughout the war, Rechlin/Lärz was the site of the research, development, and special combat operations wing of the Luftwaffe's jet aircraft, which included the Me 262 jet fighter, Arado Me 440 jet bomber, and Me 143 rocket fighter. The facility housed many buildings for maintenance, aircraft support, engine testing, technical service, personnel barracks, and underground bunkers for the storage of munitions and weapons. Rechlin/Lärz even had its own railway line connected to Germany's national railway grid.

In early April 1945, Albert Speer was alarmed at the increasing numbers of enemy bombing raids. He'd gone to Rechlin/Lärz to discuss possible strategies with Luftwaffe commanders to stem the unending tide of Allied bombers. Germany's cities were being reduced to piles of rubble. Rechlin had become an important staging area for Me 262 jet operations and the Arado jet fighter-bomber for low-level attacks on Russian troops advancing from the Eastern Front. One of the most active

Me 262 fighter groups of JG 7 was operating from Rechlin Airfield. A conventional Fw 190 fighter group, Jagdeschwader 4, was also stationed there. These fighter groups were extensively used to attack American heavy bombers. They were also heavily involved with ground support operations against the Russians.

On this mission, some elements of the 1st Air Division were to join the 2nd Air Division in attacking Rechlin, but the vast majority of the 442 heavy bombers from the 1st Division were sent to bomb targets at Oranienburg. It was there that the opening battle of the day began.

Oberleutnant Walter Schuck, commander of the III./JG 7 jet unit Gruppe based at Oranienburg Airfield, scrambled with seven other Me 262s to attack the first wave of heavy bombers. A German ace pilot, Schuck had learned how to handle the Me 262A-1a jet fighter with deadly precision against heavy bombers. His modification of the classic roller-coaster jet attack enabled him to accomplish what no other jet pilot was ever able to do: destroy four heavy bombers on a single combat mission.

Diving down at a tremendous speed from a distance of about 3,000 to 4,000 feet above the bomber stream, Schuck would select a bomber in one of the flanks of the formation, fire a short burst of cannon fire at one of the inboard engines, then quickly pull up and away before reaching within 650 feet of the bomber to avoid a collision. Because of the Me 262 jet's extreme speed, Schuck could easily climb 1,000 or 2,000 feet back up, then dive again in a matter of seconds to attack another bomber. Repeating this process, he was able to surf-ride the entire length of the bomber stream to bring down four American bombers, one right after another in a matter of minutes.

After Schuck's attack on the fourth bomber, his 206th aerial combat victory, he could see that the struck aircraft was on fire and going down, out of control. It was a B-17 Flying Fortress from the 303rd Bomb Group, named *Henn's Revenge*. Its two right engines hit by Schuck's cannon fire had burst into flames. The falling bomber suddenly exploded at 2,000 feet, breaking up into two pieces, and crashed into a lake about 17 miles northwest of Oranienburg. The pilot, 1st Lt. Robert "Boss" Murray, and six other members of the crew died. Staff Sergeant Vito J. Brunale and Technical Sergeant Carl O. Hammarlund managed to bail out. But Hammarlund was subsequently shot to death by his captors, so Brunale was the sole survivor of the attack.[1]

Flying 5,000 feet above the bomber stream, 1st Lt. Joseph Anthony Peterburs, a P-51 pilot with the 55th Fighter Squadron, 20th Fighter Group, watched with increasing apprehension over Schuck's vicious attack on the third and fourth heavy bombers. Peterburs immediately dove down full throttle at the enemy jet. Closing in fast on the jet's six o'clock position, the charging Mustang spit out machine-gun fire, with hits on the Me 262's left wing and engine. Schuck was pulling up away from his fourth kill when he noticed strikes on his left wing and the attacking

P-51 behind him. He instinctively veered away in a fast dive downward to escape Peterburs's pursuit. Heading in a southerly direction and passing over Berlin, the jet was aflame. Seeing some low cloud cover beneath him, Schuck immediately dove in and bailed out as his aircraft began to disintegrate. Peterburs could clearly see Schuck's jet burning fiercely as it quickly accelerated out of range and dove into the cloud bank.

Because his jet was in an uncontrollable dive at this point, Schuck had great difficulty bailing out of the cockpit. By the time he was successful and able to open his parachute, he was very close to the ground. Spraining both ankles from a hard landing, he managed to quickly gather his open parachute together and lie on the ground, hoping there were no enemy fighters coming around to strafe him in the open field. He was lucky—there were none. It was a standing order for all American fighter pilots to attack enemy pilots, whether in the air with their parachutes open or on the ground, whenever the chance occurred. An experienced German pilot was deemed of high value, likely to be irreplaceable, compared to the loss of an aircraft. Some American pilots followed this order, while many didn't.[2]

Schuck's fellow pilots were also successful in their attacks on the bombers of the 1st Air Division, which lost nine heavies that day. The 3rd Air Division lost an equal number as their bombers were attacked by JG 7's jets from Brandenburg-Briest and more from KG (J) 54 out of the airfield at Magdeburg. The enemy pilots fought with determination and swept into the bomber formations like voracious sharks. Bomber crews reported seeing a new type of aircraft with machine guns blazing from underneath the interceptor's wings. In actuality, they were seeing repeated salvos of R4M rockets being launched against them. Bombers were hit, and a number of escort fighters were shot down.

Our division was fortunate enough to escape jet attack, as our escort fighters did an exceptional job of keeping them at bay. The bomber-to-escort fighter ratio in our division was nearly one to one, with three hundred fifty-seven Liberators and two hundred twenty P-51 Mustangs. Our worry wasn't enemy interceptor attacks, but the heavy antiaircraft batteries surrounding the target area. Bombers from our wing suffered some moderate damage from flak, but the squadron sent to bomb the marshalling yards at Wittenburg lost a Liberator from extremely accurate flak. Nineteen Libs from our division suffered heavy damage from flak. Fortunately, we didn't, but we were hit by some close exploding shells. Raids by heavy bombers from both the 1st and 3rd Air Divisions were much closer to Berlin, and accordingly suffered heavier damage from flak. Even at this late date in the war, the deadly accuracy of the 88 mm antiaircraft guns wasn't to be taken lightly.

The raids on enemy airfields on April 10 were highly successful, with the complete destruction of several important operational bases accommodating JG 7. Despite the stiff resistance put up by enemy interceptors, the 3rd Air Division completely destroyed the airfields at Brandenburg-Briest and Magdeburg. The airfield at Oranienburg suffered heavy damage from bombers of the 1st Air Division. Our target at the Rechlin-Lärz Airfield facility was obliterated. All standing buildings, hangars, and exposed aircraft on the ground were totally destroyed. An estimated 64 aircraft of all types were put out of commission. The runways were especially hard hit and would require weeks of repair before they could become functional once again. Many of the enemy interceptors attacking the 8th's bombers had to find landing fields other than their own base. With all their air bases under constant attack, this was a common occurrence.

However, the successes of these missions came at a price. The ferocity of enemy attacks took its toll that day. The 8th Air Force lost 19 heavy bombers, the most ever by attacks from German Me 262 jet interceptors. Eight escort fighters were shot down, and a number were missing in action or had crash-landed. More than 250 bombers were damaged in the raids. Also, there were several reports of friendly fire between American and Russian fighter aircraft over Berlin. In preparation for their coming offensive to capture the German capital, the Red Army Air Force had increased its air raids in the area. In the coming weeks, virtually all bombing raids and low-level attacks in the Berlin area, and throughout the entire eastern region of Germany, would be taken over by the Russian air forces.

Despite our losses, it was JG 7, the most active Me 262 jet unit in the Luftwaffe, that would suffer the most. With the destruction of twenty-seven Me 262 jets, the unit lost more than 50 percent of their serviceable aircraft. The attacks they made on April 10 cost them dearly. JG 7 would never again be able to put up large numbers of jets to attack American heavy bombers. Inexperienced pilots, some right out of flight training school, had piloted most of the enemy jets that were shot down. Because of the overwhelming numbers of bomber escort fighters, many of the enemy jets were hit multiple times by large groups of pursuing P-47 or P-51 fighters. They never had a chance.

Included in JG 7's losses were many experienced fighter pilots who were irreplaceable. Of note were three *staffel kapitans,* jet squadron commanders. Oberleutnant Walter Wegner, of 1./JG 7, was shot down by P-51 Mustangs near Stendal during raids by the 3rd Air Division. Oberleutnant Walter Wever, of 7./JG 7, was shot down by a P-47 Thunderbolt near Neuruppin. Oberleutnant Franz Schall, of 10./JG 7, was one of the most decorated pilots of JG 7, with a total of 154 victories, which included 17 with the Me 262. Schall attempted to land on a heavily damaged runway at Parchim Airfield, lost control of the aircraft, and flipped over. His jet exploded, killing him instantly.[3]

Several other highly experienced pilots from JG 7 were also killed in the April 10 raids. The dwindling ranks of the unit's fighter pilots continued unabated. The demise of the Luftwaffe's foremost jet interceptor unit began that day. Soon, the advance of Allied troops from the Western Front and Russians from the east eliminated the availability of every jet airfield in northern Germany, forcing all remaining jet units to move south. The subsequent disintegration and end of JG 7 in April was well-documented by Oberst Hermann Buchner, one of the Luftwaffe's highest-scoring Me 262 aces. Buchner narrowly escaped death on April 8, his last combat mission, when he was attacked by a P-51 Mustang while attempting to land his burning jet. Based at Parchim Airfield, Buchner's group, nine staffel of JG 7, was forced to move to southern Germany when American bombing raids totally destroyed the air base.[4]

MISSION #22: APRIL 11, 1945
TARGET: AMBERG

We were included in what would be one of the last massive bombing raids in April, with 1,303 heavy bombers and 913 fighter escorts dispatched by the 8th Air Force. It was also the last mission by the 453rd Bomb Group, and, consequently, my last combat mission flown with the 453rd.

A wide variety of targets throughout Germany were included on this raid. The 1st Air Division, with 445 heavy bombers, attacked a munitions plant at Kraiburg, an oil depot at Freiham, another munitions plant at Landshut, and a marshalling yard at Treuchtlingen. The 3rd Air Division, with 509 heavies, sent a small force to strike marshalling yards at Landshut and Treuchtlingen, along with the 1st Air Division, while the main force was directed to bomb an airfield and marshalling yard at Ingolstadt and at Donauwörth.

Our division was assigned to attack an airfield at Obertraubling and marshalling yards at Neumark and Amberg. Transportation targets were now high on the target list to support the Allied advances to the Elbe River from the west and the Red Army advance from the east. The 453rd Bomb Group was sent to hit an important rail junction at Amberg, located 30 miles east of Nuremberg, deep in the south of Germany, only 25 miles from the Czechoslovakian border. The railway yard was a small but important rail network junction representing a vital link in providing the transport of German troops to the Eastern Front. As the Russians were preparing their assault into Germany from the Oder Front, they'd requested American assistance to bomb key transportation centers in an effort to stymie enemy troop movements. This rail center was one of them.

A force of 73 Liberators was sent to Amberg. The weather was perfect for visual bombing, and we dropped our full load of five 1,000-pound GP bombs exactly on target with excellent results. The resulting destruction of one of the few remaining rail junctions was sure to affect the movement of German troops and supplies.

There was virtually no flak. With over 900 escort fighters accompanying the three air divisions, little enemy resistance was observed in the air. Over 200 fighter escorts, composed of P-47 Thunderbolts and P-51 Mustangs, accompanied our divisional force of 346 heavy bombers. Against such numbers of fighter escorts, the few German Me 262s that were sent up to intercept the 8th turned out to be an exasperated effort. We didn't even hear of any reports of enemy fighters within range of our bomb group. As we banked around to return to Old Buckenham, I saw for the last time our squadron's bombs exploding on the ground. It seemed like such a routine after all these missions, but it was actually a new experience each time we went out.

On the same day we completed our final mission with the 453rd Bomb Group, advance units of Lt. Gen. William Simpson's US 9th Army reached the Elbe River. Late in the afternoon of the next day, on April 12, tanks from the US 83rd Armored Division raced through the suburbs of Magdeburg to reach a bridge just southeast of the city, only to find it destroyed by the Germans. It would take another day before American forces crossed over to the east bank.

Simpson had established five to six divisions across the Elbe River and was hell-bent on driving forward to Berlin. The capital was only 48 miles away. Then Gen. Bradley called him and told him to hold at the Elbe and advance no farther. He was to wait for the arrival of the Russians. Simpson was furious, telling his commander that his army could reach Berlin in two weeks, in which case it would be well ahead of the Red Army. But Bradley told Simpson the order came straight from the top, Gen. Eisenhower. The decision was made two months before, at Yalta. A sorely disappointed Simpson had to settle for sitting at the Elbe River, waiting for the war to end.[5]

On April 12, 1945, Gen. Doolittle ordered the end of Freelance operations. American fighter groups were to cease strafing enemy positions because the American and Russian ground forces were advancing so rapidly from the west and east. He wanted at all costs to prevent friendly fire on Allied troops or prisoners of war still held by the Germans. The incidence of clashes between Western Allied forces and Red Army troops did occur on occasion.[6]

On this same day, our commander-in-chief, President Franklin D. Roosevelt, passed away from a fatal cerebral hemorrhage in Warm Springs, Georgia.[7] We didn't receive notice of this occurrence until the next day, on April 13. It was a very sad day for all of us, and we vowed to commemorate his accomplishments and determination to end the war by carrying on the fight to the end.

Just three days later, on April 16, 1945, Gen. Carl Spaatz, commanding general of the US Strategic Air Forces in Europe, issued a personal message to both Maj. Gen. James Doolittle, the commander of the US 8th Air Force, and Lt. Gen. Nathan Twining, commander of the US 15th Air Force. In the message, Spaatz officially declared the cessation of the strategic air war waged against Germany by the AAF and RAF Bomber Command. The close of the strategic bombing campaign was the result of advances made by Allied forces on the ground as Germany was quickly being overrun. The Strategic Air Forces would now operate with tactical forces, such as the US 9th Air Force, in close cooperation with Allied ground forces, to complete the final phase of operations in the defeat of Germany.[8]

The US 8th Air Force completed its 10 final bombing raids in Germany within the remaining weeks of April. The last heavy bombing mission occurred on April 25, with the 2nd Air Division bomb groups hitting rail targets in Bad Reichenhall, Hallein, Salzburg, and Traunstein. There were no more major industrial targets to bomb. German plants and factories had all been destroyed or rendered unusable. All oil targets had been eliminated. The shortage of fuel was so severe that the German Air Force was essentially grounded. There was only enough aviation fuel to supply the few aircraft that were still able to fly combat sorties. The communications and transport systems suffered so much damage that movement of traffic within Germany was in a virtual state of paralysis. Most of Germany was no longer enemy territory, its major industrial cities devastated and reduced to rubble. Only tactical bombing missions in support of the advancing Allied ground forces remained to be addressed.

With the end of the Allied strategic air war, the 453rd Bombardment Group (H) was ordered to stand down. With its first combat mission on February 5, 1943, and the last on April 11, 1945, the 453rd Bomb Group had participated in 259 bombing missions with B-24 Liberators in the ETO. Our crew flew a total of 22 successful missions, and our combat tour was pretty much over. Earlier in the war, from February 1942 to April 1944, when losses were high, the operational staff and flight surgeons had established a tour of duty to be 20 missions. At that time, the loss rate was running about 5 percent MIA (missing in action) per mission. With those numbers, the chances of surviving a single mission would be 5 percent, but on 10 missions, a crew member would have used up 50 percent, or half, of their chances of survival. At 20 missions, they were living on borrowed time.[9]

As survivability increased with the added support of escort fighters, defeat of the Luftwaffe, and air superiority of Allied air forces, the tour of duty was extended to 25, then 30, and finally 35 missions. Our tour of duty was to be 35 missions, but it was cut short because of the end of the strategic air war. The estimates for determining the length of a tour of duty proved to be accurate because those who returned to the States after completing a 30-mission tour were considered very lucky and constituted less than one-fifth of all the aircrews that were sent to the ETO. Prior to April 1944, the vast number of crews lost by the 8th Air Force often exceeded 10 percent MIA on some missions.[10] We were indeed fortunate that the Luftwaffe had been defeated well before our arrival to the 453rd Bomb Group. It was the sacrifice of those crew members during the air campaigns of 1943 and 1944 that made it possible for us to achieve what we did. That was foremost in my mind as our crew awaited further orders.

OPERATION BERLIN

Joseph Stalin was ecstatic when he received the telegram Gen. Eisenhower sent on March 28, 1945, stating that the Western Allies would halt at the Elbe River and not target Berlin as a strategic objective. Ever since the Red Army had pushed the Germans out of Russia, Stalin's ultimate goal was to capture Berlin as a symbolic military and political victory for the Russian people. He felt it was their right as a nation that had suffered so much under the Nazi occupation. Stalin was therefore eager to take the German capital as soon as possible.

On April 1, he called his two top field commanders, Marshal Georgy Konstatinovich Zhukov and Marshal Ivan Stepanovich Konev, back to Moscow for a meeting at the Kremlin. Zhukov was Stalin's favorite general, a brilliant strategist and ruthless commander who never lost a battle. He could be trusted to successfully carry out any order that came from Stalin. A professional soldier, Zhukov entered military service at the age of nineteen in 1915. He then joined an elite cavalry brigade in the division commanded by Semyon Mikhailovich Budyonny, a hero of the Russian Revolution. Stalin greatly admired Zhukov's military accomplishments under Budyonny. In 1922, Zhukov attended the War Academy in Berlin to learn the techniques of modern warfare using mechanized tanks, armor, and mobile infantry tactics. He made good use of this knowledge when he defeated the mighty German Army at the battle of Kursk, one of the most famous tank battles in World War II.[11]

Compared to Zhukov, who was short and stocky, Konev was taller, more slender in build, and a year younger. Konev had worked as a lumberjack in a village near Vologda, about 250 miles north of Moscow. He was drafted into an artillery unit during the First World War and served out his tour as a noncommissioned officer. Unlike Zhukov, who continued with his military career to rise up through the ranks as an officer, Konev delayed his army aspirations by becoming a political commissar during the Russian Revolution. He then rejoined the army and was sent to the Frunze Military Academy for officer training. As a trusted member of the Communist Party, he then returned to the academy and trained as a party member for special intelligence and security operations. Then Konev rose through the ranks to become a lieutenant general.[12]

During the Russian-Japanese border conflict in 1939, Konev was sent on a special mission to dislodge the Japanese incursions into Mongolia. He was unable to accomplish his mission and was subsequently replaced by Zhukov. With his superior military acumen, Zhukov easily accomplished the task. From that point on, Konev had an intense hatred toward Zhukov. That hatred was reciprocated by Zhukov because of his extreme distaste for the infiltration of hard-core Communist Party members into the senior ranks of the military. Konev had caught Stalin's eye during the mass executions of Red Army officers when Stalin began the infamous military purges of 1939, in which Konev played a key role.

Stalin also greatly admired Konev's extreme brutality as a military commander. In February 1944, twenty thousand German soldiers were trapped in a region near Korsun in Ukraine. Konev ordered that no prisoners be taken alive, so he sent his tanks along with the Cossack heavy cavalry to cut them to pieces. This was to be known as the Korsun Massacre. Konev was every bit as brutal as any German SS commander, and he relished that fact. Stalin was keenly aware of the deep rivalry between his two top generals. He knew such animosity would benefit him in the end, so he craftily played one against the other.

At the Kremlin meeting, Stalin discussed the telegram he'd received from Eisenhower regarding plans for the Americans and Russians to link up at the Elbe River in the Leipzig/Dresden area. Stalin had lied to Eisenhower, saying that he agreed that Berlin was no longer a strategic objective and that the main Red Army forces would advance to the south. Stalin was still in a state of paranoia concerning the Western Allies' military objectives. Churchill never trusted Stalin, knowing well his intentions to subjugate the liberated countries to a communist rule. Likewise, Stalin saw the Western Allies only as an obstacle to his territorial aspirations, and he intended to use them to his advantage in the game of war. He speculated about their possible intentions to divert him from his ultimate goal of capturing Berlin. So he told Zhukov and Konev that the Allies were secretly planning to take Berlin and thus usurp Russia's ultimate prize.

Stalin then asked them who would be the first to take the city—the Allies or the Red Army? Konev was the first to answer. He said his armies could take Berlin before the Allies. Stalin reminded them of the urgency of the mission and ordered each of them to immediately draw up plans to capture Berlin. Both Zhukov and Konev worked feverishly during the next few days, and on the morning of April 3, they presented their plans to Stalin.

Zhukov's 1st Belorussian Front would have eight armies stretched along the Oder River from Gruben in the south to just above Schwedt in the north. Konev's 1st Ukrainian Front would have five armies on the Neisse River, farther south of the 1st Belorussian Front.

Stalin, from the very beginning, wanted Zhukov to be the one to take Berlin. The commander was ordered to mass his troops and attack along the bridgeheads on the Oder River north and south of Küstrin. From there, the outskirts of Berlin were only 40 miles from the Oder. This would give Zhukov's armies the quickest and shortest route straight into the capital along the *Reichstrasse 1*, the main auto-bahn to the city from the Oder River. Konev's armies were to attack westward from the Oder/Neisse River bridgeheads, targeting Potsdam and Brandenburg in the north and linking up with the American forces when they reached the Elbe River.

Stalin knew that both Zhukov and Konev wanted to be the victor, so he drew a line on the map extending from Lübben through Teupitz and Mittenwalde. He told them that the line would represent the boundary between the 1st Belorussian Front and 1st Ukrainian Front. Whoever reached that line first would be in the best position to attack Berlin. The commanders then rushed back to their respective headquarters to make the final preparations for the Russian offensive known as the Berlin Operation.

The race to capture Berlin was on.

Five days after our final mission with the 453rd Bombardment Group and the same day Gen. Spaatz ordered the end of strategic air operations, the Russian offensive began. On April 16, 1945, at five in the morning, Zhukov began his attack with a tremendous artillery barrage from thousands of guns firing simultaneously. The ground shook so violently that shock tremors were felt in Berlin. The early-morning sky lit up as bright as day. Huge mounds of dirt and dust rose quickly into the air for hundreds of feet. It seemed as if nothing could survive such devastation.

The Red Army almost always attacked with an overwhelming advantage. In this case, Stalin made sure the offensive would be unstoppable. Zhukov and Konev together had over 2.5 million men on the front lines, composed of over 17 armies totaling 190 fully equipped divisions. Along with over 16,000 tanks, self-propelled guns, and motorized vehicles were thousands of aircraft for air support. With such a formidable force, Stalin's plan was to crush all resistance and capture Berlin in a week's time.

Only one German Army group, Army Group Vistula, was to defend Berlin against the Russian onslaught. Its commander was Col. Gen. Gotthard Heinrici, a professional soldier descended from an aristocratic family consisting of military generals stretching back six centuries. Heinrici was a short, stocky individual with steely blue eyes, graying hair, and a short mustache. Unlike other officers of the Wehrmacht, he rarely wore a general staff uniform and preferred more casual attire, such as a sheepskin jacket and World War I-style leather leggings. Heinrici was noted for his outstanding ability to command respect from and authority over every-one who served under him. And he'd gained a reputation for defending untenable positions. In 1942, during the invasion of Russia under the most horrifying winter conditions, Heinrici steadfastly held the German 4th Army in sight of Moscow for 10 straight weeks while defending his command against everything the Red Army could muster against him.

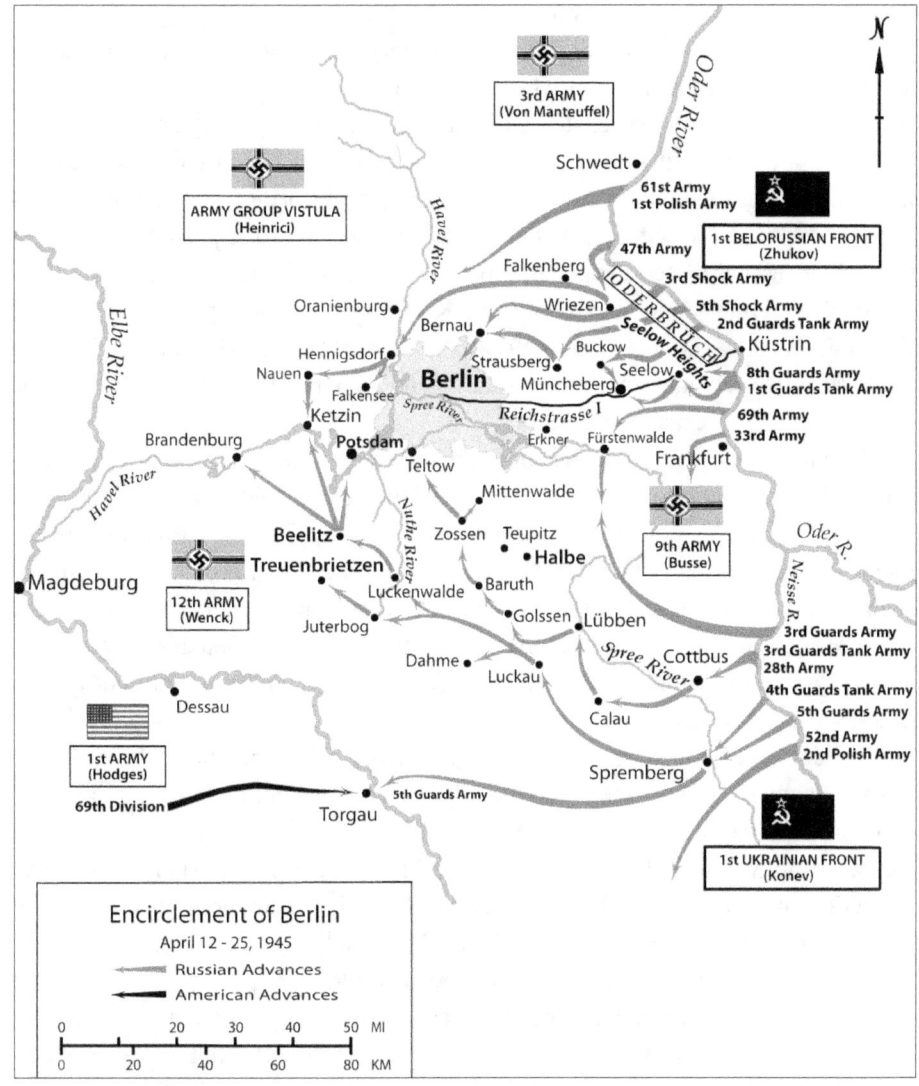

In early March 1945, Col. Gen. Heinz Guderian chose Heinrici to replace Heinrich Himmler as commander of Army Group Vistula. Guderian knew he'd chosen the right man for such a tough job, and Heinrici took command of Army Group Vistula on March 20, 1945. It would be one of the last important military decisions Guderian made as chief of staff of OKW, because just eight days later, on March 28, he was relieved of his command. This fateful event took place in a situation meeting with Hitler and his staff. The Führer was extremely upset at Gen. Theodore Busse's 9th Army's failure to prevent the loss of Küstrin on the Oder from an attack by Zhukov's 8th Guards Army.

Hitler went on a lengthy tirade lambasting Busse until Guderian stepped in to defend his general. In the conversation that ensued between Hitler and Guderian, the initially calm discussion escalated into a fiery shouting match when Guderian lost his temper. At the moment when it seemed as if a physical confrontation between the two men would ensue, Guderian's adjutant, Maj. Freytag von Loringhoven, stepped in to pull Guderian away from the meeting. An urgent message from the front had just been received, so Guderian and Von Loringhoven left the conference room. After the meeting, Hitler relieved Guderian of his position as chief of staff of OKW and forced the general to take a leave of absence for health reasons. In his place, Hitler appointed Gen. Hans Krebs, Guderian's deputy chief of staff. Krebs wasn't a Nazi, but he was well-liked by Hitler. He was also a close friend of Hitler's private secretary, Martin Bormann, and an opportunist who welcomed the chance for such an esteemed position.[13]

When Heinrici took over the command of Army Group Vistula, he and Guderian had long discussions concerning the futility of stopping the Russians from capturing Berlin. As defender of the Oder Front, Army Group Vistula was the last major military obstacle between the Red Army and Berlin. To accomplish this seemingly impossible task, Heinrici had only two armies at his disposal. In the north was the German 3rd Panzer Army, commanded by Col. Gen. Hasso von Manteuffel standing in front of Rokossovsky's 2nd Belorussian Front. South of Berlin, Busse's 9th Army faced Zhukov's 1st Belorussian Front at the Küstrin bridgeheads on the Oder River. Altogether there were only 25 divisions available to Army Group Vistula, many of which were both woefully lacking in material and equipment and composed of a large majority of inexperienced troops. At this point in the war, the lack of manpower meant that most of the Wehrmacht's army divisions were at just a fraction of their normal fighting strength. In fact, the majority of divisions of Busse's 9th Army consisted of fewer than 4,000 men.[14]

With such meager forces, Heinrici knew it would be impossible to prevent the advance of the Red Army into Berlin. He agreed with Guderian that the only way to prevent the capital from destruction was for the battle of Berlin to take place outside the city. Heinrici's main strategic objective was to slow Zhukov's armies long enough so that the Western Allied forces might be able to cross the Elbe River and capture Berlin before the Russians. If this happened, Hitler would then be forced to surrender or negotiate an armistice. In this manner, Heinrici hoped Berlin would be saved from total destruction.

Knowing firsthand the vast destruction laid waste, especially in terms of human lives, from the German forces' invasion of Russia, Heinrici wanted at all costs to save Berlin and its inhabitants from the vengeance of the Red Army. He'd seen what the Russian troops had done to the German people in Silesia and East Prussia, and he desperately wanted to prevent Berlin from becoming another Stalingrad. He would try to pull out all German troops from the city to fight the advancing Red

Army before they reached the capital. In the coming weeks, Heinrici would do everything in his power to achieve this one goal.

But Hitler, with his usual inexplicable reasons for making decisions that didn't seem logical at all, took a big step in derailing Heinrici's defensive efforts on the Oder Front. In the beginning of April 1945, the Führer ordered three of Heinrici's most powerful divisions held as reserves—the 10th SS Panzer Division, 25th Panzer Division, and 18th Panzer Grenadier Division—to be removed from Army Group Vistula and sent elsewhere. To Heinrici, Hitler's decision to further weaken the forces facing the greatest threat to the Third Reich seemed beyond normal military sensibilities. But during the final weeks of the war, Hitler's generals could plainly see he wasn't normal at all, physically or mentally. Without adequate military reserves, Heinrici knew he wouldn't be able to hold the Oder Front for long. But he formulated his plans the best he could with what forces he had.

The key sector in Heinrici's defense of the Oder Front was a natural geographical formation known as the Seelow Heights. The Heights was a steep escarpment rising to a height of 132 feet above a huge floodplain known as the Oderbruch, bordering the west bank of the Oder River. This time of year, the ground was a wet morass from ice and snow melts. The Oderbruch was made even more of an obstacle to enemy movements when the Germans opened the sluice gates of an artificial lake directly upstream of the Oder River. This flooded the Oderbruch to a level of approximately three feet in depth. The entire floodplain was now a soggy, muddy, and swampy impediment, which would drastically slow down any kind of advance made by the Red Army.

The main force facing Zhukov's armies in the Seelow defense sector was the German 9th Army's LVI Panzer Corps. It was Busse's strongest unit and would take the brunt of the initial attack by the Russian 1st Belorussian Front's 8th Guards Army and 1st Tank Army. The LVI Panzer Corps was commanded by Lt. Gen. Helmuth Weidling. Once a distinguished unit, it was now only a shell of its former self. It was composed mostly of the remnants from various divisions, including Göring's 9th Parachute Division, the 20th Panzergrenadier Division, and the Müncheberg Panzer Division. Altogether, the corps had a combined total of only about 15,000 men. But Weidling, a fifty-four-year-old veteran of World War I, was a very tough character. He sported a rimless monocle screwed onto his right eye, and as the former commander of the 56th Artillery Regiment, he was well-regarded as an experienced artilleryman.

Weidling ordered his artillery commander, Col. Hans-Oscar Wöhlermann, to place multiple batteries of the corps's 88 mm heavy artillery atop Seelow Heights. From there, Wöhlermann had a spectacular view of the entire Oderbruch, the Russian bridgeheads, and all the main roads leading to Seelow, Dolgelin, and other towns in the valley below. It would be Wöhlermann's job to put a significant dent in the well-armored advance of the Red Army tanks and infantry through the Seelow defense zone. The colonel's only worry was having enough supplies and ammunition on hand to support a prolonged and sustained effort in slowing down the enemy's advance. Like many of Busse's forces, men and material were seriously lacking, with many units having enough ammunition to last just a few days.

Heinrici had established three defense zones facing the Oder River. The first was 5.5 miles from the western bank of the river, called the Hauptkampflinie, or HKL, defensive zone. Wöhlermann and his forces were situated at the second Hardenburg-Stellung defensive zone within the Seelow sector, which was another 5.5 miles behind the HKL. The third and final Wotan-Stellung defensive zone, approximately nine miles from the second, was located at the town of Muncheberg on the Reichstrasse 1. Heinrici had placed all his heavy 88 mm guns and anti-tank artillery in the Hardenburg-Stellung defensive zone, which included Wöhlermann's units on Seelow Heights. Overlapping fields of fire from these heavy guns were to support the frontline units in the HKL defensive zone.[15]

As the HKL was intended to be the initial stopping point against the advancing Red Army forces, this defensive zone was the most fortified. It consisted of tight, interlocking strong points employing a continuous array of trenches and pillboxes. Many of the light and medium infantry artillery and anti-tank guns were placed in this sector. In front of the HKL were numerous anti-personnel and anti-tank minefields to slow the initial wave of Russian attacks. Anticipating an attack from Zhukov's bridgeheads at Küstrin, the Germans had spent most of March building up the extensive fortifications of the HKL, yet it was still incomplete when the Russian offensive began.

From his experience with Red Army tactics during Germany's invasion of Russia, Heinrici was well-acquainted with the manner in which the Russians would launch their attack. First, there would be an intensive artillery bombardment of the front lines to disrupt and decimate the enemy troops and armored emplacements. Then a massive wave of tanks and infantry would storm the shocked and dazed German troop positions. He was counting on Zhukov doing just what he was anticipating.

Heinrici was correct.

From interrogated Russian prisoners, he knew exactly when Zhukov would attack. It was to be in the early-morning hours of April 16. So Heinrici ordered Busse's frontline troops to move back to the second defensive position within the HKL defensive zone, which was approximately five miles behind the front lines. This was quietly done in the late-evening hours of April 15.

Zhukov's 1st Belorussian Front began its attack in the early-morning hours of April 16, 1945, with perhaps the largest artillery bombardment in the Second World War, if not all military history. Almost half a million artillery shells fell on virtually empty German positions on the front lines of the HKL. As Heinrici had predicted, the massive stream of tanks, self-propelled guns, armored vehicles, and infantry rushed forward. But they met little resistance until they reached the second HKL defensive position.

Then all hell broke loose.

German tanks moved in against them as heavy artillery and mortar fire rained down from above. As the roads became clogged with burning Russian tanks and hulking wrecks of armored vehicles, the withering fire from the German positions increased even more. The attacking waves of Russian infantry found themselves caught in the open with practically no cover in the soggy, flooded terrain of the Oderbruch. Confusion and chaos spread among the Russian forces as their forward advance slowed to an abysmal crawl.

Zhukov, pacing feverishly in his headquarters, was becoming more and more disgusted at the incoming reports of the slow advance of Col. Gen. Chuikov's 8th Guards Army into the Seelow sector. Zhukov had especially chosen Chuikov's army, together with Col. Gen. Mikhail Katukov's 1st Guards Tank Army, to be the spearhead of the Russian forces to break through the Seelow defensive sector. Chuikov, known as the Hero of Stalingrad, was Zhukov's top field commander, who had one of the most glowing reputations in Russia for his battlefield accomplishments. Zhukov was counting on his 8th Guards Army to quickly clear the Oderbruch of enemy resistance for an assault on Seelow Heights by the 1st and 2nd Guards Tank Armies.

Zhukov told Chuikov to move all his units forward at once, or severe consequences would follow. All of Stalin's top generals were ruthless, and Zhukov was no exception. Chuikov knew exactly what his commander meant. However, Zhukov's demands were to no avail. Chuikov's forces were completely mired in the Oderbruch. In his desperation to break the gridlock, Zhukov ordered more tanks from the 1st and 2nd Guards Tank Armies to enter the fray. This made the situation even worse. The result was a total disaster.

To rush the Red Army tanks through, the infantry vehicles and artillery had to be pushed off the roads onto the soft, muddy ground of the Oderbruch. Without artillery support, the Russian troops were at the mercy of hardened German gun emplacements as well as artillery fire from atop Seelow Heights. As a result, hundreds of advancing Russian soldiers were slaughtered. By the end of the day, Chuikov's forces had barely advanced through the German HKL defensive perimeter toward the outskirts of Seelow.

At midnight, Zhukov telephoned Stalin and informed him of the problems facing his armies at Seelow. Zhukov had grossly miscalculated the extremely strong German resistance in the Oderbruch and the fierceness of its defenders against his forces. His blunders included the ill-fated tactic of trying to punch through the German front line with the addition of more armor in an already precarious and failing situation. His forces had advanced only two or three miles, but no breakthrough was in sight. Zhukov then promised Stalin it would happen the next day.

Stalin wasn't happy at all about the situation. In fact, he vehemently reiterated the need to quickly advance as soon as possible. To increase the pressure on Zhukov, Stalin told his general that he was thinking of ordering Konev's advancing armies to swing toward Berlin from the south. Konev's lead armies, Marshal Pavel S. Rybalko's 3rd Guards Tank Army and Gen. D. D. Lelyushenko's 4th Guards Tank Army, had met little German resistance. They'd advanced to a depth of nearly nine miles in the Cottbus/Spremberg sector located south of Zhukov's 1st Belorussian Front. Zhukov didn't find out until the next day that Stalin had actually carried out his threat. Shortly after their conversation, he had ordered Konev to move two of his lead armies toward the southern suburbs of Berlin. With Zhukov's armies stalled at the Oderbruch, Konev immediately jumped at the opportunity to overtake his opponent.

In the early-morning hours of April 17, Zhukov's forces resumed their attacks. It began with a heavy bombing raid by Russian Ilyushin IL-2 Shturmovik fighter-bombers on the German fortified defenses, including Wöhlermann's artillery units atop Seelow Heights. Then an intensive artillery bombardment ensued, followed by Chuikov's 8th Guards Army and Katukov's 1st Guards Tank Army continuing their advance into the Seelow sector. By early afternoon, Red Army forces had penetrated the Seelow defensive zone and reached the escarpment of Seelow Heights. The Russian forces soon discovered that the only way to take it was with a direct assault. However, it was impossible for tanks or any type of vehicle to successfully climb the steep slopes leading up to Wöhlermann's entrenched positions. Chuikov's attack went on for hours without success.

An extremely frustrated Zhukov then ordered all his commanders to personally go to the front lines and achieve a breakthrough at any cost. To a Russian commander, this meant only one thing: throw more troops into the fight. Wave after wave of Chuikov's infantry charged forward. They were mercilessly cut down from intense enemy fire from the fortified slopes leading up to the heights. Their losses were horrific. Thousands perished. The German positions atop the heights remained unscathed. However, Wöhlermann then realized his greatest fear: his troops were running out of ammunition. In fact, all of Busse's corps in the Seelow sector were in the same position, with some units wholly without ammunition and artillery shells.

Failing to neutralize the German forces atop Seelow Heights, Chuikov's and Katukov's forces had better luck with towns near the impenetrable escarpment. The overwhelming numbers of enemy troops quickly overran the German defenders, with Dierdersdorf and later Dolgelin falling to the Russians. Seelow soon followed. Likewise, south of Seelow, Busse's XI SS Panzer Corps suffered heavy casualties from the onslaught of Red Army armor and infantry. Under the constant attack by enemy air strikes and heavy artillery bombardment, the German XI Corps was forced to fall back to the third Wotan-Stellung defensive zone.

North of Seelow Heights, a big battle developed between forces of Busse's CI Corps and two of Zhukov's armies, Lt. Gen. F. I. Perkhorovich's 47th Army and Gen. V. I. Kuznetsov's 3rd Shock Army. The terrific melee of tanks against tanks and infantry against infantry resulted in heavy losses on both sides. Many German units put up a fierce defense and fought to the last man. By nightfall, the battle continued unabated. Russian air strikes, artillery bombardments, and Katyusha rocket attacks were so overwhelming that the key defensive town of Wriezen was engulfed in a firestorm.

As bad as the second day went for the Germans, the third day, April 18, was even worse. Willing to sacrifice unending streams of armor and troops, Zhukov's armies steadily forced their way through the Hardenburg-Stellung second defensive zone. The use of heavy air strikes and artillery fire paved the way for Gen. S. I. Bogdanov's 2nd Guards Tank Army and Chuikov's 8th Guards Army on the Reichstrasse 1 autobahn to push the German defenders from the Seelow sector.

As Russian forces advanced toward Münchberg, Heinrici received a call from Busse in the afternoon, reporting several breaches in the German lines by enemy forces. The severe loss of German soldiers and equipment during the previous two days couldn't be filled by replacements. The three reserve divisions that Hitler took away from Heinrici in early April now made their absence felt. The only troops left in Berlin were several Volkssturm units. Without any more reserves on the front, Heinrici asked Hitler for more troops. Hitler assured him that they would be immediately sent to the front. As a result, Heinrici successfully removed all available fighting troops from Berlin, which was his original intention in order to save the capital. However, circumstances beyond his control would soon upend his entire plan.

Meanwhile, Chuikov's and Bogdanov's armies marched through Seelow virtually cleared of German troops. Farther north of Seelow Heights, the breach between Busse's CI Corps and Weidling's LVI Panzer Corps on the Wriezen/Buckow front line enabled Col. Gen. Nikolai E. Berzarin's 5th Shock Army and Bogdanov's 2nd Tank Army to advance unopposed toward Münchberg. German resistance slackened appreciably as their troops ran out of ammunition as well as fuel for tanks and vehicles. Busse's forces had done their best to stem the Russian advance, but they were swept aside by the sheer numbers of Russian armor and infantry. There was no other choice for Busse's CI Corps but to fall back toward the Wotan-Stellung, the third and final defensive zone at Münchberg.

With the Russians advancing north and south of Seelow Heights, the LVI Panzer Corps was in danger of being cut off from the main bulk of Busse's 9th Army. Weidling was forced to abandon Seelow Heights and retreat to a more defensible position. Busse informed Heinrici that the entire German 9th Army was being broken up into three pieces by the unstoppable waves of Russian armies. What forces remained were being inexorably pushed westward. The German retreat along

Reichstrasse 1 was both horrendous and chaotic as hundreds of vehicles, soldiers, horses, carts, and fleeing refugees jammed the road for miles.

On April 20, Münchberg fell to the Red Army, and the way was cleared on Reichstrasse 1 for Chuikov's 8th Guards Army and Katukov's 1st Guards Tank Army to advance into the eastern suburbs of Berlin. Zhukov's armies' breakthrough of the Wotan-Stellung defensive zone and the capture of Wriezen and Buckow in the north marked the beginning of the end for the battle of Berlin. With Weidling's LVI Panzer Corps pushed back to Bernau in the northern outskirts of Berlin, there was effectively no German front line extant to prevent the Russian armies from advancing into the city.

The defense of the Oder Front was now over.

What remained of Busse's 9th Army withdrew into the Spreewald forest just southwest of Berlin. Heinrici's insistence to Hitler that the German 9th Army should retreat back toward Berlin fell on deaf ears. Hitler adamantly refused. He demanded that the 9th Army stand and fight to the last man. Any officer who refused to comply with that order would be immediately arrested and executed. At that point, Heinrici realized Busse's 9th Army was doomed.

With hardly a passing concern for the collapse of the Oder Front, Hitler celebrated his fifty-sixth birthday on April 20. All the important Nazis Party officials came to pay their respects, but it was a far cry from just a few years before, when thousands cheered the Führer on such a festive occasion. In private, everyone but Hitler admitted that the war was lost. Ever since the attempt on his life in July 1944, Hitler hadn't been the same man he used to be. According to Maj. Freytag von Loringhoven, who resided in the Führerbunker with Hitler, there had been a dramatic change in his appearance since the botched assassination incident.

Major Von Loringhoven became Gen. Krebs's adjutant when Col. Gen. Guderian was relieved of his command. Krebs, along with the major, had come at the end of January 1945 to reside in the bunker with Hitler as liaison to the OKW German High Command. It was Von Loringhoven's responsibility to handle military communication reports between the front lines and the Führerbunker. When Von Loringhoven saw Hitler, he was shocked at his changed appearance.

The Führer was hunched over and walked with a painful gait, dragging his left leg behind him. His eyes were dull, and his skin had a grayish-white tinge. He used his right hand to hold his left arm to keep it from trembling. What Von Loringhoven saw in front of him wasn't the highly energetic and exuberant leader he'd seen in the past. Now Hitler seemed to be a senile old man.

When Heinrici met Hitler in Berlin on April 5, 1945, the general's observations were even more poignant. The leader of the Third Reich not only appeared to be a man who would not live more than twenty-four hours, but he resembled a walking corpse.

The assassination attempt did leave Hitler with minor injuries. But he also had a medical affliction affecting his left foot. His physical condition was exacerbated from the many years of daily drug abuse administered by his personal physician, Dr. Theodore Morell.

Being more of a quack than a genuine medical doctor, Morell had been injecting Hitler intravenously with an enormous variety of drugs, some of which the so-called doctor had concocted himself. Morell was actually slowly poisoning Hitler, injecting him with mixtures that included toxic substances, such as strychnine and belladonna. Hitler, in essence, became a drug addict.

Not a word was said regarding the obvious physical deterioration of the Führer's appearance, at least not in public.

As a gift for the Führer's birthday, the US 8th Air Force staged its last massive bombing raid on Berlin. In fact, it was one of the final raids by the 8th, which would end all heavy bomber missions on April 25. Marshalling yards and railway facilities in the Berlin area were peppered with nearly 2,000 tons of bombs. Huge fires burned uncontrollably throughout the city. The Red Army Air Force was becoming more and more active in its bombing raids throughout eastern Germany. Its bombers replaced the sight of American heavies over the skies of Berlin.

In honor of the Führer's birthday, special rations were to be given to the citizens of Berlin. After the American bombing raid ended that morning, hordes of Berliners came out from their shelters and bunkers to seek water and line up at shops distributing much appreciated meat, vegetables, and other food rations. Everyone appeared to be in a more pleasant mood while receiving such precious gifts, when suddenly the unspeakable happened. The Red Army presented its welcome to the city by firing the first salvos of heavy artillery directly into Berlin. High-explosive shells rained down over the city. The resulting chaotic, horrific effects of the barrage were ghastly and unimaginable. There were a great number of civilian casualties.[16]

The advance forces of Kuznetsov's 3rd Shock Army had reached an area west of Werneuchen, just 15 miles northwest of Berlin. Long-range artillery from the 79th Rifle Corps launched its first salvos into the city center at 1:50 p.m. By late evening, another massive barrage was to hit the area around the Reichstag. Very soon, the Red Army would bring up the heavy siege guns captured from the Germans in Silesia to bombard Berlin. From this day forward, the city wouldn't escape the pounding by Russian artillery, which was virtually continuous, day and night, until war's end. If the hundreds of air raids weren't enough, then millions of exploding shells eventually turned the great metropolis into heaps of dust and rubble.

The uninterrupted shelling by Russian artillery didn't prevent Hitler from surfacing from the Führerbunker into the Reich Chancellery garden to inspect and give medals to distinguished soldiers of the SS Frundsberg Division and young boys of the Hitler Youth brigades. Many of the Youth's "combat veterans" were of high school age and trained for one specific purpose: to attack Red Army tanks with handheld Panzerfausts. This weapon was a portable form of a rocket-propelled grenade, similar to the American bazooka but much more effective. With imminent attack by the Russians in the streets of Berlin, hundreds of Hitler Youth brigades were scattered throughout the city to destroy enemy tanks.

With trembling hands, Hitler would pin a medal onto a boy's uniform and congratulate him for his valor. With exploding shells falling all around him, Hitler then quickly scurried back down into the bunker. It was the last time he would see daylight.

With no substantial German forces inside Berlin to impede them, the Russian armies had reached the outskirts of the Berlin suburbs. All were moving in the direction of the government center, the Mitte district of the capital. In the northeast sector, Perkhorovich's 47th Army, Bogdanov's 2nd Guards Tank Army, and Kuznetsov's 3rd Shock Army advanced with little resistance, while Berzarin's 5th Shock Army drove westward through the eastern suburbs. Chuikov's 8th Guards Army and Katukov's 1st Guards Tank Army swung south of the Grosser Müggelsee to attack toward the southeastern suburbs of the city. Zhukov was keenly aware of Rybalko's 3rd Guards Tank Army's rapid advance into the southern suburbs, and he wanted Chuikov to reach the central district before Konev's lead army.

With the Red Army so close, Hitler ordered Heinrici to take command of the Berlin defensive zone. Because of Hitler's refusal to let the German 9th Army retreat toward Berlin, Busse's forces were now scattered and his main force encircled by Zhukov's 69th and 33rd Armies, in conjunction with elements of Rybalko's 3rd Guards Army attacking from the south. Weidling's LVI Panzer Corps remained the only effective unit from the German 9th Army. He was forced to keep moving his headquarters from the advancing Russian armies. Not wanting to enter the city, Weidling relocated to Köpenick from Bernau, then to Karlshorst, and finally to Rudow in the southeastern suburb of Berlin.

Heinrici had wanted the final battle to take place outside Berlin. He didn't want his troops to be involved in the destructive street-to-street fighting within the city. However, Weidling received a call from both Hitler and Gen. Busse. Hitler ordered Weidling to bring his forces into Berlin, while Busse ordered him to link up with his forces by breaking through the encircled German 9th Army. Weidling had no choice but to follow the Führer's order and would soon enter the city. There were no further communications between the other scattered units of the German 9th Army, and most withdrew westward toward Fürstenwalde. Shortly after Weidling's battered forces entered Berlin, Hitler made the general in charge of the defense of the city the battle commandant of Berlin.

This one event completely negated Heinrici's plan to save Berlin. In fact, it would completely change the course of the fight for the capital. With Weidling and his troops within the city and under Hitler's direct command, Heinrici knew the coming battle would be totally out of his control. He would now concentrate on saving Von Manteuffel's 3rd Army from being encircled like Busse's 9th Army. His goal at this point was to save as many troops as possible from the Russians. Heinrici planned to pull Von Manteuffel's army back as soon as forces from Rokossovsky's 2nd Belorussian Front broke through Von Manteuffel's defensive line at the Oder River. When that happened, Von Manteuffel's forces would initiate a fighting withdrawal to the Elbe River and surrender to the Western Allies.

Heinrici's desire to prevent Berlin from being another Stalingrad had failed. In fact, the battle would be even worse. The Russians' capture of Berlin was the greatest urban battle in military history and resulted in the complete destruction of the city.

The next day, April 21, after Hitler's festivities ended, the great exodus of Nazi officials to escape the coming battle began in earnest. In the end, they weren't willing to die for a lost cause. Reichsminister Joseph Goebbels, as the Reich commissioner for Berlin, declared that no man who was capable of bearing arms would be permitted to leave the city. Those who wanted to leave had to obtain an exemption from the headquarters for the defense of Berlin. On that day alone, over 2,000 permits were issued to high-level Nazi officials, who promptly left the city with their mistresses and other booty collected over the years. Only Goebbels and Reichsleiter Martin Bormann, who were Hitler's closest associates, were to remain in the Führerbunker with him until the end.

It wasn't until April 22 that Hitler finally allowed Busse's 9th Army to pull back from the Oder Front. Of course, it was already too late, as Zhukov's 69th Army from the north and Konev's 3rd Guards Army from the south were in their final phases of encircling the German 9th Army. With the collapse of the Eastern Front, Busse's forces were now separated into three major parts. In the north, Busse's CI Corps was in full retreat, moving westward, while the main force of the 9th Army, which included the XI SS Panzer Corps, V SS Mountain Corps, and other units from the garrison that was stationed at Frankfurt an der Oder, was being encircled by Russian forces. Within days, Busse and about 60,000 troops, along with tens of thousands of refugees fleeing the advancing Russians, would be surrounded by at least two Russian armies in the heavily wooded area of Spreewald just southeast of Berlin. In the south, Weidling and the LVI Panzer Corps were making their way to Berlin.

Hitler then ordered Busse to break out of the encirclement and attack westward to link up with Lt. Gen. Walther Wenck's 12th Army, situated at the Elbe River. Both Busse's and Wenck's armies were then instructed to attack in a northerly direction to save Berlin from the Russians. However, Busse's 9th Army was separated from Wenck's 12th Army by more than 50 miles. After fighting nonstop against overwhelming odds on the Oder Front, Busse knew that such a task would be well-nigh impossible with the reduced forces he had remaining. Yet, that was Führer's order, and Busse had no choice but to comply. OKH agreed with such a plan, and Field Marshal Wilhelm Keitel arrived at Wenck's headquarters on April 23 to personally order Wenck to move away from the Elbe River, advance to the east to meet Busse's 9th Army, and together drive north toward Berlin.

To Wenck, this was pure madness because his forces had neither the strength nor the numbers to break through the Russian lines to relieve Berlin. In reality, the German 12th Army was an entity on paper only. Composed mostly of the few remnants of German units that had survived the disastrous Ardennes Offensive, the 12th Army had little artillery, few self-propelled guns, and only about a dozen tanks. A large number of the officers and noncommissioned officers had been recruited from military training schools, and the rest were supplied by Hitler Youth brigades. In fact, the vast majority of those serving under Wenck were between seventeen and eighteen years of age. Hitler had promised Wenck 10 fully equipped divisions in early April, but he received only a fraction of what was needed to defend the Elbe River against the Western Allies.

In compliance with Keitel's order, Wenck indicated that he would attempt to advance eastward toward the Beelitz/Treuenbrietzen sector. However, instead of saving Berlin, Wenck had plans of his own. In radio contact with Busse, he told him that the 12th Army wouldn't advance eastward to save Berlin. Such an effort would be useless. Instead, he would attempt to link up with the 9th Army for the express purpose of providing an escape route to the west for soldiers and civilians facing the advancing Red Army. Wenck, like all Wehrmacht commanders, realized the war was lost and saw the futility of continued, senseless resistance. He only wanted to save as many German lives as he possibly could.

Wenck and Busse then proceeded to implement a plan to link up, which would lead to what would become known as the Battle of Halbe. Wenck would drive eastward toward Beelitz and Treuenbrietzen while Busse attempted to break through the city of Halbe and advance westward. Attack by Wenck's XX Corps began in the morning of April 24, and, in the succeeding days, they advanced as far as Treuenbrietzen. Then they ran headlong into forward elements of Konev's 4th Guards Tank Army, which was heading toward Brandenburg. Wenck's forces were repulsed with heavy losses on both sides.

The main force of Wenck's XX Corps, advancing to the east to link up with Busse, was then stalled at Beelitz. A large contingent of the XX Corps pushed north, however, and was able to reach the town of Ferch, near Schwielowsee Lake, just eight miles southwest of Potsdam. Lieutenant General Hellmuth Reymann's Army Group Spree, located at the garrison in Potsdam, was able to fight its way through the Russian lines, and more than 20,000 German troops were able to link up with Wenck's 12th Army.

Without any possibility of advancing beyond the Beelitz/Treuenbrietzen sector, Wenck ordered the German line to be held at all costs. Although most of Wenck's troops consisted of young, inexperienced recruits, they were able to hold the line for forty-eight hours against heavy Russian counterattacks until the arrival of what remained of Busse's 9th Army. Considered by many as the greatest break-out of the war, Busse's forces were able to break through three Red Army defensive lines through the Zossen/Baruth sector and Luckenwalde to reach Wenck's forces at Beelitz.

The German forces suffered horrendous losses as they pushed their way through the thick pine forests south of Berlin. They had to fight against at least six Russian armies and ferocious Red Army bomber attacks, all of which were desperate to prevent the link-up of Busse's forces with the German 12th Army. The intense ferocity of the battles was marked by the thousands of graves along the routes heading westward from Halbe to Beelitz. In Halbe alone there exist the buried remains of 30,000 men, which include an unknown number of civilians. At least 20,000 Red Army soldiers also perished.[17]

Although a narrow corridor of about only two miles wide was generated be-tween Busse's forces and units of Wenck's 12th Army at Beelitz, the link-up was a total success. By Wenck's own estimates, roughly 25,000 to 30,000 9th Army troops and 10,000 civilian refugees were rescued before the Russians severed the tenuous link between the German 12th Army and 9th Army forces.

When Busse reached the 12th Army headquarters, he looked as if he had gone through hell. There was no great celebration. Wenck and Busse just shared a glass of champagne, and Busse immediately fell asleep, not having slept for three days. His troops were so tired and fought-out that they couldn't take another step. Wenck had all of them transported to the Elbe River by rail. During the next few days, the 12th Army fell back to Tangermünde on the Elbe River in a fighting retreat from the pursuing Russians. Altogether, more than 100,000 German troops and civilians from the 12th Army, 9th Army, and Reymann's Army Group Spree crossed over the Elbe River and surrendered to the US 9th Army in early May 1945.[18]

Overshadowing the accomplishments of Wenck's 12th Army to save what was left of Busse's 9th Army were two events on April 25, 1945, that would seal the fate of the Third Reich.

The first event occurred at around noon, when leading elements of Perkhor-ovich's 47th Army from the 1st Belorussian Front, advancing from the north, met Dmitry Lelyushenko's 4th Tank Army from the 1st Ukrainian Front in the small town of Ketzin, approximately eight miles northwest of Potsdam. The linking up of Zhukov's and Konev's forces in the western outskirts of Berlin meant that Russian forces had effectively encircled the capital.

Later in the afternoon of the same day, the second event took place just 65 miles south of Berlin. The US 1st Army's 69th Division reached the small town of Torgau on the Elbe River, where American soldiers met forward units of the 1st Ukrainian Front's 5th Guards Army. American and Russian forces had linked up on the Elbe River, and Germany was now completely divided in half. All effective Wehrmacht communications between the northern and southern portions of Germany would soon cease to exist. With the Western Allied forces stationary at the Elbe River, the Red Army would complete the final phase in the defeat of Germany.[19]

The next day, April 26, Heinrici received a call from Von Manteuffel, who told him that his 3rd Panzer Army was very certain to be overrun by armies of Rokossovsky's 2nd Belorussian Front northeast of Berlin. Strict orders from Hitler remained clear: There was to be no retreat. All German units were to stand their ground to the last man. Despite this order, Heinrici gave Von Manteuffel permission to fall back and advance westward to Mecklenburg. Knowing full well about the impending consequences of his act, Heinrici did this without informing Field Marshal Keitel at OKW headquarters or Gen. Krebs at the Führerbunker. During Busse's breakout at Halbe, Heinrici realized the end was near. He'd lost all contact with the German 9th Army. In essence, Army Group Vistula was no longer a coherent entity.

Keitel didn't find out about Von Manteuffel's 3rd Panzer Army retreat until April 29, at which time Heinrici was relieved of his command. Heinrici was then told to report immediately to OKW headquarters to face what would likely have led to a military court-martial. Fearing that such an order would certainly result in a death sentence, Heinrici's senior staff begged their commander to delay his journey as long as possible. With Red Army troops fighting in the streets of Berlin, everyone knew the war would be over in days. That prediction proved to be true, and Heinrici never reached OKW headquarters in time to meet his intended fate. Thus, fifty-eight-year-old Col. Gen. Gotthard Heinrici—the ultimate professional German soldier, who'd served with distinction during Germany's invasion of Russia in 1941 and crafted the defense of the Oder Front—escaped execution and survived the war.[20]

THE FINAL HOURS OF ADOLF HITLER

By the time of Berlin's encirclement, armies of the 1st Belorussian Front and 1st Ukrainian Front had already penetrated deep within the city. In the north, Kuznetsov's 3rd Shock Army had fought its way to the Weissensee district, while Bogdanov's 2nd Guards Tank Army had reached as far as Siemensstadt, just west of the Tiergarten. Berzarin's 5th Shock Army was steadily advancing along the Spree

River toward the Silesian Station east of the city. Chuikov's 8th Guards Army and Katukov's 1st Guards Tank Army had already linked up with Rybalko's 3rd Guards Tank Army coming in from the south at the Schönefeld Airfield. Both Zhukov's and Konev's armies were now fighting their way across the Teltow Canal. All Red Army forces were now quickly converging toward the Mitte government district, where the Reichstag and Reich Chancellery were located.

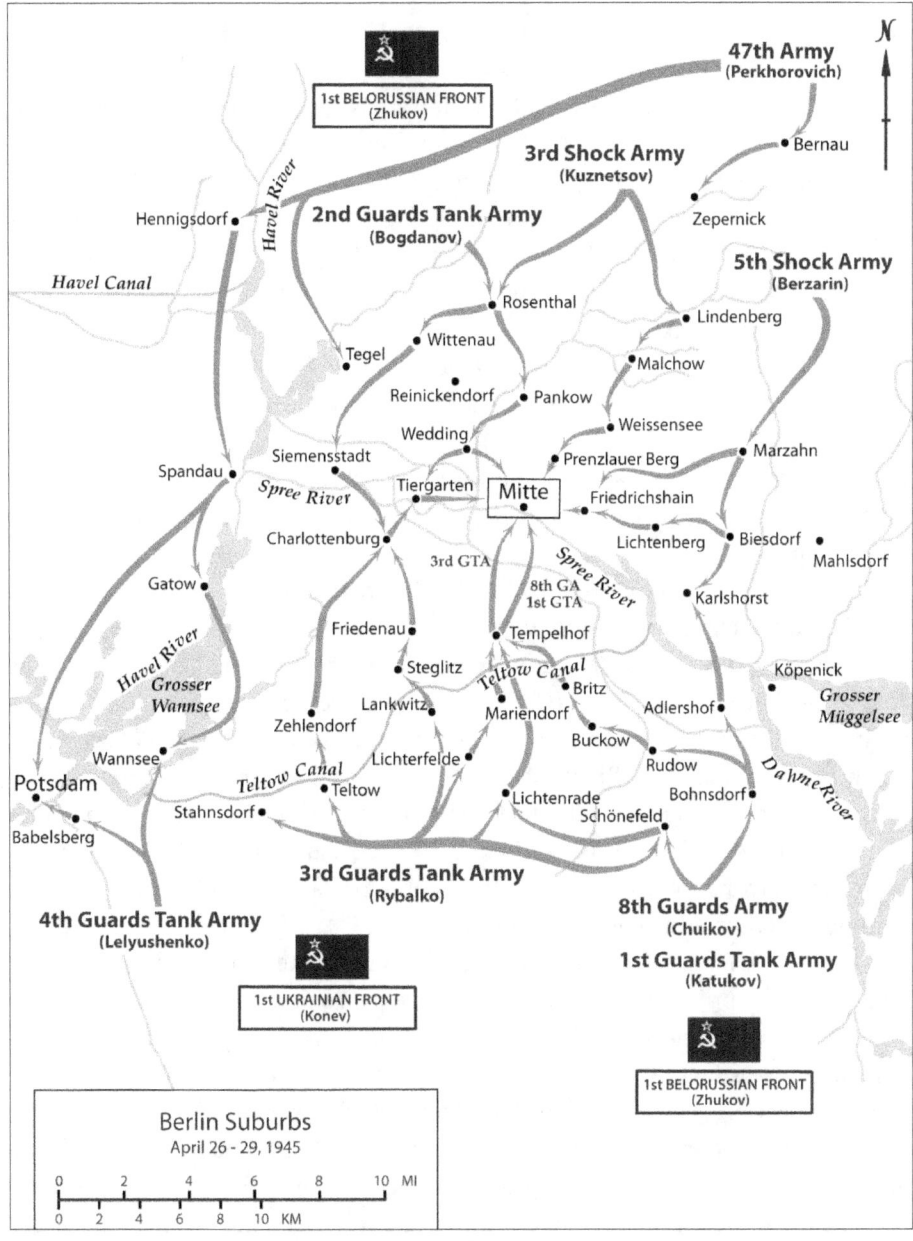

Stalin had given explicit orders to Zhukov to capture the Reichstag and plant the Red Army victory flag above the cupola of that building by May 1. The supreme Russian commander wanted that symbol of conquest to signal Russia's defeat of Germany. It would then be announced during the May Day celebrations in Moscow. As Zhukov planned his final assault on Berlin's government sector, he ordered Chuikov and his other top commanders to enhance their combat operations and continue day and night without stop until the Reichstag was taken. With an overwhelming force of almost half a million troops, 12,000 guns, 21,000 Katyusha multiple rocket launchers, and 1,500 tanks, Zhukov's armies advanced street by street, block by block, and building by building, toward Sector Z, known as the Zitadelle, the last defensive perimeter inside Berlin surrounding the central district.[21]

Within the Zitadelle were the government buildings, the Reichstag, and the Führerbunker, buried 60 feet below the Reich Chancellery. While the bombing raids by the Red Army Air Force and heavy artillery bombardment grew in size and intensity, the Führer and his most loyal Nazi officials hunkered down in the massive concrete bunker.

Hitler had returned to Berlin on January 16, 1945, for the last time and remained in the bunker until the very end. Many of the official government buildings within the Reich Chancellery complex had many of their own underground bunkers, but the sturdiest and strongest was the Führerbunker. It was built beneath another bunker, called the Vorbunker, which led farther down into the deeper Führerbunker.[22]

The Vorbunker consisted of more than 24 small rooms housing Hitler's bodyguards and military attachés from the OKW and OKH, along with a kitchen, pantry, and canteen. Other rooms were provided as living spaces for Hitler's servants and Joseph Goebbels's family. It also housed a 60-watt generator to provide electricity for both bunkers. The passageway leading from the Vorbunker to the Führerbunker below consisted of several flights of stairs and then a long corridor to the entrance of the Führerbunker. A heavily reinforced steel door protected the entrance. Six rooms were designated for Hitler's use, including a lounge and bedrooms for both him and his mistress, Eva Braun. There were other rooms available for additional occupants, bathroom facilities, and conference meetings.

Daily military situation meetings were held in the Reich Chancellery until the beginning of April, when the intensity of enemy bombing raids forced Hitler to hold the meetings inside the Führerbunker. The bunker was solidly constructed with seven-foot-thick walls of reinforced concrete. It was thus impervious to any type of aerial ordnance the Allies had. One notable feature of the Führerbunker was the location of an emergency exit at its far end. At the end of a series of long ascending staircases, an exit door provided access to the surface above and led into the Chancellery garden. Next to the exit were two observation/ventilation towers, one of which was still under construction.

As Zhukov's armies advanced closer and closer to the Zitadelle, enemy resistance stiffened and the fighting intensified. This sector was defended by the most hardened and fanatical Nazi SS troops of the Third Reich. Hitler had designated Maj. Gen. Wilhelm Mohnke as the defensive commandant of Sector Z. Several thousand SS troops were under his command, including Hitler's personal bodyguard unit known as the Leibstandarte Adolf Hitler, all of whom were willing to die without question for their Führer. More and more of Weidling's troops would also be pushed into Sector Z as the defenders fell back toward the city center under the overwhelming attacks of Red Army forces.

Soon the Russian troops were clearing each house or building and advancing block by block, faced with fierce resistance from die-hard German defenders. The battle called for a specialized form of fighting within the city. Each advancing Red Army Corps was divided into large battle groups composed of a number of assault detachments specifically designed and trained for street-to-street fighting. Most detachments were composed of an infantry company with the support of two or three 76 mm assault guns, two 45 mm assault guns, and a few tanks or self-propelled guns. Along with the infantry were two or three platoons of sappers (demolition squads) and a platoon of flame-throwers.

When the advancing units came across an enemy strongpoint—which was usually a barricaded street, fortified bunker, or building—an intense bombardment by heavy artillery preceded the attack. This was initiated by a barrage of shells from 152 mm or 203 mm Howitzers, along with a salvo of rockets from a Katyusha mobile rocket launcher. It took ten to fifteen shells from a 152 mm gun, or just six to eight from the 203 mm, to level a three-story building. Katyusha rockets were loaded with napalm to cause maximum destruction. The infantry then advanced forward with hand grenades and machine-gun fire to quash any residual enemy resistance. Very often, flame-thrower units had to be called in to eliminate the most stubborn enemy holdouts. Hitler had ordered that Berlin be defended to the last man, and many fanatical Nazi SS units took his words to heart in the most literal sense.

Although the number of German troops within Berlin was unknown during the closing days of the war, by Weidling's own estimate, there were somewhere between 45,000 and 50,000 Wehrmacht and SS troops and another 40,000 Volkssturm under his command. Only 60 tanks, mostly from Weidling's own Panzer Corps, were in combat readiness. Supplies of military munitions were low, and there were no reserves available. Because of the constant bombing raids on Berlin, the majority of supply depots were scattered among the outer suburban districts, and the Red Army captured them shortly after they entered the city.

With at least seven Russian armies advancing ever closer to the central district, Weidling was frustrated and angered by Hitler's decision to defend every inch of territory left in German hands. To the general, it was an arrogant and stupid waste of his men's lives. The final outcome was inevitable. Yet he had no choice but to follow his Führer's command. Of the five remaining divisions, Weidling placed the 18th Panzergrenadier and Müncheburg Panzer divisions in the southern districts facing the greatest threat from Konev's 3rd Guards and 28th Army as well as Zhukov's 8th Guards and 1st Guards Tank Army. The 11th SS Panzergrenadier Nordland Division, 20th Panzergrenadier Division, and 9th Parachute Division were sent to the north and east of the Zitadelle to defend against attacks from Zhukov's 3rd Shock Army and 2nd Guards Tank Army advancing down from the north, while Berzarin's 5th Shock Army closed in from the east.

At the daily conference meeting on April 28, Weidling reported the dire military situation facing Hitler. His troops could continue fighting for only another two days, at which time they would run out of ammunition. Zhukov's armies had already penetrated Sector Z. The Zitadelle was bordered in the north by the Spree River, in the west by the Tiergarten, and in the south by the Landwehr Canal. Von Loringhoven's communication with OKW headquarters revealed further deterioration of German defenses throughout the Eastern Front, with scores of Wehrmacht soldiers either surrendering or deserting their posts. But the most damaging report was that Wenck's 12th Army progress in its drive to relieve Berlin was halted at Beelitz.

This meant there was no hope to save the city. Weidling told Hitler it was only a matter of time before Russian troops were at the steps of the Reich Chancellery. Their only recourse was to break out of the encirclement. He proposed a plan for a determined attempt for all his forces to break out of the city in the evening, but Hitler refused. He wouldn't risk the threat of being captured by the Russians.

North of the Tiergarten, the 79th Rifle Corps of Kuznetsov's 3rd Shock Army had cleared the Moabit area, freeing 7,000 Anglo-American POWs from Moabit Prison. The newly freed Russian prisoners were handed rifles and recruited on the spot as cannon fodder for the coming attack on the Reichstag. Moving along Alt Moabit, the attacking Russian troops were in sight of the Moltke Bridge over the Spree River, the last obstacle to the Reichstag. The Moltke Bridge was the only remaining bridge left standing across the Spree leading directly to the Reichstag. The Germans had blown up all other access bridges.

Red Army troops from the 59th Rifle Corps of Berzarin's 5th Shock Army and elements of Katukov's 1st Tank Army were rapidly advancing from the east along Leipziger Strasse, which led directly to the Reich Chancellery. They subsequently ran into very heavy resistance from Mohnke's SS troops. Chuikov's 8th Guards Army coming in from the south attempted to force the Landwehr Canal on Potsdamer Strasse but was stopped by the determined defense of more SS troops. After a fierce fight that lasted an entire day along the entire front adjacent to the canal, the

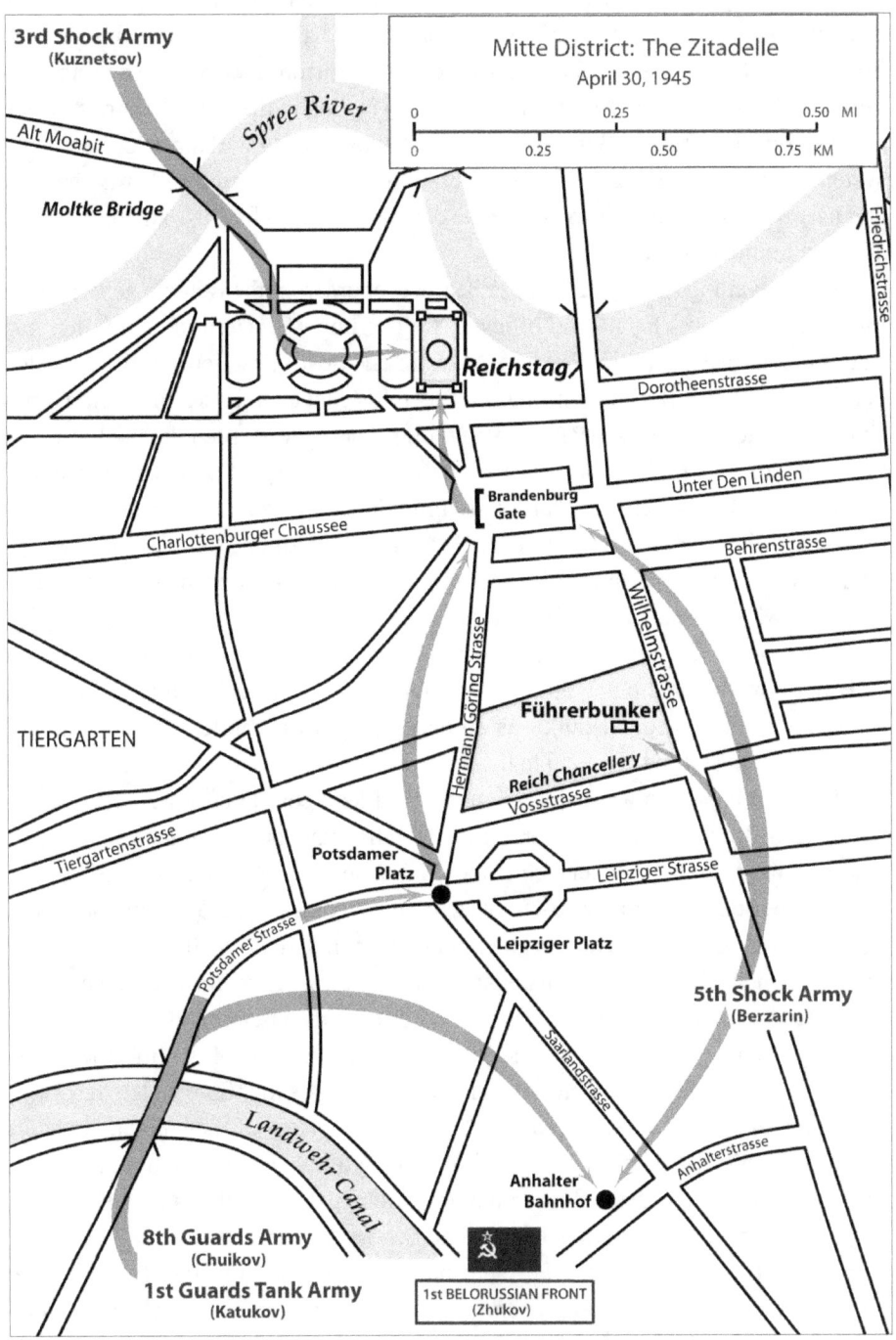

Mitte District: The Zitadelle
April 30, 1945

3rd Shock Army
(Kuznetsov)

Alt Moabit

Spree River

Moltke Bridge

Friedrichstrasse

Reichstag

Dorotheenstrasse

Unter Den Linden

Brandenburg
Gate

Behrenstrasse

Charlottenburger Chaussee

Hermann Göring Strasse

Wilhelmstrasse

TIERGARTEN

Führerbunker

Reich Chancellery
Vossstrasse

Tiergartenstrasse

Potsdamer
Platz

Leipziger Strasse

Potsdamer Strasse

Leipziger Platz

5th Shock Army
(Berzarin)

Landwehr Canal

Saarlandstrasse

Anhalter
Bahnhof

Anhalterstrasse

8th Guards Army
(Chuikov)

1st Guards Tank Army
(Katukov)

1st BELORUSSIAN FRONT
(Zhukov)

8th Guards Army and 1st Guards Tank Army were able to overcome the German forces to finally advance north toward the Reichstag. Part of Chuikov's forces were also directed to the nearby rail metro station, the Anhalter Bahnhof, to link up with troops from Berzarin's 5th Shock Army coming in from the east. This metro station was the most important underground railway hub in the central district, which consisted of the city's U-Bahn (underground subway) and S-Bahn (elevated train) systems. German soldiers and civilians alike were now packed together in the dark and narrow subway tunnels to escape the constant air raids by Russian bombers and artillery bombardments.

In the evening of April 28, Hitler heard a report from the Reuters news agency that one of his most loyal Nazi officials, Reichsführer-SS Heinrich Himmler, had negotiated a treaty with the Western Allies to end hostilities. Sensing the expected demise of Hitler in Berlin, Himmler had seen his chance to usurp the Führer's position at the top of the Nazi Party. Even though the Allies turned down Himmler's terms for surrender, Hitler became furious with this unexpected act of treachery.

But he didn't need to look far for an immediate reprisal for Himmler's despicable indiscretion. Just the previous day, Hitler's henchmen, the Gestapo, apprehended a close member of Himmler's inner circle. It was SS-Gruppenführer Hermann Fegelein, who was caught at his mistress's apartment in an attempt to flee the city. Fegelein was living in the Führerbunker as Himmler's liaison officer to the Führer, so Hitler now directed his wrath on that poor soul. Under interrogation by the Gestapo, Fegelein was found guilty as an accomplice to Himmler's treasonous act. Hitler then condemned Fegelein to death.

Fegelein had been a trusted member of Hitler's coterie because he was married to Eva Braun's younger sister, Gretl. Traudl Junge, one of Hitler's secretaries, who was living in the bunker, remembered a sobbing Eva Braun in near hysteria, who told her that her brother-in-law was to be executed. With Gretl pregnant with Fegelein's child, Braun pleaded with Hitler to spare his life. But Hitler was in such a twisted, vengeful state that he disregarded all her pleas. Fegelein's sentence was to be carried out at dawn, and that was the end of their discussion.[23]

Major Von Loringhoven was surprised to see Fegelein—his uniform disheveled, stripped of military epaulettes and decorations—as four SS men led the downtrodden man past his room and down the narrow corridor of the bunker. He had a very low opinion of Fegelein. As a dashing young officer and the commander of an SS cavalry brigade, Fegelein had won many military decorations in the field thanks to his close friend, Field Marshal Ferdinand Schörner, who was one of Hitler's most devoted and faithful generals. Fegelein had weaseled his way into Hitler's inner circle by marrying Gretl Braun in June 1944. He then became a powerful individual by being so close to Hitler. Like all SS officers, Fegelein hated the Wehrmacht and looked down on the regular German Army soldiers. Von Loringhoven had no sympathy for this man's fate. Fegelein was taken out to the Chancellery garden and shot at dawn.[24]

Himmler wasn't the only individual who wished to become Hitler's successor. Acutely aware of the Führer's coming demise, Hermann Göring sent a cable to Hitler requesting his freedom to take over the leadership of the Reich as they'd both agreed in the Führer's decree in June 1941. The decree spelled out the terms of succession if Hitler lost his ability to rule the Reich. Göring had been listed as the successor. Martin Bormann, who hated Göring, persuaded Hitler that such an impertinent suggestion amounted to treason. Bormann then ordered Göring's arrest. Stripped of all titles and powers of command, Göring was now a prisoner of the SS until the end of the war.[25]

In the early-morning hours of April 29, Hitler realized the end was near, so he summoned his secretary, Traudl Junge, to his conference room. Junge was one of a very few individuals Hitler trusted. A young lady of twenty-two, Junge had interviewed to be the Führer's secretary in 1942. She was from Munich and had been told that he had a liking for Bavarian women. But the clincher for the job was that she looked so much like Eva Braun.

In October 1929, Braun had been working in Heinrich Hoffmann's photographic studio in central Munich. Hoffman, a friend of the Führer, had asked him to accompany them to dinner. Hoffman was surprised when he noticed Hitler was smitten at the first sight of Braun and unable to take his eyes off the young beauty while trying to concentrate on his dinner. She was seventeen, and he was forty. Soon afterward, Braun became the Führer's mistress.[26]

With the sound of violent explosions above the bunker from the constant artillery barrage, Junge calmly sat down in front of the Führer. He told her he was going to dictate his political testament, followed by his personal will, and that she was to write it in shorthand. He named Grand Adm. Karl Donitz as his successor to become the president of the Reich. Joseph Goebbels was named as Reich chancellor, and Martin Bormann the party chancellor. As he was dictating his personal will, Hitler informed Junge that he and Eva Braun were to be married. This was the first time Junge had heard of Hitler's intentions concerning Braun. After he was done dictating the will, Hitler's last official request of Junge was to type the document in triplicate and bring it to him at once. Separate messengers would send the copies to Adm. Donitz, Field Marshal Schörner, and the Nazi Party headquarters in Munich.

Goebbels sent out some SS men to recruit a government official to legalize the marriage, and they returned with Walter Wagner, who was serving with the Volkssturm. In a brief ceremony, which lasted no more than five to ten minutes, the bride and groom exchanged their wedding vows in the conference room of the Führerbunker, with Bormann and Goebbels acting as witnesses. Then a wedding celebration was held in Hitler's room with a bevy of selected guests. Hitler was in his uniform, and his new wife was still in her long, black silk dress she'd worn at the wedding ceremony. It wasn't a very cheerful party, and Junge thought it was sort of a macabre event in view of the fact that they might all be dead very soon. However, Eva Braun, now Frau Hitler, was extremely happy and in a chatty mood. It was her day.

For many years, Eva Braun had stood in the shadow of Hitler's life as his mistress. She was seldom seen or even noticed by many Nazi officials. Hitler very rarely appeared with her at his public meetings and social events. She appeared in public with the Führer only once or twice in the fifteen years they were together. Von Loringhoven didn't even realize Hitler had a mistress until the major began to reside in the Führerbunker complex. A colleague told him that her name was Eva Braun. Von Loringhoven often ran into her in the bunker's main corridor, busy talking to another of Hitler's secretaries or Goebbels's wife, Magda.

Von Loringhoven found Braun to be a slim, attractive blonde with a shapely figure of medium stature. She wasn't at all like the many thirty-year-old women he knew who were associated with Nazi officials. He could never understand what Braun saw in Hitler, who was just an ordinary guy who dressed in shabby-looking clothes and often exhibited volatile episodes of extreme anger. Von Loringhoven saw firsthand this dark side of Hitler. He would watch in absolute silence, as did all others in the conference room, during those stormy military meetings when the Führer would fall into one of his uncontrollable tantrums. Hitler would scream at one of his generals at the top of his lungs in such a fit of hysteria that his face would turn beet red and he'd begin frothing at the mouth.

Junge, on the other hand, never attended military meetings and therefore never saw that side of Hitler. However, she also wondered at times what kind of relationship Hitler had with Eva Braun. During daily tea sessions after the evening meal—sessions that often lasted through the night and into the early-morning hours—Hitler would chat with his secretaries and Braun about everything except the war. He and Braun had separate bedrooms in the Führerbunker, and when he retired for the night, she would come alive and bloom like a flower at the first light of day. She then cheerfully talked about fashion, art, and the theatre.

Braun often wrote to Gretl, and her last letter to her sister was sent on April 23. She told Gretl not to destroy any of the letters, but none of them survived the war. Consequently, there's little information on what type of romantic relationship existed between Eva Braun and Hitler. Nonetheless, Hitler was devoted to Braun as much as she was to him. He often spurned the advances of other women, which included an assortment of beautiful actresses Goebbels introduced to him. Hitler often remarked that women only interfered with his political ambitions, and his desire to marry Braun at this late date was to honor her for her many years of loyal and devoted affection. He also told Junge that it was the least he could do since it was Braun's choice to come back to Berlin. He'd sent her away, but she'd returned to stay with him to the end, to her death.

Shortly after midnight, while Hitler and his new wife celebrated their wedding at the Führerbunker, the 150th and 171st Rifle Divisions of Maj. Gen. Semyon N. Perevertkin's 79th Rifle Corps from Kuznetsov's 3rd Shock Army smashed their way through the barbed-wire barricades and concrete bunkers on the Moltke Bridge. The Germans had attempted to set off the wired demolition charges on the bridge but failed to do so. This was the last remaining bridge left standing across the Spree River to the Reichstag. It was a fierce fight, with heavy losses on both sides, as the Germans were well-prepared for the attack. Tank and artillery fire from the Königsplatz, a large circular courtyard directly in front of the Reichstag building, supported the defense of the bridge.

Captain Stepan Neustroev, commander of the first battalion of the 756th Rifle Regiment in the 150th Rifle Division, was in one of the lead units that crossed the bridge. As he approached the other side, Neustroev was knocked off his feet by the explosion of a nearby mortar shell. He was still dazed when one of his lieutenants helped him up. He immediately looked around for his knapsack. It was lying on the ground next to him. Quickly opening up the partially smoking bag, the captain carefully inspected the red banner flag to see if it was damaged.

Nine red victory flags were handed out to Kuznetsov's 3rd Shock Army units for use in planting the Russian flag over the Reichstag to signify their victory. In preparation for the attack on the Reichstag the previous day, Maj. Gen. Perevertkin issued his battle orders. One of them was to issue submachine guns and hand grenades to all assaulting troops. Another was to honor the commander of any unit that was the first to raise the victory banner over the Reichstag as the Hero of the Soviet Union.

Major General Vasily M. Shatilov, commander of the Corps's 150th Rifle Division, assigned Red Victory Banner No. 5 to his 756th Rifle Regiment commander, Col. Fedor Zinchenko. Each of the regimental victory banners was passed down to the best battalion, and in this case, No. 5 was given to Capt. Neustroev's Young Communist Battalion.

Determining which regimental unit was to actually receive a victory banner was based on very specific criteria. A special committee chaired by a native Georgian—to honor Premier Stalin, who was from the province of Georgia in Russia—made absolutely sure that those troops were of pure Russian descent. Any ethnic Russians who had ever been exiled, such as Chechens or Caucasian Tartars, were excluded from receiving this special item. Captain Neustroev's unit was exceptional in that it was composed of newly recruited Russian soldiers, all demonstrating superb fighting abilities in the field of battle.

As more and more Red Army troops crossed Moltke Bridge, they came under heavy machine gun fire from the large government buildings on either side of the bridge, the most massive being the Ministry of Internal Affairs building. The three-story ministry building was known as Himmler's House. All these buildings were well-fortified, and it would take the entire day to completely clear the buildings of enemy opposition before advancing to the Königsplatz.

Farther south, Chuikov's 8th Guards Army was running into fierce enemy resistance in its advance to the Reichstag. Because more and more German troops were being pushed back from the outer city sectors into Sector Z, the advance of Chuikov's troops had become increasingly slower and slower. In the past couple of weeks, progress was rapid, with extensive gains into the suburbs. Now they had to fight for every building, block by block, leading to the Reichstag. When Zhukov reported to Stalin on his latest results in the field, his commander was furious. Zhukov was already way behind the original operations schedule laid out by the Stavka. Berlin was supposed to have been captured by April 23.

Stalin reiterated in no uncertain terms the urgency of capturing the Reichstag by May 1. If Zhukov failed to do this, there would be dire consequences. So he ordered his top field commanders to capture the Reichstag immediately at any cost. Chuikov, realizing his commander's urgency, in turn ordered the advance units of the 8th Guards Army to rush the attack on Anhalter Station. Not only was the station a vitally important military objective, it was also the final stretch of the boundary line dividing Zhukov's 1st Belorussian Front from Konev's 1st Ukrainian Front.

Now that both Zhukov and Konev's armies were racing to take Anhalter Station, their advancing units started to overlap. Confusion and chaos began to appear in the field of battle. Chuikov, in his haste to attack Anhalter Station, failed to share news of his advance with Rybalko, who was Konev's commander of the 3rd Guards Tank Army. Rybalko's forces were also moving forward to the station at the same time. Rybalko then ordered an artillery barrage to cover his advancing troops. As a result, many of Chuikov's forward units were decimated by friendly fire from Rybalko's tanks and artillery.

When Stalin heard what had happened, he immediately ordered Konev to turn his armies westward, away from the city. Konev realized that he'd been taken away from the prize he wanted more than anything—capturing the Reichstag and becoming the conqueror of Berlin. When Konev told Rybalko of Stalin's decision, Rybalko was furious beyond words. The Reichstag was just over a mile away. But both knew they had no choice but to comply without question. Even before the Berlin Operation commenced, Stalin had always wanted Zhukov to be the victor. As their commander, Stalin wanted to pit both Zhukov and Konev against each other in their race to conquer Berlin. But now there would be no contest. It was in this final gesture that Stalin insured Zhukov's victory.

Meanwhile, in the Führerbunker, the situation had grown ever more tense.

Living conditions were becoming intolerable. The bunker could withstand the constant heavy artillery bombardment coming from above, but the dust filtering down from cracks in the ceiling and exhaust fumes from the electric generators made breathing difficult. Much of the time, the ventilation system pumps had to be shut down because of the strong smell of cordite, smoke, and thick dust coming in from the outside. There was water everywhere from damaged and leaking pipes. Refuse was no longer being collected. Lighting fixtures went on and off or flickered incessantly for hours at a time.

Taking the brunt of artillery shells and bombs, conditions in the Vorbunker above the Führerbunker were even worse. That bunker was much less fortified, and the entire ceiling structure was on the verge of complete collapse.

On the morning of April 29, Col. Gen. Alfred Jodl, chief of the operations staff at OKW headquarters, was on the telephone with Gen. Krebs in the bunker. The last words Jodl said were that the German Front had collapsed everywhere. Suddenly their conversation was cut off midstream. The aerial communications barrage balloon above OKW/OKH headquarters in Rheinberg had been shot down by the Russians. The link between Rheinberg and the communications tower located next to the Zoo flak tower had been severed. The communications tower served as a relay point to OKW, where the underground telephone cables from the bunker ended.

With the loss of contact between Berlin and the German High Command, Von Loringhoven felt his military duties as the communications and intelligence officer had ended. He jumped at the excuse to leave the bunker. Explaining to Gen. Krebs the situation at hand, the young adjuvant was adamant that he didn't want to die in the bunker like a rat. He requested to be transferred to the front lines and fight to the end with his fellow soldiers.

Krebs agreed and told Von Loringhoven that he would have a chance to speak to Hitler about his intention to leave the bunker. The two of them then met with Hitler that afternoon. Von Loringhoven suggested to the Führer that it would be a good idea for him, along with Capt. Gerhard Boldt, Von Loringhoven's adjutant, and Lt. Col. Rudolf Weiss, Gen. Burgdorf's adjutant, to leave the bunker and make their way to Wenck's army to personally explain the situation at the Führerbunker. There they would inform Wenck of the best approach to reach the Reich Chancellery.

According to Von Loringhoven, in these final days, Hitler was in his own fantasy world, vacillating between the hope of rescue by his forces and contemplating suicide. Being ensconced in the bunker for so long, Hitler had completely lost the ability to comprehend what was happening in the real world above. He continued to dictate orders to his field commanders as if there were still hope of victory.

To Von Loringhoven's surprise, Hitler agreed wholeheartedly and issued an official order for the three of them to make their way out of the city to Wenck's army. Hitler still remained confident that the German 12th Army would come and save him. He asked them to convey his best wishes to Wenck, shook their hands, and wished them good luck.

Von Loringhoven couldn't believe it had been so easy. The entire meeting lasted only twenty minutes. The three young soldiers quickly left the meeting and shortly thereafter left the bunker.

With most of the city under the control of Red Army troops, the German defenders were now squeezed into an area of about 10 miles in length and 3 miles in width. This area stretched in the east from Alexander Platz, through the Tiergarten, to the Pichelsdorf Bridge in the western reaches of Berlin. Because of the shortage of military personnel available, the Volkssturm and Hitler Youth units defended much of the northern and western sectors of the city.

Von Loringhoven, Boldt, and Weiss made their way westward toward the Zoo metro station in the Tiergarten, through Charlottenburg, and arrived at the Pichelsdorf Bridge over the Havel River. The bridge was intact and still stubbornly defended by a few hundred Hitler Youth armed with rifles and Panzerfausts. On the opposite side were the Russian tanks and infantry. The German defense of the bridge began with several thousand Hitler Youth, and soon there would be none left. Von Loringhoven knew that probably all of these young volunteers were destined to die, and he cursed in disgust at the Nazis for ordering them to sacrifice their lives.

Von Loringhoven and his colleagues then found a canoe and headed south along the Havel River. Finally, they reached the German lines at Wannsee and later joined up with Wenck's army just south of Potsdam. Major Von Loringhoven eventually returned to Germany after being incarcerated for a time at an Allied prison camp and rejoined his family after the war.[27]

For the remaining individuals in the bunker, there was little hope. During the final situation meeting at 8:00 p.m. on April 29, Weidling told Hitler that hostilities against the enemy must inevitably cease in twenty-four hours because his troops would then run out of ammunition. The few tanks remaining could no longer be repaired. Russian tanks were approaching on Wilhelmplatz and were less than half a mile from the Reich Chancellery.

Hitler turned to Mohnke, commandant of the Zitadelle, and asked him for his opinion. Mohnke agreed with Weidling's assessment. Weidling then asked Hitler what was to happen when they ran out of ammunition.

Hitler told his general to have his troops organize themselves into small groups and break out of the city. They were to join the German forces still fighting against the Red Army. But he gave strict orders that there would be no surrender.

Just before the last military meeting, Hitler's personal pilot, Hans Bauer, insisted to his Führer that he had access to a new type of Junkers bomber with a range of 6,000 miles. Bauer could fly him somewhere safe, like the Middle East or

South America. But Hitler refused. He'd just received news from Reuters about the assassination of Benito Mussolini, the fascist dictator in Italy, by Italian partisans. The bodies of both Mussolini and his mistress, Clara Petacci, had been hung upside down from the rafters of a bombed-out gasoline station and been mutilated by a mad mob of partisans.[28]

Hitler's greatest fear was that he would be captured alive and tortured. In fact, Stalin had made plans for Hitler to be taken alive. He wanted to bring the Führer to Moscow and display him like a caged animal so the people of Russia could take revenge on this "fascist beast." Hitler would have to pay the price for unleashing his vicious Nazi troops, who'd tortured and murdered so many innocent people when the German Army invaded Russia.

A special SMERSH (Russian counterintelligence) unit attached to Kuznetsov's 3rd Shock Army was to go to the Führerbunker and capture Hitler if he was alive or recover any remains if he wasn't. Both Hitler and Stalin were self-imposed dictators who respected each other's bloody accomplishments in their rise to power, but they also hated each other with a vengeance.

It wasn't until 4:00 a.m. on April 30 that Himmler's House and the last of the adjacent government buildings leading to the Königsplatz were cleared of German troops. In the lull that followed, Capt. Neustroev was having a hearty breakfast with his troops from the Young Communist Battalion. As he looked around the room filled with fresh, smiling faces, he knew they were already seasoned veterans. He was glad to have such good fighters, many of whom had survived the vicious battles on the Oder Front. Today everyone's resolve would be tested to their physical and mental limits.

Unlike the Western Allied forces, the Red Army had many women soldiers on the front lines, who fought just as heroically as their male comrades. A number of them were very skilled snipers with high-powered rifles. There were also a handful of women fighter pilots in the Red Army Air Force. One of the most well known was twenty-one-year-old "Lily" Litvyak (Lydia Vladimirovna Litvyak), a highly decorated fighter pilot who shot down her share of Luftwaffe fighters and bombers.[29]

Neustroev's breakfast was cut short at 6:00 a.m., when Col. Zinchenko, the regimental commander, ordered an immediate advance to the Königsplatz. However, the first wave of attacking Russian troops was an abysmal failure. As they rushed forward, they were cut down by machine gun and mortar fire from the Kroll Opera House and fortified defensive bunkers facing the large circular courtyard of the Königsplatz. Wave after wave of Russian infantry were sent into the maelstrom without success.

Suddenly, enemy artillery shells rained down upon them from above. The artillery bombardment was coming from the heavy 88 mm antiaircraft guns atop the Zoo flak tower in the Tiergarten, nearly two miles away. It was impossible to move forward. The huge exploding shells were devastating. Neustroev lost many of his soldiers, but mostly in the first echelon of advancing troops, who were freshly recruited POWs from Moabit Prison. It would take the full morning to clear the Kroll Opera House and other German fortifications of enemy resistance before troops from the Red Army's 79th Rifle Corps could advance to the Königsplatz.[30]

When Col. Hans-Oscar Wöhlermann, Weidling's LVI Corps artillery commander, received orders to fire onto the Königsplatz, he was atop the Zoo flak tower surveying the extensive damage in the Tiergarten. Thick black smoke was rising above the Reichstag in the distance. He looked around to see the city covered in fire and smoke from the constant bombing and artillery bombardment. During the previous night, the fires had eerily lit up the sky with an unearthly red-orange glow, the partially destroyed tall, dark buildings in the background creating a grotesque scene of destruction. Wöhlermann could see the botanical gardens near his Berlin apartment, completely engulfed in flames.

The massive Zoo flak tower was under attack by bombs, artillery, Katyusha rockets, tanks, and every other kind of weapon the Red Army had at its disposal. The Russians tried their best to put it out of commission, but it was useless. The Russian tanks couldn't elevate their cannon turrets above the second-story windows. The Zoo tower was the largest flak emplacement in the central district, rising 130 feet above the air raid shelters below. Besides, any type of artillery shell the Russians had in the area could never penetrate the tower's four-foot-thick reinforced concrete walls.

Among the defenders of the Zoo tower was Wolfgang Karow, who was located in the lower section of the tower, which was more vulnerable to Russian artillery fire. Here the smaller-caliber antiaircraft guns were firing against the waves of Russian troops in their attempt to overcome the defensive barriers and bunkers around the base of the tower. It was utter chaos for Karow and his command as salvos of enemy shells continued to explode and destroy the antiaircraft guns. Yet his guns kept firing at the Russian troops. Karow felt a wave of sadness as he saw his young gunners falling right and left around him, nearly all of them Hitler Youth boys and girls who were just fourteen to sixteen years of age. The other two flak towers, in the Humboldthain and Friedrichshain districts nearby, had fallen days before. The Russians were desperate to put the Zoo tower's heavy artillery out of commission. But they weren't successful, no matter how hard they tried. It made no difference in any case. Wöhlermann's 88 mm guns had spent their last rounds firing at the Königsplatz that morning.

While Russian troops were clearing the Kroll Opera House and adjacent buildings of German troops before continuing the assault on the Reichstag, residents of the Führerbunker were preparing for the worst. With no hope of rescue by Wenck's 12th Army, Hitler made specific arrangements with Otto Günsche, his Waffen-SS adjutant, for his pending suicide with his wife. Günsche ordered Hitler's chauffer, Erich Kempka, to obtain 10 jerricans containing five gallons of gasoline per can and place them at the emergency exit entrance leading into the Chancellery garden. Their bodies were to be taken out of the bunker and burned to ashes. After their deaths, Mohnke was ordered to break out of the Zitadelle and join the remaining German troops to continue the fight against the Russians.

In the early afternoon, Hitler was having lunch with his two remaining secretaries, Gerda Christian and Traudl Junge, along with his vegetarian cook, Constanze Manziarly. He preferred to dine with his female companions, feeling they were more devoted and loyal to him. Eva would have been there as well, but she didn't have an appetite that day. The conversation was the same as the day before, the week before, and for as long as Junge could remember.

Mohnke's men were reportedly fighting in the streets above the bunker as Berzarin's 5th Shock Army tanks advanced along Wilhelmstrasse, yet Hitler calmly continued to talk as if nothing unusual was happening. Now totally oblivious to the events above the bunker, it was just another ordinary day for him. He no longer cared about the real world, nor was he even concerned that his precious Third Reich was in its final death throes. His only thoughts were solely focused on his imminent journey to Valhalla.

When they finished what Junge described as a "banquet of death," he returned to his room without saying a word. Günsche shortly thereafter went up to Junge to tell her that the Führer wanted to say goodbye to everyone. Junge went with him and found herself standing at the far end of a long processional line of people giving their farewells. She thought about how much had changed in the man she'd met in 1942, just three years earlier. He was so different now. Slowly, methodically, and painfully dragging his left foot, the Führer made his way toward her.

As Hitler gazed into her eyes, Junge hardly recognized his withered face. He had aged way beyond his years. His bloodshot eyes, encircled by dark rings, stared past her. There was no more life left in them. Then he shook Junge's hand, and it was a surreal moment for her. They both seemed far, far away from each other. This person in front of her mumbled a few words, but she didn't hear them. He then passed Junge to the next person beside her, but she stood there frozen, as if under a spell.

It was broken when Eva came up to her, smiling and embracing her as she told Junge to get out of the bunker and give her love to Bavaria.

Braun was wearing a long black gown, Hitler's favorite, with roses at the neckline, and her face was beautifully made up. Junge was taken aback at how Eva could be so calm. She seemed to have no fear of her impending death—perhaps because Eva had already attempted suicide twice before, once with her father's gun and another time with a heavy dose of sleeping pills. She would now finally succeed.[31]

Junge was sitting with the Goebbels's children on the stairs leading up to the Vorbunker from the Führerbunker. She was talking to one of them about getting something to eat when suddenly a loud shot was heard, which echoed through the rooms in the bunker. One of the children, Helmut, thought it was from an explosion outside, but Junge knew exactly where it had come from—Hitler's room. There was a rush of footsteps, with men running around.

Hitler was dead. Junge looked at her wristwatch. It was a few minutes after 3:00 p.m.[32]

However, with the intense Russian artillery bombardment above the bunker, it would have been unlikely that Junge heard a gunshot in a room located at the far end of the bunker. It's not clear if Günsche, who was waiting in the antechamber in front of Hitler's room, actually heard the fatal shot. Thus, it can't be accurately determined exactly at what time the double suicide occurred. According to Günsche, it was 3:10 p.m. when he looked at his watch while waiting in the antechamber. Joseph Goebbels's wife, Magda, went into Hitler's room briefly to give her final farewell before the door was finally closed. It wasn't until a few minutes before 4:00 p.m. that Günsche again checked his watch and entered Hitler's room. That was when he and the others discovered Hitler and Braun had committed suicide.[33]

Junge remained unmoving on the stairway. Like all the others in the bunker, she was contemplating what to do next. Escaping from the godforsaken tomb was everyone's priority. Then Günsche came up to her, his face ashen, his clothes smelling strongly of gasoline. He told her that the deed was done. He'd followed Hitler's last order to him: burn both their bodies. Hitler had given explicit orders to Günsche about what to do after their suicide, and the faithful adjutant had carried them out to the letter.

Günsche, Heinz Linge (Hitler's valet), Erich Kempka (chauffeur), Martin Bormann, and some other people had rushed into Hitler's room after he shot himself. They found Hitler on the left side of a sofa with a large bullet wound on his right temple. Blood had streamed down his cheek and neck to form a small puddle on the carpet under the sofa. On the floor next to Hitler's right foot lay two Walther pistols, one a 7.65 mm and the other a 6.35 mm. His wife, Eva, was next to him on the sofa with her legs drawn up under her with her lips pressed tightly together. She'd taken cyanide.

Linge and Bormann, with the assistance of a couple of SS guards, wrapped Hitler's body in a blanket and carried it toward the emergency exit close to Hitler's room at the far end of the bunker. Kempka followed, carrying the lifeless Eva Braun in his arms. They carried the bodies up a long flight of stairs to the emergency doorway leading into the Reich Chancellery garden. They were moving as fast as they could, expecting the Russians to burst into the bunker at any time.

However, when they reached the entrance and opened the door, they couldn't get out because Russian artillery shells were exploding all around the garden and fierce fires raged uncontrollably in the buildings next to the Reich Chancellery. Finally, during a lull in the bombardment, they were able to take the corpses out into the garden.

Bormann, Günsche, Linge, Kempka, and the SS guards then poured more than 50 gallons of gasoline over the bodies. Günsche attempted to light the gasoline with matches, but it was too windy from the raging fires. Then the artillery bombardment began anew. He grabbed a hand grenade and was going to throw it at the corpses, but Linge stopped him. Linge had successfully lit a piece of paper. He threw it onto the bodies, igniting the gasoline. Both bodies instantly burst into flames.[34]

More gasoline was added throughout the day and evening to ensure that the bodies were completely burned. Hitler had ordered Günsche to burn both his and Braun's bodies until there was nothing left, then bury their remains so that no one could find them. During the chaos of war in those final days, it couldn't be determined whether or not Günsche personally did this, but a detachment of SS soldiers did bury the remains of Hitler's corpse somewhere in the Reich Chancellery garden.[35]

Soon after Hitler's death, Magda Goebbels poisoned all of her six children. She and Joseph Goebbels then committed suicide. Rather than be captured by the Russians, Gen. Krebs and Burgdorf (Hitler's adjutant) shot themselves in the head. The remaining people in the Vorbunker and Führerbunker planned their escape from Berlin. Several large groups began to leave that evening. Junge was in the first group, led by Gen. Mohnke. The other groups made their way through the city shortly afterward. All were either killed or captured by Red Army soldiers. Junge was able to leave the capital, but she couldn't reach the American or British forces. She ended up back in Berlin, where the Russians imprisoned her.[36]

A couple of hours before Hitler committed suicide, at approximately 1:30 p.m., the final assault on the Reichstag began with a vicious artillery barrage. All the windows and doors on the front entrances of the massive building had been barricaded and sealed with brick and mortar. The attacking Russian forces trained 89 heavy weapons directly at the Reichstag. Included were 152 mm and 203 mm howitzers, tank and self-propelled cannons, mortars, Katyusha rocket launchers, and even captured enemy Panzerfausts. The intense artillery bombardment lasted twenty minutes.[37]

It was a clear, sunny day, but Capt. Neustroev and his men couldn't see the sun. The sky was full of thick dust and smoke. Hunkered down, with artillery shells whistling over him, Neustroev waited until the bombardment ended. Then he ordered his men to charge forward across the wide, circular Königsplatz, which had been heavily barricaded with concrete anti-tank pillars and anti-personnel fortifications. A hail of mortar and machine-gun fire met the front ranks. Men dropped to the right and left of him, but Neustroev and most of his men managed to get through. Their advance was stopped by the presence of a deep anti-tank ditch the Germans had flooded with water.

Tanks and self-propelled guns were then brought up to the ditch to cover the advancing troops. The last defensive obstacle to the Reichstag was an open area of approximately 660 feet covered with barbed-wire defense structures, debris, and land mines. Tank and artillery fire cleared a path through the minefield as three battalions from the 150th and 171st Rifle Divisions charged through and up the stairs leading to the front entrance of the Reichstag. Neustroev and his men had to use simultaneous mortar fire at point-blank range to blow a four-foot hole in the wall to gain entrance into the building.

Neustroev's team was one of the first to reach the large stairwell leading to the upper floors. They were met with intense fire from defenders above them using Panzerfausts, hand grenades, and machine guns. The German defenders were a mixed group of SS troops, sailors, and Hitler Youth, all fighting tenaciously to slow the advance of their attackers. The opposing fire was so fierce that Neustroev and his men had to take cover behind the statues and large balustrades all around the central staircase. With Panzerfaust shells exploding around him and bullets ricocheting all over the stairs and walls, Neustroev called for covering fire as he and his men charged up the stairs. Other divisional units were clearing the first floor, driving a large contingent of defenders down into the basement level.

As more and more Russian troops poured into the cavernous building, Neustroev's men were fighting their way up the stairs to the second floor. The German defenders were suffering tremendous losses and forced to initiate a fighting retreat up the stairs. Neustroev saw his chance. There was an opening in the German ranks. He ordered his sergeants, Mikhail Yegorov and Meliton Kantariya, to quickly advance. They all threw hand grenades and pushed their way through with submachine gun fire. Yegorov and Kantariya were able to rush to the second floor, enter a lightly defended room, and unfurl Red Banner No. 5 from the second-story window. The time was 2:25 p.m.[38]

Neustroev immediately reported their success to Col. Zinchenko, but he was shocked at his superior's reply. Zinchenko angrily told Neustroev that a flag being waved from a second-story window wasn't good enough. It had to be placed on the dome above the Reichstag. At that moment there was a fierce counterattack by the German defenders. All the Russian troops were forced to retreat and regroup. It wasn't until 6:00 p.m. that another assault on the upper floors of the building could be attempted.

Zinchenko called on Sgts. Yegorov and Kantariya for a second attempt to reach the upper floors of the Reichstag. Fighting became even more intense and chaotic. More explosive material was used in the attack, along with a large battalion

DEFEAT OF NAZI GERMANY

of flamethrowers. Soon the entire building seemed to be on fire, and the air was filled with fire and smoke. Neustroev wondered how any defender could have survived such an onslaught. Clearing each room from floor to floor necessitated savage close-quarter combat, first with grenades, then bayonets, and finally hand-to-hand fighting with knives in the dark. It took almost five hours before Yegorov and Kantariya fought their way to the top floor and broke their way into a room leading to the roof of the Reichstag.

Dispatching the final German defenders, both Russian sergeants climbed the statue of Germania on her horse, a large bronze figure on the cupola atop the dome, and finally planted Red Banner No. 5 into a shallow blast crater adjacent to the left side of the horse. At 10:50 p.m. on April 30, the Russian victory flag was waving high above the Reichstag for the first time. The deed was done, a mere seventy minutes before May 1.

But the fighting hadn't ended. There were still hundreds of German defenders in the basement. It would take another forty-eight hours before all enemy resistance at the Reichstag came to an end.

After Zhukov telephoned Stalin to tell him the good news about Hitler's death and the capture of the Reichstag, Stalin was in a very good mood for the Moscow May Day celebrations. He was a cunning and manipulating dictator, and he'd known that if anyone could accomplish the task, it would be Zhukov. He'd placed the entire success of the Berlin Operation on his favorite, hard-driving general, who was handsomely rewarded. As for those who had successfully accomplished their missions, Zinchenko, Neustroev, Yegorov, and Kantariya all received the highest military award as the Hero of the Soviet Union.

With Hitler dead and his troops defeated, Lt. Gen. Helmuth Weidling, commander of the LVI Panzer Corps and Berlin defense commandant, crossed the front line with his senior staff and surrendered to the Red Army at 6:00 a.m. on May 2, 1945.

By 3:00 p.m., the Russian guns at the capital fell silent.

The battle for Berlin had ended.

CHAPTER 6

COMING HOME

ON THE MORNING OF MAY 8, 1945, a German military delegation, composed of Field Marshal Wilhelm Keitel, Adm. Hans-Georg von Friedeburg, and Col. Gen. Hans-Jürgen Stumpff, arrived at Zhukov's headquarters in Karlshorst, a suburb in southeastern Berlin, to formally sign the Act of Military Surrender. The terms of the unconditional surrender were explained to Field Marshal Keitel, who then signed the document, followed by Gen. Stumpff and Adm. Von Friedeburg. Marshal Zhukov and Air Chief Marshal Sir Arthur Tedder, as deputy and representative of the Supreme Allied Commander Gen. Eisenhower, then penned their names. General Carl Spaatz, commander of the US Army Air Force in Europe, and Gen. Jean de Lattre de Tassigny, as representative of Gen. Charles de Gaulle, both signed as witnesses to the ceremony.

The German delegation then left the room, with the monocled Keitel maintaining an air of arrogance that had permeated the entire meeting. Suddenly, the room exploded with cheers and laughter as the Russians bear-hugged one another and the more stoic Allied representatives heartily shook hands in a celebratory mood, displaying wide smiles.

The war in Europe was over.[1]

The next day, May 9, was officially declared V-E Day, Victory in Europe. When it was announced, everyone on base began celebrating. Of course for many, this meant a fast trip to the local bar. We were given plenty of time for relaxation and recreation. I had a chance to visit the countryside and small towns near the main city of Norwich, which wasn't very far from the airfield. Southeastern England is truly beautiful in the springtime.

With the war in Europe over, procedures were implemented to transfer crews and aircraft to the Pacific Theater

I received my air medal after finishing my tour of duty in the ETO. It was a big ceremony with little fanfare, but it represented the highest honor that the 8th Air Force bestowed upon me for serving in the army.

for operations against the Japanese. However, very few actually made it before the war ended there as well, with Japan formally surrendering on September 2, 1945. Some of our guys were transferred to other bomb groups. Others, like me, were to be shipped back home. It was the end of my operational tour, and I was to return to Amarillo, Texas, where I'd trained as an air cadet. From there I would be discharged from active duty.

The war was over for me.

Like many army operations, some of which can be unnecessarily convolut-

On our way home, we had a forced landing in the Azores. We sat on the tarmac with our gear for hours before hitching another flight back to the States.

ed, it took a while before I actually reached my final destination. There was a lot of activity on the base during this transitional time after V-E Day. I was informed that I wouldn't be going back to the States on a ship, but by air transport on a Liberator B-24. It just so happened that the plane I finally boarded for my trip home was the one our crew had flown on our first mission, *Becoming Back*. We'd also been assigned to her on subsequent missions, so it was just like going home with a buddy.

It was supposed to have been a direct flight from Old Buckenham to Connecticut by way of Greenland. However, we encountered a severe oceanic storm on the way, and our flight was diverted to Portugal, where we abruptly landed on one of the islands in the Azores. Supposedly it was a beautiful place located off the west coast of Portugal/Africa, but from where I was sitting, it wasn't exactly like the pictures in tourist magazines. We had to unload all our gear onto the tarmac to wait for a flight to the States. They'd found something wrong with the Lib we were on, so we "relaxed" for quite a long time. Luckily, we were finally able to hop on another flight, which took us to the East Coast and then on to Amarillo.

When I stepped off *Becoming Back*, it would be the last time I ever saw a B-24 Liberator. I found out later that she ended up, like most of her kind, at a storage facility in Kingman, Arizona. Most, if not all, were scrapped and demolished in order to salvage their aluminum components for use in the metal industry. By the time of Germany's surrender, there were 19 heavy bomber groups stationed in England. Within those groups, the US Army Air Force inventory listed a total of 4,236 Liberator B-24 bombers. By December 1946, only five B-24 bombers remained on that list. Less than a year later, there were no Consolidated B-24 Liberator bombers on the list. They'd served their purpose well.

I finally reached Amarillo in late June, and it took another few months before I was officially discharged from the army on October 26, 1945. It was just in time to celebrate the holidays with my family, and all of them were happy to see me back. I was reunited with my brother, Edmund. I hadn't seen him for several years. He'd enlisted with the army before I did. Like me, he also wanted to become a pilot and was actually with the Army Air Corps as a cadet flying Piper Cubs and gliders. I'd received a call from him when I was in boot camp. He was somewhere in the India/Burma area at the time.

While stationed in Southeast Asia, he was in a terribly depressed state because the army had taken him out of the Air Corps and stuck him into an army intelligence unit. They told him they needed someone who could speak Chinese. His promising career as a pilot came to an abrupt end. He never flew again. To make matters worse, he wasn't at all happy about the assignments his commanders were giving him. Several missions involved chasing and apprehending known traitors or defectors, many of whom took refuge in the impenetrable jungles of Burma and China. In one instance, he caught a fellow who'd gone over to the enemy. Edmund convinced the guy to go back with him, telling him that army intelligence wanted him to spy for them. But when they both returned, the man was made a prisoner.

Although Edmund excelled in accomplishing his duties—which won him a Bronze Star commendation—it took a severe emotional toll on him. It changed him. When he was discharged from the army, the US Central Intelligence Agency wanted him to work for them, but he declined. We talked at times about his experiences during the war, and he would get emotional, so it was a subject we seldom discussed. However, he did meet some people in Southeast Asia who were very kind to him and treated him like one of the family. He eventually became close to his wartime family. One of them actually came to America for a visit, but I don't think she and Edmund ever got together.

As soon as I got home, I went to visit Betty Lee, the young lady I'd written a bunch of letters to while I was stationed in England. Amazingly, she'd compiled a huge scrapbook for me containing clippings of newspaper articles of practically all the major bombing activities of the US Army Air Force in the ETO in early 1945. She said she did it out of appreciation for all the letters and lovely gifts I'd sent to her from England. It was such a nice gesture that I was overwhelmed with gratitude.

We were together for a while until she told me she wanted to get married and start a family. Well, I felt we were still too young, and I didn't feel I was ready to make such a commitment. We'd been together since I met her in 1939 while we were both attending Francisco Junior High School. We were good friends, and the two years we were apart allowed both of us to experience new friends and visit places outside Chinatown. In essence, we were beginning to go on different paths. So we decided to go our separate ways, and our relationship ended.

Sometime after I returned home, I ran into Collin Chong's girlfriend. I'd met Collin while I was stationed in Pueblo, New Mexico. He was being trained as a pilot and wasn't happy about going into combat. His girlfriend told me that Collin was killed in action. His plane was shot down. She was still very distraught, and I tried to console her as much as possible. We started to talk. She told me there was a ceremonial plaque commemorating servicemen who were killed in World War II, and that Collin's name was on the plaque. It was located at St. Mary's Square in the heart of Chinatown.

I went to St. Mary's Park, which is located at 433 Kearny Street on the corner of California and Kearny Streets. The park itself occupies the top level of St. Mary's parking garage. Owned by the San Francisco Recreation and Park Department, St. Mary's Park is very nice, with plenty of trees and bushes, benches to sit and relax on, a playground for kids, and restroom facilities. A small war memorial plaque is nestled in some bushes directly across the large Dr. Sun Yat-sen statue. On the plaque are inscribed the names of 90 American-Chinese servicemen who made the ultimate sacrifice in the First and Second World Wars. Collin's name is indeed on the memorial. He was one of the very few Chinese American servicemen I met during my entire time in the army. I didn't even know he was from my hometown. Seeing his name inscribed on the memorial made me acutely aware of how small the world can actually be at times.

I was so glad and so lucky to be home again. Like with many of my friends, the time spent in the service changed me. I was no longer that cocky teenager I used to be. Now I wanted to make something of myself. So I enrolled at the City College of San Francisco. Just before I entered the service, while I was studying at Gompers,

A small memorial plaque located at St. Mary's Park in the heart of San Francisco's Chinatown to honor those Chinese American veterans serving in World Wars I and II. Their sacrifice will always be remembered.

We Salute these Americans of Chinese Ancestry who gave their lives for America in World Wars I and II				
Tom Kwong	Coom G. Lee	Don Tung Sing	Faye Lowe	William L. Y. Goo
Leo Sai	Chin T. Tom	Eddie Soo	Mo S. Jee	Hong S. Hoey
Bill Tom	Yuen Hop	Manuel K. Soo	Alvin Richard Wong	Yee Nee Jin
Donald Ginn Chong	Walter Tom Lum	Harry Chew	James Q. Fong	Gene F. Lay
Lincoln Mark	Tow Jer	William Chew	Lloyd Quon	Jerry M. Lum
Tung Ling Yee	Ging Gin	Richard W. Chin	Frank Wong	Rudolph Lym
Harry Wong	Benjamin Ralph Kimlau	Richard Chong	Sing Fa Ping	Jeong Wing Jeen
Daniel Lim	Samuel Choy Sin	Marshall K. Dong	Castro Yu Hing Owyang	Harry Wong
Clifford S. Low	Clinton J. Lok	Albert P. Fong	Robert W. Chin	Wesley Y. Chow
Hon Y. Lee	Choy Young	Gong B. Fong	Charles J. Chan	Fan Yee Wong
John Wing Yee	Douglas C. Foo	Lew B. Tong	William J. Quan	Jack Dai Sum Yim
Get G. Chung	Edward Dewey Quong	Wong F. Gin	Thomas Yoke Jow Lai	Lem Quock Hing
Harry Choy	Alwyn G. Wong	Lee Wong Gem	Sam Wong	Lew Hung Biew
Collin S. Chong	Tang Chu Don	Howard Lee	Taft Toy	Harry F. Lee
Alfred W. Chin	James Sing	Harold W. Young	Lee Tan	John J. Chan
Leslie Y. Gee	Yee Sing You	Hong Chew Lee	Hom Wing On	George Lew
Ed Sam Fong	Edward Yin Ong	Percy Louie	Curtis C. Wong	Bob Chan
Ah Fong	Cheng Kee	Yee Lem	Sho Ling	Yeung Yaun

List of names inscribed on the memorial plaque.

I was learning the basics of drafting, designing, and mechanical drawing. During my combat tour, I'd been able to talk at length with our copilot, Lt. Theodore Clark, who was also interested in arts and graphics.

Clark was a bit older than I—about twenty-one or twenty-two—and had graduated from St. John's College with a bachelor's degree in fine arts. He sort of took me under his wing and gave me some advice on taking the collegiate path. He told me that if I went to college, I shouldn't immediately decide what I was going to do with my life. Instead, he suggested I get a liberal arts education to expand my horizons. "Become a 'humanist' first," he said, "before going into a profession that you like best."

I didn't exactly know what he meant by that word, *humanist*, but in retrospect, it was good advice.

During our free time between missions, I would go to his Quonset hut, where he would be reading art books or painting with watercolors at his easel. We would talk for hours about life in general and the arts in particular. He had a small desk, piled with books and the paintings and drawings he was working on. He had a real passion for the arts, and I guess it rubbed off on me. It wasn't hard, because I think I already had a calling for the profession. As a fellow artisan, Clark had a big influence on me.

I also spent some time with Sgt. Melvin Weaver, who was an avid photographer. He was seldom without his trusty camera. He would take pictures of just about everything around him when the opportunity presented itself. He was even able to develop his own film and print pictures. This was amazing considering what was happening to us at the time. Weaver was kind enough to give me a big stack of photo prints as a parting gift when we said goodbye. The stack contained well over 100 photos. Unfortunately, over the years that number has been whittled down to a few remaining pictures still in my possession.

At City College, I took a liberal arts curriculum and learned as much about the art profession as I could. I also enrolled in a wide variety of courses, including psychology, history, and the social sciences. It was there where I met my future wife, Jeannie Lee. After I graduated from City College, I was intending to continue my studies at the University of California, Berkeley when Dick Whitman contacted me. He'd come from New York and had an opportunity to start a community center at Cameron House.

Also known as Donaldina Cameron House, it was built in 1873 by the Presbyterian Church. It was originally called the Occidental Mission House. Located at 920 Sacramento Street, between Stockton and Grant Streets, Cameron House is one of the oldest structures in San Francisco's Chinatown.

In 1895, nineteen-year-old Donaldina Cameron, who'd come from New Zealand with her parents when she was only three years old, joined the Mission

House's staff to work in the Youth Church Program. Eventually, she rose to become superintendent in 1900. In 1942, the Mission House was renamed Donaldina Cameron House in honor of her accomplishments in her fight against slavery in the Chinese community. In its earlier days, Cameron House was used primarily as a safe haven for girls and young women. Many of them had actively sought shelter from their unfortunate circumstances as indentured servants or prostitutes when brought over from China. The establishment eventually evolved into a public community center where people living in Chinatown could gather for social events and recreational activities.

Reverend Whitman became the superintendent of Cameron House in 1947. It was then he asked me to join the staff and work with young people at the community center. I happily accepted. With a background in art and my experiences with printing, setting type in a print shop, and working with a printing press, I was able to fit in nicely with what Whitman had in mind for the center. In the workshop I set up, we had a Chandler Price letterpress and type. The most popular printing press of its day, the first Chandler Price was built in the late 1880s. It was innovative, versatile, excellently constructed, and in use for almost 100 years. With all the equipment at hand, I was able to set up a nice working craft shop. In addition to printing, drawing, and painting, we did leatherwork, woodwork, silk-screening, and all kinds of artsy projects. It was a great experience, and when I left Cameron House, I was ready to go back to school.

However, Jeannie and I were now married, and I was in my thirties, so it was time to find work. My love for silk-screened artwork brought me to a print shop called the Bay Display on Bay Street in Berkeley. There I was able to use many of the skills I'd developed over the years. I also set up a silk screen workshop at home for my own projects, such as my annual allotment of fancy and colorful Christmas cards. With all those skills that I developed over the years, I continued my career in the arts to become a successful freelance graphic artist.

When our crew split up in May–June 1945, it was the last time I ever saw them. We'd served together for only about six or seven months, but it seemed as if we'd known one another for a lifetime. All of us were friends, and like most bomber crews on our base, we were like a family. Unlike other bomb groups in the 8th, where the distinction between officers and enlisted men was very clear—such as separate living quarters and recreational facilities—the 453rd Bomb Group had a more relaxed environment. As a crew, we were able to dine together at mess, visit each other in our quarters, and even travel off base together if we so desired.

After I came home from the war, the only member of our crew I was in contact with was Lt. John Harrington, our navigator. I believe he was living in New England at the time. We exchanged Christmas cards for a while but then eventually lost contact with each other. In early 2015, my nephew Dennis, who was helping me gather some articles related to the Second World War, came across an archival posting (Record #233) on the website www.453rd.com. Glenn Harrington, Lt. Harrington's son, had submitted a post describing his father's activities during the war.

In the post, Glenn mentioned a Chinese American member, by the name of Fong, who was the tail gunner in his father's crew. So we reached out to Glenn, and I was able to reconnect in a way with my old friend John—or, that is, with his family. Glenn and I exchanged photographs that John had kept during our tour together and photos that I had kept all those years. Glenn was also able to write down some of his father's wartime experiences while serving with the 453rd Bomb Group. Glenn was kind enough to send me some of those notes. Reading what Glenn had written brought me back to a time when we were all so young and eager to serve our country. I'm forever indebted to Glenn and his family for sharing those wartime memories with me, the same ones that John and I had shared. (See Appendix 6.)

Not long after the war, I received a letter and a pamphlet informing veterans of the 2nd Air Division of the US 8th Air Force that a memorial for our division was to be built in Norwich, England. Members of the division had established a 2nd Air Division Trust Fund, which created the financial basis for building the memorial. It was to be a tribute to honor those who'd fallen in combat. It took some time for the project to get rolling, but on January 19, 1963, the site of the 2nd Air Division Memorial was opened to the public at the newly built Norwich Central Library.

In the memorial room is the Roll of Honor, which lists more than 6,000 men in the 2nd Air Division who gave their lives in the service of our country. Included in the Roll of Honor were the names of 366 combat veterans of our group, the 453rd Bombardment Group (H). Just outside the memorial stands the memorial fountain, which was constructed using stones sent to the site from every state in America. In 1980, veterans of the 453rd Bombardment Group (H) Association established a Memorial Fund Committee to build a memorial commemorating our wartime service at Old Buckenham Airfield. On May 30, 1983, the first ceremonial reunion took place at the 453rd Memorial, which had been built as an addition to the Village Hall.[2]

At the reunion was a large number of combat veterans and their family members. The president of the 2nd Air Division Association, Maj. Gen. Andrew S. Low, was in attendance, as was a well-known veteran of the 453rd Bomb Group, Brig. Gen. James M. "Jimmy" Stewart. More widely known for his performances in Hollywood films, Stewart also had a distinguished military career. He came from a military family, with his father serving in the First World War and his grandfather in the Civil War. When he enlisted, he was eager to get to the front lines. Being an avid pilot in civilian life, Stewart was a natural fit in the Army Air Corps. He received his military wings in January 1942.[3]

Assigned to the 445th Bombardment Group (H), Stewart was promoted to the

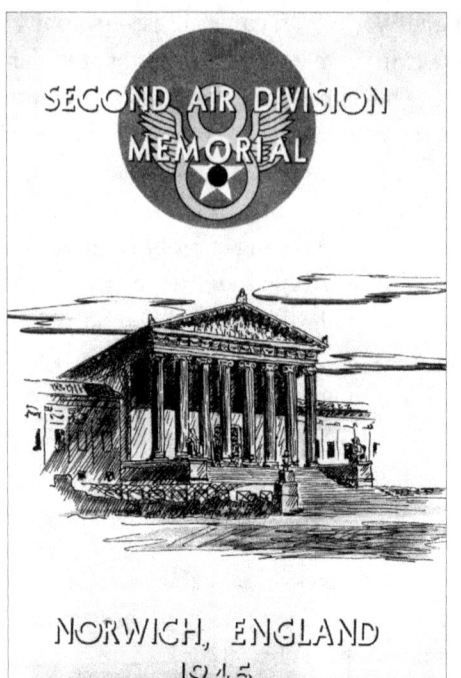

SECOND AIR DIVISION MEMORIAL

NORWICH, ENGLAND
1945

The Flame Must Burn On!

When the last bomb has been dropped, the last shot fired ; when the winds aloft have washed the last traces of this holocaust from the skies, we who are left will go home. As some returning soldier so aptly put it : " If the Statue of Liberty wants to see me again, she'll have to turn around ! "

But what of those whom we must leave here ? We all have memories of gallant comrades who paid the supreme sacrifice in war-torn hostile skies and those who died honorably in line of duty. In order to perpetuate their memory, we propose to erect a Memorial to these honored dead—*your* Memorial to *them*. This Memorial must be a spiritually living thing. The deep and sacred feeling giving birth to this Memorial, their spirit of youth, hope, and desire for a world of decency, freedom, and peace must live on—must imbue this Memorial with that same sacred spirit dedicated to oncoming generations whose way of life they died to protect. This Memorial must be a haven wherein the flame of their principles must burn brightly and eternally, wherein the bewildered, stumbling footsteps of succeeding generations can be unerringly placed on the right paths.

The Memorial will be in Norwich, England,██████ ████████████████████ It is proposed, in agreement with the Norwich City Council, who have agreed to furnish the site and build the main library building, to construct a Memorial Entrance Hall to this proposed Municipal Library, fitted with commemorative sculpture, art, plaques, and decorations, and setting forth in detail the history of the Groups of the Second Air Division, with the names of our comrades and records of the organizations.

This Hall will be flanked by two rooms fitted with literature, art, music, etc., written about America by Americans, and endowed for its continuous upkeep for generations to come. The sole entrance to the library will be through this Hall.

The estimated cost of this Memorial is £20,000 or $80,000, which, divided among the ████████ ████ personnel of this Division, brings the individual contribution to a comparatively small amount. All contributions will be voluntary and each one permanently recorded. Again . . . it is *your* Memorial to *your* friends.

Depending upon labor conditions and supplies, and priority of construction, existent in England after the War, it should take about three years minimum to construct a Memorial of this magnitude and importance. However, should the library for some unforseen reason not be built, the funds collected will remain in trust, and if another suitable memorial can not be decided upon by the trustees, the entire sum will be turned over to the United States Army Air Forces Relief Fund.

For those who survive this conflict, this Memorial will be a source of pride and enjoyment for our accomplishments. It will be a place where we can bring our families and friends in years to come and relive these days of our years.

For those who have paid the supreme sacrifice, and for whom there can be no permanent resting place, such a Memorial to their families and friends will represent tangible living evidence of the heart-felt gratitude and love of their country and comrades with whom they lived and fought—for when the airfields are plowed up, and all vestiges of the chaos of war have disappeared in time, this will remain a perpetual tribute to their memory—to their faith in an ideal

Second Air Division Memorial Committee

██████████████████
*(Obliterations made for
Security Reasons)*

HEADQUARTERS 2d AIR DIVISION
APO 558

To The Men of 2D Division :

The plan for the erection of a memorial to the men of 2d Division who have given their lives for their country has, I know, a universal appeal. All of us have friends and comrades who have been lost in action against the enemy or who have died in performance of their duty as American soldiers. These are the hard and bitter facts of war. These men live in our memory not only because of our sense of personal loss but also because of the admiration and respect we have for them and for the supreme sacrifice which they have made for their country and for their comrades. Their loss has been even more deeply felt by their loved ones at home to whom they will never return.

This memorial will be a shrine to which the families and loved ones of these gallant comrades, and indeed many of us, may return in years to come. It will be in every way worthy of the men whose memory it perpetuates and of the cause for which they gave their lives. The stately and beautiful hall of memory will furnish a harmonious setting for the Group plaques to be placed on its walls and for the bound volumes containing Group histories and the Group Rolls of Honor. More than that, however, it will be a memorial of living spiritual significance for, through the American Reference Library and the American Reading Room, it will bring a daily influence of American thought and ideals to the people of the Norwich community with whom we have been so closely associated during these difficult years.

I know that all of you will welcome this opportunity to express in concrete form what so many of you already have in your minds, and the collection of the sum required will not be difficult if the response is as enthusiastic as I expect it to be.

Together we have built the 2d Division into one of the greatest aerial striking forces in history. Together let us build this fitting memorial to its officers and men who have sacrificed their lives to overthrow the enemies of our country in order that the ideals of our American democracy, and indeed all democracy, shall endure.

W. E. KEPNER,
*Major General, USA
Commanding*

Norwich Memorial pamphlet

rank of captain as the squadron commander of the 703rd Bombardment Squadron based at RAF Tibenham, Norfolk, England. While with the 703rd Bomb Squadron, he flew 20 combat missions flying B-24 Liberators. In January 1944, Stewart was promoted to the rank of major. Soon after, on March 30, 1944, he was transferred to the 453rd Bombardment Group (H) at Old Buckenham in the role of group operations officer. There, Maj. Stewart continued to fly combat missions until June 1944, when he was promoted to lieutenant colonel and appointed as the chief of staff of the 2nd Combat Wing of the 2nd Air Division headquarters at Hethel.[4]

As the 453rd Bomb Group's operations officer, Stewart was highly respected and admired by all the crews for his commitment to the welfare of everyone who served under him. He was a serious, no-nonsense, and tireless commander who often worked throughout the night with his assistant, Capt. Andrew Low, on the morning briefings before each group's mission. Stewart was a familiar sight perched atop the control tower, where he watched each squadron take off on their mission, and then again when they returned. We were indeed fortunate to have him with us at the 453rd.

I never had a chance to visit the 2nd Air Division Memorial at Norwich, but I'm sure it's a beautiful place, a fitting gesture to honor all those who didn't make it home. When our crew began our missions in January 1945, we owed our successes to those who came before us, the ones who did the hard work. It was during the earlier years of the war, in 1943 and 1944, that the Allied Air Forces were able to defeat the Luftwaffe and achieve absolute air superiority. The price was high and resulted in tremendous losses. The US 8th Air Force suffered its heaviest casualties during those crucial years. By the time we joined the conflict, the German Air Force was no longer an effective fighting force and was on the threshold of total disintegration. With a bomber-to-escort fighter ratio of almost one to one on every mission, there was little damage overall that German interceptors could accomplish in attacking our large, heavy bomber formations.

We achieved a great victory, but I didn't realize the full breadth of our accomplishments until I had the opportunity to read the reports from the United States Strategic Bombing Survey. The purpose of these reports was to determine the effectiveness of the strategic bombing effort in the defeat of the European Axis powers. Known more widely as the USSBS, this organization was established by the secretary of war at the request of President Roosevelt on November 3, 1944.[5]

The USSBS employed hundreds of military and civilian experts to collect, collate, and compile a huge amount of evidential material from a wide variety of sources for the survey. Physical examinations and inspections of the extent of damage caused by frequent bombing raids in many of the major cities in Germany were carried out. Focus of these inquiries included hundreds of industrial plants and other vital facilities associated with the German war effort. Volumes of statistical and documentary material were obtained from captured German government documents. Included in the study were thousands of interviews and interrogations conducted on surviving political and military leaders immediately after the cessation of armed conflict.

From more than 200 reports on specific aspects of the Allied strategic bombing campaigns, some interesting facts were revealed. It wasn't until the Casablanca Directive was issued in the beginning of 1943 that a clearly established strategic bombing plan was formulated. Its goal was to eliminate Germany's ability to sustain the war by destroying its economic and industrial infrastructure. The first intensive bombing campaign began with Operation Pointblank in June 1943 against the German Air Force. The battle for dominance in the skies over Europe was a resounding success. From January through April 1944, the Germans lost more than 1,000 fighter aircraft per month.[6]

The attrition rate of German fighter aircraft and experienced pilots was so great that Generalleutnant Adolf Galland, commander of the German fighter force, admitted that from mid-1944 to the end of the war, the Luftwaffe ceased to be an effective fighting force. It was never able to recover from its losses. This fact was most evident during Operation Overlord, when very few enemy aircraft were encountered to oppose the thousands of Allied aircraft over the skies of Normandy on D-Day. The defeat of the Luftwaffe was the Combined Bomber Offensive's most important achievement of Operation Pointblank and unquestionably paved the way for the successful Allied air campaigns that followed in its wake.

Soon after the success of Operation Overlord, the next air campaign initiated by Allied air forces against the Axis oil industry went into full gear. The success of the oil campaign essentially destroyed Germany's ability to sustain its economic vitality and military operations against the advancing Allied forces. The fall and winter oil campaigns against the oil and petroleum industry in 1944 severely crippled Wehrmacht operations. By December 1944, the lack of fuel supplies led to the disaster of the German Ardennes Offensive in Belgium.

When our crew arrived at Old Buckenham in January 1945, the German war machine had already been starved for oil for many months. In February and March, when the Russians were well into their winter offensive, the German Army sent 1,200 tanks to the Eastern Front to counter the advance of the Red Army. It was a futile effort in itself, but it was compounded by the fact that they were all soon immobilized by the lack of fuel and finally overrun.[7]

Not only was the Wehrmacht suffering from the lack of oil supplies, but so was the Luftwaffe. It was Hermann Göring's opinion that the destruction of the oil industry was the most critical factor in crippling Germany's ability to maintain effective military operations. For the German Air Force, this was undeniably true. After the Russians occupied the crude oil fields in Ploesti, Rumania, and Hungary in late 1944, only 13 synthetic oil plants inside Germany were able to produce enough aviation fuel to keep the Luftwaffe in operation. By the time we started our combat missions during the final phases of the Allied oil campaign in January 1945, aviation fuel production had dropped well over 97 percent of that produced in April 1944. Every synthetic oil plant had been subjected to massive bombing raids.[8]

Yet, many of our missions, which extended well into February, were still targeting oil-producing plants. (Our last oil target was at Paderborn on February 23, 1945.) This was because of the immense German efforts to get the damaged oil facilities up and running as quickly as possible. Any other alternative would have led to disastrous consequences for the Wehrmacht. Huge numbers of laborers, as many as 350,000, were employed to salvage, repair, and rebuild synthetic oil plants that our air forces were constantly bombing. Such plants were very susceptible to air attack because of the diverse and complex industrial components necessary to produce oil and petroleum products. Oil production facilities were situated in large industrial complexes that weren't as easily dispersed or hidden as other industrial systems.

Some severely damaged oil plants were up and running within days of an intensive bombing raid. Thus, there was a crucial need for repeated attacks on the largest synthetic oil production plants. The Leuna synthetic oil industrial complex in eastern Germany was the most important, protected by smoke screens and one of the largest concentrations of antiaircraft artillery batteries in Europe. Targeted throughout 1944, Leuna was bombed 22 times, with 20 raids by the US 8th Air Force and two by RAF Bomber Command. In January 1945, Leuna was still producing synthetic oil products at 15 percent capacity. It continued its production at this rate until the end of the war despite all Allied efforts to completely destroy the facility.[9]

In essence, the oil campaign never truly came to an end, with oil targets being bombed to a lesser extent throughout March and April and until the end of the war. However, in February 1945, the next Allied air campaign came onto center stage, targeting the communication and transportation systems. The vast and intricate German railway network system, along with the crucial autobahns supporting vehicular transport, linked its major industrial cities and enabled Germany to have a thriving and robust economy to sustain the war effort. The success of the Allied oil campaign severely crippled Germany's industrial base, but the following destruction and disintegration of its railway and water transport systems finally caused its total collapse.

The bombing of communication and transportation targets began in earnest in February and continued through all of March. With good weather, the US 8th, 9th, and 15th Air Forces initiated massive bombing raids during the day, while RAF Bomber Command continued the raids by night. Every part of the railway system was struck, including railway yards, switching centers, train stations, repair shops, locomotives, and moving stock. In conjunction with rail targets, heavy attacks were made on the key inland water transport systems in western and central Germany.

Both the rail and water transport systems acted in a highly synergistic way to provide all the necessary components to support Germany's economic and industrial base. Passengers, freight, and raw materials, such as coal and steel, could be transported by both the numerous rail routes that crisscrossed the entire country and ships and barges along the extensive and well-established rivers and canals linking the major cities. The bombing of river bridges, canals, and viaducts started earlier than the railways, in late 1944. On September 23, 1944, the destruction of the crucial Dortmund-Ems and Mittelland Canals stopped all water transportation traffic between the Ruhr and major cities of the northern coast and central Germany. A key bridge over the Rhine River at Cologne was destroyed on October 14, 1944. Traffic coming out of the Ruhr dropped sharply, and the supply of coal products to southern Germany ceased completely.[10]

Approximately 40 percent of coal traffic from the Ruhr depended upon the railways. By March 1945, with the almost total destruction of the main railway networks in the Ruhr, coal traffic came to a halt. Because the German economy, with its industrial base, was powered directly by coal, it was now on the verge of collapse. Solly Zuckerman was again correct in his assessment of the importance of a viable transportation system. The railway system was the nervous system of the German economy. Coal products were the lifeblood of Germany's industrial base. When these essential products ceased to flow, it terminated the German war effort.

In mid-April, Albert Speer, Minister of Armaments and Production, told Hitler that military activities would cease in a few weeks due to the lack of supplies. It was the resounding success of the Allied air forces' transportation campaign that was the decisive blow, completely destroying the German economy. The limited amount of war goods produced by manufacturing plants and factories that remained extant became irrelevant, because it was virtually impossible to move the necessary war material to the front lines. In any case, the trickle of equipment and supplies that were able to reach the troops would have made little difference in the final outcome. The Wehrmacht was completely stymied by the severe decrease in mobility as well as impaired communications between OKW headquarters and German field commanders. This was directly due to the extreme disruption of their operational activities by the constant and relentless Allied bombing raids. The increasing lack of the supplies and war material that the German forces needed to sustain military operations soon became crucial and would finally lead to their defeat.

With the end of the Allied strategic bombing campaigns on April 16, 1945, the goals of the Casablanca Directive had been achieved. "The progressive destruction and dislocation of the German military, industrial and economic system" was now complete. (See Appendix 2.) By May 1, the remaining German armies on the Western and Eastern Fronts were eliminated, with American forces established on the Elbe River and the Russians having captured Berlin. While the Allied air forces played a decisive role in winning the war in Europe, they couldn't have done it alone. It was a combined effort of the Allied air, naval, and ground forces that ultimately led to the defeat of the Axis powers in the ETO. Each played an indispensable role in securing victory with the total destruction of Hitler's Third Reich and Nazi Germany.

As one of the three heavy-bombardment air divisions of the US 8th Air Force, the 2nd Air Division completed 493 operational missions and flew 95,948 sorties. A total of 1,458 B-24 Liberator bombers were lost on these missions.[11] As a component of the 2nd Air Division, our bomb group, the 453rd Bombardment Group (H), played its part in the success of those missions. The 453rd Bomb Group flew 259 missions, with the first at Tours, France, on February 5, 1944, and the last at Amberg, Germany, on April 11, 1945. The 2nd Air Division Memorial at Norwich, England, is a reminder of the 6,389 men who perished and made it possible for us to finish what they'd started. It's because of their bravery and sacrifice that we were able to complete our job and return home with victory.

It's for them that we can say, "Mission accomplished!"

ADDENDUM

CONGRESSIONAL MEDAL

On December 20, 2018, the 115th Congress of the United States issued a document, Public Law 115-337, which enacted the Chinese American World War II Veteran Congressional Gold Medal Act. Its purpose was "to award a Congressional Gold Medal, collectively, to the Chinese-American Veterans of World War II, in recognition of their dedicated service during World War II." (See Appendix 7.)

A large number of such medals were minted and sent, upon request, to every Chinese American veteran who served in World War II. Chester Fong received one of these medals.

Congressional Medal

Note from Letty Fong

My family and I are extremely proud of my dad for receiving the World War II Congressional Gold Medal and being one of the Chinese Americans who fought in the war. Dad absolutely hated wars and violence. He was never the type to go hunting as a sport. Yet, when he enlisted in the army at the age of eighteen, he had no reservations about the tasks required of him. Because Dad didn't want to go to war and didn't care to be a soldier, he took his time getting to his assignment in Delaware. He loved telling me how he stopped at many of the cities along the way from California via train and took it as his opportunity to travel and see the United States. As a result, when he did finally arrive at his destination, he was almost charged AWOL.

Dad was always interested in flying planes, but because of a muscle imbalance in his eye, he couldn't. So he ended up as a tail gunner in the air force. He wouldn't say too much to me about the details of his missions, although I'm sure it pained him to drop those bombs. But he knew it had to be done to end the war. He always said that in the end, it was the ordinary people, the civilians, who suffered the most in the war. I do know that he kept each pin tag of every bomb drop he did over Europe. He accomplished all his duties during those difficult and stressful times in the war, then earned a commendation for his service.

Considering he was the only Chinese American on the base he was aware of, Dad said he never felt out of place. He said he got along well with everyone he met. He spoke highly and affectionately of his crewmates. He had a lot of respect for John Harrington, the crew navigator, who taught Dad many things about the inner workings of the Liberator. Thus, it was and still is a pleasure for our family to connect with Glenn Harrington, John's son. Glenn has vivid memories about his dad during World War II, the crews, the missions, and their adventures, which we're so grateful to know about.

One thing that especially made me feel proud about Dad is Glenn telling me about this: "All the members of the Swingle Crew could fly the B-24, even Chet. When they went up practice flying or to break in an engine (called 'slow-timing,' where the engine was gradually broken in) they 'unofficially' trained each crew member at the controls so if the pilots were wounded, someone could fly the plane home. Chet could fly the plane and even land it if need be."

Even though I know the last thing in the world Dad would want to do was fight in a war, he did it with valor and dignity. And in the end, I believe he felt it was one of his proudest accomplishments. He talked a lot about his war trials and tribulations as well as his funny stories, and I know it helped shape him as the smart, confident, loving, kind, supportive, compassionate, and constantly learning man he became. Everything he did during his tour of duty, he gave 100 percent in doing the best he could while never expecting anything in return. I know Dad would have been so happy to receive the Congressional Gold Medal.

Dad, with his air force wings, is looking down on us, beaming with pride over such an honor, I'm sure!

– Letty Fong

APPENDIX 1

OUR MISSION ROSTER

MISSION	453RD BG	DATE	CITY	TARGET
1	#206	January 16, 1945	Magdeburg	Oil
2	#208	January 28, 1945	Dortmund	Oil
3	#211	February 3, 1945	Magdeburg	Oil
4	#216	February 15, 1945	Magdeburg	Oil
5	#218	February 19, 1945	Jungenthal	Munitions
6	#219	February 21, 1945	Nuremberg	Rail
7	#221	February 23, 1945	Paderborn	Rail
8	#222	February 24, 1945	Lehrte	Rail
9	#223	February 25, 1945	Giebelstadt	Airfield
10	#224	February 26, 1945	Berlin	Rail
11	#227	March 1, 1945	Ingolstadt	Rail
12	#233	March 8, 1945	Siegen	Rail
13	#234	March 9, 1945	Münster	Rail
14	#237	March 12, 1945	Wetzlar	Rail
15	#238	March 15, 1945	Gardelegen	Rail
16	#239	March 17, 1945	Münster	Rail
17	#241	March 19, 1945	Bäumenheim	Jet Factory
18	#247	March 24, 1945	DZ-Wesel	Airdrop
19	#252	April 4, 1945	Wesendorf	Airfield
20	#256	April 8, 1945	Fürth	Airfield
21	#258	April 10, 1945	Rechlin	Airfield
22	#259	April 11, 1945	Amberg	Rail

APPENDIX 2

CASABLANCA DIRECTIVE

U. S. SECRET
BRITISH MOST SECRET
C.C.S. 166   January 20, 1943

COMBINED CHIEFS OF STAFF

THE BOMBER OFFENSIVE FROM THE UNITED KINGDOM

Memorandum by the British Chiefs of Staff

It is suggested that the following directive be issued by the Combined Chiefs of Staff to the appropriate British and U. S. Air Force Commanders to govern the operations of the British and American Bomber Commands in the United Kingdom.

DRAFT DIRECTIVE

1. Your object will be the progressive destruction and dislocation of the German military, industrial and economic system, and the undermining of the morale of the German people to a point where their capacity for armed resistance is fatally weakened.

2. Within that general concept, your primary objectives, subject to the exigencies of weather and of tactical feasibility, will for the present be in the order of priority set out below. This order of priority may be varied from time to time according to developments in the strategic situation. It is not to be taken to preclude attacks on Berlin when conditions are suitable for the attainment of specially valuable results unfavorable to the morale of the enemy or favorable to that of Russia.

    (a) German submarine operational bases and construction yards.

    (b) The German aircraft industry.

    (c) Transportation.

    (d) Synthetic oil plants.

    (e) Other targets in enemy war industry.

3. There may be certain other objectives of great but fleeting importance for the attack of which all necessary plans and preparations should be made. Of these, an example would be important units of the German Fleet in harbor or at sea.

4. You should take every opportunity to attack Germany by day, to destroy objectives that are unsuitable for night attack, to sustain

86

continuous pressure on German morale, to impose heavy losses on the German day fighter force, and to contain German fighter strength away from the Russian and Mediterranean theaters of war.

5.   If and when it is decided that the Allied armies should reenter the Continent, you will afford them all possible support in the manner most effective.

6.   In attacking objectives in occupied territories, you will conform to such instructions as may be issued from time to time by His Majesty's Government through the British Chiefs of Staff.

87

APPENDIX 3

ORGANIZATION OF THE GERMAN AIR FORCE (LUFTWAFFE)

Officer Ranks

German	American
Generaloberst	General
Generalleutnant	Major general
Generalmajor	Brigadier general
Oberst	Colonel
Oberstleutnant	Lieutenant colonel
Major	Major
Hauptmann	Captain
Oberleutnant	First lieutenant
Leutnant	Second lieutenant

Tactical Units

The basic structure was the *Gruppe*, roughly equivalent to a US Air Force group. The Gruppe was led by a *Major* for bomber units and a *Hauptmann* in fighter units, but this could vary considerably depending upon the available personnel and unforeseen circumstances. Under optimal situations, the Gruppe consisted of 40 to 50 aircraft and was composed of several *Staffel*, or squadrons. The Staffel, with 12 to 16 aircraft, was split into combat formations of a *Schwarm* of four aircraft, or a pair called a *Rotte*.

In the case of *Jagdgeschwader* (JG), or Day Fighter units, which could consist of up to three Gruppen, JG 7 was the largest Me 262 jet fighter unit, with each Gruppe stationed at different Luftwaffe jet airfields.

Designation of Gruppe and Staffel Units

The Gruppe number is represented by a Roman numeral:
 III./JG 7 is the third Gruppe of the jet Jagdgeschwader 7 unit.

The Staffel number is indicated by an Arabic number:
 9./JG 11 is the ninth Staffel unit in the Jagdgeschwader 11 unit.

APPENDIX 4

GERMAN HEAVY ANTIAIRCRAFT ARTILLERY

At the start of World War II, the 88 mm Flak 18 gun was well-established as an efficient and effective weapon against heavy bombers. It went through several production modifications and upgrades to become the final 88 mm Flak 41 model, which was used extensively throughout the war. This workhorse heavy artillery piece was used in all branches of the German armed forces. Production of the Flak 41 began in 1942, and it was considered the best antiaircraft gun at the time. With an absolute firing altitude of 48,500 feet and as a very effective antiaircraft weapon at 33,000 feet, the gun was ideal for destroying enemy bombers flying at high altitudes. Firing a 32-pound high-explosive shell, the gun became a deadly menace to attacking bombers.[1]

The versatility of the 88 mm Flak 41 made it the Wehrmacht's weapon of choice, whose ground troops could use it to destroy enemy tanks, bunkers, and heavy defense fortifications. Its armor-piercing shell was capable of destroying any tank the Allied armies had at the time. Weighing in at 17,600 pounds in a stationary position, the 88 mm gun was highly mobile and transported by heavy trucks, along with the infantry. The armor-piercing shell of the 88 mm gun was so effective in penetrating enemy tank turrets and concrete bunkers that the gun was structurally modified and mounted on heavy tractors and armored vehicles as an anti-tank weapon. This led to further developments and the formation of the Kampfwagenkanone (KwK), which in essence became a highly mobile form of the cannon itself. The 88 mm KwK was then mounted on the chassis of German Panther and, eventually, Tiger tanks. The mobility of the 88 mm gun as an anti-tank weapon was now complete. The Panthers and Tigers proved to be especially devastating to Allied tanks and other armored vehicles.

Larger-caliber guns were developed during the course of the war, with German troops employing the 105 mm Flak 38 and 39 in 1940. With an increased shell weight of 57 pounds, hand-loading became unfeasible. The incorporation of a semi-automatic breech with electric firing capabilities enabled the 105 mm gun to fire 12 to 15 rounds per minute. As the heavier-caliber gun gave much more of a punch as an antiaircraft weapon than the 88 mm, the 105 mm Flaks were made mobile on specially designed tractor trailers and specialized flatbed railroad cars. In many areas in Germany, especially in the Ruhr region, scores of such mobile artillery batteries were frequently used to follow the American bomber streams as they flew to their targets. These mobile batteries of guns allowed the Germans to attack the bombers as soon as they flew into German airspace. As a result, Americans were often attacked by antiaircraft fire long before they reached their target.

The 128 mm Flak 40 was the largest flak gun developed and produced in large quantities. It was considered the best antiaircraft weapon in the war. The Flak 40 was capable of firing a 104-pound explosive shell to a maximum altitude of 48,840 feet. Electric automatic loading, combined with a specially designed electrically

128 mm Flak 40 Guns

DEFEAT OF NAZI GERMANY

powered aiming gear, made the 128 mm Flak a formidable weapon. Its rate of fire was 10 to 12 rounds per minute. On average, the 128 mm Flak 40 required 3,000 rounds to bring down a four-engine bomber, which was much more effective than either the 88 mm Flak 41 (8,500 rounds) or the 105 mm Flak 39 (6,000 rounds).[2]

Because of its heavy weight of 39,600 pounds and extreme barrel length of 26 feet, the majority of the 128 mm Flak guns produced were permanently placed in fixed positions. In 1942, the first twin-barreled 128 mm Flak 40 was delivered to the Luftwaffe's antiaircraft units. These mammoth guns were placed atop enormous flak towers built in Berlin, Hamburg, and Vienna. Some of these towers rose to heights of nearly 300 feet above the ground. They were solidly built with reinforced concrete, making their eight-foot-thick walls impervious to destruction by any artillery shell or heavy-duty bomb that the Allies had during the war.

All the flak towers were multilevel with five to six levels above ground and a large bunker below. The levels immediately below the 128 mm guns housed barracks for the gun crew and contained a hospital for the wounded. Those that followed contained emplacements for twelve multi-barreled 20 mm guns and 37 mm cannons to protect the tower from low-level aerial attacks. The bunker underneath the tower provided an air raid shelter for as many as 13,000 people, along with ample storage facilities for copious amounts of food, water, and ammunition stocks.

On top of the flak tower were positioned four heavy antiaircraft gun batteries, one on each corner of the tower. Each gun battery consisted of one twin-barreled 128 mm Flak 40 gun, for a total firepower of eight cannons. Each of the flak batteries required a crew of 21 men to operate. The heavy shell was placed on a sturdy loading tray and the fuse set. After that, everything from ramming the shell into the barrel to firing the gun became automatic and was controlled by a centralized fire-control station.

Each twinned 128 mm flak battery was able to fire at a rate of 20 to 24 shells per minute. A single salvo from a total of eight guns of the four antiaircraft batteries produced a considerable amount of firepower against enemy bomber formations. These eight exploding 128 mm shells were timed to detonate simultaneously in a specific pattern in the sky within an area of approximately 240 yards across. This area of the concentrated field of fire, also known as an antiaircraft "box barrage," presented a dense cloud of flak, which the bomber would need to fly straight through over the target. It was indeed a harrowing experience for bomber crews to see the sky thick with exploding shells all around them. It was truly nerve-wracking. We never got used to it. The amount of flak became most intense just before our bomb load was released, and all we could do was hope we didn't sustain a direct hit.

Raids on Berlin were considered the most dangerous. In 1944, the city was protected by 700 heavy flak gun emplacements, which included the four batteries of twin-barreled 128 mm Flak 40s atop each of the three immense flak towers. The Zoo flak tower was the largest, standing at 135 feet, and was located in the Berlin

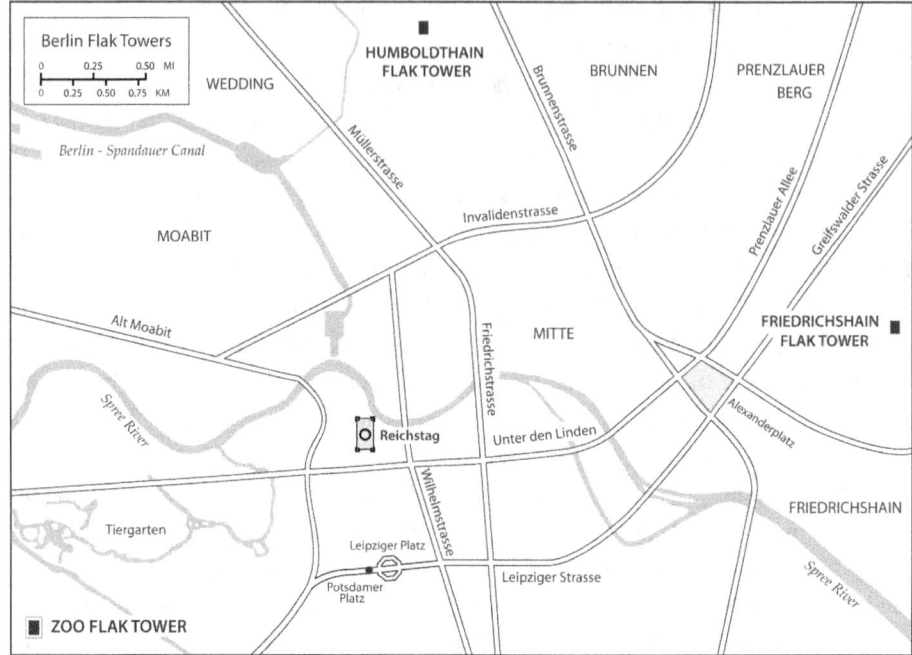

Berlin Flak Towers

WEDDING

HUMBOLDTHAIN
FLAK TOWER

BRUNNEN

PRENZLAUER
BERG

Berlin - Spandauer Canal

Müllerstrasse

Brunnenstrasse

Prenzlauer Allee

Greifswalder Strasse

MOABIT

Invalidenstrasse

Alt Moabit

Friedrichstrasse

MITTE

FRIEDRICHSHAIN
FLAK TOWER

Spree River

Alexanderplatz

Reichstag

Unter den Linden

FRIEDRICHSHAIN

Tiergarten

Wilhelmstrasse

Leipziger Platz

Spree River

Potsdamer
Platz

Leipziger Strasse

ZOO FLAK TOWER

Zoological Garden in the Tiergarten district west of the city's center. Two lesser towers were positioned in the Humboldthain district northeast of the government sector and in the Friedrichshain district nearby in the southeast. Each of the flak towers was situated between two and two and a half miles from the Reichstag. Along with the placement of the heavy flak guns were hundreds of light antiaircraft batteries. An intense flak area 40 miles wide surrounded Berlin's entire metropolitan area.[3]

By the time we began our first missions in early 1945, many of the heavy flak guns from all the major German cities were being moved to the Eastern Front on the Oder River to serve as anti-tank weapons against the advancing Russian armies. Yet damage from flak remained a constant danger. During the final months of the war, antiaircraft fire brought down more of our heavy bombers than enemy fighters did. A direct hit, or even one shell exploding within 100 or 200 hundred yards of the aircraft, could bring down a bomber. But large pieces of flying shrapnel associated with the intense barrage during a bomb run could inflict much more damage on the crew or the aircraft itself. Many times, severe injury to the pilot caused him to lose control of the aircraft, often with catastrophic results.

In earlier years, antiaircraft artillery units were within the army's domain. But in 1935, the flak units were transferred to the Luftwaffe to be incorporated into the air defense system. Members of these flak units were given a distinctive blue-gray Luftwaffe uniform with the service insignia of the flak artillery. With the horrendous losses of military personnel sustained by the German Army in 1944–1945, more and more soldiers from both the navy and Luftwaffe were sent to the front lines as replacements. Consequently, during the final year of the war, the shortage of manpower and material needed to keep the antiaircraft artillery units in serviceable operational condition became critical. Large numbers of home guard units were recruited to fill positions in the flak units. Many of these units consisted of young and untrained Hitler Youth members, mostly teenage boys and girls known as *Flakhelfer*, or flak helpers. The remaining personnel came from whatever was available, which included industrial workers, young people from occupied territories, and even POWs. Female flak helpers assisted by operating searchlights, running fire-control devices, and working as spotters for enemy aircraft.

The extreme shortage of optical and radar fire-control equipment in the final months of the war forced the flak units to rely more and more on the production of superbatteries, in which multiple flak batteries were linked together and controlled by a single fire-control station. Three of the four-gun antiaircraft batteries directed by a single, centrally located fire-control device represented a 12-gun superbattery. An improved version of the Wurzburg gun-laying radar enabled the transmission of firing data to the 12 guns located at the three separate sites. The concentrated firepower of superbatteries increased the likelihood of a successful hit against an enemy bomber. The added advantage of this system was the reduced need for personnel and fire-control equipment for each battery unit.[4]

Yet all these measures to keep the flak units fully operational to protect Germany against the increasing number of Allied bombing raids were in vain. The lack of supplies, such as an acute shortage of ammunition, and the extensive use of untrained volunteers manning the guns soon caused a steady deterioration in the quality of the flak units. The precision and accuracy needed to bring down enemy aircraft waned dramatically. The intensity of antiaircraft fire also rapidly decreased. By March 1945, we encountered less and less flak activity. On our final missions in April, flak was minimal, and in many cases there was none at all.

The final collapse of military operations and total destruction of Germany's economic infrastructure were a direct result of the devastation wrought by the massive Allied bombing raids in 1945, which were accompanied by an ineffective Luftwaffe defense and the failure of the heavy flak units to protect the cities.

APPENDIX 5

RISE AND FALL OF THE MESSERSCHMITT 262 JET FIGHTER

EARLY DEVELOPMENT

German aeronautical engineers had discussed the idea of a rocket-propelled aircraft as early as 1928. But it wasn't a reality until 1938, when Professor Willy Messerschmitt entered the scene to seriously study and develop a jet engine technology for the next generation of Luftwaffe fighter aircraft.

Messerschmitt was the brilliant engineer who designed, developed, and produced the excellent German Bf 109 fighter aircraft, which later evolved into the Me 109. He was invited to a secret meeting with the executives and researchers from the Bayerische Motoren Werke (BMW) to create and implement a working plan. Messerschmitt enthusiastically accepted the challenge. By 1939, he was able to submit his plans for a jet-propelled fighter to the German Air Ministry, also known as the Reichsluftfahrtministerium, or RLM. Reichsmarschall Hermann Göring was the head of the RLM, and all Luftwaffe activities had to be approved by him. With Göring's acceptance and support, the professor's plan went into action.

Messerschmitt and his team of research engineers decided to power the new aircraft, designated as the Messerschmitt 262 (Me 262), with turbojet engines. BMW was to build the engines and deliver them to his research team for testing at a facility located in Augsburg. In addition to the Me 262 projects, Messerschmitt was also actively involved in the development of another rocket-propelled aircraft that was fueled by a mixture of liquid hydrogen peroxide, hydrazine, and water. These studies eventually led to the production of the first rocket-propelled aircraft known as the Messerschmitt 163 (Me 163) rocket jet fighter. The fuel mixture burned for only two to three minutes, but it provided enough thrust to propel the Me 163 to an altitude of 25,000 to 30,000 feet to intercept heavy bombers. Unfortunately, the instability of the volatile fuel mixture, which tended to leak and cause fatal explosions, caused the death of more test pilots than those who actually flew the rocket during its brief operational career. It was definitely one of the Luftwaffe's more unusual fighter aircraft.

Repeated delays in the production and arrival of the promised turbojet engines from BMW forced Messerschmitt to turn to another company, Junkers, to supply the needed engines for the Me 262. The founder of the company, Dr. Hugo Junkers, had been working on a jet turbine engine even before World War I. In fact, both Junkers and Messerschmitt were competitors in the attempt to build the first jet aircraft. However, Junkers agreed to provide the latest turbojet engine, the Jumo 004, to Messerschmitt's team. Another rival company, Heinkel, was also deep into the development of their jet aircraft, known as the Heinkel He 280 jet fighter. However, the He 280 later proved to be inferior to the Me 262, and the RLM subsequently terminated Heinkel's program. It was only Messerschmitt's superior grasp of mathematics and excellence in high-speed aircraft design that allowed him to succeed in the race to produce the first operational jet fighter.

When the Jumo 004 engines finally arrived at Augsburg in late 1941, they failed miserably when submitted to a series of intensive engine tests. The heat generated in the turbojets' combustion chamber was so high that the metal alloys used to support the engine frame melted. Greater heat-resistant metallic elements—such as chromium, cobalt, and nickel—were needed. Junkers then promised to deliver a sturdier and more robust turbojet engine. However, these critical elements were in short supply, so it would take time. The result: more delays.

It wasn't until March 25, 1942, that the first prototype of the Me 262, designated as the Me 262 V1, was ready for a test flight. It occurred at the Augsburg Airfield and was manned by the renowned German test pilot Flug Kapitan Fritz Wendel. Wendel had flown every aircraft in the Luftwaffe, which included the Messerschmitt Bf 109 prototype. Rolling the jet down the runway, he increased the throttle to increase the speed. But he found the acceleration sluggish. There wasn't enough thrust from the turbojets. As he lifted off, he found himself quickly running out of runway. The aircraft cleared a fence at the edge of the airfield by just six feet.

After climbing and leveling off at an altitude of approximately 1,300 feet, Wendel decided to ease up on the throttle and vary the fuel mixture. All of a sudden, the turbojet engine under the right wing flamed out. He heard a slight *whoosh*, and then nothing. Then the left engine did the same. Without power, the jet began a rapid descent. Diving at a 60-degree angle, Wendel tried to pull the stick back to regain some flight control, but it remained frozen. He then braced himself against the cockpit and pulled on the stick with all his might. Luckily for him, he was able to move it and slowly regained level flight. With a piston engine attached to the nose of the jet as a fail-safe mechanism for instances such as the one he'd just experienced, Wendel headed for the landing strip. However, he was still unable to control the aircraft enough to prevent a hard landing, which ripped out the landing gear. The jet slid along the runway, severely damaging the turbojets. Wendel was fortunate the aircraft didn't flip over, which would have killed him instantly. He was bruised but alive.[1]

With the RLM deciding whether or not his Me 262 projects should be terminated after its first test flight resulted in a crash, Messerschmitt decided some improvements needed to be made. Junkers promised a redesign of the 004 turbojets, making them more powerful and increasing their structural strength with better metal alloys to cope with the high-temperature problems. It wouldn't be until the beginning of July 1942 that the new Junkers Jumo 004-A turbojets would be available to the plant at Augsburg for testing. Modifications were then applied to the aircraft to accommodate the heavy and sturdier turbojets. On July 8, Wendel climbed into the cockpit of the newest prototype, designated as Me 262 V3, for a second test flight. This was the jet's first unassisted flight without a backup piston engine should something go wrong. The moment of truth had arrived for the new aircraft, but Wendel was unfazed. And he was excited.

Like with the previous test flight, it took a long time before the jet gained enough speed for a successful takeoff. However, there were no problems, and Wendel climbed steeply to an elevation of 13,000 feet, where he leveled off. He was amazed at how fast and smooth the jet accelerated to reach this altitude. Flying at a speed of over 500 miles per hour without any noticeable effort was breathtaking. Easing back on the power, Wendel performed several aerial maneuvers, banking right and left and performing a wide 180-degree turn at a high rate of speed. The Me 262 remained stable, was responsive to the controls, and was remarkably easy to fly. Wendel had never experienced anything like it in any other aircraft.

After a successful landing, Wendel was happily greeted by a large contingent of spectators. Professor Messerschmitt was the first to eagerly shake his hand. Wendel was so impressed by the Me 262 that he wanted to buy one for himself. He was convinced that the jet would become a very useful addition to the Luftwaffe for attacking enemy bombers. Wendel stated in his report that it was important to pay special attention to the controls regarding the turbojets. Despite the success of the second test flight, the Me 262 was far from being ready for production status. It was to go through several more improved prototype revisions, with more than 50 test flights and nearly two more years before it would be ready to be sent to Luftwaffe units as a fully operational aircraft.

On May 22, 1943, Generalleutnant Adolf Galland, commander of the German fighter force, was able to test-fly the Me 262 V4 in Augsburg. Like Wendel, Galland was amazed at the jet's speed and performance. The general actually performed some serious aerial maneuvers with the jet, which included high-speed turns, loops, and steep dives. Being such a highly skilled and experienced pilot, he didn't encounter any major problems. Galland, like Wendel, was amazed at how easily the Me 262 responded to his control. The jet's smooth and relatively quiet movement as it sped through the clouds filled him with exhilaration and excitement. Galland immediately recognized Professor Messerschmitt's revolutionary accomplishment in creating the next generation of fighter aircraft. He realized that the Me 262 was a quantum leap in aerodynamic flight. Galland was so enthusiastic about getting the jet into the service of the Luftwaffe that he immediately sent a glowing report to Generalfeldmarschall Erhard Milch, who was in charge of the German Air Ministry.[2]

In his report, he identified the Me 262's great performance and potential capabilities as a great step forward over the current armada of piston-engine fighters. Galland emphasized the fact that this new fighter would radically change aerial warfare tactics against heavy bombers. His only reservation was the excessive length of time the jet needed to acquire enough speed to take off successfully. There were also some questions regarding such a sophisticated aircraft's requirements for a high-speed landing. Nonetheless, Galland believed that the Me 262 should be put into service as soon as possible.

After reading the report, Milch was also excited about the prospects of what the new jet fighter would bring to the German Air Force. Being an avid proponent of the new aviation sciences, Milch sought the willing approval of Göring, who'd also recently seen demonstrations of the new jet aircraft. The RLM then authorized the production of the Me 262 for the Luftwaffe.

On November 26, 1943, the first preproduction model, the Me 262 V6, was shown to Hitler at Insterburg in East Prussia. Also present were Professor Messerschmitt and General Galland. The first demonstration flight started off with some problems, as an engine flameout occurred. But the second aircraft took off without a hitch. The jet performed well, and the flight demonstration was a great success. Hitler was very impressed with it. He then turned to Messerschmitt and asked if it could carry bombs. The professor responded immediately. He told Hitler that it could carry at least a 500-pound bomb. Maybe even two. Hitler was overjoyed and said he'd been waiting for years for such a blitz bomber. The Führer then decided, on the spot, that the Me 262 would be used as a high-speed bomber.

Galland, standing next to Hitler, felt his heart sink as Hitler then ordered Messerschmitt to make the necessary preparations for the production of the Me 262 as a bomber.[3]

Galland knew without a doubt that the Me 262's use as a fighter-interceptor was the Luftwaffe's only hope in stemming the tide of the ever-increasing attacks by Allied bombers. Hitler had decided a long time ago that antiaircraft artillery would be the correct choice for defending the country against invading bombers. He considered the Luftwaffe as an offensive, rather than a defensive, weapon. Hitler's decision that day regarding the use of the Me 262 as a bomber was the beginning of Galland's long struggle to incorporate the newly christened aircraft into the ranks of the German fighter force as a successful jet interceptor.

Although the Me 262 V6 performed well for Hitler and other top Luftwaffe officials at Insterburg, there remained severe problems with the aircraft that needed to be rectified before actual production could begin. One was the performance of the Jumo engines. Individual components, like the turbine blades, often failed under the tremendous heat and pressure within the engine's combustion chamber. The damage occurred under excessive vibrations from the buckling and cracking of the turbine blades, primarily due to the lack of strength of the composite material used in the construction of these components. Because of the scarcity of vital elements, such as nickel and chromium, needed to produce the stronger and more resilient steel-based alloys that could withstand the rigors inside the combustion chamber, the problems caused by extreme temperature were never fully resolved. Thus, engine failures continued to plague the Me 262's ability to perform as expected in the field.

As late as March 1945, the Jumo engines had to be overhauled or replaced after only twelve to fifteen hours of service. Thus, the lack of engine reliability under the stress of combat operations continued to degrade the jet's effectiveness until the end of the war. At a critical time, when these jets were vitally needed in the air, many pilots couldn't fly their aircraft—aircraft that remained sitting on the ground, either being repaired or waiting for replacement parts that never came.

Another chronic problem was the throttle mechanism that controlled the turbojets. Of all the inherent dangers of flying the Me 262, engine flameouts proved to be the most deadly. Early on, test pilots quickly learned that controlling the throttle was of paramount importance in eliciting the turbojet engine's proper performance. As Fritz Wendel reiterated time and time again, the throttle must be controlled with gentleness and care. The pilot had to move the throttle slowly and carefully to control the turbojets while taking off or landing, lest a flameout occur with disastrous results. Many fatalities occurred for this very reason, even by experienced pilots. Engine failure due to flameouts often occurred at the most inopportune times. When pushed to the extreme limits of aerial combat maneuvers, engine flameouts were a constant hazard.

Despite these problems, mass production of the Me 262 went forward. There was no time for the usual research, development, and thorough testing of a new aircraft before being put into active service. The jets were rushed into service because the Luftwaffe desperately needed them. The first produced Me 262s were sent to Lechfeld on June 30, 1944, where a newly formed jet experimental unit, designated as Erprobungskommando 262 (Ekdo 262), was based.[4]

Commanded by Hauptmann Werner Thierfelder, the primary objective of Ekdo 262 was to train fighter pilots to fly the jets and test the jet's operational effectiveness in combat situations. The unit had been receiving prototypes of the Me 262 to test, but the newly arrived jets had the improved version of the Jumo 004-B turbojet engines. Each jet was fully armed with Rheinmetall-Borsig 30 mm quad-mounted cannons in the nose. Unfortunately, on July 18, 1944, Thierfelder was killed when American P-51 Mustangs attacked him above the skies of Bavaria. Ekdo 262 was then disbanded.

General Galland then formed a new jet unit, Kommando Nowotny, with many of the pilots from Ekdo 262 to carry on the program Thierfelder began. Chosen as commander of the unit was Maj. Walter Nowotny, a highly decorated fighter pilot who'd been a squadron leader with the JG 54 fighter unit. Nowotny had scored 255 victories on the Eastern Front. Units of Kommando Nowotny were relocated to Achmer and Hespe on September 26, 1944, and soon received more jet aircraft. Kommando

Nowotny had been the first Me 262 operational combat unit. Hitler admired Nowotny, and he was one of the Führer's favorite pilots in the Luftwaffe. At twenty-four years of age, Nowotny was one of the youngest German fighter aces. Galland was confident that Nowotny would prove to be successful in demonstrating his unit to be exceptionally effective in the use of the German jets against Allied heavy bombers.

Throughout October 1944, Kommando Nowotny showed itself to be highly successful in using the Me 262 fighter jet to attack and destroy Allied aircraft. Twenty-two enemy aircraft, which included both heavy bombers and their P-51 fighter escorts, were shot down. Nowotny's pilots had learned to develop new tactics and combat techniques against the heavy bombers. Relying on the jet's superior speed and utilizing its formidable quad-mounted 30 mm cannons, the pilots demonstrated this combination to be exceptionally deadly. The firepower of these explosive cannon shells was capable of downing a bomber with three direct hits, or completely destroying an enemy fighter with a single hit.

Galland was glowing at the success of the newly formed jet unit. Then disaster hit. On November 8, 1944, Nowotny was killed in an attack by American fighter aircraft while returning to base.[5]

JAGDGESCHWADER 7

With the loss of Nowotny, his unit was disbanded. The fighter pilots of Kommando Nowotny were then used to form the nucleus of the first regular jet unit. It was designated as Jagdgeschwader 7, or JG 7. The first Gruppe of JG 7, designated as III./JG 7, was formed in mid-November 1944. This Gruppe was commanded by Maj. Erich Hohagen and based in Lechfeld. Two new Gruppe were soon to be added to JG 7—I./JG 7 and II./JG 7—both of which were moved to Brandenburg-Briest Airfield. To command JG 7, Galland chose a willing and capable German ace pilot he'd known for many years, Oberst Johannes Steinhoff. He'd served at every front and destroyed 176 enemy aircraft while flying over 900 missions. Considered by many to be one of the Luftwaffe's most versatile fighter pilots, Steinhoff had flown both day and night fighter aircraft and become an accomplished pilot of the Me 262.

By January 1945, Steinhoff had built JG 7 into an effective and highly destructive force against Allied bombers. Due to Galland's concerted efforts to supply his fighter forces with the needed Me 262A-1a fighter jets, JG 7 was receiving the jets as soon as they became available. When Hitler ordered all Me 262s produced to be used as bombers, Galland had to find a way to work around this obstacle to fulfill JG 7's needs. He contacted Professor Messerschmitt and Albert Speer. They all agreed on how important it was to produce the Me 262 as a fighter-interceptor.

Messerschmitt stated that he would accelerate the production of a new jet bomber, known as the Arado Ar 234, to satisfy Hitler's request for such an aircraft. Speer, with his dispersed aircraft production sites throughout Germany, produced the Me 262A-1a jet fighter for Galland's jet units. Both Galland and Speer tried, time and time again, to convince the Führer of the need for an effective jet fighter against Allied heavy bombers. But Hitler would hear nothing of it. Galland remarked that it was like talking to a deaf man.

With the success of Ekdo 262 and Kommando Nowotny jet units in their ability to consistently destroy Allied bombers and fighters, Hitler began to appreciate the usefulness of the Me 262 as a jet fighter. Speer finally convinced him to release one Me 262 fighter to Galland's fighter units for every other Me 262 jet bomber that was being produced. Although Speer's production efforts were able to produce over 400 jet fighters per month till the end of the war, it still wasn't enough to fill the void created by combat losses. However, despite the limited availability of jets, Galland's jet fighter units proved to be a serious weapon against the Allied air forces.

With the ability to put up to 30 jets to attack Allied bombers at any one time, field operations of JG 7 increased dramatically in February 1945. Although Steinhoff had about 60 pilots on hand, most of them were new, inexperienced recruits still in the process of training on flying the jets. However, many of the squadron leaders were skilled in combat with the Me 262. Almost all of them had come from Ekdo 262, and then Kommando Nowotny. Some, such as Erich Ruderffer, Theodore Wissenberger, Franz Schall, Walter Shuck, George-Peter Eder, and Hermann Buchner, were all German aces. All flew with JG 7, and they represented the best of the Luftwaffe's fighter pilots. Their keen ability to develop new tactical maneuvers and increasing experience with the jets in attacking heavy bombers paid off substantially. But the incorporation of a new and deadlier form of weapon system employed by the Me 262 grabbed the immediate attention of the commanders of the US 8th Air Force. It was the R4M air-to-air rocket.

THE ORKAN HURRICANE

Professor Messerschmitt and his team had long considered the potential use of air-to-air rockets on German fighter aircraft. It began with the development of unguided rockets such as the Werfer-Granate-21 (Wrg-21) and R100BS, which were primarily used for ground assault. Luftwaffe fighter aircraft used the Wrg-21 in 1944. It was simply a tube-launched projectile of a modified army mortar shell. They proved to be highly inaccurate and made little impact when used against enemy aircraft.

In early 1945, the professor's engineers came up with a more feasible air-to-air rocket design they thought might prove workable when used by the Me 262. The engineers named it *Orkan*, which means "hurricane." Its technical designation was the Rakete 4 kg Minenkopf, or simply the R4M rocket. It was simply a slender steel tube approximately three feet in length and filled with a solid-fuel propellant. An impact-fused warhead was attached to the front end of the weapon. The rocket itself weighed a mere 7.7 pounds.[6]

Initial tests with the R4M proved the weapon to be unstable and wildly inaccurate. But as the engineers honed the working model, they made improvements to stabilize the rocket's flight. Eight slender fin-like structures were attached to the tail end of the rocket, which popped out immediately after the rocket was launched. This provided the needed directional control for the rocket's flight to its target. The tail fins didn't give the R4M pinpoint accuracy in hitting its target, but it did prove to be highly effective. Fired in salvos of 12, the R4M rockets gave the Me 262 a very deadly weapon against heavy bombers. A single rocket hit could destroy a bomber. Even a near hit was enough to disrupt the entire bomber formation and, in some cases, induce fatal air-to-air collisions.

The R4M air-to-air rocket's warhead contained an armor-piercing 55 mm caliber shell containing a little over one pound of hexogen, also known as RDX (the agent in the plastic explosive C-4). Twelve R4Ms were fitted onto a wooden rack under each wing of the Me 262 jet fighter. When loaded onto the rack, the eight fins of each rocket were folded down and bound together by a spring steel wire. As soon as each rocket was fired, the eighth fin was designed to spring free and, in the process, release the other seven fins. This normally occurred after the rocket had flown about eight feet from its launch point. The R4M had a rated maximum velocity of 1,772 feet per second.[7]

The beauty of the R4M rocket was that its effective range was 3,300 feet. Consequently, the attacking Me 262 jet fighter could fire its rockets well beyond

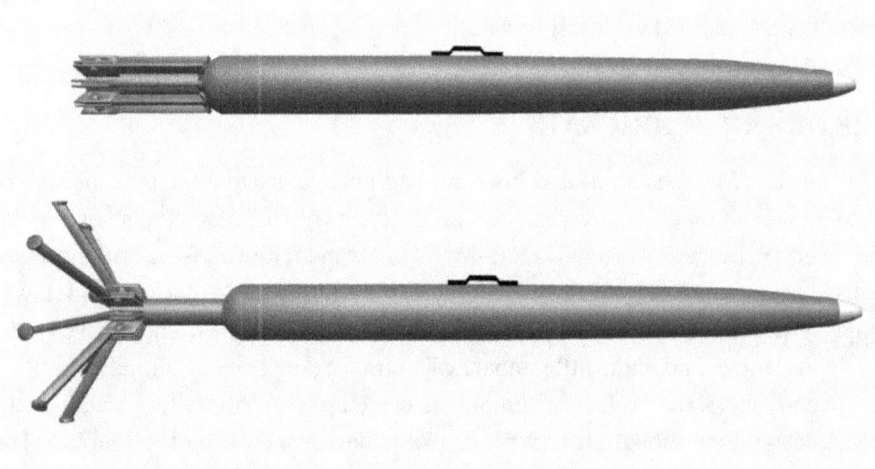

R4M Tail Fins: Folded/Expanded Positions

Me 262A-1a Firing R4M Rockets

the range of the bomber's .50-caliber machine guns. Soon after JG 7 received the R4Ms, other jet units were issued the lethal weapon system. The use of these rockets gave the jets the means to effectively break up the integrity of the closely knit bomber formations. Waves of attacking enemy fighters launching multiple salvos of rockets into the formation almost always created utter chaos and confusion. The bombers were then vulnerable to attack by cannon fire.

On March 18, 1945, JG 7 units had their first chance to use the R4Ms against the US 8th Air Force bombers targeting jet airfields around the Berlin area. The effects of German jet fighters' devastating attacks with R4Ms were clearly evident, not only on the heavy bombers but also their P-51 and P-47 escorts. From that point forward, the origin of a true air-to-air missile against enemy aircraft revolutionized aerial combat.

Realizing that the R4M rocket was capable of being the ultimate weapon against heavy bombers, Professor Messerschmitt personally supervised the construction and implementation of the wooden launching racks underneath each wing of the Me 262 jet. Each rack contained 12 rockets, each of which was carefully slid into the rack's guardrails through a sliding lug on top of the rocket. Each rocket thus hung freely in the rack's slot, with its eight rear stabilizing fins folded in place. Electronic ignition of the rockets was accomplished through cockpit controls initiated by the pilot. The R4Ms could be fired in salvos of six or twelve under each wing at any one time.

JAGDVERBAND 44

Perhaps the most famous Me 262 jet fighter unit was Gen. Adolf Galland's squadron of *Experten* (ace) fighter pilots, known as Jagdverband 44 (JV 44). The origin of JV 44 began at the end of December 1944, when Hermann Göring telephoned Galland to tell him that he'd been relieved of his command as general of the Fighter Force. Göring had no clear reasons why Galland had to go, but the move was obviously a political one. The Luftwaffe's high command structure had been greatly influenced by SS officers close to Hitler and his associates, especially Heinrich Himmler.

Galland had a long history of problems with these Nazi officials, who knew nothing of the German Air Force and its day-to-day operational activities. Then there was Göring himself, who bore the brunt of Hitler's fury over the Luftwaffe's inability to effectively deal with the Allied bombing raids. Of course, Göring blamed Galland and his fighter pilots for not doing their duty. Göring went so far as to threaten Galland's pilots with execution. This led to an increasing degree of personal animosity between Galland and Göring. In any case, Galland could not offer any kind of defense in this matter, and he accepted his fate.

When Albert Speer discovered what had happened, he immediately confronted Hitler, who himself knew nothing of the conversation between Göring and Galland. Using his amiable influence on Hitler, Speer convinced the Führer of the injustice placed upon Galland. Hitler then agreed to drop all charges against Galland, and the general was ordered to report to the Reich Chancellery to meet with him. Upon arrival, Galland discovered that Hitler was away on business, and he consequently met with Oberst Nickolaus von Below, who was Hitler's Luftwaffe adjutant. Von Below told Galland that he was to set up a jet unit to prove the superiority of the Me 262 as a fighter aircraft. Galland thought such an order was very strange because Kommando Nowotny and JG 7 had already proven the jet aircraft's capabilities. Yet, he accepted. It was a far better choice than any other alternative left for him.

On January 23, 1945, Göring officially announced that Galland had been dismissed from his post as general of the Fighter Force, and Oberst Gordon Gollob, who had close ties with the SS, was appointed to take over Galland's duties and responsibilities. Upon Hitler's order, Galland's unit was formed on February 24, 1945. Galland chose the name Jagdverband 44 for his unit, and its base of operations was Brandenburg-Briest Airfield. Located just 30 miles west of Berlin, JV 44 was well-positioned to defend the Berlin area from enemy bombing raids. Generalleutnant Karl Koller, the chief of the general staff of the Luftwaffe, ordered Galland's unit to be formed as a *Staffel* (squadron) with a complement of 16 operational Me 262 jets and 15 pilots. This meant that Generalleutnant Adolf Galland was now the commander of a mere squadron of jet fighter pilots!

JV 44 was designated as an independent unit, outside the general purview of the Luftwaffe's high command. This suited Galland just fine because he now had the opportunity to run JV 44 as he saw fit. The first action he took was to enlist his friend and fellow ace pilot Oberst Johannes Steinhoff as JV 44's principal training commander. At the time, Steinhoff was the head of JG 7, and when he was offered the position at JV 44, he jumped at the chance to be with Galland's squadron. With his extensive combat experience with the Me 262 jets, Steinhoff was well-placed.

His first task was to enlist as many pilots for the unit as he could find. Galland wanted the best fighter pilots Steinhoff could scrounge up to join JV 44. Steinhoff eventually built up an impressive team of fighter pilots he recruited from other Luftwaffe units, experienced instructor pilots from flight schools, and even wounded veterans recovering in hospitals. Eventually, more than 40 pilots served in JV 44, although only fewer than half that number was actively engaged in combat operations at any one time. Seven of these were of Experten caliber—highly decorated fighter pilots with over 100 confirmed victories under their belts. Steinhoff himself had 176 victories.[8]

On March 28, 1945, the German High Command ordered Galland to move JV 44 farther south from Brandenburg-Briest to Lechfeld. Much of the industrial centers in northern Germany had been almost totally destroyed by Allied bombing raids. Defense of the jet airfields and vital military production facilities in the south had to be defended. Galland then decided that Lechfeld wouldn't be suitable and chose to send JV 44 to the large airbase at Munich-Riem, which was situated less than five miles east of Munich. It was one of the few jet bases that remained fully operational. Months of intensive efforts by the US 8th Air Force to destroy every other base in northern and central Germany were so successful that most, if not all, existing Luftwaffe jet units were forced to move south.

On April 5, 1945, five Me 262 jets from JV 44 took off from Munich-Riem on their first full combat missions against American bombers. Their pilots made a good account of themselves, destroying at least six heavy bombers. The succeeding days of April 7, 8, and 9 were also successful interceptions. It was on April 16 that Galland, for the first time, led his squadron against a group of American B-26 Marauder medium bombers. Armed with R4M rockets, Galland brought down two Marauders by firing a salvo of rockets into their tight formation. Hauptmann Walter Krupinski, flying next to Galland, was amazed at the R4Ms' tremendous destructive power. One Marauder received a direct hit and just disintegrated in midair. Another had its entire tail blown off and immediately turned downward through the clouds.

Tragedy then struck on April 18, 1945, when JV 44's field headquarters received a call that enemy heavy bombers were over Stuttgart, heading for Regensburg. Galland and his pilots immediately responded by rushing out to their aircraft. Galland was to take the first flight of three Me 262 jets, and Steinhoff was to take the second three. Galland's group had just taken off and watched in horror as Stein-hoff's jet hit a recently patched bombed-out crater on the runway during his takeoff. His jet veered out of control, lifted off the ground, nosed back down, hit the ground, and exploded. Seeing thick smoke rising from the crashed aircraft, Galland was in tears, convinced that Steinhoff was a dead man. The other pilots who witnessed the accident felt the same.

However, Steinhoff miraculously survived, and his account of what happened that day described his harrowing experience. As his jet was gaining sufficient speed down the bumpy runway, he had to get it off the ground as he approached the end of the runway. Just at that moment, the jet's left undercarriage hit a poorly covered bomb crater. The left wheel came flying off, and the aircraft was propelled about three feet into the air. Without sufficient speed to take off, Steinhoff knew he was going to crash.

Hauptmann Walter Krupinski was on the runway to the left and behind Stein-hoff when he crashed. Krupinski had to veer sharply to avoid colliding with the doomed aircraft. As Krupinski's jet took off, he could see Steinhoff's plane hit the ground and explode. He felt the shock wave of the blast as his jet climbed away. In fact, the pilots taking off after following Steinhoff's lead were also buffeted by the shock of the explosion, and they felt the intense heat, even though they were over 100 feet away.

As his jet crashed hard onto the ground Steinhoff felt the stinging heat of flames burning through the canopy. He was trying to unfasten his safety belt when the plane suddenly exploded and became engulfed in flames. He managed to force open the canopy and climb out. Covered in flames, he fell down and rolled on the ground, but its surface was covered with burning jet fuel. As the twenty-four R4M rockets and 30 mm cannon shells exploded around him, Steinhoff tried to run from the burning wreckage but was repeatedly knocked down by the concussive blasts. Everyone on the airfield immediately rushed to his aid. They managed to pull him away from the burning wreckage, and in doing so, some of his rescuers suffered severe burns.

Steinhoff was barely conscious while his fellow pilots tried to calm and reas-sure him as they quickly carried him from the field and into a vehicle. There was no ambulance at the airbase. It took an hour to get him to a hospital in Munich. Suffering third-degree burns over much of his body, it was an excruciating journey. His rescuers attempted to remove his smoking outer clothes but stopped when they found that his skin was so badly burned that it just peeled off. His odds of survival were slim at best. However, the doctors at the hospital managed to save his life. When Galland and his pilots returned from their mission, they couldn't believe Steinhoff survived the crash. Galland immediately went to the hospital. His friend was a very lucky man. But it took many years of medical care before Steinhoff eventually recovered from the horrific incident.[9]

Galland was to lose more of his fellow pilots in the days ahead. As with the other jet units still capable of launching attacks, every interception with Allied heavy bombers resulted in an ever-increasing loss of both Luftwaffe aircraft and pilots. Galland realized that the war was lost and coming to an end. So he gathered his men and told them that he didn't want them to sacrifice their lives needlessly. They were free to go home. The war would be over for them. He wanted only volunteers to carry on the fight to the end. But all his pilots refused to leave. It was now clear that Germany was defenseless against the continuing Allied bombing raids. They only wanted to prevent more death and destruction.

On April 26, 1945, Galland flew his last mission. He led the first group of six Me 262 jets to intercept 16 American B-26 Marauders northwest of Munich. The bombers were on their way to bomb the Lechfeld Airfield. Galland's force ran head-long into the bomber stream. Closing in fast at 990 feet per second, he swooped down from a twelve o'clock high position to attack. Flicking off the safety switch on the control to launch the R4M rockets, he pressed the firing button. But nothing happened. He'd failed to switch off the second safety switch. But he still had his cannons. With his gunsight focused on the bomber, he fired a volley of cannon shells from all four of the 30 mm guns. With a direct hit, the B-26 exploded.

Galland then flew through the group of bombers at a high rate of speed, banked around, and headed toward the rear of the formation. He picked out a bomber and fired a salvo of rockets into the formation. A B-26 took a hit, but Galland didn't have time to see if it was fatal. As he passed through the bomber formation, he felt his plane shudder as a number of .50-caliber shells struck it. Even with the damage sustained by the defensive machine gun fire from one of the bombers, Galland was determined to see the fate of the second bomber he'd hit. So he banked steeply to port and observed the B-26 stagger out of formation, ablaze and spewing thick black smoke. The stricken bomber then began spinning downward, out of control. Galland had his satisfaction of a confirmed kill, but it proved to be a big mistake.

As he flew through the formation of the 8th's 17th Bomb Group to see the results of his second kill, T.Sgt. Henry Dietz, the waist gunner aboard the lead ship of the 34th Bomb Squadron, caught a glimpse of his jet. Galland had flown right into the sights of Dietz's .50-caliber gun, so he immediately fired a few bursts, but nothing happened. Then Dietz just kept firing above and below the flying jet, hoping for a hit. Dietz noted that the tail gunners in the flight of bombers above him were also firing at Galland. That's when Galland felt the hits on his jet.

Noticing the increasing loss of fuel, Galland decided to break off the attack and veered away. Then a stream of machine-gun fire pounded his jet, piercing the canopy and smashing the instrument panel in front of him. A sharp pain shot through his leg as a shell grazed his right knee. Lieutenant James Finnegan of the 50th Fighter Group had watched Galland's attacking jet hit the second bomber. Finnegan was at 13,000 feet, high above the bomber stream. Seeing Galland's Me 262 being hit several times by bomber defensive fire, Finnegan saw his chance and dove steeply in his P-47 Thunderbolt to attack the jet. At extreme speed, Finnegan gave a short burst of fire from less than 300 feet away. Shells from the P-47's guns smashed through the jet's canopy, wounding Galland.

The sky suddenly became filled with bomber escort fighters. Galland's jet was now severely damaged, with multiple hits on both his left and right engines. He was running out of fuel, his leg was bleeding profusely, and his only chance of survival was to escape as fast as possible. As much damage as his jet had sustained, Galland pushed for full throttle. Surprisingly, he was still able to outrun the pursuing Mustangs. He immediately headed for home.

But upon arrival, he found the airfield under attack by a group of American P-47s that were strafing and bombing everything in sight. Coming in fast, Galland landed the jet hard. He quickly jumped out of the canopy and dove into a nearby bomb crater. That probably saved his life, as bullets whizzed past his head and bombs burst around him. He was taken to the hospital and would recover from his wounds, although it left him with a slight stiffness in his right knee for the rest of his life. He would never fly combat again.[10]

The next day, Oberleutnant Heinz Bar took over the command of JV 44 while Galland was recuperating in the hospital. With the war ending in a matter of days, Galland's Verband 44 unit fought on despite the increasing losses of pilots and aircraft. On April 30, the 45th Infantry Division of the US 7th Army met heavy resistance from determined SS Wehrmacht units in the Oberschleissheim area, but the Germans were defeated. The 45th Division was able to capture Munich. Anticipating the capture of Munich-Riem by the advancing American army, JV 44 had made its final move from the airfield the day before to Salzburg, Austria. It would be their last place of refuge.

THE DISINTEGRATION OF JG 7

As with JV 44, other jet units were forced to move from one airfield to another as the Allies advanced deep into the heart of Germany. All units remaining in active service headed south as northern Germany was quickly being cut off from the south. JG 7 was the largest operational jet fighter unit in the Luftwaffe. Its Staffel units were also forced to move farther and farther south from their main bases in Brandenburg-Briest and Parchim. They relocated first to Plattling, then Mühldorf, Landau, and finally Prague-Ruzyne. The end of JG 7, during its chaotic and unorganized forced evacuation from northern Germany, was fully documented by one of its foremost pilots, Oberst Hermann Buchner.

Buchner had flown over 600 missions during the war and was a leading ace pilot with the Me 262 jet. He was one of the original pilots who served with Kommando Nowotny. After the death of Nowotny, he moved on to the newly formed JG 7 in December 1944. Buchner was assigned to 9 Staffel of JG 7 at Parchim, while 10 Staffel was based at Oranienburg and 11 Staffel at Brandenburg-Briest.

In early March 1945, Buchner asked for a transfer to 10 Staffel. By the time he arrived at Oranienburg on March 18, the airfield had been put out of commission for a length of time by the American bombing raids. Returning to Parchim with the ground crew, Buchner flew subsequent missions from that airfield. By early April, American bombing raids against the existing jet airfields had intensified, especially those where operational units of JG 7 were located. Worse yet, American fighter aircraft made it a practice of constantly loitering around the airfields to attack jets that were taking off or returning to land after a mission.

On April 7, Buchner was returning to Parchim from a mission against an 8th Air Force bombing raid in the Hannover-Magdeburg area. His Schwarm[11] received a call on their radio to avoid landing at Parchim and instead go to Wismar on the Baltic. Parchim Airbase was under attack. On the way to Wismar, a group of American P-47 Thunderbolts was seen approaching Buchner's unit. Quickly landing on a grassy area beside the runway, Buchner could see that the airfield was already under attack by enemy fighters. By the time his jet came to a complete stop, several aircraft on the runway and ground crew vehicles were aflame. With a P-47 coming around for a second pass, Buchner jumped into an open trench just in time to escape the enemy fighter's strafing fire.

All through March and April 1945, hundreds of American fighters hunted German jets in the air and on the ground. Almost half of all casualties incurred by jet pilots happened while being attacked in their attempt to take off or land. JG 7 lost many of their pilots in this manner—a number that included experienced commanding officers. Slowly but surely, the grinding loss of aircraft and pilots weakened and ultimately destroyed the operational capabilities of all the jet units.

Buchner and his fellow pilots were fortunate that day because the thick smoke from the burning wreckage on the airfield prevented the enemy fighters from coming around again and again to strafe them on the ground. Their aircraft were functional enough to return to Parchim. On return, they found the airfield severely damaged by the 8th's air raid. The bombed-out runways were being repaired by engineers, forced laborers, and American prisoners of war. Buchner sadly found out that the commander of his Staffel, Oberleutnant Franz Schall, had been killed earlier that day. Running short of fuel, Schall had tried to make an emergency landing outside the airfield. His jet was damaged and an attempt to make a fast belly-landing resulted in the loss of control and a fatal crash. Schall died in the burning wreckage.[12]

The next day, April 8, Buchner and his Schwarm took off from Parchim to attack American bombers in the Bremen area. He was able to score hits on several heavy bombers, but, due to the great number of American escort fighters covering the bombers, he couldn't determine the success of his encounter with the bombers. He had to break off the attack because he was low on fuel. Looking for an airfield near Bremen, he couldn't find any. The Allied forces had already occupied many of the remaining airbases. Finally, he found one at Rotenburg an der Wümme, in the Lüneburg Heath. With the last drops of fuel in his tank, Buchner was coming down toward the runway when he saw something blazing on his right wing. Seeing hits on the ground in front of him, he realized that he was under attack by an enemy fighter. A P-51 Mustang had appeared from nowhere. Its pilot was most likely following Buchner to his home base. With his aircraft coming to a stop, Buchner's jet engines took successive hits from the marauding P-51, causing his aircraft to quickly catch fire.

As his jet became enveloped with intense flames, Buchner had to thrust himself out of the cockpit. Bouncing off the wing, he fell hard onto the ground. He realized that he still had his parachute on while he picked himself up and sprinted away from the burning aircraft. He ran on pure adrenaline for about 150 feet before collapsing, unconscious. Rescued by medics and taken to the airfield's medical facilities, Buchner was more in shock than seriously injured. The ground crew told him that the enemy Mustang came back around to finish off his burning aircraft.

Again, Buchner had managed to survive an attack while landing his jet. Considering how many jet pilots were killed by enemy fighters in such a manner, he couldn't believe his good fortune. It would be the young pilot's last combat mission of the war.[13]

After making his way back to Parchim from the airfield at Lüneburg-Heath, Buchner was ordered to drive with two other pilots to the JG 7 jet unit at Brandenburg-Briest and fly three Me 262 jets back to Parchim. Yet, when Buchner and his accompanying pilots arrived at Brandenburg-Briest, it was under heavy attack. An ongoing American bombing raid was destroying everything in sight. The remaining Me 262s that were supposed to have been flown back to Parchim were now a pile of burning wreckage. The situation was getting worse by the day. Buchner soon realized that combat operations of JG 7 in northern Germany were quickly unraveling into a complete state of dissolution.

Buchner was able to confiscate a Bücker Bu 181 Bestmann that had just landed at the airfield. The small twin-seated monoplane was used extensively to train new cadets at the Luftwaffe's flight training schools. The pilot, in fact, was a student who'd flown the Bu 181 from the flying school at Magdeburg East. American troops had just taken Magdeburg (April 11, 1945), and the student was told to immediately take off to escape capture. Buchner convinced the pilot to exchange his Bu 181 for a moped, which the pilot immediately hopped on and drove straight home. Buchner was then able to fly back to Parchim from Brandenburg-Briest on the next day.

Another surprise awaited him when he arrived at his home base. Parchim Airfield had been completely destroyed by bombs. The flying elements of his Staffel had to land at Alt-Lankwitz, and the unit's ground elements relocated to Prague and other airfields in southern Germany. Buchner was then ordered to lead a truck convoy to the Prague-Ruzyne airfield. But upon reaching it, he was ordered to drive to Deggendorf, where JG 7 had set up its new headquarters. By now, Buchner's multiple journeys had been increasingly dangerous and deadly due to enemy attacks by both fighters and fighter-bombers of the US 9th Air Force. Travel could be accomplished only at night, since it was suicidal for any moving military vehicles to be on the road during the day.

It was now April 21, and at Deggendorf, Buchner discovered that the remaining elements of JG 7 were being moved to Mühldorf in Bavaria. Buchner was ordered to undertake another long, tortuous journey, during which he had a close call from an attack by American fighter-bombers. A truck in his convoy loaded with R4M rockets exploded when hit by enemy bombs. The massive explosion destroyed a number of vehicles and even some houses nearby.

Buchner finally arrived at Mühldorf Airfield around April 24 or 25, just about the time when Berlin was completely surrounded by Russian forces. As far as Buchner was concerned, the situation with operations within his own unit had become intolerable—and even essentially nonexistent. It didn't matter much anyway, since he knew the war would soon be over. In fact, he, along with his fellow officers, wasn't the least bit surprised when the commandant announced to everyone that there would be no more operations at Mühldorf. The few flying jets of what was left of JG 7 were now at Prague-Ruzyme, where they would continue combat operations, primarily against the advancing Russian troops. The remaining elements of JG 7 in Mühldorf were to be disbanded and enlisted personnel released from active duty. For Buchner the war was over.

By May 3, 1945, Buchner had arrived home in Salzburg, Austria, and reunited with his wife and family. He heard that some Me 262 jets had recently landed at the Salzburg airport. Out of curiosity, Buchner and his wife went out to the airfield. Upon arrival, they saw ten Me 262 jet fighters parked neatly in a row near a local inn. It turned out that the inn was the headquarters of what was left of JV 44. There he met some old friends, including Maj. Erich Hohagen, who'd been Buchner's commander of Gruppe III./JG 7, before Hohagen joined Galland's JV 44 unit. It was, however, a short reunion, as American troops marched into Salzburg two days later, on May 5. Just before the Americans took possession of the airfield, Oberleutnant Heinz Bar, as acting commander of JV 44, ordered the ground crew to destroy the last of the Me 262 jets in their unit.[14]

Thus, the amazing saga of the first successful combat jet-propelled aircraft in the Second World War came to its fruitful conclusion. The legacy of the German Me 262A-1a jet fighter would continue to live on for decades after the war, as air forces around the world continued the evolution of jet aircraft. But the Me 262's success against the Allied air forces was undeniable. It had served the Luftwaffe well during its brief operational existence.

APPENDIX 6

DAD'S WARTIME SERVICE: PLOWING THE RUTABAGAS
(GLENN HARRINGTON)

Some of this might be true . . .

Swingle Crew in front of B-24 Wandering Wanda. Dad is second from left, standing. Chet Fong is kneeling at the far left, front row. (USAF photos)

JOHN T. HARRINGTON,
2ND LT. UNITED STATES ARMY AIR CORPS, SN: 07072724

I want to tell the story of Dad's wartime service, a series of vignettes and impressions I grew up hearing about. Unlike many wartime vets who seldom talked about their experiences, Dad talked about his often. The events were constantly on his mind, and he was outspoken about his service with the US Army Air Corps (USAAC), 8th Air Force.

The internet has much information available to augment the stories and give them relevance. There are blogs and websites with scanned documents and photos posted, including official unit histories. Many armchair historians have tracked down, scanned, and posted every scrap of information for the greater good. Because of this, I have found mission reports, crew lists, and photos to use as references. I am eternally in their debt.

I was able to make contact with the last surviving member of Dad's crew using a blog entry. His relatives came across a post I made and were able to make contact. I'm thankful for that.

TWENTY-THREE TRIPS BUT NEVER LANDED

Dad went overseas in 1945 and flew 23 combat missions, all over Germany. His last mission, in fact, was the last heavy bombing mission flown by the 8th Air Force, to Bad Reichenhall. He was haunted by his experiences and suffered occasional nightmares the rest of his life.

FIRST, AN ENLISTED MAN

Dad got drafted into the US Army as an enlisted man. He could have received a deferment since he worked as a tool-and-die maker, a critical wartime skill. One of his projects was to design an underwater cable cutter to cut through mine anchor cables and underwater entanglements. It was a handheld device that would hook around a steel cable, and with a blank shotgun shell would shoot a hardened steel cutting blade to cut through the cable so the mine would float free. It could be operated by one hand and was disposable for single use. It was supposed to be used by US Navy frogmen, UDT personnel (precursor to the US Navy SEALs). A key feature was that it was sealed so no bubbles were given off that could reveal the frogman's position.

TRAINING

During basic training, Dad received a battery of tests, which revealed a high mechanical aptitude. So he was selected to train as an aircraft and power plant mechanic. He later found out the basic classes in front of and behind his ended up in the D-Day Normandy Invasion.

After basic training, he ended up in Charleston, South Carolina. When his unit arrived during the heat of the day, they entered the barracks and were astounded that there were several blankets at the foot of each bed. "Typical stupid army," they muttered, "giving us blankets in hot weather!" Later that night, every blanket was in use as the nighttime chill descended.

Another issue Dad encountered in the south was the segregation of that era. He found that restrooms and other facilities for Black people were designated as "colored." He thought that was ridiculous and used colored restrooms anyway, even though he was white. Several times he was called out by the locals. Someone would say, "You went into a COLORED restroom!"

His reply, with typical Dad humor, was, "Yes, I saw it was colored. It was painted yellow inside."

This went on until some Black people tipped him off that the Southerners took segregation very seriously and would even kill him if they thought he was making a joke out of it.

He stood guard duty in Charleston, enforcing nighttime blackout regulations. Lights from the shore could silhouette the many transport ships and make them easy targets for German U-boats. His orders were to first give out a warning and then shoot out any light that was visible. He had several altercations with civilians who wouldn't shield their lights from view. He was astounded that they wouldn't follow regulations.

Dad liked to target shoot, and he made friends with the base armorers. (This was a recurring theme.) One of them had built up a personal M1 carbine that was reworked to match-grade perfection, combined with hand-built ammunition. Dad shot it and said, "You couldn't miss with it." Later in the war he shot all kinds of guns and ended up with two .45-caliber automatic pistols.

When they enlisted, the men received batteries of tests to determine their best assignment for the needs of the service. Dad later was sent to aircraft mechanic's school to get his A&P (aircraft and power plant) rating. He also was promoted to corporal. He was more proud of that promotion than becoming an officer after going through the aviation cadet program. His A&P rating came in handy later on when he was flying combat missions.

Dad applied for navigator school and was accepted to the nine-week program. He also entered cadets for OTS (Officer Training School) in Michigan. So he was commissioned to second lieutenant from corporal. OTS was like boot camp on afterburner—lots more yelling and an extremely accelerated pace. Anyone who couldn't keep up washed out. There were always minor made-up infractions that had to be worked off by walking a post with a seat-pack parachute strapped on that thumped the legs with every step. Dad soon became accustomed to walking posts.

He also received flight training as a pilot, which was part of the requirements to be a navigator. He trained in a Porterfield aircraft, similar to a Piper Cub. It was a two-place, tandem-seat, single-engine, and high-winged light aircraft. Once when he was up with an instructor above the airfield, the instructor spotted another rival instructor coming in to land. The instructor told Dad, "Spin it! We're going to land ahead of him!"

Dad protested that they were right over the field, but the instructor said again, "Spin it! That's an order!" So Dad landed the plane ahead of the other, and the two instructors jumped out of their planes and traded harsh words on the tarmac. Dad and the other student pilot just stood at attention. Being lowly cadets, they were left out of the argument and could only stand there and watch. Neither of them ended up in any trouble.

Later on, he got his multi-engine rating and transitioned to the B-24. A little-known fact is that the B-24 could be flown like a fighter plane when stripped down (no guns, armor plate, heavy fuel load, or bombs aboard). On training flights, the instructor would flip the plane around, and Dad had to recover to level flight, even with an engine feathered. It taught him great respect for the bomber's capabilities.

Since Dad scored high in mathematics, for a time he taught the subject to other army personnel at Michigan State University. One of his greatest shocks was when the entire room came to attention as he entered the classroom to give the day's lesson, even though some of the students outranked him.

Training also included many movies about various aspects of military life and special subjects. One film was about venereal disease. The movie so shocked some in the audience that several men passed out; others threw up on the spot.

GOLFING AND OTHER RECREATIONAL ACTIVITIES

Dad learned how to play golf as an officer. The base had many recreational activities to try out, all taught by expert instructors. He learned how to play golf from a man who'd been a golf pro in civilian life, with all golfing equipment provided. Because of that, Dad had a lifetime hobby as a golfer. He even joined the golf club at Sikorsky Aircraft when he worked there later in life. The army took great pains to have its officers be refined gentlemen, like making sure they learned to play golf. Dad also played some informal baseball and softball games. The army included one left-handed glove with every dozen ball gloves. Dad was amazed. "The army thinks of everything," he said. "Even supplying bats, balls, and gloves for use."

CHEATING AT CARDS

The army recruited a card-trick magician (I believe it was John Scarne, a famous magician of the era) to travel around to various bases to warn servicemen about crooked card games. With a standard deck of cards, he was able to shuffle the deck and deal himself any hand he wanted. He could deal himself four aces, or someone else four kings or a royal flush at will. Then he'd shuffle the deck and deal himself or anyone else blackjack every time. His motto was, "If I can do it, so can anyone else. And you'd never know it. So don't get into card games, and you won't get cheated." Dad met him while in the service. He played blackjack a few times and won a few hands, but he wasn't much into gambling.

BUILDING A PLANE

After Dad got commissioned and received his navigator's wings, he was assigned to an air base where there was a big lag in orders coming through. He was palling around with a group of fellow officers when the light bulb went on.

It was a training base for the A-26 aircraft, a hot twin-engine ship. Turns out there was a large junkyard of damaged aircraft that had suffered training mishaps. Dad had his A&P and was a scrounger, so he rounded up some friends and set about making a flyable aircraft out of all the junked ones. Fuselage, wings, tail, engines— they borrowed all the tools and fixtures. They ended up with a good plane and got it flying. They were able to get fuel and supplies since it looked just like any other US Army aircraft on base. Who would suspect anything?

One of the guys was from Texas, so on one trip, they flew to his hometown and ate authentic Mexican food for lunch. They flew around on other trips, with Dad doing the navigating. That is, until one day when they were in the plane, ready to take off, and the base commander showed up. He sat in the pilot's seat and said, "Let's go flying."

The men were all dumbfounded and stricken with fear of a massive court-martial. Somehow word had gotten out they had their own private A-26. The base commander started up the engines, taxied out, and took off. He flew a few maneuvers, entered the pattern, and landed. He gathered everyone together and said, "This is the best A-26 I've ever flown. Everything on it is perfect and rigged just right. But it doesn't have a tail number, so officially it doesn't exist. So it is hereby grounded!"

They had to take the plane back to the junkyard and leave it there. No action was ever taken against any of the men. That was the informal culture that existed in wartime.

GOING OVERSEAS

Dad shipped out on the liner *Aquitania* for Europe, a luxury cruise liner that had been converted to a troop transport ship. It sailed alone, relying on its speed for protection against U-boats. His berth was far below the water line, below decks. As the responsible officer he was assigned to be the last one out of his section if the ship were hit and sinking, to make sure everyone got out in case of "Abandon Ship." He recalled being out on deck to get fresh air and seeing the sun go from one side to the other as the ship sailed a zigzag course. No one was allowed on deck after dark so there would be no risk of anyone showing a light, such as a lit cigarette, that would give away their position to a marauding U-boat. While on board, he ran into one of his high school classmates, who was also in the army. The ship arrived on New Year's Eve in 1944; the next day was January 1, 1945.

Dad was assigned to the 453rd Bomb Group, part of the 2nd Air Division, 8th Air Force. The Mighty Eighth had three air divisions, the 1st and 3rd flying the B-17, and the 2nd flying B-24s. Each air division flew a common type. At the time there were two heavy four-engine bombers in the ETO: the Boeing B-17 and the Consolidated B-24. The B-24 was the most-produced American combat aircraft of all types during WWII. Since it had a large twin tail, the bomb group designation was painted on the tail with colorful stripes or patterns, for identification.

THE SWINGLE CREW

Many aircrews were assigned to fly together as a unit, even if they didn't always fly the same plane on every mission. Dad's crew was named the Swingle Crew after the aircraft commander 1st Lt. Raymond R. Swingle. The Swingle Crew was happy in that everyone got along well (with one exception, noted further on). Dad always spoke fondly of the tail gunner, Chet Fong, a Chinese American. I was able to get a list of the Swingle Crew with ranks and serial numbers as of April 20, 1945, from a personnel memo transferring them from the 453rd to the 458th Bomb Group.

Here are the members:

Raymond R. Swingle	1LT	O632278	Pilot/Aircraft Commander
Theodore W. Clark	2LT	O830823	Copilot
John T. Harrington	2LT	O7072724	Navigator
Ralph S. Gardy (748)	TSGT	18186688	Aerial Engineer/Gunner
John M. McCarl (757)	TSGT	13188051	Radio Operator/Gunner
Arthur W. Simpson (612)	SSGT	36866701	Armorer/Gunner
Melvin Weaver (612)	SSGT	18124999	Armorer/Gunner
William F. Hicks (748)	SSGT	18248529	Aerial Engineer/Gunner
Chester Fong (612)	SSGT	39135989	Armorer/Gunner

The officers have the letter *O* in front of their serial number, while the enlisted men have just the number. All the enlisted crew members were sergeants. This was for recognition of their special skills and training. In addition, if they were shot down and became a POW, they would secure slightly better treatment in the Luft Stalag. The number after their name is their MOS, or Military Operational Specialty.

Chet Fong was the last surviving crewman from the Swingle Crew. I'm in contact with his relatives, and we trade photos and memories. Chet saved a bomb tag from every mission as a souvenir. He was the tail gunner, who had the critical job of performing oxygen checks while flying at altitude. Periodically, the tail gunner would say, "Oxygen check," over the intercom, and every member had to check in. Above 20,000 feet or so, if someone's oxygen system malfunctioned, he would pass out from anoxia and could die within minutes.

Chet folded his wings on February 3, 2017.

Dad always referred to himself as belonging to the 458th Bomb Group, but he started out and flew most missions in the 453rd. The reason for the transfers was at that time in the war, the ETO was running out of targets, as the Nazis were being pushed back on all fronts and the occupied countries were liberated. It was realized that most crews would soon transition to the Pacific Theater of Operations (PTO) and the war in Europe would be over. Hence, personnel with fewer than 15 missions were reassigned to the PTO. Those with over 15 missions were reassigned to a different bomb group as time permitted. So the Swingle Crew was transferred to the 458th. While there, they flew one mission, which turned out to be the last heavy bomber mission flown by the 8th Air Force. The 453rd flew its last mission on April 12 and was withdrawn from combat operations for transition to the Pacific.

In a mechanized war such as WWII the people involved identified themselves as belonging to a unit and their hardware (ships, tanks, planes, etc.). It was realized that crew integrity was important to combat survival, so (as much as possible) crews were formed and stayed together throughout their tours, even if they flew different planes. Dad identified himself with the B-24 and thought it was the best plane ever. There was a friendly rivalry among heavy bomber crews, such as the B-17 and B-24, over which plane was better. Each thought the other had the inferior plane. The B-24 crews called the B-17 the Flying Outhouse, while the B-17 crews called the B-24 the Big-Assed Bird, due to its twin tail.

Dad was twenty-one years old when he went overseas in 1945 and was called Pops since he was actually one of the older men in the unit. He also had the nickname Red due his flaming red hair, before going mostly bald later in life.

The radio operator carried sets of extra crystals to tune in on different frequencies. He was able to get music from Switzerland and pipe it over the intercom to the crew, as well as talk to the fighter escort groups and others.

NINE MEN? WHY NOT TEN?

The crew list reveals nine instead of the traditional ten-man crew. The bombardier is missing for two reasons. First, each plane usually carried a bombardier, but at that stage of the war, bomb groups bombed as a unit, with all bomb squadrons dropping their loads with the lead ship in the formation. That meant the lead ship (plus an alternate) was the only plane that really needed a bombardier. The squadron would either all hit on target or all miss. When they missed, the term was "plowing the rutabagas," since any scrap of open land was planted with rutabagas, a root crop, to feed the German people.

The other reason Dad refused to fly with a bombardier came about on one mission, when the assigned bombardier went berserk on the way to the target. The nose of the B-24 had barely enough room for the two crewmen—the navigator and the bombardier—behind the nose gunner, especially since everyone was encumbered with heavy flying suit, flak jacket, helmet, Mae West inflatable life preserver, pistol, and oxygen equipment. The bombardier had the Norden bombsight up front, below the nose gunner. The navigator sat behind the bombardier with a tiny desk and seat for performing calculations.

On one mission, Dad was sitting at the desk when he heard over the intercom, "I'm going to kill you!"

He looked up, and the bombardier was pointing his .45 automatic right at Dad's head from inches away. Then the bombardier turned to the nose gunner and said, "Then I'm going to kill YOU!"

The nose gunner looked back over his shoulder in terror from the turret, which he'd entered through two tiny saloon-type doors. It was very difficult to squeeze through to sit at the gun controls. He never would have had a chance to get away.

The bombardier then scooted down through the small tunnel under the flight deck to get to the pilot and copilot. Dad followed, and as the bombardier pointed his gun at them, Dad jumped him and wrestled him to the floor, taking away the .45. Other crewmen jumped in, and they tied the bombardier up with intercom wire and put a spare oxygen mask on him. It was long flight to the target and back, with the bombardier screaming out and struggling to get loose.

Dad went back in the nose and dropped the bombs on the lead ship. The radio operator radioed ahead what was going on, and their plane was directed to land and taxi to a remote area of their base. From there, MPs met the plane and took the bombardier away. The crew never saw him again.

Dad taught himself how to use the Norden bombsight, and from then on he dropped the bombs. Several times his plane was the lead ship, and he toggled the bombs for the entire squadron. I have the bombardier's name but won't release it for privacy reasons. His episode could have been an anoxia-induced breakdown from oxygen starvation. It was also not uncommon for men to crack up under the strain of combat flying.

TWO .45S

That's how Dad ended up with two .45 automatic pistols: his own and the one taken off the bombardier. He wore them in twin shoulder holsters, one on the left and one on the right, over his leather jacket.

Dad liked shooting the .45. He made friends with the group armorer, and they'd go out to a revetment, where each would shoot a case of ammo, 500 rounds each, for target practice. He could shoot well with either hand. The armorer also had Thompson submachine guns that fired the same round. Dad liked shooting the tommy gun and could accurately fire three-round bursts with it.

Since Dad was a scrounger, he also tried to smuggle the .45s back home to keep. Returning GIs were told their belongings would be searched upon return to the States for any contraband, such as weapon bring-backs or government property. When the crew flew their plane back home on the ferry flight, Dad hid the pistols under the Norden bombsight. It was held in place by two thumbscrews. Once removed, there was just enough space to nest the two guns unseen after the bombsight was reinstalled.

After they landed and were searched, Dad expected to go back to the plane and pick up the guns. As it turned out, when they landed, they weren't searched at all. Instead they were whisked away from the plane and prevented from going back inside. Dad could have kept the pistols in his baggage. The plane went straight to the scrap area, so some lucky airman who removed the Norden bombsight to prepare the plane for scrapping got the two pistols.

SWINGLE CREW PLANES

Dad's crew flew missions in several different B-24s. Even though they flew together as a crew, they didn't always fly the same plane. The 453rd flew out of Old Buckenham Air Base. In the 453rd: B-24H-25-FO SN 42-95214, built by Ford (hence the "FO" code for Ford) at their Willow Run plant in Michigan, named "Wandering Wanda" after a popular song of the era.

We have a crew photo taken with *Wandering Wanda* in the background. There was another B-24 with the same name, but it was in the Pacific Theater of Operations and assigned to an entirely different bomb group.

The Swingle Crew also flew a B-24J-1-DT SN 42-51270 built by Douglas Aircraft Company in Tulsa, Oklahoma ((hence the "DT" code for Douglas Tulsa). It was named *My Bunnie II*. It featured a fully naked woman on the nose art. This wasn't unusual, but later in the war a directive came out to paint at least a bikini over any X-rated art. The high command didn't want the enemy to think our fighting men had pornography on their minds.

Chet's relatives have identified another aircraft, B-24J-65-CF SN 44-10575, built by Consolidated Aircraft in its Forth Worth, Texas plant. Its name: *Becoming Back*. The CF code was for Consolidated Fort (the "Worth" part not included in

Becoming Back (with the 453rd Bomb Group) nose art.

order to have a two-letter designation).

After transferring to the 458th, the crew flew out of Horsham St. Faith Air Base. I don't know what plane they flew for the one combat mission they had in the 458th.

After the war ended in Europe, the ferry flight home was in a B24H-15-CF SN 41-29567 built by Consolidated in Fort Worth. It was named *My Bunnie* and had been transferred over from the 34th Bomb Group, which originally trained in B-24s but was reassigned to fly B-17s.

JUDAS GOAT MISSIONS

Dad also flew some *Judas Goat* missions in the squadron B-24 assembly ship. The *Judas Goat* was a war-weary aircraft no longer combat-capable that was used as an assembly ship for the squadron to form up in the air before heading out on their mission. It was a stripped-down aircraft painted in bright, garish colors so the squadron could see it and gather round after takeoff. The name comes from a trained goat, called the Judas Goat, which would lead sheep into the slaughterhouse to their unsuspecting demise. Sheep and cattle would not go into a slaughterhouse alone, but would readily follow a goat.

Stripped down, a B-24 could be flown like a fighter plane. There was a friendly rivalry between the British RAF and American bombers. Turns out the British Avro Lancaster bomber (nicknamed the Lanc) had far superior performance to any American heavy bomber in terms of speed and bomb load. The British usually bombed at night but many times could be seen flying over the countryside.

One time, returning from a *Judas Goat* mission, Dad's crew spotted a Lanc flying around. They pulled up next to the Lancaster and feathered the two engines closest to the British plane. They gestured to the

The colorful "First Sergeant" B-24 Liberator was used to organize formations during the assembly of bombers in the sky. Bulb sockets were attached to the sides that lit up at night for night formations. January 1945. (NARA)

British crew to fly faster. The British then slammed their throttles wide open. As the British plane started to pull ahead, Dad's plane gunned its two operational engines and pulled ahead, climbing above the British crew to tease them.

BAD LANGUAGE

On one mission, the plan was to have a number of different bomb groups hit the target from different altitudes and directions so as to confuse the German defenses. Split-second timing would enable them to bomb the target in successive waves. Naturally, as it happened, all the groups arrived over the target at the same time and dropped their bombs through each other. It was a miracle no plane got hit by a falling bomb or had a midair collision. While this was going on, the planes were radioing each other over the command channel with lots of profanity, and worse, questions about which idiot had dreamed up this mission. The top brass were especially subject to abuse, and the crews named names over the airways, which was a security violation. Unbeknownst to them, all the radio chatter was being recorded on a wire recorder back in England. When the groups returned from that mission, they were assembled, had what they'd said played back to them, and got a severe tongue-lashing.

IRON PANTS/HOT TIP

Dad inherited a cute little dog as a pet from a crew that had rotated home. The dog would leave puddles in their hut, so it got the name Iron Pants. Later on, Dad changed its name to Hot Tip for the latest hot tip rumor about when the war would end. When Dad rotated home, he handed off the dog to someone else.

SPARE COMPASS

Dad always flew with a spare compass. The guys would sneak into the planes and drink the alcohol in the liquid-filled ship's compass. Alcohol was used to dampen the compass so it wouldn't freeze up at altitude. Once emptied, the compass would freeze up at altitude and be useless. Dad scrounged up a British Army Mark 1 prismatic marching compass with radium-painted needle and compass points to use in the plane. It was very well made and is still in the family today.

GEE NAVIGATION SYSTEM

Dad was trained on the Gee navigation system, a primitive LORAN system but high-tech for its day. It consisted of synchronized radio signals sent out from ground stations located a known distance apart. An aircraft equipped with Gee had several radio sets tuned to the different frequencies. When the two directional signals matched the crosshatched lines on a chart, the position could be known with some accuracy. Depending on the distance from the ground stations, it could be used for bombing when the target was obscured by clouds.

OUT AND ABOUT

Many times Dad received leave to go to London or other areas. On one trip, he visited Wales and thought that area was completely beautiful, with rolling hills and quaint towns.

The army gave lectures about interacting with the British civilians when on leave. The British people were grateful and were welcoming toward Americans. Army personnel were supposed to be good guests, especially at mealtimes. Due to wartime rationing, a family might have a single small piece of meat for Sunday dinner that had to last them all week—a serving that was far smaller than a single serving in the mess hall. And in the mess hall, second servings were available. So, if servicemen were offered a platter, they were to size it up and take only a small portion of the serving divided equally among the diners. Also, if offered a friendly drink, they were to accept only in moderation so as not to use up the host family's supply of spirits, which were extremely difficult to replace.

The army warned servicemen about the prostitutes (known as Piccadilly Commandos) and told them not to become romantically involved with British women in time of war. Yet, I've met a number of British women who immigrated to the United States as a war bride, and many of those marriages stood the test of time. I've also met couples in which the wife was Japanese, Korean, or Filipino, depending on where the serviceman was stationed. Cupid's arrow never misses.

Dad had several buddies he would go into town with on leave in Britain. One of them carried a British Army revolver with the barrel that had been cut down to about two inches with a hacksaw so it could be concealed. Why the guy felt the need to carry a gun was a mystery. Maybe to fight off some Piccadilly Commandos. One day, they took the gun to the range and test-fired it. The guy took careful aim at a fifty-five-gallon drum from about 10 feet away, and fired all six shots. Only one bullet hit the drum, off to the side, making a small dent. Not much of a defense gun.

BIRTHDAY IN LONDON: TURNING TWENTY-TWO

Dad's birthday was May 17, a few days after V-E Day (Victory in Europe Day). To celebrate, he went on leave in London, where he got a hotel and had a nice meal.

When the waiter asked if there was anything else, Dad mentioned that it was his birthday and asked if they had any strawberry shortcake. He always had strawberry shortcake on his birthday. Due to wartime rationing, he realized it was an impossible request. However, the waiter brought out a huge slice of strawberry shortcake topped with a heaping mound of the most succulent, delicious strawberries with whipped cream. How they got them in wartime was a miracle. Dad left a tip that was bigger than the cost of the entire meal. So there's an unknown waiter who made a lonely GI's birthday far from home a memorable one.

GROWING UP IN THE ARMY

When Dad graduated high school in 1941, he was exactly five feet tall. By the time he mustered out at war's end, he was five feet, nine inches tall. His mother grew to only four feet, eleven and a half inches and always said he would grow, to comfort him. Dad had to continually get new uniforms the entire time as he grew. He had huge hands and gorilla-sized arms that came in handy when he was flying the B-24, since it was heavy on the controls. Normally, the span of outstretched arms is equal to the person's height. Dad's span was just over six feet. When shooting the .45 automatic pistols, he said it felt like shooting a cap gun in his large hand.

LETTERS FROM HOME

Dad saved all letters he got from home. They were from both his dad and my mom. (They were high school sweethearts and got married July 4, 1945, when Dad came home on leave.) The letters he sent home were also saved.

He received boxes of cookies from Mom. They were called crazy cookies because, with wartime rationing, she couldn't get butter, eggs, or sugar to make them with, yet they were good. Mom and Dad had to hurry up and get married since he was due to be sent to the Pacific to bomb Japan. Thankfully, the war ended when the atomic bombs were dropped soon after their wedding. Postwar, Dad stayed in the US Air Force Reserves and flew around one weekend each month.

When my brother came along in 1948 (their firstborn), Dad would fly over the house and rock the wings so Mom and the baby could go outside and see him. Dad dropped being in the reserves, which was perfect timing because he would have certainly been called up for the Korean War.

Mom became a bank teller during the war, since the men were all called up or doing war work. At that time, there was a custom against women handling money, but the war put an end to that. In today's world, women are heavily represented in banking and other sectors of the economy, and it seems ridiculous nowadays to have a prohibition of that kind.

FLYING AROUND

Dad liked flying around. He said that other than getting shot at, it was very nice. Many times his plane had an engine shot out and they had to slow-time the replacement, so they got to fly all over the British countryside. (Slow-timing a replacement engine meant flying the engine at reduced power settings, gradually increasing the power to break it in.) While on missions, they flew to many spots on the European continent. They flew near Berchtesgaden (Adolf Hitler's mountain retreat) but were forbidden to bomb it. Violating this rule would have brought a court-martial. On occasion they flew near the Swiss border. The Swiss were expert gunners and would put up a few shots close by as a warning. If a crew entered Swiss airspace, the Swiss would shoot them down. But Switzerland was a safe refuge for a plane that had battle damage or was out of fuel. It was far better to be interned by the Swiss than be a POW held by the Germans.

If they had trouble over Switzerland, the crew was to drop the plane's landing gear, and Swiss fighter planes would escort them to an airfield. By war's end, the Swiss had a large collection of aircraft, some of them German. Dad's crew also flew over Peenemunde, the German rocket-science base headed by Werner von Braun (later of NASA fame). They were forbidden to bomb that base; it was left to the British RAF.

When they flew into Germany, they always fought a headwind. Dad said, "You'd crawl into Germany." He had to take periodic sun sightings with his octant to calculate position, and he had a small periscope pointed down to view features on the ground for navigational landmarks. In one case, he spotted a farmhouse far below that didn't appear to budge for a good fifteen minutes due to the headwind. They were red-lined at an indicated airspeed of 170 knots but usually flew slower to conserve fuel. A stripped B-24 could make 300 knots at full power. They had strict rules about maintaining formation. A lone plane was easy prey for lurking fighters.

The USAAC had strict rules about what to bomb. If the primary target was socked in, they would go to a secondary target or target of opportunity. If that was obscured, they would head back. Any spare or hung bombs were to be dropped in the English Channel rather than dropped at random or brought back. No bomber was allowed back to base with spare or hung bombs. There was too great a risk of crashing and blowing the place up.

There were strict rules among the gunners about not securing the guns until after landing. The Germans had a practice of sneaking planes into the landing pattern and shooting down a plane or two before high-tailing it back. By that stage of the war, the Luftwaffe wasn't as powerful as it had been earlier in the war, but it still could put up a fight. Some gunners would start cleaning the guns after crossing the English Channel, leaving the plane defenseless.

For another plane to join up in the formation, the rule was it had to fly a parallel course out of range and tip the wings up so it could be identified as friendly. Any plane flying directly at the formation to join up would be fired upon, since there was almost no time to tell friend from foe until too late. Dad said the enemy fighters came at them so fast that there was little time to react. In the 458th, a general got shot down that way. He and another pilot were flying an RAF Mosquito twin-engine fighter-bomber as a roving observation plane scouting around the mission. The general decided to join up with one of the squadrons and was promptly shot down by the B-24s. The two men in the Mosquito ended up parachuting to safety and became POWs. After the war, they tried to find out who'd shot them down so they could issue reprimands, but they were told they were in the wrong for not joining up the right way.

When slow-timing an engine, the crew often took passengers on board for sightseeing. In the B-24, if you shook the yoke fore and aft, the wings would flap up and down due to the thin, high-aspect ratio Davis Wing design. The crew would tell the passengers to watch the wing tips. If they flapped up and down, it meant big trouble. The guests were told to tell the crew right away because they might have to bail out right then and there. So the crew would shake the yoke a little, and the passengers would come up to the flight deck in terror, screaming about the wing tips. Of course, by then, the wing tips had settled down. So when the pilots looked out, there was nothing to see. After a few times, they would let the passengers in on the joke.

Dad flew the B-24 quite a bit. He actually had more time at the controls than the normally assigned copilot.

The Luftwaffe had several fighters to put up against the bombers. Their main single-engine fighters were of two types: the Messerschmitt Me 109, and the Focke-Wulf 190. They had a points system in which a German pilot received not just a kill but also more points for shooting down a bomber versus a fighter. Shooting down a bomber took 10 men and a larger, four-engine airframe out of the fight, not to mention something that could drop bombs and shut down a factory. Shooting down a fighter took one man and a single-engine airframe out of the fight.

As time went on, more and more experienced German pilots were killed in action. That loss, combined with less fuel available for training, meant the Luftwaffe diminished as a fighting force. From about late 1944 until V-E Day, the Luftwaffe became less and less potent. That didn't mean they were ineffective; fighters still claimed many a bomber. The fighter armament usually was a combination of aerial cannon and machine guns. It turned out that it took cannon fire to bring down a heavy bomber. This was usually a 20 mm or 30 mm cannon. Some fighters carried a 50 mm cannon. When so armed, the German fighters had greatly reduced maneuverability and needed escort fighters themselves to be protected while attacking the heavy bombers.

American fighters took a heavy toll on the Luftwaffe once our production and training ramped up. We rotated experienced pilots back home to train new pilots. The Luftwaffe kept their experienced pilots in the fight until killed or wounded, rendering them unable to pass on knowledge to new pilots.

EVERYBODY A PILOT

Every man in the Swingle Crew knew how to fly the B-24. The reasoning was, if the flight deck got shot up, one of the other crewmen could at least fly the plane back to Britain. So if they were up slow-timing a replacement engine, the crew would take turns at the controls and practice landings. Flying the plane without a bomb load and light on fuel was much easier. And there was no need to practice taking off—just flight maneuvering and landing. Chet's family was surprised he also could fly and land the B-24.

Dad also test-fired the 50 caliber machine guns, thought they were a potent weapon.

LET'S GET THE HELL OUT OF HERE

After dropping the bombs, the crew had an expression: "Let's get the hell out of here!" They would make the turn away from the target and head for home. When I was growing up, Dad used that expression a lot when we were somewhere and had to get out and away.

FLAK

Flak is a German word, short for *fliegerabwehrkanone*, which literally means "flier defense cannon." By 1945, the Luftwaffe was losing planes and pilots faster than they could be replaced. Flak was always a danger and became the nemesis of many a plane. The Germans ran short of trained pilots as they were shot down and didn't have much fuel for training flights. It took two years to train a pilot, but only two weeks to train a flak gunner. The Germans used the very capable 88 mm anti-aircraft gun, accurate and potent. Later on, they also developed a harder-hitting 105 mm gun. At times, the flak was so heavy, Dad said, "you could get out and walk on it." Flak was aimed from the ground and walked into the formation.

The crew had a gallows humor about flak. If the bursts were far away and hopelessly out of range, they'd say Adolf himself was shooting at them. As the bursts got closer, then Adolf had been replaced by a buck private. As the shots came in closer, the man at the trigger was replaced with successively higher ranks: the private was replaced with a corporal, then a sergeant, then a *Leutnant* (lieutenant), a *Haupt-*

mann (captain), and an *Oberst* (colonel). Finally, if the bursts were all around them with deadly accuracy, "fatso Goering" himself was doing the shooting.

TWICE LUCKY

Twice Dad got hit by flak, both times near misses.

Once he was seated at his desk, making a calculation, and a shell exploded right outside the plane. A piece of shrapnel came through the side of the plane and ripped the glove right off his hand, leaving a small scratch on one of his fingers. It was "not worth a Purple Heart," he would say.

Another time, he stood up to take a sighting on the octant, which meant standing on two small tabs to get up to the astrodome window on top of the nose. A shell hit the nose landing gear and exploded, taking the entire nose gear and the bottom of the nose away in one big bang, along with his desk, charts, and instruments. Dad said he looked down and saw nothing below him except Germany as he stood on the two small foot tabs. That flak hit came after they started flying without a bombardier. Had a bombardier been in the nose, he would have fallen to his death.

Dad wasn't wearing a parachute, since the parachutes were stowed separately and clipped on just before bailing out. The space was so cramped that a parachute was too cumbersome. Dad was able to climb down and make his way to the flight deck. On landing, the plane was diverted to a plowed field. They landed on the main landing gear, keeping the nose up as long as possible before settling down.

I believe this was the *Wandering Wanda*, since one mission report had battle damage noted. The plane was repaired and sent back in service. At other times, there was damage from flak in other parts of planes they flew. Thankfully none of the Swingle Crew was ever wounded, except the scratch on Dad's finger.

THE TRIP HOME: ONE CHANCE MIGHT BE ALL YOU GET

At the war's end, Dad and the crew flew back to the States by way of the Azores, a group of islands off the coast of Africa. They received briefings on how to make the trip. The engine carburetors were re-jetted for maximum fuel economy. They were told to fly at such low power settings that it made them gasp that the plane would fall out of the sky at that speed! But the Air Transport Command pilots stated, "That's what we do, get distance on long flights and conserve gas. So can you." Also, in the Azores, the runway was at the top of a cliff overlooking the sea. They were told to fly directly at the cliff edge. Due to prevailing winds, it was explained that an updraft would lift the plane up and position it for landing. If they tried to make a normal landing and drop down on the runway, the updraft would balloon the plane up and cause it to land far down the runway, leading to an overshoot. For the ferry flight, they carried extra GIs who had priority to get home. I believe the aircraft is My Bunnie, since there is a ferry flight photo with that aircraft and the Swingle Crew with extra passengers.

As it turned out, they took off and immediately found themselves in heavy clouds flying on instruments. They also couldn't find a homing beacon on the radio. They were flying blind, relying on dead reckoning to estimate their course and position. Dad was

The flight home. Ferry Flight Aircraft: *My Bunnie*. Dad is in the middle of the back row, standing. I believe Chet is sitting at the far left, front row. (USAF Photo)

sitting there as the hours went by, making calculations on their estimated route, but he had no idea if their position was any good. Suddenly, the plane broke out to a clear spot. Dad jumped up and was able to get just one sun sight on his octant before the clouds socked in again. Usually the navigator takes a number of sightings and averages them together for better accuracy. From that one sighting, Dad made a position calculation and ordered a course change. After dead reckoning a few more hours, he told the pilot to drop down to look around. A few minutes later, the plane broke out in the clear with the airfield right ahead of them.

Dad tried to pass that on to us kids—that one chance might be all you get.

THE CHAPLAINS

Dad's group had a chaplain who was a Jewish rabbi in civilian life, a very capable man sought out by many of all denominations for words of comfort. Dad rated the rabbi better than many Catholic priests he encountered. The air base also had a chaplain who would stand on the side of the runway to greet returning planes. He would have several bottles of whiskey and a large glass with him. As each plane landed, he would go to the plane and allow any of the men to drink as much whiskey as they wanted out of the glass before heading off (probably staggering off) to debriefing. As a result, the men were very talkative in post-mission interrogation after a few drinks. Unfortunately the Women's Christian Temperance Union (WCTU) found out, and there was a big scurry to stop the practice, since, as the WCTU claimed, "They're turning our boys into drunks!"

There was heavy drinking in the Officer's Club. Sometimes the men were so hungover that they had to be helped into the plane to fly the mission. But one cure was breathing oxygen as soon as they got on board, which instantly revived them. The rule usually was to go on oxygen as soon as the plane got above 10,000 feet for daylight missions. At night, oxygen was supposed to be used from the ground up. Many crews used oxygen from the ground level up for maximum alertness.

HORRORS OF WAR: THE UNKNOWN AIRMAN

When Dad landed in theater, before even flying his first mission, he had a gruesome task. Since he was the most junior officer, he got an immediate lesson in the horrors of war. One of the aircraft that came back had a direct flak hit on one of the gunner positions. The dead gunner was pulverized and unrecognizable as a human being. Dad had the grim job of washing the airman out of the aircraft with a fire hose and collecting the remains in buckets for burial. That haunted him the rest of his life.

This man, who I now call the Unknown Airman (similar to the Unknown Soldier) reminds us all of sacrifice. His name is certainly recorded in the official records, but to me he stands for the many lost in aerial combat. The 8th Air Force lost more men killed in action than the Marines and Navy combined, and also suffered far more wounded and captured. Dad hated the Nazis with a passion from then on. He didn't hate the German people themselves, but their political system and leaders who brought unspeakable evil to the world.

HORRORS OF WAR: OPERATION VARSITY

Operation Varsity was the last airborne operation of the ETO. The plan was to force a crossing of the Rhine by an airdrop at Wesel (both parachute and glider regiments), combined with a river crossing. The key was to cross the Rhine River and invade Germany proper. An earlier attempt, Operation Market-Garden (described in the book and movie *A Bridge Too Far*), had failed.

During Operation Varsity, the 453rd had a resupply mission to drop supply canisters by parachute. The parachutes were different colors to signify what was inside—red for ammunition, white for medical supplies, green for food, etc.—so the paratroopers could tell at a glance what was inside the canister and get what supplies they needed. During the mission, the group flew below treetop level to avoid flak, which was intense and accurate. They flew so low that they had to dodge trees and haystacks, pull up over fences, and look up at rooftops.

They made the drop but were horrified at the carnage. Dad said he could look out the astrodome and see the faces of dead paratroopers hanging in their chutes from trees and telephone poles mere feet away. Also, there were many C-46 and C-47 aircraft, as well as gliders, shot down and burned out, with hundreds and hundreds of bodies scattered about. When they got back, the crew chief called the crew over and showed them battle damage to the wing. The wing (where the gas tanks were) had taken numerous 20 mm cannon-fire hits, but without effect. The self-sealing feature of the gas tanks had saved them. Also, at that stage of the war, the Nazi munitions were being made by slave labor; they played their own game of sabotage by leaving out the explosive compound in shells. One explosive shell in the wing would have caused a fuel explosion that would have blown off the wing. At that low altitude, none of the crew would have been able to bail out.

Since Dad was trained as a mechanic, he sometimes helped the maintenance crews work on planes when he wasn't slated for a mission. The ground crews liked him for that; he didn't pull rank as if he were too good to swing a wrench. After the Wesel mission, Dad helped repair his own aircraft.

ATTACKED BY ME 262S

The first operational jet fighter of the war was the German Messerschmitt Me 262. It outclassed anything the Allies had but made its appearance too late in the war to make much of a difference in the outcome. By then, the Nazi regime was certain to be defeated, and they didn't have enough fuel or trained pilots to put up many planes. The Me 262 did shoot down a number of bombers, but it couldn't stem the tide of defeat.

It had two axial-flow jet engines, very advanced for its day, and packed various cannon sizes of 20 mm, 30 mm, and even a 50 mm cannon, depending on armament.

The Luftwaffe tactic was to get a group of fighters and attack a bomber formation head-on, each plane picking out a bomber to fire upon. If the bombers weren't immediately shot down (and many were, using this tactic), the Germans would disrupt the formation into individual planes, which were much easier to pick off one by one. On one mission, a group of Me 262s formed up in front to make a head-on pass. The group made frantic calls for help using their call sign (Silver Dollar), and from out of nowhere, a group of P-51s flew right over the top of their formation head-on into the jets. Dad's group flew through the resulting furball of fighters and emerged unscathed.

OBSERVED THE ME 163 KOMET

The Germans also developed a rocket-powered aircraft called the Messerschmitt Me 163 Komet. It was a single-seat aircraft that was fueled by a hypergolic mixture of hydrogen peroxide and hydrazine hydrate. It had enough fuel for only three minutes, so it would take off and fly almost vertically to the 30,000-foot altitude of the bomber steam, and make one or two passes before gliding back down to land. It carried a potent 30 mm cannon armament to attack bombers.

Dad saw them taking off with their long, vertical plume of white smoke trailing behind. The Me 163 was actually more dangerous to the pilot than anything else. If anything went wrong, the plane could explode. If the concentrated rocket fuel leaked into the cockpit, it would actually dissolve the pilot's body while he was alive. The Me 163 had a (thankfully) short and unsuccessful career, making few kills.

SAW V-2 ROCKET LAUNCHES, V-1 BUZZ BOMBS

Dad witnessed a number of V-2 rockets launch. The V-2 was a primitive, but innovative, theater ballistic missile with a 2,000-pound warhead. He said the smoke trail would go up 30 miles and arc over to the target (mostly London and later Antwerp) until the fuel burned out. It actually killed more German than British people, since it took most of the potato crop to make the alcohol for fuel, leading to massive starvation. Not to mention, manufacturing the rocket took slave labor; they were worked to death as a matter of policy.

The Germans also made a primitive cruise missile called the V-1 buzz bomb. It carried a 1,000-pound warhead using a pulse-jet engine. The only guidance system was to aim it in the general direction of the target, and an onboard timer would cut off the fuel and jam the controls so it would spin into the ground and blow up. It made a loud buzzing noise as it flew—hence the nickname "buzz bomb." Once the sound cut off, everyone would dive for cover, awaiting the inevitable explosion. Since the V-2 rocket arrived at the target over the speed of sound, there was no warning at all.

RED TAILS

Dad stated that at least once the Red Tails, who are now known as the Tuskegee Airmen, saved them. This was a group of all Negro pilots (what they were called at the time), since the armed forces were segregated. They were trained as fighter pilots to see if Black men could perform as well as whites. As is now known, they performed brilliantly in combat. Dad gave them his highest praise, saying, "Gee, could they ever FLY!"

As a mark of distinction, they painted the entire tail of their aircraft bright red. There are documented cases of enemy fighter pilots bailing out upon seeing the red tail, since they knew what they were up against.

The Red Tails were highly educated (all had college degrees) and well-spoken. But, once in combat, they would switch to heavily accented jive talk, since they knew the enemy was listening in on the radio chatter. Dad's bomb group issued a standing invitation to any Red Tail to land at their base for a drink or dinner. The bomber crews would talk to the Red Tails over the radio to let them know what was on the menu for dinner. Sometimes, if the meal was particularly good, several of the fighters would have "engine trouble" and land at Dad's base. None of them could buy a drink at the Officer's Club; they were held in such high esteem that the other men would buy their drinks and not let them pay. After the war, they unfortunately had to endure segregation when they went home. Thankfully, much of segregation was overturned as civil rights kicked in over many decades after the war.

After the war ended and Dad was back in the States, he was eating lunch in the mess hall with some other officers when in walked one of the Red Tail pilots he knew. Dad immediately invited him over to their table to eat. Several others at the table also knew the pilot. They were talking about their exploits when someone at a different table shouted out, "You guys are eating with a n-----r!" as if that mattered. Dad's whole table stood up as one, carried their plates over to a different table, and sat down to eat and resume their discussion to get away from the idiot.

JIMMY STEWART, OPERATIONS OFFICER

Of special note is that the famed actor Jimmy Stewart was an operations officer in the 453rd and flew many tough combat missions before being promoted up to Wing. But he still was involved and gave mission briefings. I attended a 458th Bomb Group reunion with Dad, and the people there remembered Jimmy. They said he occasionally came to reunions and was just one of the regular guys. There were no autographs or talk about Hollywood—only about the missions, friends, and families. He retired a brigadier general in the USAF reserves. Also, he flew combat missions in the Korean War and over Hanoi in the Vietnam War.

THE MISSIONS: TWENTY-THREE ROUND TRIPS

Dad flew 23 combat missions over Germany. His comment was, "I bombed Magdeburg visual three times!" with a somber expression. Magdeburg was a heavily defended, high-value target as important to the German war effort as Detroit was to the United States. Bombing visual meant being able to see the target in the bombsight, as opposed to bombing through the overcast using radar. It meant the target could see you and shoot back, as well.

The combat missions were all in 1945:

Jan. 16	Magdeburg	Industrial targets
Jan. 28	Dortmund	Oil refinery
Feb. 3	Magdeburg	Marshalling yards
Feb. 15	Magdeburg	Industrial targets
Feb. 19	Jungenthal	Munitions
Feb. 21	Nurnberg	Marshalling yards
Feb. 23	Paderborn	Bridge
Feb. 24	Lehrte	Railroad marshalling yards
Feb. 25	Giebelstadt	Airfield
Feb. 26	Berlin	Rail yards
Mar. 1	Ingelstadt:	Marshalling yards
Mar. 8	Siegen	Marshalling yards
Mar. 9	Münster	Rail yards
Mar. 12	Wetzler	Rail yards
Mar. 15	Gerdelegen	Marshalling yards
Mar. 17	Münster	Communications center
Mar. 19	Bäumenheim	Jet aircraft airfields
Mar. 24	Wesel	Air-drop supplies in Operation Varsity
Apr. 4	Wesendorf	Airfield
Apr 8	Fürth	Airfield
Apr. 10	Amberg	Marshalling yards
Apr. 25	Bad Reichenhall	Troop concentration, with the 458th BG

The mission on February 15 to Magdeburg coincided with the famous event of the Dresden bombing by the RAF at night and 8th Air Force 1st Air Division (flying B-17s) the next day. The Dresden bombing created a massive firestorm and caused tens of thousands of casualties, which is very controversial to this day. My opinion: If it shortened the war by as little as one minute, it was worth it. Dad never thought twice about the missions he flew. To him they were out to destroy the Nazi regime and all it stood for. Since the tragedy of the Holocaust came out near the end of the war, many crews throughout the 8th Air Force were on a rampage to get Hitler. The commanders had to call briefings where the men were ordered not to bomb Berchtesgaden or try to get Hitler by bombing away from their assigned target.

END-OF-THE-WAR PARTY

The Officer's Club saved a bottle out of every case of liquor for an end-of-the-war party. When V-E Day finally came, there were wild parties at every air base that lasted for days on end. Dad's crew stayed together and made the rounds, visiting other air bases and fellow airmen in the group. In another crew, one of the men had to be carried around in a chair since he was passed out drunk. When he came to, he would drink until he passed out again, with a big smile on his face. Few planes were flying until the festivities died down. Chet Fong didn't drink at all, but he nevertheless took part in the party.

THE HOLLYWOOD WAR

Few Hollywood movies featured the 8th Air Force, although I can recall several classics: *Twelve O'Clock High*, *The War Lover*, and *Command Decision*. *Twelve O'Clock High*, made in 1949, is perhaps the most realistic. The movie was used for many years at UCLA for leadership training in business classes. Dad didn't like it since it featured the B-17, but he always watched it with a somber expression. Every scene in the movie was taken from actual events.

Later on, a TV show called *Twelve O'Clock High* (Quinn Martin Productions, also featuring the B-17) came out, and we watched it together, with Dad giving a running commentary on some aspects of the show. One of the episodes featured the use of chaff, thin aluminum strips that were thrown out to float gently back to earth. This was used to block enemy radar from picking up attacking formations.

In a rare moment of factual reality in film, in the movie *The War Lover*, actor Burt Kwouk starred as a Chinese American navigator.

Few movies have featured the B-24, even though more of them were made than the B-17 and it was used in more applications. I can recall the movie *Unbroken*, featuring the life of Olympic runner Louis Zamperini. They used CGI B-24s, since of the thousands built, only two are flying today. The movie *To End All Wars* depicts a POW camp being bombed by CGI B-24s, killing and wounding some allied POWs.

The British bombing effort included such classics as *Target for Tonight* and *The Dam Busters*.

The 1960s had a great many TV shows featuring WWII: *Hogan's Heroes*, *The Gallant Men*, *Combat!*, and *McHale's Navy*, among others. Some were comedies, and there were others that were dramatic presentations. The star of *Hogan's Heroes*, Robert Crane, was an almost exact twin of Dad's younger brother, our Uncle Jimmy. His family also noticed the resemblance. Uncle Jimmy was a naval aviator in the Pacific, flying fighter planes off a carrier. He was on a carrier headed to Japan when V-J Day took place.

The Tuskegee Airmen were featured in two movies: *Red Tails* and *The Tuskegee Airmen.*

There are also a number of excellent documentaries available for viewing on YouTube; some were made during the war (*Target for Today, The Last Bomb*). There's even some footage on the B-24, including the 453rd Bomb Group's Operation Varsity supply drops at Wesel.

CONTEXT

WWII was the first war in which air operations played a large role. Many think in an air war that one stroke would end the war. In actuality, an air war is a brutal and lengthy war of attrition. Air power theorists tried different targeting methods for the knockout blow, such as oil refineries, aircraft production plants, ball-bearing manufacturing plants, electrical power grids, dams (the RAF dam buster raids in particular), area bombing, and transportation, among others.

Postwar criticism of air operations in the ETO was that there was no focused strategy; targets were selected at random based on the flavor of the month. In reality, it took a combination of targets that, when combined, gradually reduced the Nazi war machine. Analysis of the effects of bombing immediately after the war declared it was relatively ineffective for the resources spent. In recent years, however, new research has revealed that the air war was a large part of the victory in Europe.

For instance, the D-Day cross-Channel attack could never have succeeded without complete air supremacy. That meant destroying the Luftwaffe by denying it the fuel to fly, the factories to build aircraft, and the air bases to fly from. Some missions were selected to bait the Luftwaffe by selecting targets they HAD to protect, so they would come up and be shot down by bomber gunners and escort fighters. Railroad marshalling yards became an effective target, since the German war machine relied heavily on train transportation. They were large targets that could be easily hit, and their destruction caused great disruption of the supply chain. In addition, destruction of boxcars and the completed war goods and munitions denied their use at the front.

Top Nazi war production was achieved in 1944, but by then, fuel and manpower shortages meant reduced effectiveness. The Nazi war machine was very resilient at staying alive when being pounded by day by American air power and by night by the RAF over many years, not to mention losses on the Russian and other fronts. But in the long run, they were doomed. Both the Nazis and the Japanese Empire were great evils that had to be destroyed; air power was a great contribution to that.

MORE CONTEXT

Operations research and statistical analysis revealed that survival was heavily weighted by chance. Whether you lived or died or were able to parachute to the ground and become a POW was mostly random.

The B-24 had an unfortunate habit of exploding without warning due to all the fuel lines being routed through the bomb bay. Fumes would accumulate, and a spark would set them off. There were heavy losses from both combat and operational accidents.

Dad had survivor's guilt and survivor's trauma because he was somehow selected to live. He had too many close calls, and for his entire life, he suffered occasional nightmares. He had a suitcase of war memorabilia that he would sometimes take out and go over, commenting on what each souvenir meant. He had a large collection of business cards from fellow officers he'd served with. Many of them were marked with an X in the top corner. When I asked about them, he said those were the ones who didn't make it.

Dad with Hot Tip.

He made his telling comment about his entire service with a haunted expression: "I bombed Magdeburg visual three times."

APPENDIX 7

CONGRESSIONAL GOLD MEDAL

PUBLIC LAW 115–337—DEC. 20, 2018   132 STAT. 5029

Public Law 115–337
115th Congress

An Act

To award a Congressional Gold Medal, collectively, to the Chinese-American Veterans of World War II, in recognition of their dedicated service during World War II.

Dec. 20, 2018
[S. 1050]

Chinese-
American World
War II Veteran
Congressional
Gold Medal Act.
31 USC 5111
note.

Be it enacted by the Senate and House of Representatives of the United States of America in Congress assembled,

SECTION 1. SHORT TITLE.

This Act may be cited as the "Chinese-American World War II Veteran Congressional Gold Medal Act".

SEC. 2. FINDINGS.

Congress finds that—

(1) Chinese Americans served the United States in every conflict since the Civil War, and distinguished themselves in World War II, serving in every theater of war and every branch of service, earning citations for their heroism and honorable service, including the Medal of Honor;

(2) Chinese nationals and Chinese Americans faced institutional discrimination in the United States since before World War II, limiting the size of their population and their ability to build thriving communities in the United States;

(3) the Act entitled "An Act to execute certain treaty stipulations relating to Chinese", approved May 6, 1882 (commonly known as the "Chinese Exclusion Act of 1882") (22 Stat. 58, chapter 126), was the first Federal law that broadly restricted immigration and a specific nationality, making it illegal for Chinese laborers to immigrate to the United States and limiting the Chinese population in the United States for over 60 years;

(4) major court decisions such as the decisions in Lum v. Rice, 275 U.S. 78 (1927), and People v. Hall, 4 Cal. 399 (1854), found "yellow" races to be equal to African Americans with regard to "separate but equal" school facilities, and prohibited Chinese Americans, along with "Black, mulatto, or Indian" persons, from testifying against White men;

(5) Chinese Americans were harassed, beaten, and murdered because of their ethnicity, including the Chinese Massacre of 1871, where 17 Chinese immigrants in Los Angeles, California, were tortured and murdered, the Rock Springs Massacre of 1885 where White rioters killed 28 Chinese miners and burned 75 of their homes in Rock Springs, Wyoming, and the Hells Canyon Massacre of 1887 where 34 Chinese gold miners were ambushed and murdered in Hells Canyon, Oregon;

(6) there were only 78,000 Chinese Americans living on the United States mainland, with 29,000 living in Hawaii,

at the start of World War II as result of Federal and State legislation and judicial decisions;

(7) despite the anti-Chinese discrimination at the time, as many as 20,000 Chinese Americans served in the Armed Forces during World War II, of whom, approximately 40 percent were not United States citizens due to the laws that denied citizenship to persons of Chinese descent;

(8) Chinese Americans, although small in numbers, made important contributions to the World War II effort;

(9) of the total Chinese Americans serving, approximately 25 percent served in the United States Army Air Force, with some sent to the China-Burma-India Theater with the 14th Air Service Group;

(10) the remainder of Chinese Americans who served in World War II served in all branches of the Armed Forces in all 4 theaters of war;

(11) the first all Chinese-American group was the 14th Air Service Group in the China-Burma-India Theater which enabled extensive and effective operations against the Japanese military in China;

(12) Chinese Americans are widely acknowledged for their role in the 14th Air Force, widely known as the Flying Tigers;

(13) Chinese Americans assigned to the China-Burma-India Theater made transoceanic journeys through hostile territories and were subject to enemy attack while at sea and in the air;

(14) in the Pacific Theater, Chinese Americans were in ground, air, and ocean combat and support roles throughout the Pacific including New Guinea, Guadalcanal, Solomon Islands, Iwo Jima, Okinawa, Philippines, Mariana Islands, and Aleutian Islands;

(15) throughout the Pacific and China-Burma-India theaters, Chinese Americans performed vital functions in translating, coordinating Nationalist Chinese and United States combat operations, servicing and repairing aircraft and armaments, training Nationalist Chinese troops and sailors, delivering medical care, providing signal and communication support, gathering and analyzing intelligence, participating in ground and air combat, and securing and delivering supplies;

(16) Chinese Americans also served in combat and support roles in the European and African theaters, serving in North Africa, Sicily, Italy, the Normandy D–Day invasion, which liberated Western Europe, and the Battle of the Bulge, occupying Western Germany while helping to liberate Central Europe;

(17) Chinese Americans flew bomber missions, served in infantry units and combat ships in the Battle of the Atlantic, including aboard Merchant Marines convoys vulnerable to submarine and air attacks;

(18) many Chinese-American women served in the Women's Army Corps, the Army Air Forces, and the United States Naval Reserve Women's Reserve, and some became pilots, air traffic controllers, flight trainers, weather forecasters, occupational therapists, and nurses;

(19) Captain Francis B. Wai is the only Chinese American who served in World War II to have been awarded the Medal of Honor, the highest military award given by the United States

(20) Chinese Americans also earned Combat Infantry Badges, Purple Hearts, Bronze Stars, Silver Stars, Distinguished Service Cross, and Distinguished Flying Cross;

(21) units of the Armed Forces with Chinese Americans were also awarded unit citations for valor and bravery;

(22) the United States remains forever indebted to the bravery, valor, and dedication that the Chinese-American Veterans of World War II displayed; and

(23) the commitment and sacrifice of Chinese Americans demonstrates a highly uncommon and commendable sense of patriotism and honor in the face of discrimination.

SEC. 3. DEFINITIONS.

In this Act—

(1) the term "Chinese-American Veterans of World II" includes individuals of Chinese ancestry who served—

(A) honorably at any time during the period December 7, 1941, and ending December 31, 1946; and

(B) in an active duty status under the command of the Armed Forces; and

(2) the term "Secretary" means the Secretary of the Treasury.

SEC. 4. CONGRESSIONAL GOLD MEDAL.

(a) AWARD AUTHORIZED.—The President Pro Tempore of the Senate and the Speaker of the House of Representatives shall make appropriate arrangements for the award, on behalf of Congress, of a single gold medal of appropriate design to the Chinese-American Veterans of World War II, in recognition of their dedicated service during World War II.

(b) DESIGN AND STRIKING.—For the purposes of the award referred to in subsection (a), the Secretary shall strike the gold medal with suitable emblems, devices, and inscriptions to be determined by the Secretary.

(c) SMITHSONIAN INSTITUTE.—

(1) IN GENERAL.—Following the award of the gold medal in honor of the Chinese-American Veterans of World War II, the gold medal shall be given to the Smithsonian Institution, where it shall be available for display as appropriate and made available for research.

(2) SENSE OF CONGRESS.—It is the sense of Congress that the Smithsonian Institution should make the gold medal received under paragraph (1) available for display elsewhere, particularly at other locations associated with the Chinese-American Veterans of World II or with World War II.

(d) DUPLICATE MEDALS.—Under regulations that the Secretary may promulgate, the Secretary may strike and sell duplicates in bronze of the gold medal struck under this Act, at a price sufficient to cover the cost of the medals, including labor, materials, dies, use of machinery, and overhead expenses.

SEC. 5. STATUS OF MEDAL.

(a) NATIONAL MEDAL.—The gold medal struck under this Act shall be a national medal for the purposes of chapter 51 of title 31, Unites States Code.

(b) NUMISMATIC ITEMS.—For purpose of section 5134 of title 31, United States Code, all medals struck under this Act shall be considered to be numismatic items.

Approved December 20, 2018.

NOTES

CHAPTER 1: OFF TO WAR

1. Whelan, *Hunters in the Sky*, 65.

2. Whelan, 67.

3. Douglas, *Consolidated B-24 Liberator*, 55.

4. Chant, *Warfare and the Third Reich*, 171. The origin of the Waffen SS goes back to 1933 during the rapid rise of Adolf Hitler as the Chancellor of Germany. At that time, the Nazi Party had a paramilitary army known as the SS (*Schutzstaffel*), or Protection Squad, for the security of Nazi officials. Hitler had a regiment of SS troops known as the Leibstandarte Adolf Hitler (LAH), which was essentially his personal army of bodyguards. The regiment started out with 120 soldiers commanded by Josef "Sepp" Dietrich. At the beginning of the war, the LAH, now designated as Leibstandarte SS Adolf Hitler (LSSAH), merged with three other SS military groups to form the basis of the Waffen SS. At this stage, the LSSAH was a fully equipped armored division. The Waffen SS was completely autonomous with no interaction with the regular German Army and under the direct control of Hitler. It was the SS troops from the Waffen SS divisions that were responsible for much of the atrocities committed during the Second World War. Eberle, *The Hitler Book*, 3–5.

5. Bradley, *A Soldier's Story*, 465.

6. Eisenhower, *Crusade in Europe*, 350; Beevor, *Ardennes* 1944, 189–90.

7. Goolrick, *The Battle of the Bulge*, 110–11.

8. Larrabee, *Commander in Chief*, 415–16.

9. Goolrick, *The Battle of the Bulge*, 121.

10. Goolrick, 58.

11. Wood, *Hitler's Luftwaffe*, 114.

12. Goolrick, 163.

13. Bradley, 482.

14. Eisenhower, 365.

CHAPTER 2: OUR FIRST MISSION

1. Benarcik, *In Search of Peace*, 58.

2. Neillands, *The Bomber War*, 293.

3. Craven, *The Army Air Forces in World War II*: Vol. 2, 353–58.

4. Craven, Vol. 2, 374.

5. Craven, *The Army Air Forces in World War II*: Vol. 3, 173.

6. A *Gruppen* is roughly equivalent to a US Fighter Group and consists of three or four *Staffels*, or squadrons.

7. Craven, Vol. 3, 642–46.

8. Overy, *The Bombers and the Bombed*, 203.

9. Neillands, 159.

10. Kershaw, *The End*, 168–69.

11. Erickson, *The Road to Berlin*, 456.

12. Erickson, 467.

13. Pogue, *The Supreme Command*, 411.

CHAPTER 3: MAXIMUM EFFORT

1. Nisbet, *Roosevelt and Stalin*, 84.

2. Craven, Vol. 3, 654–57.

3. The Gestapo (*Geheime Staatspolizei*) was the state secret police under the control of SS Reichsfuhrer Heinrich Himmler. SS Gruppenfuhrer Heinrich Muller was chief of the Gestapo. Gestapo headquarters was located on Prinz-Albrechtstrasse in central Berlin.

4. Overy, 55.

5. Friedrich, *The Fire*, 15.

6. Friedrich, 305–06.

7. Freeman, *The Mighty Eighth War Manual*, 224–25.

8. Overy, 174–75.

9. Craven, Vol. 3, 8.

10. Craven, Vol. 3, 47.

11. USSBS, "Defeat of GAF" in *The United States Strategic Bombing Survey*, 1.

12. USSBS, "Overall Report" in *The United States Strategic Bombing Survey*, 22.

13. NARA, 2nd Air Division, 453rd Bomb Group: Mission Report #223.

14. Neillands, 150–51.

15. Freeman, *The Mighty Eighth War Diary*, 450.

16. Pogue, 412.

17. In late 1944, Hitler issued an order that all men between the ages of 16 to 60 would be drafted into the *Volkssturm* (People's Storm), known as the people's militia, to defend the homeland. A great number of battalions were subsequently formed throughout Germany. The Volkssturm units were under the direction of the Nazi Party, not the army. Of course, party officials were exempt from being inducted. Himmler's SS officials were delegated to train and equip the Volkssturm. However, these militia units remained poorly organized, almost never trained, and lacked even the basic essentials of weaponry. Most were given old and unreliable rifles or merely a handful of grenades, and quickly sent to the front lines. In the vast majority of cases, their only "uniform" was a Nazi armband.

18. Bessel, *Germany 1945*, 60.

CHAPTER 4: THE FINAL CURTAIN

1. Craven, Vol. 3, 658; Rumpf, *The Bombing of Germany*, 47.

2. Heaton, *The Me 262 Stormbird*, 72–73.

3. Harvey, *Sharks of the Air*, 261–62.

4. Harvey, 277.

5. Heaton, 67.

6. Foreman, *The Messerschmitt Me 262 Combat Diary*, 298.

7. Buchner, *Stormbird*, 224–25, 188.

8. The designation of this Luftwaffe fighter aircraft unit I./KG (J) 54 is as follows:
I. refers to the unit's *Gruppen* (group) number. A roman numeral character represents a Gruppen, while an arabic number designates a *Staffel* (squadron). *KG* (J) 54 indicates that the original KG 54 bomber unit had been converted to an Me 262 jet fighter unit.

9. Steinhoff, *Voices from the Third Reich*, 409–11.

10. Eisenhower, 380.

11. Hitler had total control over the country with his personal paramilitary army, the *SS Schutzstaffel* (Protection Squad) and the Gestapo. The latter was established to control subversion and root out all political or dissident individuals who opposed the Nazi state, including religious leaders. With offices, prisons, and concentration camps throughout Germany and the occupied countries, the Gestapo and the SS were instrumental in the Holocaust. As the political police force of the Third Reich, the Gestapo was given extraordinary powers. Individuals could be arrested, imprisoned, or summarily executed without any judicial recourse. In essence, the Gestapo was above the law.

12. The German military had four separate high command structures: OKH (Oberkommando des Heeres) the Supreme Command of the Army, OKL (Oberkommando der Luftwaffe) the Supreme Command of the Air Force, OKM (Oberkommando der Marine) the Supreme Command of the Navy, and OKW (Oberkommando der Wehrmacht) the Supreme Command of the Armed Forces. Hitler never trusted the German Army, so he placed his two most devoted and loyal generals, Field Marshal Wilhelm Keitel as chief and Col. Gen. Alfred Jodl as the chief of operations at the head of OKW. The OKH, OKL, and OKM were all subordinate to the OKW, and thus Hitler had direct control of all the armed forces. This might have been prescient on his part, because the major conspirators of the assassination plot on his life on July 20, 1944, were all high-level officers of the German Army (OKH).

13. Von Loringhoven, *In the Bunker with Hitler*, 139.

14. Harvey, 325.

15. Kershaw, 216.

16. Speer, *Inside the Third Reich*, 442, 447.

17. Speer, 455–58.

18. Pogue, 438–39.

19. Berthon, *Warlords*, 287.

20. Ambrose, *Eisenhower and Berlin 1945*, 29.

21. Pogue, 446.

22. Eisenhower, 400–02.

23. Bradley, xiii.

24. Ambrose, 89.

CHAPTER 5

1. Heaton, 225–26.

2. Heaton, 227.

3. Foreman, 243; Harvey, 344.

4. Buchner, 240–51.

5. MacDonald, *The Mighty Endeavor*, 480–81; Richie, *Faust's Metropolis*, 553–54.

6. Pogue, 461.

7. MacDonald, 484.

8. Craven, Vol. 3, 754.

9. Benarcik, 184.

10. Overy, 164.

11. Chaney, Jr., *Zhukov*, 9, 14.

12. Read, *The Fall of Berlin*, 192–93.

13. Read, 275–77.

14. Hamilton, *The Oder Front 1945*, 103.

15. Hamilton, 100–01.

16. Richie, 573.

17. Beevor, *The Fall of Berlin 1945*, 337.

18. Soviet General Staff, *The Berlin Operation 1945*, 343–51; Hamilton, 220–31.

19. MacDonald, 496–97.

20. Beevor, *The Fall of Berlin 1945*, 338.

21. Erickson, 595.

22. Ramsey, *After the Battle*, 31.

23. Junge, *Until the Final Hour*, 180.

24. Von Loringhoven, 173.

25. Göring was taken prisoner by American soldiers on May 3, 1945. At the Nuremberg trials, he was sentenced to death by hanging, to be carried out on October 15, 1946. As befitting for a field marshal, Göring requested that he be executed by a firing squad instead, but was refused. So he committed suicide just a few hours before his execution by ingesting a cyanide capsule that he'd been able to conceal during his imprisonment. Brown, *The Epic of Flight*, 170.

26. Gortemaker, *Eva Braun*, 13.

27. Von Loringhoven, 189.

28. Best, *Five Days That Shocked the World*, 3–9.

29. Soviet General Staff, 378; Whelan, 52.

30. Beevor, *The Fall of Berlin 1945*, 355.

31. Gortemaker, 48, 94.

32. Junge, 186–88.

33. Eberle, 269–70.

34. Eberle, 271–72.

35. Soldiers from the special SMERSH counterintelligence unit attached to Zhukov's 3rd Shock Army were reported to have discovered remnants of Hitler's remains in the Reich Chancellery Garden on May 5, 1945. SMERSH officials supervised all the forensic

analyses of the remains. The alleged pieces of Hitler's skull were eventually sent to Russia and a report issued to Stalin. However, for many years after the war, Stalin never truly believed that Hitler committed suicide. He was convinced that Hitler had escaped from Berlin to a distant country like so many Nazi officials did during the end of the war. Even direct eyewitness accounts of Hitler's suicide remain controversial to this day, because shortly after the war, there were very few survivors who actually witnessed the Fuhrer's corpse. Traudl Junge, who was in the bunker during the afternoon of April 30, didn't actually see the bodies of Hitler and Braun being taken out of his room, although she did enter the room afterward and noted the bloodstain on the upholstery of the bench where Hitler was thought to be sitting. Junge, 188. The validity of the actual recovery of Hitler's remains and their subsequent forensic analysis also remain questionable and mired in controversy. For further discussions of Hitler's alleged suicide and his remains, see Beevor, *The Fall of Berlin 1945*, 399–400, 431; Eberle, 268–74; Hugh Trevor Roper, *The Last Days of Hitler*, 230–35; Joachim Fest, *Inside Hitler's Bunker*, 110–22, 159–64,177–79.

36. After being incarcerated in various criminal institutions in Russia, Junge was released. She finally made it home to Bavaria on Easter Sunday of April 1946.

37. Soviet General Staff, 382.

38. Read, 454.

CHAPTER 6

1. Pogue, 490–93.

2. Benarcik, 274–75.

3. Douglas, 41.

4. Harrison, *Kassel*, 154; Wright, *An Emotional Gauntlet*, 176–78, 268, 291.

5. USSBS, "Summary" in *The United States Strategic Bombing Survey*, 3.

6. USSBS, "Summary," 19.

7. USSBS, "Summary," 23.

8. USSBS, "Summary," 21.

9. USSBS, "Summary," 22.

10. USSBS, "Summary," 32–33.

11. Benarcik, 268.

APPENDIX 4 FLAK GUNS

1. Muller, *The Heavy Flak Guns 1933–1945*, 5.

2. Muller, 137.

3. Westermann, *Flak*, 230–31.

4. Westermann, 157.

APPENDIX 5 RISE AND FALL OF THE ME 262

1. Harvey, 113–15.

2. Harvey, 143–44.

3. Harvey, 194–97.

4. Heaton, 42.

5. Heaton, 127–33.

6. Harvey, 323–24; Forsyth, *JV44 The Galland Circus*, 159.

7. Forsyth, 160.

8. Forsyth, 332–33.

9. Heaton, 181–85.

10. Forsyth, 246–55; Heaton, 199–202.

11. In the Luftwaffe there were three basic combat formations. A single pair of aircraft was called a *Rotte*, while three aircraft were termed a *Kette*. A *Schwarm* was composed of four aircraft. A typical operational *Staffel* (squadron) formation for fighters consisted of several Schwarm or Rotte, and for bombers, one or more Kette.

12. Buchner, 240.

13. Buchner, 241.

14. Buchner, 251.

BIBLIOGRAPHY

Ambrose, Stephen E. *Eisenhower and Berlin, 1945: The Decision to Halt at the Elbe*. New York: W. W. Norton, 1967.

Anonymous. *A Woman in Berlin: Eight Weeks in the Conquered City, A Diary*. New York: Metropolitan Books, 2005.

Beevor, Antony. *Ardennes 1944: Hitler's Last Gamble*. New York: Viking, 2015.

Beevor, Antony. *The Fall of Berlin 1945*. New York: Penguin Books, 2002.

Benarcik, Michael D., and Major General Andrew S. Low, Jr., eds. *In Search of Peace: A Review of Events and Emotional Experiences Endured by the 8th Air Force Bombardment Groups in World War II*. Wilmington: Michael D. Benarcik Foundation, 1989.

Berthon, Simon, and Joanna Potts. *Warlords: An Extraordinary Re-Creation of World War II Through the Eyes and Minds of Hitler, Churchill, Roosevelt, and Stalin*. Boston: Da Capo Press, 2006.

Bessel, Richard. *Germany 1945: From War to Peace*. New York: Harper Collins, 2009.

Best, Nicholas. *Five Days That Shocked the World: Eyewitness Accounts from Europe at the End of World War II*. New York: Thomas Dunne Books, 2012.

Bowman, Martin W. *B-24 Combat Missions: First-Hand Accounts of Liberator Operations over Nazi Europe*. New York: Fall River Press, 2009.

Bradley, Omar N. *A Soldier's Story*. New York: Modern Library, 1999.

Brown, Dale M., ed. *The Epic of Flight: The Luftwaffe*. Fairfax: Time-Life Books, 1982.

Bruning, John R. *Bombs Away! The World War II Bombing Campaigns over Europe*. New York: Crestline, 2013.

Buchner, Hermann. *Stormbird: One of the Luftwaffe's Highest Scoring Me 262 Aces, Oberst (i.R.) Hermann Buchner*. Manchester, UK: Crecy Publishing, 2000.

Chaney, Jr., Otto Preston. *Zhukov*. Norman: University of Oklahoma Press, 1971.

Chant, Christopher, ed. *Warfare and the Third Reich: The Rise and Fall of Hitler's Armed Forces*. London: Salamander Books, 1998.

Conquest, Robert. *Stalin: Breaker of Nations*. New York: Viking Penguin, 1991.

Craven, Wesley Frank, and James Lea Cate, eds. *The Army Air Forces in World War II*. Vol. 2, *Torch to Pointblank: August 1942 to December 1943*. Washington, DC: Office of Air Force History, 1983.

Craven, Wesley Frank, and James Lea Cate, eds. *The Army Air Forces in World War II*. Vol. 3, *Europe: Argument to V-E Day, January 1944 to May 1945*. Washington, DC: Office of Air Force History, 1983.

Dorr, Robert F. *B-24 Liberator Units of the Eighth Air Force: Osprey Combat Aircraft 15*. Oxford: Osprey Publishing, 1999.

Douglas, Graeme. *Consolidated B-24 Liberator: 1939 Onwards*. Newbury Park: Haynes North American, 2013.

Eberle, Henrik, and Matthias Uhl, eds. *The Hitler Book: The Secret Dossier Prepared for Stalin*. London: Public Affairs, 2005.

Edmonds, Robin. *The Big Three: Churchill, Roosevelt and Stalin in Peace and War*. New York: W. W. Norton, 1991.

Eisenhower, Dwight D. *Crusade in Europe: A Personal Account of World War II*. New York: Doubleday, 1948.

Erickson, John. *The Road to Berlin: Continuing the History of Stalin's War with Germany*. Boulder: Westview Press, 1983.

Feis, Herbert. *Churchill Roosevelt Stalin: The War They Waged and the Peace They Sought*. Princeton: Princeton University Press, 1957.

Fest, Joachim. *Inside Hitler's Bunker: The Last Days of the Third Reich*. New York: Farrar, Straus and Giroux, 2004.

Foreman, John, and S. E. Harvey. *The Messerschmitt Me 262 Combat Diary: The Story of the World's First Jet Fighter in Battle*. London: Air Research Publications, 1995.

Forsyth, Robert. *JV 44: The Galland Circus*. Lancaster, UK: Classic Publications, 1996.

Freeman, Roger A. *The Mighty Eighth War Diary*. Osceola: Motorbooks International, 1993.

Freeman, Roger A. *The Mighty Eighth War Manual*. London: Cassell, 2001.

Friedrich, Jorg. *The Fire: The Bombing of Germany, 1940–1945*. New York: Columbia University Press, 2006.

Gilbert, Martin. *The Second World War: A Complete History*. New York: Henry Holt, 1991.

Goolrick, William K., and Ogden Tanner. *The Battle of the Bulge*. Linden: Time-Life Books, 1979.

Gortemaker, Heike B. *Eva Braun: Life with Hitler*. Translated by Damion Searls. New York: Alfred A. Knopf, 2011.

Hamilton, Stephan A. *The Oder Front 1945: Generaloberst Gotthard Heinrici, Heeresgruppe Weichsel and Germany's Final Defense in the East, 20 March–3 May*. Warwick, UK: Helion & Company, 2011.

Harrison, Tom. *Kassel*. Bloomington: Xlibris, 2013.

Harvey, James Neal. *Sharks of the Air: The Story of Willy Messerschmitt and the Development of History's First Operational Jet Fighter*. Havertown: Casemate, 2011.

Hastings, Max. *Inferno: The World at War, 1939–1945*. New York: Alfred A. Knopf, 2011.

Heaton, Colin D., and Anne-Marie Lewis. *The Me 262 Stormbird: From the Pilots Who Flew, Fought, and Survived It*. Minneapolis: Zenith Press, 2012.

Junge, Traudl. *Until the Final Hour: Hitler's Last Secretary*. Edited by Melissa Muller. Translated by Anthea Bell. New York: Arcade Publishing, 2004.

Kershaw, Ian. *The End: The Defiance and Destruction of Hitler's Germany, 1944–1945*. New York: Penguin, 2012.

Larrabee, Eric. *Commander in Chief: Franklin Delano Roosevelt, His Lieutenants, and Their War*. New York: Harper & Row, 1987.

MacDonald, Charles B. *The Mighty Endeavor: American Armed Forces in the European Theater in World War II*. New York: Oxford University Press, 1969.

Muller, Werner. *The Heavy Flak Guns 1933–1945: 88 mm 105 mm 128 mm 150 mm, German Guns and Ballistic Directional Equipment*. Atglen: Schiffer Publishing, 1990.

Neillands, Robin. *The Bomber War: The Allied Air Offensive Against Nazi Germany*. New York: Barnes & Noble Books, 2005.

Nisbet, Robert. *Roosevelt and Stalin: The Failed Courtship*. Washington, DC: Regnery Gateway, 1988.

Overy, Richard. *The Bombers and the Bombed: Allied Air War over Europe, 1940–1945*. New York: Viking, 2013.

Pogue, Forrest C. *The Supreme Command: United States Army in World War II, The European Theater of Operations*. Washington, DC: Center of Military History, United States Army, 1996.

Ramsey, Winston G., ed. *After the Battle: The Reichs Chancellery and the Berlin Bunker Then and Now*. Number 61. London: Battle of Britain International, 1988.

Read, Anthony, and David Fisher. *The Fall of Berlin*. New York: W. W. Norton, 1993.

Richie, Alexandra. *Faust's Metropolis: A History of Berlin*. New York: Carroll & Graf Publishers, 1998.

Rumpf, Hans. *The Bombing of Germany*. New York: Holt, Rinehart and Winston, 1963.

Sion, Edward M. *Through Blue Skies to Hell: America's "Bloody 100th" in the Air War over Germany*. Havertown: Casemate, 2007.

Soviet General Staff. *The Berlin Operation 1945*. Translated and edited by Richard W. Harrison. Warwick, UK: Helion & Company, 2016.

Speer, Albert. *Inside the Third Reich: Memoirs*. New York: Macmillan, 1970.

Steinhoff, Johannes, Peter Pechel, and Dennis Showalter. *Voices from the Third Reich: An Oral History*. Washington, DC: Regnery Gateway, 1989.

Trevor-Roper, Hugh. *The Last Days of Hitler*. Chicago: University of Chicago Press, 1992.

Von Loringhoven, Bernd Freytag. *In the Bunker with Hitler: 23 July 1944–29 April 1945.* New York: Pegasus, 2006.

Westermann, Edward B. *Flak: German Anti-Aircraft Defenses, 1914–1945.* Lawrence: University of Kansas Press, 2001.

Whelan, James R. *Hunters in the Sky: Fighter Aces of WWII.* Washington, DC: Regnery Gateway, 1991.

Wood, Tony, and Bill Gunston. *Hitler's Luftwaffe: A Pictorial History and Technical Encyclopedia of Hitler's Air Power in World War II.* New York: Crescent, 1977.

Wright, Stuart J. *An Emotional Gauntlet: From Life in Peaceful America to the War in European Skies.* Madison: University of Wisconsin Press, 2004.

INDEX

Ekdo 262 Jet: 96, 213, 215

Fegelein, Hermann (SS-Gruppenführer): 166-67

Firestorms: 73-74, 90, 153

Fischer-Tropsch Plants: 38-39, 42

Focke-Wulf 190: 77, 94

Fong, Edmund: 4, 6, 182-83

Freelance Operations: 78-79, 95, 120-21, 142

Führerbunker: 90, 111, 154-55, 157, 160, 162, 166-71, 173-74, 176-77

Fürth Mission: 135-36

Galland, Adolf (Gen.): 96-97, 132, 190, 211-15, 218-22, 225

Gardelegen Mission: 108-11

Gestapo: 69, 105, 107, 124, 166, 258-59

Giebelstadt Mission: 86-87

Goebbels, Joseph (Reichsminister): 124, 157, 162, 167-68, 176-77

Göring, Hermann (Reichsmarschall): 149, 167, 190, 209, 212, 218, 260

Guderian, Heinz (Col. Gen.): 57, 111, 147, 148

Günsche, Otto: 174-77

H2X Radar: 50-51, 83, 85, 89-90, 100, 108, 112

Halbe, Battle of: 158-60

Hamburg: 73-74, 89-90

Harrington, Glenn: 187
    See also Appendix 6

Harrington, John T. (2nd Lt.): 9-10, 49, 186-87

Harris, Sir Arthur (Air Chief Marshal): 31, 33, 37, 72-74, 90

Heinrici, Gotthard (Col. Gen.): 146-50, 153-54, 156-57, 160

Himmler, Heinrich (Reichsführer-SS): 57, 123, 128, 147, 166-67, 170, 173, 218, 258

Hitler Youth: 74, 100, 102, 105, 155-56, 158, 172, 174, 178, 207

Hitler, Adolf
    attempted assassination: 154-55, 259
    marriage: 167-69

suicide: 171, 175-77, 260-61

Hodges, Courtney H. (Gen.): 16, 20, 121, 126

Ingolstadt Mission: 96-101

JG 7 Unit: 7, 97-98, 113-14, 117, 120, 132-34, 138, 139, 140-41, 201, 214-15, 217-19, 222-26

Jodl, Alfred (Lt. Gen.): 171, 259

Junck, Werner (Lt. Gen.): 80

Junge, Traudl: 166-67, 175, 261

Jungenthal Mission: 70-75

Junkers: 209-210

JV 44 Squadron: 132, 218-222

Kantariya, Meliton (Sgt.): 178-79

Keitel, Wilhelm (Field Marshal): 158, 160, 180, 259

Kempka, Erich: 175-77

Kepner, William (Maj. Gen.): 76-78, 87

Konev, Ivan S. (Marshal): 53-56, 58, 59, 144-46, 152, 156-59, 161, 164, 170

Krebs, Hans (Gen.): 111, 148, 154, 160, 171, 177

Küstrin: 56, 59, 92, 125, 145, 147-48, 150

Lee, Jeannie: 185-86

Lehrte Mission: 85-87

Lelyushenko, D. D. (Gen.): 152, 159

Linge, Heinz: 176-77

Ludendorff Bridge: 101, 104-05, 121

Magdeburg Missions: 40-42, 51-52, 67-70

Malmedy Massacre: 17-19, 20, 27

Marshall, George (Gen.): 62, 129

McAuliffe, Anthony C. (Brig. Gen.): 24-25

Me Jets, design and fighting strategy
    Me 109: 78, 94, 135-136
    Me 163: 163, 110, 209

Me 262: 95-98, 113-21, 132-34, 137-38, 209-26

Messerschmitt, Prof. Willy: 114-15, 209-12, 215-17

Mickey Scope: 50, 85, 108

Middleton, Troy H. (Maj. Gen.): 15-17, 20, 24

Model, Walter (Field Marshal): 16, 126, 127-28

Mohnke, Wilhelm (Maj. Gen.): 163-64, 172, 175, 177

Montgomery, Bernard (Field Marshal): 90, 121-22, 128-30

Munich-Riem Airfield: 219-22

Münster Missions: 106-07, 111-12

Nero Order: 124-25

Neuberg Airfield: 100, 118-20

Neustroev, Stepan (Capt.): 169, 173-74, 177-79

Norden Bombsight: 48-50, 85-86, 112

Normandy Invasion: 6-7, 13-14, 38, 65, 80, 190

Norwich Memorial: 28, 181, 187-89, 193

Nowotny, Walter (Maj.): 96-98, 213-15, 218

Nuremberg Mission: 80-81

Oderbruch: 149, 151-52

Oil Campaign: 38-40, 63-64, 66-67, 190-91

OKW (German High Command): 108, 110-11, 147-48, 154, 160, 162, 164, 171, 192, 259

Old Buckenham: 28-30, 40-41, 142, 181, 187, 189, 190

Oranienburg Airfield: 108-09, 113, 134, 137-38, 140, 223

Overlord, Operation
See Normandy Invasion

P-47 Thunderbolt
design: 76
See also Freelance Operations

P-51 Mustang
design: 77-78
See also Freelance Operations

Paderborn Mission: 83-85

Stalin, Joseph V. (Marshal): 30, 53, 55-63, 92, 128-29, 144-46, 151-52, 162, 169-70, 173, 179, 261

Stavka: 53, 56-59, 170

Steinhoff, Johannes (Oberst): 117, 132-33, 214, 219, 220, 259

Stewart, James M. "Jimmy" (Brig. Gen.): 187, 189

Swingle, Raymond R. (1st Lt.): 9-10, 41, 84, 87, 99, 106, 134, 195

Tedder, Arthur (Air Marshal): 64, 66, 180

Togglelier Bomb Release Method: 49

Transportation Plan: 63-64, 66-67

Twining, Nathan (Lt. Gen.): 39, 78, 142

Varsity, Operation: 122

Volkssturm: 92, 102, 121, 123, 153, 163, 167, 172, 258

von Loringhoven, Bernd Freytag (Maj.): 111, 148, 154, 164, 166, 168, 171-72, 260

von Manteuffel, Hasso (Col. Gen.): 17, 19, 20, 22-27, 128, 157, 160

von Rundstedt, Gerd (Field Marshal): 15-17, 27, 65

Vorbunker: 162, 171, 176-77

Wagner, Walter: 167

Weaver, Melvin (S. Sgt.): 9-10, 185

Wegner, Walter (Oberleutnant): 140

Weidling, Helmuth (Lt. Gen.): 149, 153-57, 163-64, 172, 174, 179

Wenck, Walther (Lt. Gen.): 157-59, 164, 171-74

Wendel, Fritz (Flug Kapitan): 210-11, 213

Wesel River: 71, 84-85, 122
    See also D-Z Wesel Mission

Wesendorf Mission: 133-35

Wetzlar Mission: 107-08

Wever, Walter (Oberleutnant): 140

Winter Offensive, Russian: 14, 20, 28, 53-56, 61, 136, 190

Wöhlermann, Hans-Oscar (Col.): 149-50, 152, 174